Two Hogs, Two Dogs, and a Country to Cross

Two Hogs, Two Dogs, and a Country to Cross

Rediscovering the Heart of America

Janet Charbonneau

Front and Back Cover Photos: Blaine Parks and Jay Schwantes
Cover Design: Klassic Designs
Interior Map Design: Jay Schwantes

Published by:
Janet Charbonneau
PO Box 449
Willow Spring, NC 27592

A portion of the proceeds from book sales will be donated to organizations who train and place Assistance Dogs or Guide Dogs.

Disclaimer

This book describes the author's experience during the 2004 Hogs for Dogs charity ride and reflects her opinions relating to those experiences. Some names of people and organizations have been changed at the author's discretion. Descriptions of experiences and locations visited were based on experiences in 2004. Please research any place for the current situations.

Dedication

This book is dedicated to my family that is no longer with me but was key in creating who I am today.

My brother, Den, was the one who took me for the ride that day in September 2003 that started the conversation for our ride. Without you, there would never have been a ride, charity, or this book. I miss you dearly and wish you were still alive to see this book being published.

In memory of my brother, Paul, I have the adventurous spirit that you had. You would have joined us in a heartbeat!

My Dad gave me my strength. He taught me the ability to endure, and I would not have been able to have completed this trip without that quality. This was a very difficult ride and he prepared me for being able to handle those adversities.

One of my most heartfelt dedications is to my Mom. She always believed in us and never called us crazy. Her support was amazing as we moved forward with our crazy idea.

"Move to the right, move to the right!" I heard Blaine frantically screaming in my ear! He was yelling at me in a sudden panic via the CB. As his urgent message reverberated through my earpiece and into my brain, I looked around, trying to figure out why he was yelling at me and started to move right. Glancing in every direction, I saw nothing near me, so I was really confused. Why was he so adamant at making me move over? Suddenly, coming out of my blind spot on my left, I saw it, but it was too late! Panic engulfed me. I had a pickup truck right beside me within inches of my bike and he was moving into me! Terrified, I envisioned the wreck that was about to occur. I tightly gripped the handlebars to attempt to remain on the highway as the truck sideswiped me and then swerved to the left.

Blaine had seen this whole frightening episode pan out as he was following me. He saw the truck veer to the left, then veer to the right, and hit me as he suddenly scooted again to the left.

His worst fear of the ride had become real!

Table of Contents

Acknowledgements

My sincerest thanks go to Blaine Parks who came up with this crazy idea that started this whole story. As the big picture thinker, he did an exceptional job with marketing and organizing our adventure. That 48-state journey with you was the best time of my life! Thanks for the endless work to support our ride and for being the best partner ever as we ventured into the unknown. I can't thank you enough for everything that you did on our ride that allowed me to write this book. The pictures that you took and the daily journal that you wrote are what I used to invoke my memories of our journey. Thanks for cheering me on as I persevered in writing this book. I don't have enough words to be able to express my gratitude for everything you've done.

Next, I want to thank Jay Schwantes who was invaluable for our ability to market this charity. He created our logo and the extraordinary picture of Max and Bailey in front of the flag that was on the back of our T-shirts and is on the cover of this book. Thanks for creating our website and moving that darn paw print on our website map every day as we moved throughout the US. Your advice was greatly appreciated to help us prepare for being on the road daily on our motorcycles. The initial route idea was perfect and your continuous encouragement kept us going when we wanted to quit. Thanks again for the map which is included in this book.

Deb Davis was another significant factor in the success of our trip. Thanks for believing in us when we presented this crazy idea to you. You followed us daily and connected us with Paws With A Cause representatives throughout the U.S. for school visits and events. Having reps with demo dogs at school visits was priceless! Thanks for the daily encouragement and for promoting our ride which greatly contributed to its success. Thank you also for being a reviewer of my book to make sure that I represented the Assistance Dog community well and that my information was accurate.

Our events coordinator, Steve Metz, was phenomenal in organizing the major events that volunteers throughout the U.S. held for us. He consistently promoted our ride and was better than our marketing firm. Thanks for being our rode captain for our ride out of town and the ride back home. I am grateful for everything you did to support us.

Thanks to JoLee Southard for organizing our initial kickoff event and for handling everything that came into our PO Box.

Our lawyer, Seth Cortigene, helped us get everything in order so we could create the Hogs for Dogs charity. Thanks for handling all the details to allow us to concentrate on organizing the ride and not worrying about the paperwork.

Thanks to our CPA, Terry O'Malley, who helped me with all the financial details to make sure we obtained our 501(c)(3) status and were compliant with the IRS and all the states.

A huge shout out to April Fort, Annette Newman, and Beth Cassels. These three ladies did a tremendous job of helping us sort out the continuous emails with all the volunteer and school visit requests. Beth helped us coordinate all of our school visits which allowed us to teach the younger generation about Assistance Dogs and charity. April and Annette sifted through all our volunteer requests and coordinated everything for our events throughout the U.S. For larger events, they passed it over to Steve, but for the plethora of other events, they were key in their success. If it wasn't for them, then those events would not have happened, and we would not have had T-shirts at our events and in our Tour-Paks to sell daily. These three ladies made it happen! Thank you!

Thanks to Dr. Melissa Hudson for making sure Max and Bailey were ready for our ride and for being our veterinarian on our board. That was vital in ensuring the wellbeing of Max and Bailey.

While my Mom passed away in 2020 at the age of 94, I still want to thank her for her support. She let us set up a home base at her house while we planned this journey and handled our personal mail and well needed mail drops during our ride. She never called us crazy and always supported us in our wild ride.

Thanks to Mary Ann Tormey who helped keep us organized. This ride was a stupendous undertaking and she made sure all the various parts and pieces were working together.

Brad Parker was a key person in making our charity auction a success. Thanks for your support throughout our ride.

Thanks to all our charity partners who believed in us and helped us with events and marketing our ride. Blaine and I appreciated your support, and we were grateful to be able to promote you as we trekked through those 48 states.

The Harley-Davidson dealerships that we visited for service were exceptional! We were hard on our motorcycles with over 25,000 miles in seven months loaded down with everything we needed for our journey. The Harley-Davidson dealerships always worked with us to do their best to keep us on our schedule. They were excellent to work with and always very supportive. You rock!

Thanks to all the volunteers throughout the U.S. that supported our ride. They created events, offered school visits, and opened up their homes for our weary bones to rest. Our ride would not have existed if not for you. For you, I am forever grateful!

A final thanks to my reviewers for giving me excellent, honest feedback and making sure the grammar was correct. My book was tremendously improved with your input!

- Susan Morrison
- Julie Thorington
- Kathy Hart
- Jean Kurpiel
- Deb Davis
- Blaine Parks
- Erica Smith

Introduction

The story you are about to read is based on an unbelievable journey that I took with my then-husband, Blaine Parks, and our two Golden Retrievers, Max and Bailey…2 Harley-Davidson motorcycles with the dogs in their sidecars, 48 states visited, 218 days on the road, and 25,000 miles driven. Our motorcycle ride took place in 2004 before social media and smartphones. The non-profit that we created was a grassroots organization which relied on friends, family, and word-of-mouth to advertise our ride. Back then, a website and emails were the best way to market our cause. Crowdfunding websites, such as GoFundMe, did not exist.

Smartphones with GPS apps did not exist either. The GPS that I used was a detachable device fastened to my handlebars. I carried a large Rand McNally United States Road Atlas that I also used for route planning. Google Maps did not exist, so I depended extensively on my clunky GPS software and paperback atlas.

To find motels where the dogs were allowed to stay, I used a couple of dog-friendly accommodation websites that I found on the internet, but I relied heavily on chain motels/hotels that I knew were usually pet-friendly i.e. Motel 6, Red Roof Inn, Super 8, Comfort Inn, Days Inn, and LaQuinta.

Despite the lack of social media and crowdfunding sites, the news spread about our ride.

Our passion was like wildfire, and we were astonished with how it propagated across the United States by word-of-mouth…with just a website and emails.

We discovered the heart of America; come along for the ride!

NOTE: Dear Reader, the pictures in this book were from a digital camera in 2004. Therefore, the resolution is low on them, so they are lower resolution than images from today's cameras. However, I chose to include them because they still provide excellent visualizations of our adventures and who doesn't want to see Golden Retrievers in goggles?

Map of our Route

The map of our route is included on the following page. We started where the pawprint is in North Carolina and headed west. From there, you can follow our route and see where we were at the first day of each month, ending back at the same place in North Carolina seven months later.

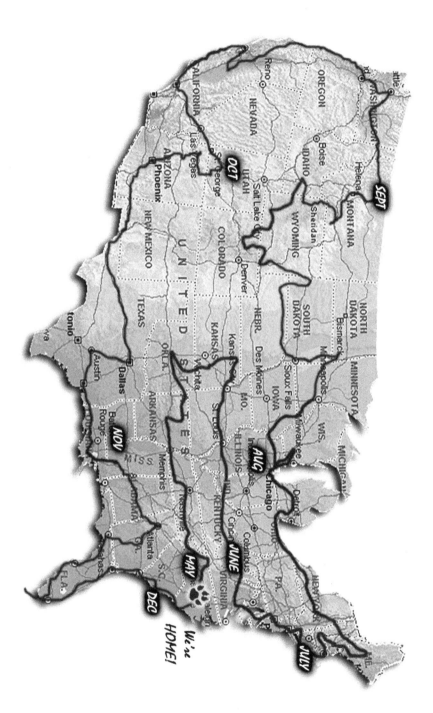

September 2003 - Where It All Began

Have you ever been sitting around the dinner table with a bunch of friends, and you blurt out a really crazy idea? And then everyone adds extra details to it to make it even more insane. Then you all laugh about it and continue to chuckle about it the next day, wishing you had enough guts to try it but knowing you will never do it. Well, that is how this entire trip began.

It was really all my brother's fault. After being without a motorcycle for 25 years, my 54-year-old brother decided he was going to get a motorcycle. Not just any motorcycle, but a beautiful Harley-Davidson Heritage Softail motorcycle. My husband, Blaine, and I were out on vacation visiting him and my sister-in-law, Debbie. Earlier in the day, my brother Den had taken Blaine and me (separately, of course) on a motorcycle ride through the beautiful mountains of Northern Arkansas. I had only ridden on a motorcycle once in my life. Balanced on the gas tank with my brother holding me, I had ridden slowly through the small town of Adams, MA, when I was 5 years old. Therefore, this had been my first REAL ride on a motorcycle, experiencing all the phenomenal sights, sounds, and smells of being out on the open road on a gorgeous fall day.

As we glided through the curvy back roads of northern Arkansas, I realized I was destined to be a Harley babe. You need to have experienced a motorcycle ride through the country to REALLY realize what I was feeling. The wind in your face, all the great (and not so great) smells, just being out in nature; it can really be addictive! I laughed at the cows, who haphazardly scattered throughout the grassy pastures as we passed by. I do not think they loved the boisterous sound of the Harley tailpipes like I did.

Along with the excitement of my first actual ride, I also realized the seriousness of dropping your bike as Den almost lost balance of the bike while we were sitting in a cemetery. OK, so that sounds like a weird place to be on a motorcycle, but it was a perfect place to stop to stretch our legs. Since there was not much around us except for forests, I learned that if you drop a large bike for whatever reason, you will need more than one person to upright it again. I did not know if I would be strong enough to help Den upright it if it happened to us and there was not much traffic flowing along this serene spot to be of any help. Not a pretty thought...I made a mental note to always keep my balance, so I did not have to sheepishly recruit volunteers to pick up my bike. Thankfully, we did not need to find recruits. So onward we continued for a joyous ride through the scenic mountains of Arkansas. I was hooked!

That evening, after a great steak dinner (remember those cows?), we were sitting around the kitchen table, drinking our fruity, tropical rum drinks, and discussing how awesome the motorcycle rides were that day. Well, maybe I should not have blamed my brother; maybe I should have blamed the rum drinks. As we continued talking about the fun rides, Blaine said that he had always wanted to ride across the country by motorcycle. I contemplated the idea. It would have never occurred to me before that day to even consider an idea like that, but after a few rum drinks, that was sounding like a pretty darn good idea. However, we had two Golden Retrievers, Max (age 10) and Bailey (age 9), at the time, and, since they were still fairly young, we knew we could not do a ride like that any time soon. Then the crazy idea came to us that we could take them with us. How? In sidecars! We all laughed at the thought of the four of us riding across the country with two motorcycles and our two huge Goldens in sidecars. We could even throw some goggles on the dogs. We howled even louder at the vision we were creating. Another round of rum! Howling with laughter could make you very thirsty!

The next morning Blaine brought up the idea again. Remember the part where you laugh about the insane idea, but know you will never do it? Well, Blaine forgot that part...he said, "Why couldn't we do it?" I guess I also had temporary insanity because I responded with, "Well, I guess we could." So, the adventure began. (Well, I should not use that phrase because that phrase is now taboo to us since it was the start of a harrowing trip to the British Virgin Islands many years earlier, but that is another story in itself.) Our adventure did indeed begin from that day on.

Did I mention to you that I had only been on a motorcycle once before this trip? Blaine had ridden dirt bikes when he was younger, but I had never really ridden a motorcycle before that day, much less driven one! Now I was considering riding across the country on my own bike with a sidecar attached to it and my Golden Retriever, Bailey, hanging on for dear life beside me. Most grown men will not even attempt to drive a sidecar rig and here I was, contemplating that very idea. I'm glad Bailey could not talk because I'm sure he would have said, "No way, man; are you insane?!"

We already had the time available to do a trip like that. Blaine and I had invested early in life to be able to take a few years off to fulfill another dream of Blaine's, cruising the open seas on a sailboat. I fell for that crazy idea as well. We had just spent three and a half years aboard our 40-foot Island Packet sailboat after cruising the east coast of the U.S., Nova Scotia, and the Bahamas with our two Golden Retrievers, of course. But I will save that story for a different day (and a different book as well).

As we discussed this adventure, we talked about the possibilities of rediscovering the heart of America. Before we went cruising, we felt like the old-fashioned ideals had been lost on the new generation. Everything these days seemed to be oriented towards being faster, relying on movies and computers for entertainment, and having an "It's all about me" mentality. While cruising, we realized you could still depend on your neighbor in the cruising community and could still enjoy the simple things in life: playing card games with good friends, watching the changing colors of a phenomenal sunset, curling up with a good book on a rainy day, feeling the gratification of lending a helping hand to someone in need, etc. We wondered if we could still find the satisfying qualities of cruising in the neighborhoods of small-town America. We decided we wanted to explore as many small towns as possible to see what we could discover.

October - The First Step

With our minds set on this trip, our extensive planning began. First step: elementary, my dear Watson (or dear Bailey as the case may be); learn how to ride a motorcycle. Without this extremely crucial step, we would not get very far on our adventure. My sister-in-law, Debbie, told us about a Beginner's Motorcycle class that was offered by their local community college. Since our visit with them, Debbie had taken one of these classes and now owned her own Yamaha 650. While we were out cruising on our sailboat, she signed us up for a class. So, in October 2003, we journeyed back out to Arkansas to take our motorcycle class.

There were only about seven of us in the class, but it included another husband-and-wife team from Little Rock, Arkansas. I was thankful that I was not the only crazy female in the bunch. We had a great instructor that started us out with the basics on paper and then gave us some hands-on experience. He assumed we had never been on a motorcycle during those hands-on sessions, so he started us off slowly with the basics. Having never grown up around motorcycles, I did not realize which way the throttle needed to be turned to give it gas. Blaine grew up mimicking being on a motorcycle, and it was second nature to twist the throttle backwards towards him to give it gas. For me, that was totally opposite to what I had imagined, so I was not getting very far as I rolled my hand forward to give it gas. Inevitably, I was going nowhere, since I was not giving it any gas at all.

When I got nervous and was hanging on for dear life, I was turning the throttle towards me (backwards) and giving it gas! And I planned to cross the country on this thing?! Yikes! Well, it was not as bad as it sounded. Thankfully, my actions only scared Blaine a couple of times. He really only thought I would quit just one time when I panicked on a figure 8 course. I nearly lost the motorcycle as I revved the engine wildly, trying to slow myself down with the wrong, backward motion. I eventually got the hang of it and passed my course with flying colors. Imagine that...I felt I may actually be able to handle one of these machines!

Next, we had to buy our own motorcycles and start practicing our riding skills. Debbie was ready to upgrade to a bigger bike, so we tested hers out to see if we were interested in buying it. Blaine test drove it and thought it was perfect for him. SOLD! I tried it and was WAY too intimidated by it. And I was going to cross the country on a motorcycle twice the size of this one? Was I insane? What had I gotten myself into? I began having some serious doubts about this trip.

I convinced Blaine that I needed a smaller bike to practice on, since I wanted to spend a lot of time riding by myself. I needed something that I felt confident riding. Answer...one of the bikes from our class! We looked locally in North Carolina for a bike like we had in class and could not find one available. As luck would have it, the school we attended was selling some of its bikes and I was able to purchase one of the training bikes, a Yamaha Virago 250. Perfect! My brother brought it out to my Mom's house in eastern North Carolina, packed in his motorcycle trailer along with Debbie's 650 and his own Harley.

Thankfully, I could practice a few days on my own to get familiar with the back roads in the local area. That prepared me to be a tour guide for Blaine and Den on their motorcycles when we had a chance to ride together. Remember my comment of the good and bad smells experienced while riding a motorcycle? Well, we experienced all the unpleasant smells that day. Eastern North Carolina is home of the pig farms, chicken farms, and cow pastures and we passed plenty of those along the way. Needless to say, it was a very aromatic ride! As we sat at one of the quaint little country stores outside of Seven Springs during a rest break, Den commented that he did not think I could find a smellier ride than I had taken them that day. Hey, that was a true southern North Carolina experience! You cannot say you rode the back roads of North Carolina if you did not pass a few stinky chicken houses.

After Den left, it was time to practice, practice, practice. Isn't the old saying that "Practice makes perfect"? Well, I was still working on perfection. I graduated from my 250 to sometimes riding Blaine's 650. It was still an intimidating bike, especially during windy days. We spent the next three months riding almost every day to gain the experience we needed for this trip.

We also learned a lot about the motorcycle world. Motorcyclists were a unique group. Most of them had big hearts, as they were often part of motorcycle events that raised money for charities. We learned that motorcyclists came from all walks of life. You would meet a guy decked out in his leathers and tattoos, looking like a rough dude, and then find out he was a CEO of a large corporation. It was like an alter ego on weekends. There was also a special wave when you passed another motorcycle rider. It consisted of a low wave, arm out down by your side in either a wave or a peace sign. The sign acknowledged the other rider and was a silent "Hello, stay safe" signal. It was an interesting group.

November - The Charity Idea

While contemplating the ideas for the trip, we thought it would be awesome to have a worthy cause to promote along the way. We knew we would attract a lot of attention with two dogs in sidecars. That attention would obviously allow us to easily promote a charity. We had been donating to and supporting an Assistance Dog non-profit organization for years called Paws With A Cause (PAWS) and we were very passionate about what an Assistance Dog could provide for someone with a physical disability. What a fantastic way to raise money and awareness for this noble cause, we thought. As we continued to discuss the idea, we decided to make them our major charity partner and to find several smaller organizations that also trained Assistance Dogs to have as our minor charity partners. The proceeds of our ride would go to these organizations that trained and placed the Assistance Dogs with our major partner receiving 70% of our proceeds and the rest evenly divided among our minor partners.

What exactly is an Assistance Dog? Most people were familiar with guide dogs which assist people who are blind or visually impaired. However, we realized that many people still did not know about Assistance Dogs. Along with guide dogs, there are also hearing dogs which are trained to assist people who are deaf or hard of hearing, seizure dogs which are trained to assist people with seizures, and service dogs which assist people with other physical disabilities. These dogs are trained for the specific needs of the person with the disability. A guide dog for a person who is blind is trained for completely different skills than a hearing dog for a person who is hearing impaired or a service dog that is trained to assist someone in a wheelchair.

A hearing dog is trained to alert the person to sounds such as a doorbell, a fire alarm, a crying baby, or a ringing telephone.

A seizure dog is trained to react to a person experiencing a seizure by activating a device, getting help, or retrieving items such as medication or a phone. Remarkably, some seizure response dogs can even learn to predict a person's seizures due to slight nuances or changes in their scent or personalities. This is because of the remarkably close bond they develop with their person. This can give a person a chance to get in a protected area to reduce the possibility of being hurt during the seizure. Amazing!

A service dog can be trained in up to ninety commands. Examples of what these dogs can do are turning on and off light switches, retrieving an item as small as a dime or as heavy as a briefcase, opening a door, retrieving an item out of the refrigerator, loading a clothes washer, unloading a dryer, providing balance and stability, providing help with dressing or undressing, and assisting a person to get back into a wheelchair.

The Assistance Dog does not just assist that person with specific tasks; it gives that person more independence and a better quality of life. The person is no longer dependent on another person and can go out of their house independently or go back to work. The dog also provides a bridge to new friendships. For instance, many people do not know how to approach someone in a wheelchair, so that person is often ignored. Add an Assistance Dog in that same situation and most people will start a conversation with the person in a wheelchair to ask questions about their dog. It makes that person more approachable.

Consider what that really means. Having that Assistance Dog allows them to get their dignity back. It may help them reduce or eliminate their depression. They can finally do things on their own without depending on another person.

The cost of training an Assistance Dog can range from $15,000 to $40,000. The organizations we partnered with provided these dogs to the recipients free of charge or with just an application fee or small donation. These organizations did not receive any funds from the government. They relied solely on donations from individuals, businesses, and grants. We wanted to raise funds for these organizations to help them be able to train more dogs.

Another goal we had for our journey was to raise awareness throughout the U.S. Most people were familiar with guide dogs, but most people did not know about other Assistance Dogs. During our journey, I always got frustrated when I saw a sign in a public building that stated that guide dogs were allowed. They obviously had no clue about other Assistance Dogs! We wanted to educate as many people as we could about Assistance Dogs. This awareness would also help those that already had Assistance Dogs. Many people with Assistance Dogs were denied access to public places because of their dog. Imagine being thrown out of a restaurant because they thought you brought your pet inside! If we could raise awareness about these dogs, then more people would know that they are assisting that person. Even though the Americans with Disabilities Act (ADA) states that businesses open to the public must allow service dogs into their establishment, many business owners and managers were still unaware of this law and were refusing services to those individuals coming in with Assistance Dogs. We wanted to eliminate that problem!

While I believe Assistance Dogs are more widely known today, I feel that there are still a lot of misconceptions of what an Assistance Dog really is and what rights the Assistance Dog user has. According to the ADA, "a service animal is defined as a dog that has been individually trained to do work or perform tasks for an individual with a disability. The task(s) performed by the dog must be directly related to the person's disability." The key here is that the service dog must perform an action to assist the person with the disability.

The ADA also states that "dogs whose sole function is to provide comfort or emotional support do not qualify as service animals under the ADA". Emotional support dogs provide comfort by being near their person. Therapy dogs are trained to provide comfort, affection, and support by going with their owners to volunteer at schools, libraries, hospitals, nursing homes and disaster areas. Both emotional support dogs and therapy dogs do not perform tasks for owners with disabilities, so they do not have the same rights as service dogs.

Service dogs must be allowed in all public places, according to the ADA. To know if the service dog is legitimate, you can ask the person two questions: (1) is the dog a service animal required because of a disability? and (2) what work or task has the dog been trained to perform? These are the only two questions you can ask to determine if it is indeed a real service dog. You cannot ask about the person's disability or require them to demo the task that the dog can perform. There is no requirement for the dog to be wearing a vest or have any specific ID. Their handler must also keep their dog under control. If a service dog is out of control, then they can be asked to leave the premises.

In order to raise money for these charities that trained Assistance Dogs, we decided we needed to create our own non-profit organization. That would allow all the donations to be tax deductible. First, we needed a name. After throwing around names for many days, it came to us…Hogs for Dogs! We were going to be riding Harleys, which are nicknamed Hogs, and raising money for charities that trained Assistance Dogs. Hence, Hogs for Dogs. Perfect!

Since we wanted to have PAWS as our major charity partner, we wanted to make sure they would support our crazy idea. We contacted them and they seemed interested. Thankfully, they did not laugh at us and toss our number out the window. Instead, they invited us up to visit their headquarters in Wayland, Michigan to see their organization, learn more about what they do, and make sure we were serious about this trip. We packed our stuff and the dogs into our minivan and off to Michigan we went. Since we had so much planning to still accomplish, we made it a quick trip. They were gracious enough to host us in one of their partnering hotels.

We ended up meeting with Deb Davis, Development/Communications Coordinator, and Mike Sapp, the co-founder and CEO. They gave us an informative tour of their facility with demos on what the Assistance Dogs could do. Then we sat with them and explained our organization and our tour ideas. We knew our idea sounded a little insane and they could just call us crazy and throw us out the door. Instead, they realized that we really were serious about this endeavor and decided to give us a chance. We had the opportunity to promote their organization throughout the country and raise money for them. The highlight of the day was attending the graduation and placement of a mobility assistance dog with his new owner. Witnessing that placement was heartwarming, as it represented the reason that we would do the ride. Here was one more person who gained their independence with an Assistance Dog.

Our drive home was an exceptionally long thirteen-hour ride, but we were excited to have solidified one of our charity partners. We used our travel time throwing out ideas and trying to come up with slogans for our website and T-shirts. The two that stuck were "Helping People with Disabilities Get a New Leash on Life" and "Two Dogs Crossing the Country to Help Others Simply Cross the Road".

Once we got home, we knew we needed to get serious about our ride planning. We started making a list of everything we needed to do before our ride started. First, the normal items for a new business: get an EIN, register with the state, create the corporation documents, file to be a 501(c)(3) non-profit organization, create a logo, and build a website. Then the items for our journey: figure out how to get the word out, create events, plan the route, create fundraising ideas, etc. Plus, we still needed to find our minor charity partners. How were we going to get all of this done in a few short months with just the two of us?

As we were trying to figure out how to plan the trip on motorcycles, including items to bring and route planning, we knew we needed to connect with an expert. Blaine decided to talk to a friend of ours who had been riding motorcycles for years. Jay Schwantes had been Blaine's manager when they worked together at Glaxo in the Security department. Jay had been taking extended motorcycle rides for years and Blaine knew he would be an excellent mentor for helping us plan the motorcycle part of the trip. Blaine called him up and explained what we planned to do. After a quiet pause, the next words out of Jay's mouth were "Fuck you!" and he hung up. Blaine looked at his phone in dismay and I asked him what happened. He exclaimed, "he hung up on me!" I asked him why and he said he had no idea.

Several minutes later, Jay called Blaine back. He explained that, after we had spent a few years at a young age sailing on a sailboat, we were now planning to embark on his dream ride. He was jealous and mad as hell that he was not going with us. After he settled down, he started giving Blaine a lengthy list of things that would need to be done before we left.

It was time to share the news with our family and friends on our website. When we had embarked on our sailboat adventures on our Island Packet 40, Charbonneau, we had created a website so friends and family could follow our experiences and enjoy our journey from the safety of their homes. During our three and a half years of cruising, we had met many fellow Island Packet owners at rendezvous events and countless other cruisers on our daily adventures. Therefore, the website had a good following, so it was the perfect place to get the word out about our charity ride. (Remember that social media as we know it today did not exist at that time, so websites were the way to spread the word.)

Solutions began coming our way before we even knew we had problems. Shortly after posting our upcoming adventure on our website, we received an email from a friend of ours in Texas. Seth Cortigene said he had enjoyed following us on our sailing website and thought he could help with our charity ride. He is a lawyer and volunteered to be our lawyer for the organization. He said he would start working on our Articles of Incorporation and Bylaws for us. We were certainly grateful to have that task off our plate!

December - Motorcycle Purchase

Purchasing motorcycles was next on our planning list. We already knew that we had to take the trip on two Harleys...if you are going to rediscover the heart of America, then it had to be on American-made bikes! We decided on the Harley Ultra Classic for our motorcycles. Since we were going to ride thousands of miles over a course of seven months, we needed to have the most comfortable Harleys available.

Next, we needed to choose sidecars. We researched numerous brands of sidecars and ended up having to select one sight unseen, since sidecars are a rare breed, especially on the east coast of the U.S. We chose the Harley sidecar since we knew we would have plenty of Harley dealerships available throughout the country if we had any problems with the bikes. Before committing to buying them, we tried to get dimensions of the seating area to make sure our 100-pound Golden Retrievers would fit in them. We got some dimensions but were still not sure they would fit. Our insanity continued, and we decided to spend thousands of dollars on the most expensive sidecars out there hoping our Goldens would fit in them. We just had to cross our fingers and pray that they would fit! What if we ordered these two sidecars and our dogs did not fit comfortably in them? No wonder we had so many sleepless nights waiting for these motorcycles and sidecars to arrive!

Once we decided on which motorcycles and sidecars to purchase, we had to pick a Harley dealer. We decided on Ray Price Harley-Davidson in Raleigh, NC where we used to live. The reason we picked them was that we had lived in Raleigh for many years, knew lots of the Harley Owners Group members, and knew Ray Price was famous for drag racing. We headed up to Raleigh to purchase our bikes. As I sat on one of the Ultra Classics, I made a couple of small modifications to mine to make it easier for me to ride. I changed out the handlebars to pull-back handlebars to accommodate my short arms. I also added an easy clutch to make the clutch more manageable. If not, I would have had to use one of those funky hand grip exercisers to strengthen my hands. We both had reversing gears added to our bikes, so we could drive forward and reverse instead of pushing the rig backwards like you would on a normal bike. Can you imagine me pushing that rig to make my bike move in reverse? I would have had to bring an entourage with me on the entire trip just to push my bike in reverse! Last, we selected our colors: black for Blaine and a deep blue for me. After placing our order, we received an estimated delivery date of January 30th, giving us three months to get comfortable riding our new rigs with the dogs.

As we completed the bike orders, we told them about our story and walked away with a great deal on our bikes. They even ended up being one of our sponsors, so we displayed their logo on the back of both of our sidecars.

We decided it would be nice to protect the dogs' eyes with some goggles, so we started researching it. Blaine ran across a product called Doggles which were goggles for dogs and they came with interchangeable lenses. Blaine contacted the company and told them about our charity ride. They donated a few sets of Doggles for Max and Bailey to use on our ride, including two sets with flames on the side. They sent three different color lenses (smoke mirrored, orange, and clear) which allowed us to switch them depending on day or night riding. To get them used to wearing them, we would put them on and immediately take the dogs for a walk so they were too busy walking to paw the Doggles off. After a few days, they were getting used to them and we felt they would keep them on while riding.

Susan Sims, who was the creator and editor of FIDO Friendly magazine, contacted us and was interested in being one of our sponsors. FIDO Friendly is an American dog travel and lifestyle magazine published bimonthly, including hotel and destination reviews along with health and wellness topics, dog training advice, celebrity interviews, and the latest fashion trends. Blaine had written a few articles for the magazine while we were sailing, so they wanted us to write some articles during our journey and, in exchange, they would place a full-size ad in their issues that advertised our trip and our charity cause. Blaine agreed, and we became excited that the word was getting out about our trip. Susan also offered us a place to stay with them when we made it to Fresno, CA.

Good friends of ours, Jim and Sue Taylor, contacted us about an Assistance Dog organization that they volunteered with. We knew them from our sailing days and our sailing website was again connecting us to friends that were willing to help our cause. We were thrilled! Jim and Sue were our neighbors at the boat dock in Washington, NC where we kept our first sailboat. Many a day they rescued us as we learned to back our sailboat into our slip with the currents of the river challenging us constantly. They lived in Deep Gap, NC and helped raise dogs that were eventually trained and placed by an organization called New Life

Mobility Assistance Dogs (NLMAD). Jim and Sue connected us to NLMAD, and we shared the details of our planned ride with them. They were thrilled to hear of our ride and wanted to be one of our minor charity partners. Everything was falling into place, and we already had two charity partners to ride for and who supported us.

Since Jay's business was web design, he offered to design and host our website for free. He already had a website that he had updated for years about his motorcycle adventures. With his wonderful creative flair, he designed an amazing website for us. Blaine provided him with the content and Jay made the content shine!

Seth continued to work on the paperwork and filed the articles of incorporation, setting us up as a Texas organization. He also submitted the IRS application for our Employer Identification Number (EIN).

Blaine and I made a good team. Blaine was the "big picture" kind of guy, so he had the vision of where we, as an organization, needed to expand. He was in charge of the marketing and events side. He figured out how to move this idea into fruition. I was the details person. When it came to finances or the details needed to keep our organization intact, then I managed those tasks. We complimented each other in order to handle all aspects of the organization.

January 2004

As we entered January, we received our official EIN number from the IRS. Since I was the numbers and details person, it was my job to make sure I registered our organization in North Carolina so we could solicit funds in that state. I filled out the paperwork to register Hogs for Dogs as a "Foreign corporation" in North Carolina so that, even though we were incorporated in Texas, we could do business in NC. Once that was done, I realized that in order for us to raise funds in every state we visited, we would have to register to be able to solicit funds....in EVERY state we visited! Good grief! What had we gotten ourselves into? And again, since I was the details person, that task fell upon me. Talk about a daunting task! Where did I even begin? I began to research it and there was no easy way to do this. You could pay big bucks to an organization to do it for you, but we did not have the funds to do that and did not want to throw our funds into that, anyway. We wanted our profits to go to our charity partners. Therefore, I continued to research it. Every state had their own process. Some were easy, and some were difficult. There was no uniformity of the applications. They were all completely different for each state. Most of them also required that you get the application notarized. Most of them also required a fee. There were only a few states that did not require any registration. I was grateful for those wonderful states!

I created a spreadsheet to document all the states requiring registration for solicitation to track when I mailed the application and the status of each. I organized them in the order that we would visit them. As the registration numbers came in, I also documented them in this spreadsheet.

Seth introduced us to a CPA, Terry O'Malley, who was a friend of his. After Seth told him about our plans, Terry offered to become our financial consultant for the organization. He started working on the paperwork for the application for our 501(C)(3) status. This was extremely important to us because we wanted all donations to be tax deductible. We were ecstatic to have both a lawyer and a CPA volunteer to help us through the legal and financial processes in setting up the organization. We continued to attract the right people to help us achieve our goal.

After collaborating with us for a while, Terry agreed to become one of our board members.

We decided we needed to have a fundraising event before we left on our ride to raise initial funds. Another friend of ours, JoLee Southard, offered to be the organizer of the event. Blaine met JoLee when he worked at Glaxo. She worked in the Records Information Management department, so Jay and Blaine had worked with JoLee. Since they worked in sister departments, Jay, Blaine, and JoLee often were at the same company retreats. Therefore, Blaine and JoLee became good friends. JoLee loves dogs and when she heard about our ride, she immediately volunteered.

After several discussions, we chose a formal affair with an auction, both a silent auction during the event and a live auction to close out the event. JoLee found the perfect venue and booked it for the evening of April 23rd. My sister, Lois Rains, heard about the event and immediately offered to make a novelty-themed cake for it (which she specialized in as a side job) and to help with the decorations for the event. Our next steps were to visit the venue to plan the layout of our event and to gather donations for the auctions. Since we had a tentative ride kickoff date of mid-April, we pushed the kickoff date to May 1st for our official ride out of town.

We needed to get a bank account set up for the organization, so we researched banks to find the one which had locations in the most states. Bank of America was the winner, and we opened an account with them. However, there were still many states throughout the country that did not have any Bank of America locations. When we had fundraisers in those states, we decided to get a money order for the donation money and mail that back to JoLee so she could deposit it into the Hogs for Dogs checking account.

JoLee also volunteered to monitor our post office box. Therefore, we opened one in Raleigh close to where she lived, so that it would be convenient for her. She would document all the mail that came in by sending emails to us and then deposit the donations into our bank account.

Since our organization finally existed legally, it was time to create our board of directors. It was logical to ask the people who had been helping us the most, so our initial board consisted of the following people:

- Blaine Parks
- Janet Parks
- Jay Schwantes
- Seth Cortigene

- JoLee Southard
- Terry O'Malley

During our first board meeting, we decided that this would be the executive board and Blaine would be the Chairman. Also, we all agreed that we needed to continue to expand the board and to seek others to join. The following mission statement was approved: "Hogs for Dogs leverages partnerships with canine-related, not-for-profit organizations by amplifying their awareness programs and creating fundraising opportunities on their behalf through unique charity motorcycle rides across America."

A little later in the month, one of my childhood friends, Mary Ann Tormey, joined our board as a general member. Mary Ann and I had known each other since before we were in grade school because we lived only a couple of houses apart. She was excited about helping with promoting our ride and was already working on getting donations for auction items. She eventually became our office manager, helping us stay organized while we were on the road.

Our next team member, Amanda MacDowell, is my niece and Lois's daughter. She joined our general board. She had print media editing experience and immediately started helping edit the brochure that Blaine had been working on. We received permission to use the PAWS logo on our brochure and our website, so our marketing plans were panning out nicely.

Deb Davis introduced us to Jan Santel, the North Carolina Field Trainer for PAWS. After we chatted with her and told her about our ride, she agreed to join our general board.

Other volunteers were showing up as well because we had announced our trip on our sailing website. Penny Zibula and her husband, Simon, who were fellow Island Packet owners, contacted us since they had been following our website. Penny is blind, so she wanted to volunteer with our organization. She agreed to come up for our auction and be one of the guest speakers to tell others about her guide dog, CJ. We were excited to have her join us!

Through a mutual friend, Blaine was connected to an organization called KSDS which was previously called Kansas Specialty Dog Service, but since they were placing dogs throughout the U.S., they changed their name to KSDS. The acronym was more generic instead of stating it was just for Kansas recipients. We researched their organization and they fit our criteria. We preferred partnering with organizations that did not charge their recipients thousands or tens of thousands for their service dogs. Blaine contacted them and told them about our project. Since they did not laugh at us, we figured that we again had a possibility of our second minor charity partner. They reviewed our information and agreed to be one of our partners. We were again excited that our vision was coming to fruition, and we had three charity partners to ride for.

Our excitement continued to grow as we got our first pledge for the ride. We received an email from a couple who said that they would pledge $500 per month for 10 months, accumulating to be $5,000 at the end of our ride. It started to sink in on how much we could raise to help others receive Assistance Dogs!

I was in charge of the route planning and eventually the daily navigation. We chose to ride through all lower 48 states, so I needed a route that would touch all 48 states and would also put us in the best regions at the best time of year. We decided to be out for 7 months and be back before the Christmas timeframe. We felt people would start spending their charitable dollars to help those in need at Christmas time, and we agreed with that philosophy. Jay produced the perfect route for us. I asked him how he came up with it and he was free in admitting that he was sitting on the toilet one day staring at the atlas when the route just came to him. Therefore, we deemed it "The Shitty Route." But it allowed us to venture to all lower 48 states at the best weather times of the year. I took it and ran with it.

With our goal of visiting all lower 48 states during the best seasons, Jay's idea took us west from North Carolina to Oklahoma, up one state to Kansas and then back east to the east coast, visiting new states on our easterly trek. This would be one of our most difficult legs weather-wise because we would go through tornado states during their tornado seasons. Once we got back to the east coast, we would head north to Maine and then go counterclockwise around the country, zigzagging a little along the way to make sure we touched each state. Jay even created a map of the United States with our route on it and could put a paw print on it for our current location so people could follow our progress via our website. That was cool!

Jay gave me the general route as a template, but I needed to figure out what towns in each state we wanted to visit to make a more definitive route. I started with towns we were interested in visiting along with towns that had friends or relatives that volunteered a place to stay. We decided we had to see the famous landmarks i.e. D.C., St. Louis arch, Golden Gate bridge, Mount Rushmore, Grand Canyon, Route 66. Plus, we wanted to visit the not-so-known places such as towns with interesting names and towns off the beaten path. I had been reading a delightful book called Road Trip USA by Jamie Jensen to help me find the interesting yet unknown places. It contained 11 routes across the country: five routes traversing east to west and six routes traversing north to south. It helped me find the interesting and odd places, such as Carhenge and Ed Galloway's Totem Pole Park. Upon Jay's suggestion, I began using Microsoft's Streets and Trips software to plan our route and figure out each day's itinerary and how many miles we needed to drive to get to our daily destination. This was an extremely daunting task, and I had to keep reminding myself of that old saying…How do you eat an elephant? One bite at a time. I was just starting to nibble on this elephant of a task. Holy smokes! What had I gotten myself into?

Blaine collaborated with Jay to create a logo for the organization that we could use on the website, marketing materials, and T-shirts. We wanted to have something Harley looking that related to our cross-country ride. We ended up incorporating the shape of the U.S. highway sign and the look of the Harley logo along with a little of a winged motorcycle feel into an incredible logo.

We used that on the back of our original T-shirts, but then decided we wanted something with Max and Bailey's picture on it. Blaine took a picture of Max and Bailey wearing their Doggles along with their red, white, and blue flag bandanas and sent it to Jay. The picture totally exuded their behaviors. Max had his regal look, and Bailey had his usual goofy grin. In less than an hour, Jay had an incredible version with a waving flag behind Max and Bailey and our logo underneath them. It was perfect! That was the design that we knew had to be on the back of all our T-shirts that we sold for the ride.

Bailey   Max

www.HogsForDogs.com

Since our logo was complete, Blaine could finish working on the brochure for us as well as the ad for FIDO Friendly. He ordered polo shirts with our logo embroidered on the front and T-shirts with our new picture of Max and Bailey on the back of them. We knew we had a hit with our Max and Bailey T-shirts, so we wanted to sell them both on our website and in person during our ride. Blaine researched the best way to do this and then opened a merchant account for us so we could accept credit cards. We also wanted to offer credit card purchases for our in-person sales during our ride, so he purchased a mobile credit card machine. It was about the size of a brick, but it was our best option at the time. To fulfill the online orders, Blaine found a company that would provide an online store for us which included store design using our graphics, screen printing and embroidery services, warehousing, fulfillment services, and reporting tools.

After three months of riding our motorcycles and getting comfortable with them, it was time for us to get real motorcycle licenses instead of just the driver's permits. Actually, in North Carolina where I was getting the license, they just added the letter "M" to your license...just one letter, but a very important "M". Blaine and I headed down to the DMV to take our tests and get our licenses. Now for the lesson learned...had we taken the motorcycle class in North Carolina, instead of Arkansas, we would not have needed to take the skills part of the tests...just vision, signs, and the written test. I do not know why you had to take the class in the same state as your license. Since we had taken our class in Arkansas, we were required to take the skills test as well.

We knew they only gave the skills tests at certain hours of certain days, so we had come during one of those times. Since the times were so restricted, I have no idea why the usual person was not there to give the tests. We ended up instead with a substitute. I was the first one who would go through the test course, followed by Blaine. When the instructor got to the course, she reprimanded me for practicing around the cones on the course. We were never told not to practice on the course and there were no signs stating that rule either. Not a great start to my test!

I was using my little 250 to maneuver through their course. One task was to speed up and then slow down quickly, hand signal for a right turn and then make the turn. OK, I have had turn signals on all my bikes and now you want me to hand signal on a turn...which I, of course, forgot to do. That along with one other minor mistake and she failed me on the test! Grrr! She knew I had the skills but was being extremely picky on it.

As I passed Blaine on his way to take the test, I said, "Do not forget that hand signal!" He came back with a passing grade. Now I had to wait 2 weeks before I could come back and try again.

Exactly two weeks later, I was back at the DMV. Boy, was I nervous! What if I could not pass this test and get my license? I was starting to really get concerned that I would not be able to go on our trip because I could not pass the skills test, even though I knew what I was doing on the bike. Thankfully, the usual DMV testing person was back, and I went to take my test with her. I completed all the other tasks with no problems, and it came back to this same final task. And what did I do? I once again forgot that darn hand signal. Ugh! She knew I had the skills, and she allowed me to retake that one task which I finally accomplished perfectly, and she passed me! Yay! I walked out of the DMV office proudly holding my new driver's license with the coveted "M" on it and a picture of me grinning from ear to ear.

Part of our planning was to make sure we had the right gear with us for the distance we were riding and the weather conditions we would be in. Leather jackets were a big decision since we would be wearing them daily in hot and freezing weather, and we wanted ones that would help protect us in case of an accident. After many shopping trips and extensive research, we selected Fox Creek Leathers because of their quality and since they were made in the USA. Blaine and I both opted for the classic motorcycle jackets. We chose these jackets since they had zip-in liners for freezing weather and vents in the front, back, and sleeves for hot weather. They were extremely heavy weight for extra protection. Mine had laced leather sides to give it a more fitted and feminine look.

Gloves were also important to protect our hands. Ultimately, I ended up with three pairs. One was a standard set. The second set stopped halfway down my fingers to protect my palms but exposed the tips of my fingers to help me stay cooler. The last pair was a set that extended a few inches over my wrist/arm to help me stay warm in freezing weather.

We purchased rain gear but could not store leather chaps on our bikes since they would take up too much space. For chilly weather we opted for layering, using our rain gear as an extra layer. I also brought my wind-resistant leggings for one more warm layer under my jeans.

Finally, at the end of January, we got our first hack rig (motorcycle lingo for a motorcycle with a sidecar attached). Compared to what we had been riding, these things were huge! Wow! Blaine's motorcycle was the first one to come in and Blaine rode it back to my Mom's house where we were staying while we prepared for our trip.

We took turns driving this huge rig around the neighborhood while the other person sat in the sidecar. After driving your own motorcycle, it was quite unnerving to be sitting in a sidecar, really low to the ground, and being at the mercy of the driver, who was new to the rig. We had to get used to riding on the left half of the road, so the entire rig was on the road. No more riding on the right third of the street. If you did that, then your sidecar was on the curb! My Mom lived in a neighborhood called Walnut Creek, which was a few miles outside of Goldsboro, NC. It was a quiet, peaceful neighborhood, and it was the perfect place to practice. Thankfully, there were no concrete curbs in this neighborhood, so we just drove on the grass on the side of the road a bit too often. Soon we got the hang of it, keeping the entire rig on the road.

February

Even though we only had one hack rig, we needed to get some photos with it and the dogs for the FIDO Friendly ad and our new brochure. We went out in the neighborhood and found a place for the photo shoot. Max sat in his sidecar and Bailey sat next to it. We did not even have our logos on the bike yet, so we had to Photoshop the logo and Max's name on the sidecar. It worked, and it ended up being one of the pictures on our brochure and our giveaway postcard. We designed a giveaway postcard as a souvenir that we could give out easily. It had this cute picture of the dogs, one of our hack rigs, and our website, plus it was a lot less expensive than our brochures. I could easily walk into any Walmart in the country and purchase copies of this picture, so it was simple to replenish anywhere we traveled.

Our charity partner connections were rolling in. We met Canine Partners for Life through a mutual friend. Blaine contacted them and told them about our ride. They jumped at the chance to be part of our ride and asked how they could assist us. It was amazing how these partnerships were coming to us via friends of ours. They were our third minor partner and fourth overall charity partner.

We received our Foreign Non-Profit Certificate from North Carolina, so we were finally eligible to raise funds in North Carolina. Blaine had to rewrite our Bylaws to conform to the verbiage that was needed for the IRS. Once completed, our application for 501(c)(3) status was submitted. The feeling was sinking in that we were going to accomplish this status and all the donations to our organization would be tax deductible. This was huge!

We knew we would need help with marketing, so we contacted a marketing company to see how they could help us. After an initial discussion, we planned to have dinner with them to discuss all the details of our ride. Our dinner was successful, and we awaited their proposal for our marketing plan. They wanted to target markets like the Today Show and The Tonight Show with Jay Leno. We hoped they would be successful in getting the word out to the world.

A couple of weeks after taking possession of the first hack rig, my rig finally arrived! The dealership asked if they could display it at one of their open house events and we immediately agreed. It was a terrific opportunity to attract attention to our cause.

Since we had brought Blaine's motorcycle up to Raleigh to have a couple of issues checked, we needed to move both motorcycles back to Goldsboro. Since I was not comfortable riding it that distance yet, we asked Jay to ride my motorcycle back for me. I followed in my car. I had a good laugh all the way back as I followed behind Jay. You see, Jay had been riding motorcycles for many years and was well known by many in the motorcycle world as just Muthuh. With all that experience, he knew that when he stopped he had to put his feet down to keep the bike balanced. Remember my fear of having to sheepishly recruit volunteers to pick up my bike if I lost balance? With all those years of experience on his bike, it was just second nature to put his feet down when he stopped. Which is what Jay did all the way back to Goldsboro. He realized along the way that he did not need to put his feet down on a sidecar rig...it does not fall over. Therefore, each stop suddenly became a stretch like he had planned to put his feet down to stretch. I laughed the whole way; old habits are hard to break.

On our way back, we stopped for a quick lunch at a fast-food restaurant. A gentleman approached us as we parked. He worked for one of the local TV stations, WRAL in Raleigh, NC, and he asked about our rigs. We told him about our upcoming ride, and he said he thought it would make a remarkable story for them. He promised to pass along our info, and we hoped this would be the start of our media interest.

The next step was changing the sidecars, so the dogs had nice comfortable beds to ride on. Blaine was the wizard behind this invention. He took out the "people" seat and the stereo speakers to make room for the dogs. The "people" seatback had a locking mechanism to provide locked storage behind the seat and we wanted to keep that feature. Blaine designed a great dog seat that was comprised of a long plywood floor and a cushioned lockable seat back. This provided our lockable storage on the aft part of the sidecar. We made vinyl-covered cushions that sat on top of the plywood and made a great dog bed platform for them to sit comfortably or lie down on their ride. We attached removable fleece covers to these cushions, and the cushions came out to provide us with portable dog beds we could use anywhere along our trip. Blaine also cushioned the dashboard and side handrails so they could rest their chins on them as they watched the world go by. After finishing these modifications, we got to the moment of truth. Would they fit in these sidecars? Bailey was the guinea pig. Blaine picked him up and in he went. He laid down on his newly designed cushion and he fit! Hallelujah!

Now that they fit, the next question that was begging to be answered was, "Will they ride in the sidecars?" We put them both in their respective sidecars, Max with Blaine and Bailey with me. It was easy to decide which dog rode with each of us. Before we were married and while we were dating, Blaine got Max. We broke up for a while and I missed Max, so I went looking for a Golden Retriever pup like Max and I found Bailey. Later, we started dating again and eventually married. Therefore, originally Max was Blaine's dog and Bailey was mine.

As we rode down the driveway for the very first time, Bailey turned all the way around in his sidecar, so he was facing backwards. He looked at Blaine with an expression stating, "Are you sure she knows what she is doing?!" Obviously, he sensed my apprehension! I had just gotten my brand-new hack rig. Blaine had just installed speakers in my helmet, so I could use the CB radio to communicate with him. I also had the controls for the CB, cruise control, radio, CD player and separate turn signals on each handlebar. With all these new gadgets, along with a dog who had never been on a motorcycle, I felt I had the right to be a bit nervous! OK, I was petrified! However, Bailey and I sucked it up and gave it a try. Within a few minutes and a couple of laps around the neighborhood, Max and Bailey were looking bored and ready for the open road. We decided to immediately attempt one of the back roads to that great little country store that we had visited during our ride with my brother. And away we went. The dogs absolutely loved it! With noses in the air and wind whipping their ears back, they were in heaven! They rocked their new Doggles and comfortably enjoyed the ride. When we stopped, they remained peacefully in their sidecars. Yep, we believed this was actually going to work! We were extremely grateful for getting over one more hurdle which would have been a showstopper.

Jay created designs for decals for our bikes and then found a place that could print them for us. We put our logo on the side and rear of the sidecars and the dogs' names were located just under the area where they were sitting. On the back cargo area of the sidecars, we put logos from our sponsors. Both sidecars had a Ray Price Harley-Davidson decal. On the back of Max's sidecar, we put the logo of Jay's web design business, WebEFX, and the logo for MadMaps, who had also become our sponsor. Bailey's sidecar sported a decal for FIDO Friendly. On the back of our motorcycles on the tour packs, we added our website URL and the CB channel we monitored so truckers could chat with us.

We were down to just a couple of months before our ride, so we constantly went riding to get used to handling these huge rigs. One day we traveled up to Raleigh to go to a biker party, visit Ray Price Harley-Davidson and stop at a biker shop in Clayton, NC. Nearing home after our day trip, I exited off Hwy 70 onto a small back road leading to my Mom's house. It was a sharp right-hand turn, and I took it too fast. When making right-hand turns, the weight shifts to the left of the rig; when doing so with great speed, it shifts it so much that it makes the motorcycle lean to the left and picks the sidecar off its wheel. With that dynamic on the three wheels, I lifted Bailey and his sidecar, which then put me only on the two wheels of the motorcycle. The steering is completely different on two wheels versus three, and I could not stay in my lane. Thankfully, no one was coming the other direction, and I was able to slow down and get the sidecar back on the road. I quickly learned that I needed to be diligent in slowing down for curves to keep the sidecar on the ground. Bailey was all for that idea!

Our planning continued with finding a place to host our kickoff ride. Since we had purchased our motorcycles and sidecars from Ray Price Harley-Davidson, that was a logical place to start. We met with Chris Haddock, Ray Price's Operations Manager, and he thought it was a great idea! He said they would be happy to sponsor it. We also secured a booth at their Open House the week before our kickoff ride.

JoLee plowed full steam ahead on organizing our auction and set up a meeting at the venue, Sisters' Garden, to understand the layout of the place and to work on the details with their event coordinator. Several of the board members and volunteers attended the meeting, and the creative juices started to flow. We selected a scrumptious menu which included a cheese display, vegetable display with the dips served out of dog bowls, raspberry brie, spring rolls, beef skewers, chicken Florentine, penne pasta station, chicken Piccata with capers, crabmeat fondue, and a roast beef carving station. No one would go home hungry. Blaine and I also bargained and traded two Max and Bailey T-shirts for an addition of five pounds of boiled shrimp. Three hundred drink tickets were also included. We received permission for my sister to bring the cakes and they would provide a coffee bar. It was going to be an impressive event!

The word about our auction was getting out and again the grapevine of word of mouth was spreading. We received an email from a lady who wanted to donate an item to our auction, and it was quite unique. It was a toilet seat cover that had an engraving of a Harley on the top and an engraving of a flag on the underneath side. It was quite different, but we jumped at the chance of the uniqueness and told her we would love it as an auction item.

We started attending the Raleigh Harley Owners Group (H.O.G.) meetings and Butch Evans, the Raleigh H.O.G. Director, gave Blaine the opportunity to tell the group about our ride. Blaine offered to write an article with some pictures for their upcoming newsletter and they agreed. They were incredibly supportive of our upcoming ride. Steve Metz, their Activities Director, was a program manager at IBM who ensured that IBM's websites and applications were accessible to people with disabilities. He loved the idea of our ride and our cause and offered to be the road captain for our ride out of town.

On one of our daily rides, we met a lady name Peggy Zionts who was a breeder and heavily involved with many Golden Retriever organizations. She spread the word about our ride, and the AKC Gazette and the Golden Retriever News contacted us to submit articles to them, which Blaine quickly sent in.

My sister contacted the local paper in Goldsboro where she and my Mom lived, and they too seemed interested in our ride. The media was starting to learn about our ride!

We knew it would be a very long and difficult ride and that it would take some toll on our bodies through long miles and the stress of planning and participating in the hundreds of events across the country. It was important that all four of us received physicals before our ride to make sure we were all healthy. The dogs were first as we took them to their vet, Northwoods Animal Hospital, in

Cary, NC where we used to live. The dogs had been going there ever since they were puppies. Even when we lived on our sailboat, we took a yearly trip to go back there for their annual physicals. Their usual veterinarian, Dr. Melissa Hudson, DVM, examined them and declared them healthy for the ride. She loved the idea of our journey and said she would set up a display in their waiting room to highlight our trip and provide brochures to their customers. We knew we would get questioned about the safety of the dogs in their sidecars and thought it would be beneficial to have a veterinarian on our general board. We asked Melissa if she would join the board and we were delighted when she said "Yes"!

Blaine did a tremendous amount of research on the internet and found a website, Global SchoolNet (GSN), that would allow us to partner with hundreds of schools throughout the U.S. This is the description from their website:

Mission: Global SchoolNet's mission is to support 21st century learning and improve academic performance through content driven collaboration. We engage teachers and K-12 students in meaningful project learning exchanges worldwide to develop science, math, literacy and communication skills, foster teamwork, civic responsibility, and collaboration, encourage workforce preparedness and create multi-cultural understanding. We prepare youth for full participation as productive and effective citizens in an increasing global economy. Founded in 1984, GSN is a 501(c)3 non-profit education organization. Let's work together to give youth the skills they need.

Online Expeditions: Thanks to the Internet, you can have incredible adventures in exotic locales without spending a dime or leaving the room. Whether explorers travel the Silk Road of China or climb Mt. Everest, learning becomes an unforgettable adventure as students join thrilling, real-time expeditions to remote and fascinating locations. Observe daily progress and read field dispatches. Best of all, interact with real world adventurers through intriguing dialogue as they re-enact history—or even make history!

Blaine contacted them and they were extremely interested in our journey. It would give their students a chance to learn about Guide and Assistance Dogs and the geography of the United States as we traveled through each state. Blaine solidified our partnership with them, and they added us to their website. We ended up with daily offers from schools for us to visit them and speak to their students about Guide and Assistance Dogs. It was dawning on us that anything was possible on this ride. We just needed to believe that it was possible, and it showed up for us.

As we continued our marketing plans, we decided to have Max and Bailey be the stars of our ride while Blaine and I were merely the chauffeurs for them. It was going to be all about what our pups were doing to spread the news about Assistance Dogs.

While Blaine promoted our charity with marketing and planning, I continued to work on our route throughout the U.S., changing it as schools and event volunteers asked us to visit. As funds were starting to come in, I realized I was going to need a professional software application to help me keep track of the organization's finances. I decided on QuickBooks, so I purchased the not-for-profit version and installed it on my laptop. I did not have experience in formal accounting, so I had to learn quickly. I was grateful that I had an extensive math background. I had to make sure I set it up properly to be able to track donations individually in all 48 states that we would travel through, knowing I would have to report the donations made by each state come tax time.

Since we did not have a guide dog partner yet, we had been trying to solidify a minor partnership with Guiding Eyes for the Blind, who we had supported via donations in the past. It had been exceedingly difficult to get in touch with the decision makers in the organization. Thankfully, Sherry Dodson, who was the region coordinator for the North Carolina Puppy Raiser Program for Guiding Eyes, contacted us. Sherry and her husband, Don, managed their own dog training business, and we met with them to discuss our ride and our charity partnerships. Sherry helped us to solidify our partnership with their organization to be one of our minor partners.

Along with all our planning, we continued to ride daily. After receiving invites from a few friends of ours, we spent a three-day trip visiting friends to see how we would do with the daily rides and spending the night in a different place each night. While our evenings were long, as we spent some well-needed relaxing time catching up with our friends, we got back on our bikes each day, ready for a new adventure. It was a successful trip, and we felt we were going to be able to manage the daily routines.

The list of items that we needed to accomplish before our ride was overwhelming. We were working in the sunroom at my Mom's house and many nights I would leave Blaine still working there and head to bed with Max and Bailey. I often woke up in the middle of the night and turned over to cuddle with Blaine, only to find him not there. Lonely, I would roll back over and worry about him. Many mornings I would find him asleep on the couch, still in the sunroom. The stress of everything that needed to be done before we left was taking its toll on him.

March

As we transitioned into March, a representative from WRAL contacted us. Their employee whom we had met in the Arby's parking lot had indeed told them about our ride and we were invited to do an interview with Scott Mason. We were excited and nervous as we drove up to Raleigh to meet Scott and his cameraman in a local park. The interview process was lengthy as Scott asked us numerous questions while we sat on our motorcycles with the dogs in their sidecars. After the multitude of questions were done being asked, then the cameraman started taking various videos of the dogs, different angles of the motorcycle rigs, and then of Blaine and me in various acts of getting ready for our ride such as putting on our helmets, zipping up our jackets, and starting our motorcycles. Once the exhaustive video shoot was over, we then went on various rides around curves and along streets, including an extensive drive with them filming us as they rode alongside in their car. After approximately 3 hours, we were finally done and were looking forward to seeing our interview on TV. About a week later, it aired during the evening news, and Max and Bailey's ride was seen throughout the Triangle (Raleigh, Durham, Chapel Hill). They put together very professionally the interview segment, and we were excited about the new publicity advertising our ride.

Next, the online store officially opened, and we could sell our Hogs for Dogs logo gear and T-shirts with Max and Bailey on the back. We had a meeting at Ray Price Harley-Davidson to solidify and organize our kickoff event and our spot at the open house the week prior.

Our list of minor partners expanded when Rick Hairston of Carolina Canines for Service contacted us. He had heard about our ride from a friend of his and was interested in becoming one of our charity partners. Blaine researched his organization located in Wilmington, NC, and then called Rick to tell him more about our ride. After a productive conversation, Blaine emailed the board with information about Rick's organization and once approved, they joined us as a minor partner. Rick then invited us to come down to the Azalea festival at the beginning of April to join his organization in walking in the parade, except we would actually ride our motorcycles in it so everyone could see Max and Bailey.

The Raleigh H.O.G. group also invited us to join them in riding in the Raleigh St. Patrick's Day parade. Blaine's journal entry explains the fun day we had:

The U.S. Hogs For Dogs team wishes everyone a Happy St. Patrick's Day. After the week we've had, I have to believe that Max & Bailey once visited the 15th century Blarney Castle and kissed the Blarney Stone. The legend says that anyone who kisses the stone is henceforth endowed with the gift of eloquence and persuasive flattery. And there is no better description of how people around the country have responded to Max & Bailey's big debut on TV and through our educational partnership with Global SchoolNet.

But the biggest story of the week was Max and Bailey's ride in the Raleigh St. Patrick's Day Parade. Before the parade, Max and Bailey were the star attraction for several hundred kids and adults. The dogs just soaked up all the attention with the grace of real celebrities.

We had been invited to be a part of the parade as part of the Raleigh Harley Owners Group and were expected to be in the #11 spot in the parade. Well, somehow, in all the parade confusion, the Raleigh H.O.G. group landed in the #3 position, right behind the Parade's Grand Marshall and Raleigh's Mayor, Charles Meeker. The Grand Marshall, none other than NBC 17's Bill Gaines, spent several minutes talking with us about the upcoming charity ride while Bailey enjoyed lots of Bill's loving attention. And the icing on the cake was when Bill promised to join us on the May 1st ride out of town.

Thousands lined Raleigh's downtown streets to cheer and watch the parade. And, when the bagpipes announced the beginning of the parade march, Max & Bailey were right up near the front, smiling and wagging their tongues while wearing their goggles. The reactions were the same everywhere we looked: smiles, laughs and cheers for Max and Bailey - the dogs they had seen in the WRAL interview on TV. The next thing you know, Max and Bailey will want their own agent!

I'll close this entry with a St. Patrick's Day thought: If you travel to the Blarney Castle in county Cork of Ireland, be careful when kissing the Blarney Stone. You may find that there is a little dog slobber still on the stone from Max & Bailey's big, good luck kiss.

In the middle of the month, we received a school visit invitation from one of our friends, Paul Taubner, who we had met while cruising on our sailboat. His girls were attending Benson Elementary School, and he arranged for our very first school visit. As we headed up there, it began to rain. We did not have rain covers for the dogs, so we ducked under the cover of an abandoned gas station. We called Paul, who had arranged the visit and told him our dilemma. We were panicking because we were going to be late, and we did not want Max and Bailey to arrive soaking wet! Paul saved the day as he offered to come pick up Max and Bailey and take them to the school while we followed on our Harleys. A little while later, Max and Bailey arrived nice and dry, and we sloshed in with our rain gear on. Blaine gave a presentation for the fourth-grade class and the rain had stopped by the time we were done, so the students could see Max and Bailey in their sidecars. Despite the challenge of getting there, it had been a successful visit, and we knew we were going to make a difference throughout our journey, one student at a time.

While Max and Bailey had passed their physicals with flying colors, Blaine and I still needed to get ours completed. Mine was first, and they gave me the green light to go on our ride. Blaine completed his round of physicals and he only had one issue. He had an elevated level of uric acid, so there was a possibility of getting gout. He had never had it before, so we felt confident that it would not be an issue. Dr. Griffin, our doctor, was proactive and gave Blaine a prescription for gout medicine, which we filled before we left just to be on the safe side. That completed our physicals. We were all healthy and ready to hit the open road.

We were astonished as our auction items continued to roll in; items received this month included a flag and flagpole (installed), certificate for new shutters, special events cake, UNC signed basketball, UNC football tickets, one-day rental of a Harley-Davidson motorcycle, Rider's Edge New Rider Motorcycle course, four Jimmy Buffett concert tickets, teeth whitening certificate, ½ day fishing or eco-tour charter for two, and tennis lessons and golf lessons at Walnut Creek Country Club. Since we had remained friends with our salesman from our BMW purchase a few years earlier, we managed to get a two-day use of a brand-new BMW donated. A friend of ours, who was an avid NC State fan, vowed to get some NC State donations to compete with all the UNC donations…the rivalry between schools transformed into a rivalry of auction items, so we knew we still had more items coming in.

Our list of auction items gathered by JoLee, Mary Ann, Amanda, and the other volunteers along with Blaine and me, was impressive. Then we received a list of items that Steve had gathered, and it doubled our list in number of items. He got the following donations: golf for four at two different golf courses, state and federal tax preparation certificate, a limo for the Jimmy Buffet concert, a team-signed hockey stick from the Carolina Hurricanes, three expensive bottles of wine, $100 Ace hardware certificate, plus several restaurant gift certificates. That was impressive!

As I envisioned our auction night, I knew we needed to have a true auctioneer for the live auction part of our event, so I started calling auction firms. Miraculously, I talked to a gentleman at Stone Auction and Realty who loved the idea of our ride. Not only did he agree to be our auctioneer, but I was able to get him to donate his time, so our auctioneer was free for us. Wow...that was certainly an unexpected bonus!

More media opportunities showed up. Jay received permission to submit an article about our ride to Thunder Press, a motorcycle magazine, so he submitted the article which was due to be published in their May magazine, which would be out mid-April. Also, the local Goldsboro newspaper, The News Argus, interviewed us and took pictures, but we did not know when it would appear in the paper. Another TV station, WWAY, out of Wilmington, NC came up for an interview as well. The spring edition of FIDO Friendly came out and Max and Bailey were in a full-page ad for our charity. The word was miraculously getting out to the media, and they loved Max and Bailey!

The school invites were steadily coming in and we did our best to work them into our schedule. I was constantly tweaking our route when a new school came up where we thought we could visit. Some invitations we could not make, especially if they were in a town where we were scheduled to be during the summer months when they were out of school. We scheduled about 50% of the invitations before our ride began and we knew we would continue to get more invitations as the word was spreading about our ride.

April

On April 2nd, we headed down to Wilmington for the Azalea Festival the following day. This was the first time we were relying on my new GPS for directions as we were traveling to our first unknown place with the motorcycles and dogs, so I was extremely nervous about getting us to where we needed to go. We headed down using only back roads to avoid the interstate.

Pat Nowak, the office manager for Carolina Canines, had emailed us before our trip to let us know we would have a complimentary stay at the Jamison Inn, which was pet friendly. We had never stayed at one before and were excited to try it. The hotel was easy to find, and we quickly hauled our stuff into the room and got Max and Bailey settled in. They were used to traveling and staying in hotels, so they quickly laid down and relaxed. Bailey was happy I had brought some of his toys with us.

A little while later, Pat and Rick picked us up so we could spend the evening getting to know each other over dinner. We swapped stories about how each of our organizations was founded. Rick said that he had volunteered for several years with a service dog organization in St. Louis, MO. When he moved to Wilmington, NC, he found that there were no formal service dog training programs in southeast North Carolina. He felt God was calling him to start a new service dog training program, so he started with one black Labrador puppy named Moses, and Carolina Canines was born. They decided they would give all future Carolina Canines service dogs biblical names.

Carolina Canines not only trained service dogs, but they also trained owner/dog teams to become therapy dog teams. One program that was spawned off the therapy dog teams was their Paws for Reading program. This program would allow therapy dog teams (the therapy dog and handler) to go into schools or libraries and work with children that were reading below their grade level by letting them read to the therapy dog. The program worked well because, while a child may be intimidated by reading to an adult, the child was more relaxed and had fun reading to the therapy dog. This program made it enjoyable to read and soon the children in the program were reading at or above their grade level.

While we knew how amazing Assistance Dogs were, we had not realized the tremendous impact a therapy dog could have on a child by improving their love of reading. Our dinner was highly informative, and we had fun getting to know our new friends.

The next morning, we were up bright and early and joined the Carolina Canines crew at the parade start location. We got to meet so many lovely people, including many puppy raisers and several recipients of service dogs from Carolina Canines. It was so touching to hear the recipients' stories and to learn how the service dogs completely changed their lives and the independence and comfort they received from their dogs. This was just the tip of the iceberg, since we would spend our entire journey with stories like these that always brought tears to our eyes.

Blaine's journal entry after our adventures at the Azalea Festival shares the story of one of the service dog recipients:

Yesterday, at the North Carolina Azalea Festival Parade, I met a man that I could really look up to. That may seem unusual, however, because I had to look down to speak with him since he was unable to rise from his wheelchair. He has no use of his legs due to Multiple Sclerosis and is dependent on a motorized wheelchair for his mobility. His name is Edmond Kent.

I was immediately drawn to Edmond in the early morning hours as we waited to ride in the Azalea Festival Parade. He arrived almost unnoticed at the designated parade gathering spot, where Carolina Canines - one of our charity partners - was assembling for the parade, and he simply sat off to one side of the sidewalk, out of the way of passerby traffic. Yet, his quiet confidence, bright spirit and silent determination left a palpable feeling in the air from the first time he smiled and said hello. He had come to march in the parade with his wife Brenda and Gideon, his Assistance Dog that was trained and provided by Carolina Canines.

Edmond told Janet and me how he and Gideon had first met. Carolina Canines had worked with Gideon for his initial training for several months before he and Gideon were introduced. At the introduction, there were four clients in the room. Gideon walked into the room and immediately walked up to Edmond. And although Carolina Canines had already decided that Gideon would be placed with Edmond, nobody had told either of them. Gideon just seemed to 'know'. Their partnership continues to have that unique bond that is sometimes unexplainable by simple logic and understanding.

But it was not until Gideon's trainer Cynthia Mackie joined the conversation that we learned how this partnership of man and dog had changed Edmond's life. I'll admit to you that I was wondering just what Edmond was doing with a service dog because he had great use of his upper body and hands. What could Gideon really do for him? Well, my ignorance was rewarded with a story of how prior to Gideon's placement it would take Edmond almost two full hours to get back into his wheelchair when he would fall. Two hours of dragging himself to the nearest wall, pushing himself back into a sitting position and then struggling to pull himself into his chair. Without the use of his legs, Edmond would be exhausted after such a fall. Enter Gideon.

During their first training session, Cynthia asked Edmond what his most difficult task was. Edmond mentioned the long struggles after a fall. Cynthia then said, "let's see it" and put Edmond on the ground with Gideon. Gideon spent a while trying to figure out how to help Edmond back into his chair, but eventually they worked it out together - in much less than two hours. With great joy and satisfaction, Edmond rewarded Gideon by praising him with the words, "You're the man, Gideon. You're the man."

I feel very fortunate to have met Edmond. Having learned the depth of his daily challenges, I was impressed with how his perseverance keeps him going with a positive outlook on life and a smile for all those around him. And though I think Gideon is an amazing dog, I'd like to say something to Edmond in this journal - "Thank you for your inspiration and for reminding me that this ride is about helping people reclaim their independence." And lastly, "You're the man, Edmond. You're the man."

So with less than a month to go before we begin this 25,000-mile journey for charity, I have another role model to help keep me focused on how important it is that we succeed in educating the public about the largely unmet needs for Assistance Dogs to be trained and placed with people just like Edmond. And while words and education help improve the understanding of these needs, it takes donations to solve the problem; donations from people like you and me. I made another financial donation today. I'm now asking you to do the same.

If you're still struggling to decide whether you should make a donation today, why not try falling on the floor and then spend the next two hours getting back into a chair without using your legs before you decide? And it's not fair to ask your dog for help because without your donations there won't be any Assistance Dogs to help the millions of Americans who are waiting to have a Gideon of their own.

Therapy Dogs

During our visit with Rick and Pat, Rick mentioned getting our dogs certified as therapy dogs. Unlike service dogs who are allowed in all public places per the ADA, therapy dogs are not allowed in all public places; however, the certification would give us a better chance of being able to take the dogs into schools, hospitals, and nursing homes where therapy dogs are often allowed. We thought it was a wise idea. At the time, we had no idea how helpful those certifications would become to us during our journey and the doors it would open for unique visits as we crossed America.

Rick stepped us through the therapy dog certification process. Since our final certification would be through the Delta Society, we had to follow the requirements for their process. We took a home study course to learn responsibilities of therapy dog handlers, how to interact with clients, ways to handle different situations, and recognizing stress in dogs to know when to take a break or retreat on a visit. When we were done with the course, we were grateful that Rick drove up to Goldsboro to give Max and Bailey their final tests. It was an interesting test process, including basic commands and many distractions, such as being crowded and petted by multiple people, being bumped from behind, and having a metal ball full of chain dropped behind the dog. With a possibility of being extremely startled and bolting when the ball was dropped, Bailey just looked at it with a "so what" attitude. When they were aggressively petted during the test, both dogs loved it. Goldens just love attention!

The dogs did great with all their tests and qualified for the "Complex" certification level, which had no restrictions. If there were certain circumstances that the dog could not handle, then the dog could be certified with restrictions, such as "one-on-one work only". Max and Bailey handled all situations well, so no restrictions were required.

After we had finished all the qualifications, we filled out our applications. We had to submit four applications pairing Max and Bailey with each of us so that both Blaine and I could be the handlers for both of them. Once certified, we received two badges for each of us with our pictures on them. For example, I received my two ID badges, one with a picture of Bailey and me and one with Max and me. That certified me to be the handler for either dog.

The Shakedown Trip

Slowly, our trip began to take shape. Now we needed to figure out how we were going to carry everything we needed for seven months on two motorcycles. Thankfully, I have never been one of those women who packs for a weeklong trip in a suitcase the same size as me. I have always been a great packer for traveling. When I graduated from college, I went on a 30-day trip to Europe with only one medium-sized suitcase and one toiletry bag. However, now I had to pack for seven months into one small suitcase that would fit into the passenger seat of my motorcycle, along with a toiletry bag strapped on top of it. That was going to be a challenge! We had to pack for all weather conditions, including our rain gear.

We not only had to pack personal items, such as clothing, toiletries, rain gear, etc., but we also had to take everything required to run a business, such as laptops, a printer, a credit card machine, etc. along with all the stuff for the dogs, such as food, water, bowls, and toys. We made lists of everything we wanted to take with us and pared it down. Then we pared it down again and then once more.

We planned a shakedown trip to the Outer Banks of North Carolina for the Outer Banks Bike Week. This would be a daunting test for us! We would try to pack everything as if we were leaving on our 7-month trip. We would travel with a few other bikers to the Outer Banks, and then we would be at a huge rally with hundreds of other bikers.

I was extremely nervous about this event. Our first biker rally…Yikes! Would they accept us into the community? Blaine looked like Opie trying to appear as a tough biker dude and I felt I was doing a poor impression of a biker babe. Would they find us out? Would they realize we were new to this biker world? I was also the only female in this group traveling to the rally. I have always worked in male-dominated environments, so I believed I was prepared for it, but was I?

We met up with the group outside of Greenville, NC. It consisted of our board members, Jay and Steve, and one of their fellow H.O.G. members, Jesse, who wanted to join us for this ride. They were laughing at Jesse as we approached, since he was shivering so hard his coffee was spilling over the edges. It was quite chilly that morning. Jay and Steve had larger cruising motorcycles and stayed pretty warm behind their fairings, which protected them from the chilly wind. Fairings are protective paneling that wrap around the frame of the motorcycles to reduce aerodynamic drag for fuel efficiency; however, they also provided excellent protection for the motorcyclist. Jesse, on the other hand, was riding a sweet custom Fat Boy which had no fairings, so he could not stay shielded from the cold. Poor guy was freezing!

As we got off our bikes to join our crew, a crowd gathered around our bikes to see Max and Bailey, so we spent some time spreading the word of our charity ride and cause. Our new group was starting to find out that a quick stop was not always going to be so quick! After chatting with several people and receiving some donations, we continued on our way.

Our next stop was in Bath, NC, the oldest city in North Carolina. We wanted to stop at the Bath Harbor Marina and check on our sailboat. It had been a while since we saw her and wanted to ensure she was doing fine in her current slip. Max and Bailey got to stretch their legs, and we showed off our home for the past four years.

Then we were off for a lunch stop. Just a mile down the road was one of our favorite Mom and Pop joints, Old Town Country Kitchen, famous for their cheese biscuits that had so much cheddar cheese in them that they became bricks if you let them cool off. It was our favorite breakfast stop whenever we were cruising on our sailboat and stopped in Bath. We parked the bikes in the shade for the pups and went inside for a great southern lunch.

After our stomachs were full and we had caught up with each other, we headed down U.S. 92 and then Hwy 264 towards the Outer Banks, passing through the Mattamuskeet National Wildlife Refuge and flirting with sights of the Pamlico Sound off our right side. It was a long ride with one rest stop along the way, but it was a beautiful scenic ride through the eastern part of the state. As we approached Manteo, NC, I got the whiff of the ocean breeze and Jay, our ultimate tour guide, planned our next stop, The Weeping Radish, for a beer and a midday snack of German sausages and onion rings. We relaxed and chatted about our plans for the next day at the rally. Max and Bailey were amazing as usual as they chilled in their sidecars and were rewarded with a bite of sausage before heading back on the road.

We headed into Manteo and parted ways for the next couple of hours while they found their hotel and we went to find the condo, which was generously offered to us by a great friend of ours. We got settled into the condo and made sure Max and Bailey were comfortable; then we headed back out to meet the crew for dinner. Since it was just the two of us, we decided I would just ride on the back of Blaine's bike.

Our crew was waiting for us at Tortuga Lies and we had a delicious seafood dinner. We wanted to check out the beach party at Kelly's, so we headed back out on the bikes. Blaine and I were in for a shocking surprise as Blaine took a right-hand turn out of the parking lot. Seems we both forgot that the bike rides differently with no weight in the sidecar and this effect is exaggerated when someone (me) is riding on the back of the bike in the passenger's seat. The effect is that the sidecar easily lifts off the ground, leaning the bike quickly to the left side. We almost tipped over! Thankfully, both of us were quick to react and put our left feet on the ground to keep the bike upright. Jesse was waiting to follow behind us and was rolling with laughter as he saw our expressions when we realized what was happening and shifted our weight to right the bike as we continued through our turn. Holy smokes, that was a close one! We chuckled all the way to our next stop and retold our near mishap to the rest of the crew when we stopped. Jesse was still laughing at us!

We hung out at Kelly's for a bit, where Jay appropriately described it as "too many people, too loud, and too many guys in one room". I was enjoying it, but my male crew ended up hanging out in the parking lot and shooting the breeze with newfound friends out there.

The next morning, Jay picked up a couple dozen eggs, bacon, bread, and OJ and came over to the condo, where I whipped up a substantial breakfast for the crew. We then headed to Nag's Head Harley-Davidson, where the crowd gathered for the start of the Poker Run. After a ride around the parking lot, we found a spot and parked our new hack rigs in the middle of the event. We realized that trying to find parking for these two huge rigs was going to be a challenge. Next, we prepared for the true test. How would the biker world react to the dogs in sidecars? Answer: They were a HUGE hit! Everybody loved the dogs and thought they were the coolest things as they hammed it up in their sidecars. The pups adored the attention and hundreds of pictures were taken of them.

Photo credit: Jay Schwantes

To promote our non-profit organization and our purpose, we had made brochure holders to snap onto the sidecars and decorated a bin to collect donations. Seeing the newfound attention, we snapped our brochure holders onto each sidecar, and I propped up our donation bin on the back of my sidecar.

Media attention found us as we got reps from Thunder Roads and Pampered Pooch stopping by for pictures and info about our ride. Jay knew the owner and general manager for the dealership and introduced them to us and the pups. They offered their support if we wanted to do an event at one of their east coast dealerships on our return leg of the trip.

Bikers started heading out to begin the Poker Run, and the surrounding crowd started to quickly decline. Since we finally had time to catch our breath, Blaine came over and told me about one biker that he spoke with about the reason for our ride. One of the male bikers handed Blaine a donation with tears in his eyes and a heartfelt "Thank You". The charity hit close to home as his father was physically disabled, so he knew how much these dogs could help. He was so choked up as he talked to Blaine that Blaine too became misty eyed. After relaying this story to me, we also were both choked up. It was a preview of the many times we would be touched by stories relayed to us about the lives these dogs would touch. This was confirmation that our purpose was spot on.

After most of the bikes headed out for the Poker Run, we headed out as well for a 60-mile ride to the Hatteras lighthouse, skipping most of the Poker Run stops along the way. We stopped at the 4th stop of the Poker Run, The Reef Restaurant, and backed our bikes up to the restaurant porch railing. There was a crowd of bikers standing in line to get their next card for the Poker Run, but we believe Max and Bailey had an even bigger crowd around them. We were seeing how popular those two pups were going to be in their sidecars.

We finished our ride to the Cape Hatteras Lighthouse and took a few pictures of us, the pups, and the rigs in front of the lighthouse.

After a remarkably successful weekend, we headed home. We started to feel like real bikers and learned the hazards of biking as well. As the dark clouds rolled in, we donned our rain gear. I worried about trying to find cover for the dogs, since we had not made sidecar covers for them yet. I did not want their sidecars to fill up with rain and to have them riding around in swimming pools. At one point, we had to duck into an abandoned gas station to hide from the rain; it was short lived, so we continued our ride. I realized this was the second abandoned gas station that we had ducked into for rain protection. I was hoping this would not become a trend.

Finally, we needed a break to stretch our legs and grab a quick bite to eat, so we all piled into a McDonald's. After finishing my meal, I stepped out of the restaurant to call my Mom to let her know we were heading back and were still safe. As I walked back in, all the guys were chuckling. I was infused with the laughter and, chuckling myself, asked what was so funny. While I was gone, Steve wanted an apple pie for dessert. He did not want the whole thing, so he offered Jay the other half. He took out his pocketknife and cut it into two halves and shared. While they were chatting, he cleaned his knife and continued to play with it...flicking it open, flicking it closed, flicking it open, flicking it closed.

Blaine noticed a couple trying to find a seat near them and, nervously eyeing Steve, they immediately went to the other side of the restaurant. Then another couple got up mid-mouthful and moved to another table! Seemed everyone saw this unruly biker crowd with one biker threatening with a knife. When in reality, it was Steve, a manager for IBM, and Jay, owner of a website management company, trying to share an apple pie. I learned of the reactions of the customers and just burst out laughing!

The Final Weeks Before the Journey Began

As we continued with our daily practice rides, we quickly came up to our 2500-mile service. We took our motorcycles back up to Ray-Price for that service so we would be ready for our May 1st kickoff.

As the weeks were ticking down to our kickoff, we were still figuring out logistics. While we had been cruising on our sailboat, my Mom had been receiving our mail and paying bills as needed. She had a power of attorney for both of us in case she needed to sign something for us. We continued with this arrangement and planned for mail drops to us when we would stay with family or friends. We also knew that we were going to need supplies like the dogs' heartworm meds and joint care meds during our journey. With limited storage space on the motorcycles, we mailed the needed supplies to family members at strategic places so they would be waiting when we arrived.

A few more volunteers joined us. We met April Fort when we were visiting our sailing friends, the Taubners. They were neighbors, and Paul and Colleen had told April about our ride. April was already familiar with Carolina Canines, knew Rick Hairston, and had volunteered at some of their events. We went over to April's house to meet her Golden Retriever and Saint Bernard and to discuss our organization. After meeting us and hearing more about our ride, she was excited to volunteer with us.

Annette Rowan was a long-time friend of mine. We met in ninth grade before both of us went to different high schools and parted ways. Years later, I moved to Cary, NC and picked the State Farm agent that Annette was working for. What a coincidence. We remained friends, and she followed our sailing website. She volunteered to help us with our auction and kickoff events

Jay had created a form on our website where interested people could fill out a volunteer form if they wanted to volunteer for an event, school visit, or host us for an evening. Both April and Annette started reviewing all our volunteer requests that were coming in. For each one, they contacted the volunteer for more details and to see if they were somewhere close to our route. The volunteers were setting up events and meet and greets for us. If the volunteer event looked doable, then they would pass the info along to Blaine, so he could coordinate further with the volunteer. April and Annette stayed in the loop to assist with the event details and to make sure our brochures and logo gear would be sent to the location in time for the event. If it was a major event, then it was handed over to Steve Metz, who had become our events coordinator. While this was going on, I was changing our route to the specific event areas. We knew this was going to be ongoing with our route constantly changing.

Beth Cassels, a previous coworker of Blaine, had also been following our sailing website and, since she and her husband were Harley riders, she fell in love with the charity ride. She joined our general board and offered to coordinate our school visits that were coming in through GlobalSchool.net. She took those invites, matched the location to see if our route would pass by the school area within the school year timeframe, and connected Blaine and me with the school volunteer to see if we could change our route to make a school visit. Many of these school visits would also spawn fundraising events as well.

A trickle of donations began coming into our website, but we knew we needed to have more cash flow for our ride to be successful. We were relying heavily on the charity auction that the board and volunteers were planning. We continued to get items donated for the auction, including a signed NC State basketball, an NC State mini football helmet signed by coach Chuck Amato, and tickets to the NC State vs. Miami football game; our avid NC State fan delivered. Go Pack! Larry Johnson, Frank Vester, and Pete Oakley donated a southern pig pickin' for the auction. I used to work with the three of them at IBM and we became good friends. Blaine and I used to have a yearly party at our house in Willow Spring, NC and we always asked them to roast a pig for us for a good ol' pig pickin'. It was my favorite time of year. We were excited to have that as an auction item. Blaine and I also donated our timeshare week in Harborside at Atlantis in Nassau, Bahamas and a one-week chartered sailing vacation on our sailboat.

We started receiving the newsletters from our charity partners and they were including information about our ride to get the word out.

Finally, the auction day arrived. It was time to get prepared for the "Tail Wagging Affair." Unfortunately, the forecast was for rain that day, so we tried to get one of our motorcycle rigs inside the event space. We finally figured out how to get it inside and the preparations continued.

Our volunteers were amazing! My sister brought three cakes decorated in honor of our ride. There were two round cakes, one with red and white wavey stripes and the other was blue with white stars. She topped each one with a figurine of a Harley with a sidecar attached. The third cake was decorated with the map of the U.S. with sections of the country decorated to represent the atmosphere of the areas. She also helped with all the decorations throughout the event space.

The tables were covered with elegant white tablecloths and decorated with motorcycle and dog related items. There was a silent auction that would allow people to sip on drinks, munch on hors d'oeuvres, and place their bids on the auction items. A live auction would follow, being led by our auctioneer from Stone Auction and Realty.

The silent auction items had been placed on long tables covered in white tablecloths. Each item had a bid sheet with the recommended starting bid and lines where the bidders could place their bid. Blaine had created the booklets that would be given to all the attendees. It contained information about our ride, our charity partners, and descriptions of all items that would be available during the live auction. There was a bar set up along with stations of hors d'oeuvres and a beautiful buffet of delicious food.

We had sold a large number of tickets, but as the start time of 7:00 pm approached, there was only a trickle of people coming in. The rain was coming down steady and hard and we were nervous that this would keep our attendance down. Blaine had several phone calls throughout the day as people called to apologize that they would not be attending. As time passed, we knew we were going to have a much smaller turnout and Blaine and I were nauseous as we envisioned small or non-existent auction bids. By 7:30, we still only had about 40 people at the event. At 8:00 p.m. we had reached almost 70 attendees, which was a far cry from the 150 we had hoped for. Deb Davis from PAWS had flown down from Michigan and we had several client/dog teams who had joined us. We hoped our event would not be a disappointment.

Our good friend Brad Parker showed up and gave us encouragement, as he told us that many of his friends were coming. He had been incredibly supportive in getting donations for us and he continued to support us by rallying up a crowd for the event. As we chatted with Brad, we saw his friends begin to trickle in. Brad had already browsed the charity items up for auction and we bantered about which ones we wanted to bid on, hoping we were not bidding on the same items for a bidding war.

Despite the small crowd, everyone was mingling, sipping on bar drinks, and bidding on the silent auction items. Blaine and I joined them, and I enjoyed a friendly bidding war with April's husband, Mike. We were bidding on a double magnum of 1998 Chateau Barreyres Haut-Medoc. Every time I placed a bid and walked away, I would see Mike approach it and outbid me again.

Brad and Dr. Melissa also had their own bidding war over the Parrothead basket, which included two tickets to the Jimmy Buffett concert for the following Tuesday, a pinata, and salt and pepper shakers to avoid Buffett's Margaritaville "lost shaker of salt". They were getting serious as each of them continued to outbid the other person.

Since the crowd was not too big and many of them were our good friends, the atmosphere became less formal and more like a party atmosphere...just a lot of fun. There were no long lines for food or drink, and you could feel the excitement in the air as participants bantered over the silent auction items and subsequent bidding wars.

Soon the silent auction ended, and it was time for the live auction to begin. Since we had lots of action on the silent auction items, we were hopeful. Before the auctioneer began the bidding, Blaine asked the auctioneer if he could say a few words before we started the auction. He knew he needed to relay the heartfelt reason for the ride.

He stood up in front of the crowd and talked about the many people we had already met and the amazing things that service dogs were doing to give them independence. Story after story, his words tugged at the hearts of our attendees. He described the tasks that these incredible dogs could complete, but he also emphasized the feelings the recipients felt with these dogs. They were finally empowered to lead a life without depending on another person to constantly help them. He finished with the story of Edmond. You're the man, Edmond, you're the man. There was not a dry eye in the crowd.

Blaine introduced our auctioneer, and the bidding war began. While we had a small turnout, they had certainly come out to support our cause. The bidding for each item remained steady and Blaine and I were hopeful for successful end to the evening. The last two items were our big-ticket items: the sailing vacation and the Bahamas timeshare week. The bidding for the sailing vacation started and there was a frenzy of activity as many bids came in. Brad finally won top bid for the vacation at $2,100. Thank you, Brad! The last item auctioned off was the week at the Harborside Resort. Our jaws dropped as we watched the bidding war for this last item. The winning bid was $4,700! Nancy Livesay was the winner and Blaine had worked for her at Cisco. Thank you, Nancy! Blaine and I sat there in shock…$6,800 in just the two items alone.

We pulled all the silent bidding sheets and the list of live auction winners and tallied up the amounts owed by each person. I was pleasantly surprised that I was the winner of the double magnum of wine! Brad and Melissa both came over to check their final tallies and Melissa was extremely disappointed that she did not win the Parrothead package. She really wanted to go to the Buffett concert. Brad asked for her phone number and said he would see what he could do about getting tickets for her since he had some connections. I was curious what the outcome would be for that.

While we had fretted over the small turnout, the crowd had shown their enormous hearts. The final total was over $20,000 in profits! Blaine and I were astounded at the final tally. What a way to kick off our ride!

The next day, we headed to Ray Price Harley-Davidson for their open house event. They had a table set up for us, so we could sell our Hogs for Dogs logo gear and tickets to our kickoff event. Our table stayed crowded all day long as we told them about our ride, sold logo gear, and raised excitement about our kickoff ride the following weekend. Our volunteers were impressive and Blaine's journal entry described one of them.

I really enjoyed the surprised looks on people's faces when they realized that Penny Zibula, the volunteer taking their money and packing their shirts and ride registration items, was blind. She had the help of her guide dog, CJ, and several volunteers, but Penny proved that having a disability, like blindness, does not mean that a person cannot make great contributions. She is just one example of what is possible with a good attitude, a willing service dog and a supportive community.

There was still a crowd at our table as the event organizers started closing the event and trying to take away our table. We moved everything to our boxes and kept on chatting about our ride and our kickoff event. By the end of the day, we had pre-registered 55 riders for the event the following week.

As we approached our minivan the next morning, I noticed broken glass around it. Running around to the other side, I saw that someone had broken into our van during the night. We had loaded it with boxes and boxes of T-shirts for our kickoff event. Thankfully, the burglar realized he could never sell those T-shirts with Max and Bailey's picture on the back, so he left all the merchandise there.

Blaine gave me a hug to comfort me as I was shaking at the thought of the near loss. We were frustrated that we had to deal with getting a window fixed during our last week of preparations. However, we were incredibly grateful that we did not lose our T-shirts that we needed for our event the following Saturday!

After a tough morning, we headed back to my Mom's house where we were greeted with a fantastic surprise. The article about our ride was in the Sunday paper of the Goldsboro News-Argus. We were on the front page of the feature section with an eye-catching color picture of Max in his sidecar at the top of the page.

We spent the next week gathering everything we would need for the trip and then continuously pared it down so we could fit everything in our bikes. Thankfully, there was storage behind the sidecar seats, so that was helpful. The list of items needed went on and on: clothes, shoes, toiletries, rain gear, leather jackets with liners, multiple gloves, helmets, dog food, dog treats, jug of water for dogs, dog toys, first aid kit, tools, two laptops, a digital camera, a small portable printer, a credit card machine, donation bin, brochures, logo gear (t-shirts and hats), atlas, and the list continued on.

For our clothes, we had purchased T-Bags Route 66 bags for both of us. They had wheels and telescopic handles like most rolling luggage, but they were made to fit in the passenger seat and be strapped to the bikes. An optional saddle roll could be attached on the top and we both opted for those. It contained a built-in rain cover to protect our clothes from the rain. Since we had to pack light, we both brought 3-4 pairs of jeans, several T-shirts, a pair of shorts, sweatpants, a denim shirt, tennis shoes, and undergarments. Our leather jackets and boots were worn daily.

Our toiletries were kept in the saddle roll bags and I had to be minimalistic. After living on the boat for four years, I was used to wearing no makeup, so I did not bring any with me. My long hair was always back in a ponytail, so hair care was also basic.

All week long we packed and rearranged things, trying to figure out the most efficient way to put everything according to frequency of use. We stored a soft-sided container of dog food in the back of the sidecar of my bike and refilled a Ziploc every few days from it. That Ziploc was kept in a zippered bag made into the shape of my side saddlebag. All the other daily dog supplies such as dog bowls, treats, and toys were also in there. Therefore, at the end of the day, I just had to pull out that one zippered bag, and we had all the dog supplies needed for the night. The packing and repacking continued all week long as our minds repeatedly went through our new daily routine.

On Tuesday, we took one night off our trip planning and went to the Jimmy Buffett concert. Since several of our friends and board members were going to the concert, we decided we were all going to tailgate together before the concert.

Brad owned a limousine business, and he usually was the chauffeur for Jimmy Buffett when he was in concert in the Raleigh, NC area. This night, one of Brad's other drivers, Johnny, was the one to chauffeur Buffett. We had found out about this and knew that Buffett owned a Golden Retriever. Therefore, we arranged for Johnny to give Buffett a PR package including one of our T-shirts with Max and Bailey on the back of it along with some information about our ride. We never knew when our marketing ideas would work, but we at least had to try!

Brad had donated a limo ride to the Buffett concert as a charity auction item and Blaine and I had won it. Brad was our chauffeur for the evening. He had come through on his promise to Melissa about getting tickets for her. Not only was he able to score a couple of tickets for her to the concert, but he also offered to pick up her and her boyfriend in the limo. We were elated to see them in the limo when Brad came to pick us up. What a great surprise!

As Brad drove us into the parking area, we ended up with a prime spot for tailgating. Our other board members, Jay and Steve, had also come out to tailgate with us. Everyone had brought snacks and Brad came prepared with his portable blender powered by a weed eater motor. He was extremely popular as he blended up delicious frozen margaritas for our crew. We started drawing a crowd who was interested in these popular margaritas.

After several months of non-stop stress as we worked day and night to organize this ride, this was the absolute perfect way for us to de-stress and enjoy a night with our friends before our 7-month journey began. For Blaine and me, this night was priceless!

The rest of the week flew by and suddenly it was the Friday before our kickoff event. Blaine and I discussed the impending start of our trip and gave each other moral support as our nerves started to kick in. We did not feel like we were ready at all, but we had run out of time. With no choices left, we took a deep breath and started packing the remaining stuff on the bikes. We spent an extra hour or two trying to get everything into its place. There were things we decided that we just had to leave behind since they did not fit. It was extremely difficult to pare down the things we could take and hope we would not need the items we left behind. We managed without them, so I believe we made the right decisions.

When it was time to leave my Mom's house, I hugged her tightly. With tears in my eyes, I tried to be brave. It broke my heart knowing I would not see her for seven months. I assured her we would stay safe, not really knowing myself if we would. The fear of the unfamiliar territory ahead gripped me, but I did not let her know of my uncertainties. I told her we would check in often with her and keep her updated on our adventures.

With the unknown weighing heavily on us, we then headed to Raleigh. I had butterflies in my stomach. Actually, instead of butterflies, I think I had elephants rumbling around in there. When we got to our hotel, we realized how much stuff we were going to have to lug into the hotels each night: two suitcases on wheels with toiletry bags strapped on top, two tour pack units filled with T-shirts for sale, two laptops, dog supplies bag, dog water jug, helmets, and one purse. Were we really going to be able to manage moving this much stuff into the hotel each night? Of course, that meant that we had to lug that much down the next day and pack it nicely back onto the bikes. This was going to be a long 218 days of travel!

May - The Adventure Begins

May 1 - Day 1: Raleigh, NC - Climax, NC

We awoke the next morning to the sound of rain on the roof. Ugh! Our big kickoff event and second major fundraiser was going to be rained out. We were devastated! Who would be crazy enough to head out in the rain to ride around on their motorcycle for an unknown charity event? We had not finished our dog rain covers, so we attempted to get those ready as we headed to Ray Price's for our event. It amazed us that there were people who still came out for the event.

Just before it was time to head out, Butch Evans and Steve Metz got the attention of all attendees. They asked us to join them and then presented us with a $2,000 check on behalf of the Raleigh H.O.G. organization. We were very touched by the generosity of the H.O.G. group, who had been giving us moral support for the past few months, and now they were also donating money to help our cause. Choked up by how much this meant to us, Blaine and I were glad it was raining as we left the building so they would not see our tears of gratefulness.

The rain had been falling on and off as our event unfolded. We said farewell to our friends who would not be riding to the second venue of our kickoff event, and we got in line for our "Get Out of Town" ride. I was extremely nervous as we waited for them to start the ride. Our ride was escorted out of town by several Raleigh City Police and Wake County Sheriff cars with handoffs scheduled for county sheriff cars of the counties we would be traversing. This was the first organized motorcycle ride we had been on, and we were at the head of the line behind our road captain. The road captain was the leader of the ride, so I just needed to keep up with him. Would I be able to handle my big sidecar rig and keep up with all these experienced Harley riders? Oh boy! Those elephants were back in my stomach!

It was time! Steve was our ride captain, and he rolled out of the parking lot behind our police escort as I followed behind him with Blaine and Max behind us. Thankfully, we were followed by a small group of motorcycle riders and Corvette owners who braved the rain to support our first ride of the trip. It was exhilarating to be escorted by the blue lights and sirens alerting other cars and to see intersections blocked off for us as we went, so our entire motorcade could pass through. I was so grateful for the Harley Owners Group escort so I could enjoy the ride and not worry about routing us.

Since we had CB capabilities on our Harleys, we could communicate with many of the other riders as we took the first ride of our trip. It was awesome to hear the support. With the police escort, it was just a phenomenal feeling! We were off! No turning back now! We traveled along the back roads for a little over an hour to The Garage Motor Sports Bar in Burlington, NC for a fun time with a live band and plenty of food and drink. Some of our volunteers sold our logo gear out of the back of an SUV. We had a superb turnout there despite the rain. Max and Bailey got to park under the event tents and soaked up all the attention again. They were in heaven and more than happy to be the ambassadors for this charity ride!

While I was chatting with people who came up to visit Max and Bailey, a group of lady riders from the H.O.G. group pulled me aside. Since motorcycle riders are predominantly male, they told me I was an inspiration to all the female riders out there and that they admired how brave I was to take on this adventure. I had not felt so brave, so their support meant the world to me!

After a fun time was had by all, Blaine, Max, Bailey, and I headed to Climax, NC to stay with my sister, Sue Charbonneau, and her daughter, Jennifer, at their house. Both had attended the events of the day to support our send off. This town fit the scheme of unusual town names. We were ready to embark on the first night of our 218-day trip. As we settled in to our first night on the road, it was comforting to be in a familiar place with family by our side to enjoy our excitement. Before we could relax, we had to start our daily evening routine. Blaine had to download our pictures of the day and continue responding to emails and planning new school visits. I had to count and document the money we made at our events and on T-shirt sales, plan our route for the next day, and download the route onto my GPS. Once accomplished, we could kick back, enjoy the rest of the evening, visit with my sister and niece, and try to ignore the anxious feelings from thinking ahead of the following day. Our next day would be our first day by ourselves and my first day routing us.

May 2 - Day 2: Climax, NC - Mount Airy, NC

As we left the next morning, our butterflies continued. I had done my research and found a dog-friendly hotel in Mount Airy, NC, otherwise known as Mayberry. This was the town where Andy Griffith grew up and from which The Andy Griffith Show was designed. As we started our route through the back roads of North Carolina, we started our daily routine. I would ride in front as "The Navigator." Blaine would follow behind as "The Protector"...keeping an eye out for me and Bailey, watching out for him and Max, and switching lanes first to allow me to move lanes easily and continue my routing.

On this day, I learned that my GPS software did not always match the roads and the road names in the program were not always the same on the road signs. For some insane reason, instead of saying "Turn right in half a mile onto Hwy 220", it would say "Turn right in half a mile onto Battleground Avenue". Of course, all the road signs would say "Hwy 220", not "Battleground Avenue", so I would just have to guess on the road and see if I was following the GPS arrow properly.

Needless to say, I was pretty stressed out at trying to follow this route with Blaine behind me asking me if I knew where I was going. He did not understand the difficulties I was having with the GPS. After a couple of U-turns on missed roads, we had a beautiful ride through the country lanes of North Carolina and made it to Mount Airy safely. Lesson of the day for me was to create my route in the GPS software as well as Microsoft Streets and Trips and become familiar with the next day's route to ease my stress each day.

After unpacking the bikes, the four of us settled into our small room. It was going to be close quarters for the next 216 days as Blaine and I shared one room with nowhere to go if we had a disagreement and needed a time out. Thankfully, we had been living on our sailboat inside close quarters and had learned how to give each other "space". I felt our boat living had prepared us for this ride.

May 3 - Day 3: Mount Airy, NC - Deep Gap, NC

After a good night's sleep, we packed the bikes for another day's adventures. We were starting to feel a little more confident about our new daily routine and being on the road. As we were getting the dogs loaded into their sidecars, we got a visit from the hotel manager and one of the cleaning staff. They loved the dogs and had to come out and see what our story was. After hearing our story, the hotel manager said she would pay for our hotel bill, so we ended up with the night's stay for free. We were feeling the generosity of small-town America.

We then headed to the quaint town of Mount Airy for a brief visit before we turned west. We found the downtown area where we could eat at Snappy Lunch, made famous on The Andy Griffith Show. We navigated the downtown streets and found the well-known little sandwich shop. Thankfully, we found an excellent parking spot near the entrance, so we went inside and found a seat where we could keep an eye out for our pups in the sidecars. Both of us ordered the legendary pork chop sandwich. We ate a delicious lunch in the nostalgic ole place and then headed out to join our pups for an afternoon ride. As we headed out, we saw a large group of elementary students heading our way. They saw Max and Bailey and we were an immediate hit! We began introducing Max and Bailey and telling the students why we were riding around the country. We explained what Assistance Dogs do and let Max and Bailey greet all the kids. The dogs loved all the "free pets" and did not realize what they were doing to spread the word on Assistance Dogs. What kind of impact would they make on the young generation that we were meeting? No one would ever know what they were able to accomplish! It was an eye-opening introduction to the impact we would soon make on students across the country.

When we spied a picture of Opie on a wall in town, we knew we had to get a picture of Blaine next to it. Growing up, he looked like Opie and was told that on a consistent basis. See the resemblance?

We wandered around town and found "Wally's Service Center and Comfort Station." It was closed but was the perfect little gas station you would expect in Mayberry. We took our picture in front of it and wondered what the "Comfort Station" would have provided on another day.

Our long trek for the day took us into the Blue Ridge Mountains as we headed to Deep Gap to visit the Taylors who had introduced us to our charity partner, NLMAD.

By early afternoon, we had reached the Blue Ridge Parkway, and we looked forward to the scenic drive.

As we ascended to the top of one of the mountains, it began snowing. Chills ran through me. Not because of the colder temperatures, but to think of possibly having to navigate on snow-covered roads. I became genuinely concerned that we would not make it to our friends' house for the evening. Where would we go if the roads became treacherous? At the top of the mountain, we stopped for fuel and to discuss our route. This would have been a perfect time to look at a weather app to see the current conditions ahead and the futurecast, but this was 2004 and we did not have smartphones with those awesome apps. We finally decided that the snow did not look like it would be too bad, and we hopped back on our bikes to continue our trek.

As I heard Blaine start his bike, I overheard his music. Country music? What the heck? He hated when I played country music in prior years and now he was listening to it? I asked him over the CB "You're listening to country music? What happened?" He came back with the response, "Well, we are traveling across this great country, so it just seemed logical to listen to country music and I am enjoying it!"

The snow stopped as we rode through the curvy, small back roads to find our friends' house. I continued trusting that the GPS would lead us to their house, but I was nervous because there was not much around us except for endless forest.

Finally, we found our friends' driveway tucked away in Deep Gap, NC. As we approached it, I realized it was a steep gravel driveway going up a mountain. I was happy we were on three wheels, as it could have been extremely difficult on two wheels.

We cautiously moved up the desolate driveway. As we approached their house, our friends of old times greeted us! It was so nice to unpack and chill in their house for the evening and relive old times on our boats. We had a very relaxing dinner with them and a very enjoyable evening. These were the times we would cherish on our journey!

May 4 - Day 4: Deep Gap, NC - Boone, NC

Our morning plan was to visit one of our minor charity partners, NLMAD. Karen Brown, the founder, was diagnosed with Muscular Dystrophy at age 28. With the help of her first Assistance Dog, Ozzie, Karen overcame many of her everyday challenges. Years later, Karen opened her own Assistance Dog training facility to help others suffering with physical disabilities to achieve that same independence. Her story, as told by her, was featured on our website:

COURAGEOUS BEGINNINGS

Limb-girdle Muscular Dystrophy were the words the doctor calmly announced, as if I had a common cold. As I listened to the explanation of this disease, a rush of panic came over me. The disease was progressive and would first rob me of the use of my legs and arms, then eventually touch other muscles affecting my heart and my ability to swallow. This is not a reality easy to face, but I now look it in the eye with the strength of a tiger. Upon reflection, my life's experiences have all led me to the founding of New Life Mobility Assistance Dogs.

During my school years, I was drawn to books about animals and people with disabilities. Eventually, my love for dogs filled me with aspirations of becoming a guide dog trainer. I set up a training course in my backyard and practiced teaching my dogs and cats tricks. I was a typical child with unbounded energy.

At the age of twelve, a high fever and strep throat left me visibly weakened. I began having great difficulty getting up from the floor and climbing stairs. Despite my difficulties, I managed to make it through high school doing gymnastics. However, the bounce I once had in my legs was gone. I hid a lot of my physical symptoms simply by avoiding doing the things that might reveal a problem.

As an adult, I was an entrepreneur involved in business ventures with a friend. I continued to lead a pretty normal life, but always tried to hide my mobility limitations. However, I eventually became unable to hide the difficulties I had in doing some simple things. When people began asking what was wrong, I finally had to face my fears and go to a doctor.

I was 28 when I was diagnosed with muscular dystrophy. Dealing with this disability was not easy. Depression, loss of confidence, and self-esteem played roles in isolating myself from society. I quit driving and going out. I filled my time with reading, writing, crocheting afghans by the dozen, and watching television.

One day while watching TV, I saw a girl with muscular dystrophy talking about her assistance dog. The dog was helping her walk and pulling her wheelchair. Immediately, I knew an assistance dog was the answer for me. I applied for a dog with one of the few programs in the country. Within a year I was accepted into the program and placed with a beautiful Collie named Ozzie, trained as a walker dog. While in training with Ozzie, I found people were not looking at me and my disability, rather the focus was on my dog and our partnership. I liked that aspect! Ozzie and I became very independent engaging in activities like walking the one-mile track at our local community college and going for a three-month solo stay in Florida every year for the first four years. I also started to drive again. Ozzie became my "Wizard of Oz", granting me back my independence.

As my disease progressed, Ozzie had to meet the challenges of my ever-changing needs. I taught him to pull a wheelchair because my balance was getting worse. He also learned to retrieve dropped items and the phone, carry in groceries, and retrieve sodas from the refrigerator.

In 1996, I became a Humane Society of Wilkes member. Visits to the local animal shelter were a real eye-opener for me as to the number of great dogs being euthanized. While visiting a Florida Humane Society shelter, a lovely shepherd/husky mix named Jessie stole my heart. After five months of intense training, Jessie was ready to replace Ozzie upon his retirement.

Jessie was very affectionate, and her antics made me laugh. It was a devastating loss to me when Jessie was hit and killed by a car in the chaos of moving to a new home. It is a tribute to Jessie that New Life Mobility Assistance Dogs was founded. Since I had been successful in rescuing and training Jessie, I wondered what other untapped potential lay behind shelter doors.

This is how Summer entered into the equation. She was a yellow lab found running at our county landfill. The animal control truck was dumping its weekly load of euthanizations when the landfill operator asked him to take Summer before she was hit by a bulldozer. The tailgate of the truck was lowered, and Summer eagerly jumped in, eyes twinkling and tail wagging.

Her fate was essentially sealed with that leap of faith. Summer was scheduled to be put down on the day of one of my visits to the shelter. I knew with one look at her that she was the dog for me.

I am rarely out of my wheelchair these days. My arm and leg muscles have really begun to wither. I can no longer transfer from a seated position. Summer has always been on call, ready and eager to help when I need her. She never grumbles or complains and is really at her best when we are working together for some chore. She has been my assistance dog for almost eight years and is beginning to slow, her vision starting to fail. I have only recently *and reluctantly retired Summer. Eight to ten years is the average working life of a healthy assistance dog. With Summer by my side, I have been fully confident. She has been the joy of my life. Since her retirement, Summer spends her days lounging about the house, sleeping in front of sunny windows.*

I have been so fortunate with the success of New Life Mobility Assistance Dogs. I have made many good friends and met some truly amazing people. I have realized some of the potential within myself and have been able to see and help others achieve some of their goals. I also have access to a supply of wonderful dogs to assist me temporarily until they go on to their permanent homes with others who need them. Often times, despite the fact that I am in a wheelchair, people have said to me, "But you do not seem disabled." I proudly answer, "It is because of my dog." Life sure has its twists and turns. I came full circle from wanting to train service dogs to needing one myself and finally founding NLMAD, creating the opportunity for others to share the same successes that Ozzie, Jessie, Summer, and I have shared.

Karen Brown
President and Founder, New Life Mobility Assistance Dogs, Inc.

Two of the dog stories on our website were from NLMAD recipients. Here are their stories:

9-11 Puppy:

My name is Diane and I live in North Carolina. I have a Golden Retriever service dog named Lacy who was trained by Ann-Marie and Karen of New Life Mobility Assistance Dogs, Inc. Lacy was just meant to be a service dog. She was born on September 11, the day of the terrible terrorist attacks in New York. She was donated to NLMAD as a puppy and was placed in the home of the most wonderful couple -Jim & Sue- who were her puppy raisers for one year.

Lacy is my best friend and right arm. Without her I would not be able to function as well as I do. She is my mental and physical support every day. Lacy has been trained as a mobility assistance dog. She responds to over sixty commands which include things like bracing for me to walk, pulling my shoes and socks off, pulling my wheelchair, getting drinks out of the refrigerator, turning lights on and off, retrieving a cordless phone, opening and closing doors, and -her favorite- retrieving anything I drop. Lacy is also very much in tune with my emotions. She has been there every time I've needed her, even at times when I didn't realize that I needed her!

Service animals change people's lives for the better and they need to be promoted as such. Far too many service dog organizations have to close their doors forever because they cannot find the funding to continue. Most are nonprofit organizations but there is no government funding available for them at this time and because the service dog industry is still somewhat new, these organizations don't fit neatly into the criteria of most grant foundations. Finding the money to operate on a daily basis is the most difficult thing these wonderful organizations have to do. There are many disabled people who are forced to live in homes where nurses can help them, and there are many more who sit home alone all day relying on their families and perhaps an aide to help them with day-to-day chores. A service dog can frequently provide these people with enough assistance that they are able to lead independent lives. That independence equates to better living conditions, happiness, and pride in one's accomplishments for these people. This is what these wonderful helpers can do! In my case that wonderful helper is Lacy. Without her, I would have to depend on my 17-year-old daughter and my husband all the time. With her, I lead a full life and am able to care for myself.

Diane & Lacy

Lewis and Cinder:

My name is Brenda and I'm writing to tell you about my father, Lewis. He is the proud recipient of a wonderful service dog named Cinder. Service dog is such a simple term for miracle! New Life Mobility Assistance Dogs, Inc, Karen Brown, and Cinder have had a profound effect on my father's life and on mine too.

At 57, a stroke took my father's sight and left him in a wheelchair. After three years of struggling and a lot of therapy, he began to realize that he was as good as he was going to get. People who lose something as precious as their sight and/or mobility go through a grieving process. That is very traumatic to watch. Finally, a very deep depression set in for my father. Absolutely nothing helped. At 60, he wanted to be dead and cursed the three years of hard work he had done.

Then came NLMAD. Daddy was eligible but wondered where he would get the money to pay for Cinder. Fundraising was started and with a lot of help from Karen, the money was raised! Daddy had a blast! His life once again had purpose and meaning.

When the training started, we had hope again. Dad worked so hard and Karen was wonderful with him. I must admit I had some concerns with the thirty commands that Dad had to learn along with all the physical stuff. But with Dad's hard work and Karen's patience and understanding, it all went very smoothly.

Cinder and Dad have been together now for almost six years. With Cinder's help, Dad is now very active. They live alone and together they can conquer anything. They go shopping, to the park, and they talk. I think they talk about me sometimes! The companionship alone would be enough, but the other things that Cinder can do is amazing. She can open and close the icebox, pickup anything -even a dime, she even picks up her toys.

There is a lot of care in having a dog, but Dad relishes every second. He brushes Cinder every day and takes her for long walks. Cinder knows well over thirty commands but most importantly, she knows how to make Dad smile.

Thank you New Life Mobility Assistance Dogs, Karen, and Cinder for giving my Daddy back!

Sincerely,
Brenda

With an escort from our friends, we went to meet the folks at NLMAD. As we arrived, we were greeted by Karen Brown and her dog, Cookie, both all decked out in their leather biker-looking outfits. This was our first visit on our ride to one of our charity partners and we were excited to give them a check for $1,000, which was our starting donation for each minor partner we met during our ride.

After our wonderful visit, we said a tearful goodbye to our friends and headed on our way to Boone, NC and to visit the infamous Mast General Store, another idea from the Road Trip USA book. The Mast General Store opened for business in Valle Crucis, NC in 1883 and quickly grew in reputation for carrying everything from "cradles to caskets". It has been known for the slogan "If you cannot buy it here, you do not need it." The store contains the post office as well. There is a delightful story about this post office. It was said that the post office changed locations - from the Farthing Store (staunch Republicans) to the Mast Store (dyed-in-the-wool Democrats) - depending upon what political party was in power. How would you like to get up in the morning after an election and not know just exactly where to go to get your mail?

We were curious to see this genuine country general store that was on the National Register of Historic Places. As we were winding our way up the mountain through the hairpin curves of Watauga County to find this gem, I got the strange feeling that we were being followed. At each turn, this same vehicle kept taking the turns with us. "I think we are being followed, " I said to Blaine on the CB. He agreed. Well, we were a sight, so hopefully they were just enjoying the entertainment and would not harm us. As we finally arrived at the Mast General Store, the vehicle stalking us pulled over too. Yes, they were following us. The lady wrote for the local newspaper and wanted to get pictures of us and find out our story. A perfect opportunity to teach the community about our ride for Assistance Dogs and how they could bring independence to someone with a disability. After chatting with her for a bit, posing in front of the general store and doing a couple "drive-bys" for pictures, we got to visit the general store and see all the great unique items they offered. We grabbed a soda, gave the dogs a slurp of water, and plopped down on the bench in front of the store, as so many had done for over a hundred years. We reveled in the store's history.

Next, it was off to find our motel for the evening and the continual search for the next meal. We found our motel, the Scottish Inns, and decided we could endure it for one night. Definitely not one to write home about. We agreed some nights were going to be difficult and we would just have to make the best of it. Since we did not want to spend much time in this motel, we headed out to find dinner for the evening. We found a lovely home-cooking type of restaurant called the Mountain House Restaurant and had a relaxing meal before heading back to our not-so-lovely motel.

Since Brad Parker had been so extremely supportive in our cause so far (including donating items to our auction, being an important action attendee, and joining us for our rainy Get Out Of Town ride), after discussing the idea with Brad, Blaine had emailed our Executive Board with a request to add him to our General Board. The board members agreed, and we added Brad as our eighth General Board member.

May 5 - Day 5: Boone, NC - Maggie Valley, NC

We got up the next morning with a long trip ahead of us, 150 miles. But first, we were on a mission for breakfast and a copy of the local newspaper, the Watauga Democrat. We found a copy, sat down for a fast-food breakfast, and enjoyed the article. Max made the front page! We were featured on half a page on the front and the back page with pictures of Bailey and me in front of the mast general store and a picture of us cruising down the street. That should get the attention of Watauga County! They even listed our website, so everyone could continue to track us on our journey and spread the word to their friends. We also spent some time chatting with a couple of nice guys at the restaurant, so we got a late start for our long day ahead.

We had planned to continue on the Blue Ridge Parkway to enjoy the scenery with a stop at Linville Falls. It was a beautiful drive of miles and miles of lush green forest on a two-lane road with very little traffic. Ah, what a ride! Just as I was getting comfortable and really enjoying the ride, I had to play a game of chicken with a wild turkey. We had been seeing the wild turkeys on the side of the road along the way. They usually heard us coming with our loud Harley tailpipes and ran into the woods. Well, this one was confused. It ran onto the road, straight for me! It felt like slow motion. I watched this gigantic bird running towards me. I was trying to decide what to do to avoid it. Which was the best direction to move? I felt if I aimed for him that I would hit him, but if I tried to avoid him that he would make the same avoidance maneuver and still run right into me. Just as I was thinking this monstrous bird was going to run right into my windshield and fall into my lap, he managed to fly up and out of the way. That turkey sure could move fast for an enormous bird! Blaine was back there laughing at me. "Did you see that crazy bird trying to kill me?!" I exclaimed. "I thought you were about to buy the farm.," he snickered. We spent the next ten minutes chuckling about that crazy bird. Boy, I thought I was toast!

We continued to Linville Falls for a well-needed break. I had been to the Falls many years earlier with my college roommate, so I was excited to make another visit. We spent some time enjoying the falls and stretching our legs by walking along the scenic pathways. Since we still had a ways to go, we packed ourselves back onto the bikes to continue our trek.

I had mapped out our route for the day and analyzed where we were going and what towns we would pass by. I noticed we would go by a town called Little Switzerland. It is called that for a reason. I remembered many years ago going through this same town. I recalled having my fingernails dug into the dash of the car as we swerved around a narrow, two-lane road up and down these gigantic mountains. I was always on the outside lane looking over these massive cliffs...only I was not looking because my eyes were closed most of the time. Thankfully, I was not driving.

Because of this previous experience, I was extremely nervous to go near this town again...since this time I was driving! Bailey was depending on me to not be driving with my eyes closed around steep mountain cliffs. I exhaled with relief as we passed by Little Switzerland on this day, as it was totally different. Since we were on the Blue Ridge Parkway, it was still the same two-lane road with lush forest on both sides. Yes...no steep cliffs lurking! I could now breathe again.

We found a great little pull-off parking area on top of one mountain and pulled over for a well-deserved break and spectacular view of the valley below. We let Max and Bailey stretch their legs at this stop. Bailey, our notorious free

68

spirit, trotted off without his leash and immediately rolled in the grass. Ah, grass! He rolled, and rolled, and rolled, kicking his hind feet up in the air every so often. Blaine and I just had to laugh…that was so Bailey! Oh, to be a dog and enjoy a carefree roll in the grass!

As we were letting Bailey enjoy his roll and were enjoying our view of Mount Mitchell, we met four bikers from California, who fell in love with Bailey's free spirit. We told them about our ride, and we immediately sold four T-shirts. Amazing how addicting the Max and Bailey T-shirts could be! More income going to our beloved charities for which we were riding.

We were grateful that we had figured out how to carry a decent amount of merchandise for sale on our bikes. We both had a rectangular T-Bags Dekker Supreme bag that attached to the luggage rack on our bikes' Tour-Paks. We were happy they came with rain covers to protect the bags and T-shirts from rain. Each of us carried a substantial number of T-shirts and a few logo gear baseball caps. I carried the small and medium sizes and Blaine carried the large, extra-large, and XXL sizes. The T-shirts came in three colors: black, blue, and gray. We would replenish our T-shirt stocks at our events or have T-shirts shipped to us as needed. With it only being our fifth day on the road, we saw how popular these T-shirts were going to be

After a quick break, we continued on our way because we still had a long way to go to get to our destination for the night. As we traveled through Asheville, we looked at our timing and realized we would get into Maggie Valley a bit late. We decided to stop for a quick dinner, finding a fast-food restaurant with outdoor seating so we could eat and keep our eyes on Max and Bailey. While we ate, they received lots of attention and were treated with a couple of French fries when we were done. They were both thrilled.

With full stomachs, we rode to the small Mom and Pop motel in Maggie Valley. It was called the Applecover Inn. We were getting there a bit late, so I was worried about trying to check in. We made it there in the nick of time and checked in before they closed for the night.

It was a quaint little motel, white with red trim and red doors. I read they were biker-friendly, and they really were...even had bike rags available to be able to wash your bike and dry it without having to sacrifice the hotel towels. How awesome was that! The parking lot was quiet, so Bailey wandered back and forth with me as I unpacked my bike and settled into room #7 for the night. He enjoyed the ability to follow me around the parking lot. Normally he had to stay in the room and guard the door, so he was loving the freedom.

We enjoyed our stay as we sat in the lovely rocking chairs on the porch outside our room. Bailey joined us on the porch to enjoy the relaxing evening. Ah, life was good!

May 6 - Day 6: Maggie Valley, NC - Knoxville, TN

We woke early, packed our bikes, and headed out for breakfast. We had a 93-mile trip ahead of us in order to arrive at the Knoxville Montessori School for our first school presentation on our journey. We wanted to have plenty of time for breakfast and a couple of stops in the Great Smoky Mountains on our way to Knoxville.

We headed back up the road to find the Country Vittles restaurant that we had passed the previous evening. It looked like the perfect Mom and Pop restaurant for breakfast. As we were attaching our brochure holders to the bikes and taking the Doggles off the dogs, a reporter from The Tourist News spotted us and came over to see the dogs. We chatted with her for a while and told her about our trip.

She took notes and a few pictures of the dogs. She told us she would run our story in a future edition, follow our progress, and post updates periodically.

We finally got a chance to go into the restaurant to sit down for a delicious breakfast. While we were waiting for our food, the owner of the restaurant, Judy Miller, visited us. She went out to meet the dogs, and I gave her a brochure. She loved the dogs and our cause and gave us a $100 donation! This certainly had been a very productive stop for breakfast.

As we finished breakfast, we realized we were now running short on time. We had to hustle to not be late for our school visit. There would be no stops in the Smoky Mountains. I suddenly realized that one of our drawbacks of our journey was having to miss sightseeing opportunities in order to stay on our schedule.

Can you say CURVES? Yes, that was our word for the day! We headed through the Great Smoky Mountains National Park. One part of our trip looked like a shoe...we headed down the leg towards the ankle, then 90-degree turn to the left and moved to the toe, then reversed and moved to the heel, then a 90-degree turn to the right up the ankle and leg. Our trip included many sections where we doubled back and then back again to ride three sections that made the distance of one. I felt like every turn seemed to be the well-known hairpin turn. I kept thinking "Boy, am I going to have great arm muscles when I get done with this trip"! Since we were on sidecar rigs, there was no lean on our bikes. Therefore, instead of using the lean to help steer the bikes, we needed to use our arms and upper body strength to steer through the curves.

Because of the school visit, we did not have time to stop and enjoy the numerous turnouts. We saw all kinds of waterfalls and phenomenal scenery and were so discouraged that we could not stop and enjoy it! Definitely a disadvantage of this charity ride!

We traveled through Gatlinburg and Pigeon Forge and were chomping at the bit to stop. The streets were covered with tourists, and it would have been the perfect place to stop for a while and get the word out about our trip! We were dedicated to making our school visit on time, so we barreled on towards Knoxville, devastated to miss the scenery and marketing opportunities.

We made it to the school on time and quickly got the dogs out of the sidecars and into the school. They gathered all the students together, and we started into our routine, which would become an old habit by the end of the journey. Since I was deathly afraid of public speaking, Blaine was nominated (by me) to do the speaking at all of our presentations. My job was to find a nice place up front to have Max and Bailey lay down in clear view of the students. I would then go find a good spot in the room to take pictures of the students and of Blaine speaking to them. Sneaking back to Max and Bailey if either of them got restless and decided to go off for a walk.

Blaine began speaking to the students and found out one of the difficulties of speaking in schools. The students here were preschool to fifth grade. It was a wide range of ages and learning levels, so he had to make it understandable and interesting to all in attendance. The younger they are, the harder to keep their interest in your speech. He did a great job keeping them interested and teaching them about Assistance Dogs.

As we got ready to leave, we put Max and Bailey in their sidecars and let the students come up to pet them. We were also pleasantly surprised by our host, who gave us a $285.52 donation from the students and faculty.

Then we were off again to find our motel for the next couple of days. Thankfully, we had traveled many times through Knoxville on our way to visit my brother and sister-in-law in Arkansas. This was a good middle point, and we had stayed many times in a very nice Red Roof Inn, so it was familiar territory this evening. We got the dogs settled in for the evening and then walked on over to Famous Dave's for dinner. We had not eaten since breakfast, and we were starving! Baby back ribs...yum!

May 7 - Day 7: Knoxville, TN

Today was a day of errands, email, laundry, event planning, and paperwork. The dogs lounged in the hotel for a day of rest, but Blaine and I had a full day ahead. We took our afternoon break to go to the bank to make a deposit. We learned a tough lesson on the way back to the motel. There was an accident, and we should have gotten off the road and found a cool spot to take a break, instead of waiting in the traffic. The day was HOT! After way too much time sweating and daydreaming of cold drinks and air-conditioning, we finally made it back to our hotel.

May 8 - Day 8: Knoxville, TN - Leiper's Fork, TN

Our destination for the day was a little town called Leiper's Fork. It was south of Nashville and was where a previous co-worker of Blaine lived. We took Hwy 70, which paralleled I-40 on an east to west route. As we wound our way through this quaint little road, we really felt like we were going through small town America. Not far into our journey for the day, we stopped in Kingston, TN at a little diner called Nana's Country Kitchen for breakfast. The smell of bacon wafted into our noses as we entered the café. We had a scrumptious breakfast and were fortunate enough to meet the owners of this cool little diner. No, it was not Nana, but was owned by four sisters. It used to be 5, but one had retired. They were sweet as we told them about our journey. I did not even have to save Max and Bailey a bite or two from my breakfast because the owners graciously sent us back out to our bikes with a mound of bacon for Max and Bailey. Boy, were they lucky dogs that day!

We then continued to head to our destination while enjoying the phenomenal scenery along the way. The countryside along our ride reminded me of what I had imagined Kentucky to look like...rolling green pastures, horses, and red barns. This was definitely God's country...absolutely breathtaking! We stopped along the side of the road so Blaine could take a picture of a beautiful red barn with the American flag on the side of it. Yes, this was what America was all about. We later passed a red barn with a horse statue on top of it. The scenery never failed, and we had a glorious trip for the day.

We headed into the little town of Leiper's Fork, and I used my trusty GPS to get us to our destination. Along the back roads we went until we finally found our home for the night...a sweet little horse farm with our friends inviting us in. We received the tour and introduced Max and Bailey to the horses. They did not faze Max, but Bailey was not sure what to do with an animal three times his size. He attempted to growl at them, but they did not budge, so he went up to sniff them. He finally decided they were OK and proceeded to explore his new home for the night.

We went to go explore the small town of Leiper's Fork. We followed our hosts into town and parked our motorcycles outside a neat little art gallery. We were right next to the Backyard Café and wandered over to see if they were open for lunch. It was a little late for lunch, but we ended up talking to the owner and introduced her to Max and Bailey. Even though she was just closing up for the day, she reopened just to serve us lunch. She served an awesome lunch and even sent us away with a little to-go box each for Max and Bailey. Each box consisted of a small, clear, hard plastic sandwich box with two perfect rolls of turkey. We presented our gourmet goodie boxes to Max and Bailey and they were instant hits with them! YUM! Talk about spoiled pups...bacon for breakfast and gourmet turkey rolls for lunch. What a day for Max and Bailey!

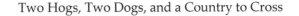

But the day did not end there. As we were chatting with visitors who were exploring this quaint little town, we ended up meeting their local celebrity, Uncle Lester. He brought over his silver rhinestone dancing shoes and talked about what a celebrity he was, which I thought included being on Hee Haw. However, after searching for his info, it appears he was just a local legend who had a dance night named after him. He was quite the character, though. Later we headed out to visit Leiper's Fork Choppers to see the sweet-looking motorcycles they had. We ended our evening by hanging out with our friends and enjoying their warm hospitality.

As I tried to figure out our route for the next day, I realized how challenging this was going to be each night. Each evening I had to set our waypoints on the route for the next day, calculate our route, and then download everything to my GPS. As the cities became bigger or our route spanned an enormous distance, I had to download multiple sections of maps. They were beginning to take longer each day, sometimes taking an hour to download properly.

May 9 - Day 9: Leiper's Fork, TN - Memphis, TN

After a fun stay with our friends, we packed our gear on the bikes and headed out for our 205-mile trip via the Natchez Trace Parkway. The parkway starts in Natchez, Mississippi and ends in Nashville, Tennessee. According to the National Park Service, the Natchez Trace Parkway is "a 444-mile drive through exceptional scenery and 10,000 years of North American history. Used by American Indians, Kaintucks, settlers, and future presidents, the Old Trace played an important role in American history. Today, visitors can enjoy not only a scenic drive but also hiking, biking, horseback riding, and camping." It sounded like a perfect ride for two motorcycles and the map showed the infamous green dotted line marking a scenic drive.

As we came upon the entrance to the Natchez Trace Parkway, we saw the sign and a great little grassy area in front of it. A perfect spot to park our bikes and get pictures of us and the sign. After the obligatory pictures, we rode 60 miles through the parkway. Along the way, we stopped at the memorial for Meriwether

Lewis of the Lewis and Clark expedition. The memorial was located at Lewis's grave site. Since my heritage traces back to Sacagawea and her husband, Toussaint Charbonneau, who were on the Lewis and Clark Expedition, I was very interested in visiting this memorial to Meriwether Lewis.

One sign at the memorial states:

This plainly visible, though long deserted road is a section of the Natchez Trace, evolved from Buffalo and Indian Trails, into the National Highway of the South-west, cut and opened under authority of the United States Government, after treaties negotiated with the Chickasaw and the Choctaw Indians, in 1801.

Designed to meet early necessities of trade between Nashville and the Country of the Lower Mississippi, it is an abiding footprint of the bold, crude commerce of the Pioneers: yet it is not without military significance in the history of our Country. Over it passed a part of Andrew Jackson's army in his campaign against the Creek Indians in 1813, and again on his return from the battlefield of New Orleans in 1815.

But, before Talladega and New Orleans - before the soldiers of Jackson had given renown to the Natchez Trace, it received its immortal touch of melancholy fame when Meriwether Lewis, journeying over it on his way to Philadelphia, to edit the story of his great expedition, here met his untimely death on the night of Oct. 11, 1809.

Lewis had been traveling from St. Louis to Washington, D.C. to document and defend spending of government funds after payment vouchers approved by President Jefferson were denied by the new Madison administration, leaving him liable for those bills. He also planned to publish his expedition journals. He stopped at Grinder's Stand for the night. Later that evening, gunshots were heard, and Lewis was found with a shot to the chest and one to the head. There is still uncertainty about his cause of death. Some say that he was murdered while most historians believe it was suicide.

We wandered around the memorial for a bit and then headed back on the trail. It was a beautiful ride through rolling grassy hills and lush green trees. We finished our 60 miles of the parkway and turned west onto Hwy. 64. That road was a lovely ride as well and, even though it was a long ride for us, we thoroughly enjoyed it! It was a quiet ride since we did not really run into many people along the way. Nice to spread the word about our cause, but some days it was nice to just be invisible and be able to enjoy the scenery. We stopped in

Memphis for the next couple of nights with a planned service stop at the Harley dealer the following day.

May 10 - Day 10: Memphis, TN

Our primary mission for the day was to get the bikes serviced for one of their 5000-mile checkups. We had made an appointment with Bumpus Harley-Davidson, so they were expecting us when we arrived in the morning. They would need to take most of the day for the servicing, but they knew we were on a tight schedule, and they promised to have the bikes done by the end of the day. Since we had many errands and loads of paperwork to get done, we decided to rent a car so we could get all our errands accomplished and not be stuck at the dealership all day. We called Enterprise to come pick us up.

One of the important things that we needed to accomplish was to get some of our solicitation applications notarized. Thankfully, we could go to our bank and get them to do it for free. We found the closest Bank of America and brought my huge stack of paperwork into the bank. We asked to meet with someone who was a notary at the bank. We met with a young lady and told her we needed to get all our documents notarized. She asked me what the documents were, so I explained that in order for us to solicit in many of the states, we had to register in those states, and these were some of the applications. She then refused to notarize the applications because she did not know and understand what they were. I explained to her that, as a notary, she did not need to know or understand any of the papers. She was only there to acknowledge that I was the one who signed the paperwork. She was totally clueless about what her responsibility as a notary was and continued to refuse to notarize my documents. I was furious! I had worked really hard on these documents and needed to get these mailed out to several states and she had just extended this painful process, so I would have to go in search of a notary again. Hopefully, the next one would actually understand her job! I walked out of the bank furious! If we were not in the middle of a 218-day journey where we were moving on a daily basis, I would have taken the time to change banks! Thankfully, a few days later we found a Bank of America branch who had a notary that finally notarized my signatures, and I could mail off another set of requests to solicit funds in several more states.

We finished running the rest of our errands while I slowly calmed down after our morning's ordeal. When we arrived back at our motel to work on more paperwork, finances, and routing, we found Bailey stretched out across the entire bed! The pups were definitely enjoying their day off!

We had a friend of Blaine's family drop by for a visit since she lived in the area. She was able to meet the dogs and even bought a couple of T-shirts from us. Later that afternoon, we got a call from the Harley dealer saying that our bikes were done. We headed on over to pick them up. They were great to us, and the manager and technicians came out to pose in front of the dealership with the bikes, dogs, and me.

Since it was dinner time again, we went next door to the Sidecar Cafe. We could not resist eating in a place with sidecar in its name! We, of course, had to pose the bikes and the dogs in front of the building with the words Sidecar Café in huge red letters hanging over their heads.

We then moved the dogs to a great little spot in the back where we could keep an eye on them from the back patio entrance.

While we were there, we met a couple who had seen us at a restaurant the previous night. They had seen the dogs outside in their sidecars. They joined us for dinner and went outside to meet Max and Bailey. They were an awesome couple, and we really enjoyed our chat with them.

The waitresses at this restaurant were all wearing tight sexy little red shirts with a picture on the front of a lady with long flowing blond hair riding a sidecar. On the back were the words "Come along for the ride". I fell in love with the T-shirt. The theme fit me perfectly! I wanted one of the T-shirts, so I chatted with our waitress about the shirt. I tried to buy one, but it was not for sale, so I began bargaining. We made a deal, and I traded one of our Max and Bailey T-shirts for one of their Sidecar Cafe T-shirts. It became one of my favorite shirts from our trip!

We ended up with a really great day despite our challenges with certain aspects of the business.

May 11 - Day 11: Memphis, TN - Little Rock, AR

I awoke for the day with butterflies in my stomach again. Today was the day I had to overcome another great fear of mine...large bridges. Most people will find this silly, but somewhere along the way in my life I developed that fear. I was fine in my 20s. I could drive anywhere with no problems at all. Somewhere in my 30s, I developed the fear, and I could not drive over the huge bridge on Interstate 40 that crosses the Mississippi River, just west of Memphis. Whenever Blaine and I would go out to visit my brother and sister-in-law in Arkansas, I would always arrange my driving time so that Blaine was the one driving when we got to the bridge. I would start sweating and get light-headed just thinking about it.

Therefore, I was extremely nervous about driving a huge motorcycle over the bridge with my beloved dog beside me. Thankfully, Bailey did not seem to sense my fear. I knew I had no choice but to drive across it. I would have another even longer bridge in Maryland, so I needed to eliminate this fear. I knew the Chesapeake Bay Bridge had a drive over service where someone would drive over for you, but they would not be able to drive my motorcycle...and I was determined not to let that fear hinder my journey.

Our route for the day would be 163 miles and we would do most of the travel via Hwy 70 that paralleled Interstate 40 out to Little Rock. The first hurdle was tackling the busy loop around Memphis, and then we rode down Beale Street. Blaine and I had been to Beale Street before and we wished we could have stayed the evening there to experience some blues, but we had to keep going. We had a pleasant cruise down memory lane as we passed the places we had visited previously and, of course, we had to get the obligatory picture of the dogs in their sidecars on Beale Street!

Since we were down near Beale Street and wanted to travel on Hwy 70, we took the Interstate 55 bridge across the Mississippi River. This bridge was smaller than the Interstate 40 bridge, so it would hopefully be easier for me to cross. Blaine knew about my fear of bridges, so, as we got closer, he said "Are you going to make it across the bridge?" I told him that I would (hoping I was correct).

We approached the bridge; I took a deep breath and then...I crossed the bridge with no problems at all. Go figure! I do not know if it was the openness of the bike or what it was, but I had no anxiety or fear at all with crossing it while driving the motorcycle. Whew!

Now it was off to an enjoyable ride along Hwy. 70 in our 3rd state, Arkansas. I was expecting more of the same type of beautiful, serene scenery as we had in Tennessee, but it was very different. We had switched states and this smaller road was not taken care of very well. It had broken pavement and was not anywhere near as nice as the roads from which we had come. The scenery was very bleak as well. Miles and miles of farmland and scrub brush with an occasional house sparsely surrounded by only a few trees.

A few minutes down the road and the clouds started piling up. We entered the normal debate on when to put on rain gear and put the dogs' rain covers on. It was not long before we felt the rain begin and we found an overpass to park under until we were all covered up. We spent the rest of the ride in the dreary day with off and on rain.

Soon, we were at our destination for the night. We had the pleasure of staying with Barry and Kathy Travis, who were in our riding class. They had graciously offered a room in their home to stay for two nights for our events in Little Rock. Another example that the heart of America is still out there. They enthusiastically welcomed us into their home and told us about the plans for the next day. It was a fun evening catching up with them.

May 12 - Day 12: Little Rock, AR

We started off our day early and in the pouring rain! Our hosts had arranged for an interview with one of the radio stations, KKPT 94.1FM, in Little Rock. We would quickly learn to suck it up for days like this and still get on the road in the dismal rain in order to spread the word about our charity ride. Thankfully, we had a fun interview and could tell Little Rock about our ride.

We spent most of the day relaxing back at their house because of the heavy rains. The rain let up in time for our ride out to our evening event at Cruisin' in the Rock at their Riverfront Park. It was a monthly event where they had all sorts of classic cars, trucks, and cool motorcycles. The dogs were again the hit of the show and we ended up winning the Best Motorcycle Award! We were handed the award, which was a blue, clear glass plate with the event name and Best Motorcycle Award etched onto it.

May 13 - Day 13: Little Rock, AR - Jordan, AR

Our route for the day was 140 miles on the beautiful back roads in Arkansas. We took Interstate 40 a short way to US65 and then onto State Road 9. Unfortunately, we did not get to see the beauty of the scenery because it was raining cats and dogs! It was raining so hard that it might as well have been cats and dogs because we could not see a thing. This 3½-hour trip felt like it took six hours.

Once we turned onto State Road 9, we had no choice but to trudge on. It was an extremely small two-lane road in the middle of nowhere. There was no place to pull over, and the road contained endless curves. My goggles were constantly fogging up to the point where I could barely see. I could not attempt to vent them to unfog them because I had to use both hands to maneuver the motorcycle through the curves. I prayed constantly to stay on the road, for a break in the rain, or for a place to pull over to rest!

We finally found a small gas station where I could strip my goggles and just use the face shield on the helmet. We trudged on further in the sheer torture of the torrential rain. I'm not sure how I stayed on the road since I could not see it. Our visibility was essentially zero. Soon, the lightning began as well, and I was becoming terrified of being out on the road.

We eventually got to a small town called Mountain View, and I rejoiced because I was familiar with where we were and felt we were back in civilization! We stopped at a Sonic and parked under a covered area for a break from the rain. I was so excited to be out of the challenging rain for a while. Max and Bailey enjoyed the fresh air as we opened their rain coverings. While they were nice and dry in their sidecars, I'm sure their areas were fogging up as well.

In our ride journal, Blaine summed up the route:

After today's ride, we'd like to nominate Shirley, Arkansas as the town with the most twists and curves in America. There's no need for the police; you simply cannot go much faster than 25 mph without killing yourself.

After a small snack and waiting out the rain, we finally got a break with lighter rain, so we headed out again towards my brother and sister-in-law's house. I was familiar with the route to their house from Mountain View, since I had ridden it many times while visiting with them. Even though it still had some curves, it was nothing like those we had ridden earlier in the day. We were so excited to finally be at Den and Debbie's house for a couple of days. Before we could rejoice at getting to their house, we had to climb their twisting gravel driveway. They had built their beautiful house at the top of a mountain, and it was a steep climb up. I was nervous heading there on the wet gravel, but we maneuvered up the driveway with no problems. They heard us coming and opened the garage so we could drive right into the dry area. It was so nice to be with family once again!

After many hugs and explanations of our events for the day, we were told that there was a news crew coming to interview us in less than an hour. Ugh! We just wanted to strip our wet clothes, get comfortable, and have one of those great rum drinks that started this entire trip. Instead, we had to put on our marketing hats and get ready for another interview. It was still raining, so it would have to be done in the garage. We did not have time to get into dry clothes, so we did the interview in our wet clothing with our wet hair matted to our heads. Guess we represented the hurdles of our trip that day. Max and Bailey were dry in their sidecars, and they were, of course, the stars of the interview.

We finally were done with our publicity obligations and could change into dry comfortable clothes to relax. It was exciting to visit with family and have a great home-cooked meal. Bring on the rum!

May 14 - Day 14: Jordan, AR

We awoke with unsure plans for the day. We were hoping to visit a school and spread the word about service dogs and eventually we got confirmation that we could make the visit. In the afternoon, we headed to Arrie Goforth Elementary School in Norfolk, Arkansas to teach the kindergarten through third graders about service dogs. Debbie joined us on the trip. Max and Bailey were again a hit as they reveled in getting lots of pets while all the students visited them in their sidecars after the presentation.

Once our presentation and visits with the pups were complete, we headed back to Den and Debbie's house for a quiet evening. Again, we enjoyed another home-cooked meal, rum drinks, and great conversation with my dear family.

May 15 - Day 15: Jordan, AR

I love a good parade, don't you? It is even better when you are in the parade and get to hang out with all the parade participants before it starts! We were invited to join a motorcycle group that was going to be in the Pioneer Days Parade in Norfolk, Arkansas, and we all gathered near the starting point. Our motorcycle group was hanging out near the fire trucks and a group that looked like they had just fought in the civil war when along came a clown riding in his mini Model T.

His signs said he was with the Twin Lakes Shrine Clowns from Mountain Home, Arkansas. There ended up being a few of them that came to say hi to Max and Bailey, but my favorite was the one who drove up in the car. An older gentleman dressed in dark pants, purple and white striped shirt, rainbow suspenders, multi-colored diagonally striped tie, red hat, and neon orange gloves with the clown white lips and red nose. He was so cute that I had to get a picture with him and Bailey. He was happy to oblige as he came over to greet Max and Bailey. I had to put Bailey's Doggles back over his eyes for the picture. He had learned to shake his head just the right way so his Doggles would end up on top of his head when he was tired of wearing them over his eyes. Thankfully, he only did this when we were at events, never when we were riding.

After a while, they finally lined us up to start the parade route. I was positioned behind the fire trucks, and we proceeded on our way. The dogs were an enormous hit to the parade viewers! Since this was not our first parade, it finally dawned on Blaine that since both sidecars were on the right side of our motorcycles, then only the people on the right side of the parade route could see the dogs, so shortly after we started, he made a U-turn and started riding backwards. Since he had a reversing gear on his motorcycle, we was able to drive in reverse at a decent speed to keep up with the parade participants. As soon as he made that 180-degree turn, a cheer came from the crowds as they finally got a glimpse of Max in his sidecar. This would become a norm for our future parades so both sides of the parade could enjoy seeing Max or Bailey.

After the parade, we set up our bikes near the festivities to spread the word about our journey to all the people who enjoyed seeing Max and Bailey in the parade. We had a group of scouts come for a visit and even got a picture of all of us with the Pioneer Day Queen. We had a lot of fun taking part in another event in small-town America. What a great day!

After a couple hours of meeting and greeting the festival participants, we headed back to Den and Debbie's for our last night in their house. I was melancholy knowing we would be leaving the next day. As we prepared for the next day, I asked Debbie if she could package up the glass plate award that we had won in Arkansas and ship it to my Mom's house. I realized we would probably have to ship items back as we accumulated stuff along the way, since we had very limited storage on our bikes.

Our prior interview proved to be fruitful as we ended up on the front page of the weekend edition of the Baxter Bulletin newspaper. This time Bailey's picture was the feature picture along with Blaine and me next to his sidecar.

May 16 - Day 16: Jordan, AR - Fayetteville, AR

It was time to pack up again and get on the road. Thankfully, Den and Debbie were coming along for the ride. As I went into the garage to pack up Max and Bailey's things, I ran across Bear with his head stuffed into the saddlebag that I had Max and Bailey's treats stored. Bear was Den and Debbie's large German Shepard. He was large for a German Shepard and had big ears that just made him look adorable. I managed to get a picture with his head buried in the bag and then when I said "Bear, what are you doing?" he pulled his head out of the bag and gave me the cutest, sheepish "who me?" look. I could not help but laugh at him. This is the memory I will always hold of him. What a sweetie!

After packing up the bikes, we headed down the steep, winding gravel driveway. I was so excited...I did not have to navigate today! My brother was leading the pack, so I got to follow along and really enjoy the scenery. We crossed the Norfork Dam near their house and followed the curvy, steep road. A few miles later, we stopped in Salesville (population 490) for some fuel. We were the hit of the gas station and the two ladies working there had to come out and see Max and Bailey!

Shortly after that, we drove through Flippin, AR. Now, there is a town with an unusual name; just what we were looking for. Several miles later, we rolled into the parking lot for the Front Porch restaurant in Yellville, one of the favorite breakfast spots of Den and Debbie when they went out on their bikes. We parked our bikes under some cool shade trees for Max and Bailey. A few minutes later Blaine was saying "Come on, let's go eat!" as I was in an extensive discussion with my brother over gloves to wear in the rain.

We had a delicious breakfast, and we discussed our plans for the day. I knew where we were ending up since I had to make reservations in a dog friendly hotel, so I told Den that I was following him and Debbie...and happy to do so! I was always more relaxed when I did not need to pay constant attention to the GPS to route us.

We had a phenomenal ride! Rode next to green pastures filled with black grazing cows and passed a group of riders on horseback. We continued through beautiful mountains filled with lush green trees and saw quaint little country stores. We stopped at a turnout on top of one mountain and enjoyed the breathtaking view. The blue sky was dotted with white, puffy clouds; each cloud making a shadow on the green valley below. After the dogs got a slurp from their water bowl, we were on our way again.

We wound through the mountains on roads with streams alongside. About an hour later, we stopped for a break at the general store in the Lost Valley Canoe and Lodging in Ponca, AR. It was a classic old-time general store. Max and Bailey were an enormous hit again, and they enjoyed the attention. All of us enjoyed some ice cream. After the dogs got to stretch their legs a bit, we were back on the road. Another hour into the ride, we found a great little park with picnic tables and a little cover provided by an overhang of a huge rock mountainside. It was a peaceful spot for a break.

We ended our ride in Fayetteville, AR where we had reserved our hotel rooms for the night. We enjoyed one last evening with Den and Debbie before we had to say goodbye yet again. This had been a very special day. I was so excited to share a bit of the ride with my brother and sister-in-law, who started the spark that allowed us to make this trip possible.

May 17 - Day 17: Fayetteville, AR - Muskogee, OK

It was another tough day for me because I had to say goodbye to Den and Debbie. As Blaine, Max, Bailey, and I would continue on to Muskogee, OK entering our 4th state, they would turn around to go back home. We decided to do a little shopping with them before we left, as well as to drop by the bank to make another deposit. As we were leaving the bank, we had a very steep drop on the pavement and I bottomed out the bike, breaking my kickstand. While I did not need my kickstand with the sidecar attached, it was still a hindrance since it was dragging the ground! Den had scraped along the bottom of his bike, so he knew what my problem was when I lagged behind a bit. I was holding the kickstand up with my foot. We pulled into another parking lot quickly and thankfully we had come prepared for those types of emergencies. Good ol' tie wraps! You know those plastic ties that you use to tie up electrical wires? Well, they also work great to tie up broken kickstands! We would find these to come in handy several times during our trip.

A little later in the day, we had to say goodbye to my brother and sister-in-law and travel out by ourselves again. It was a tearful farewell, and I wished they could continue further with us.

As we traveled on, we found a nice, shaded area for a break on our journey where the four of us could take a much-needed water and stretch break. I pulled out the jug of water and water bowl for the pups. Blaine and I grabbed our water bottles, and we went to go sit in the shade for a bit. My sweet Bailey gave me kisses as I relaxed on the sidewalk with him.

With our tough day, our journal update looked like this:

It was a tough day in other areas. Janet busted her kickstand when she bottomed out leaving the bank, our school visit in Tahlequah was cancelled, and we had a few national media opportunities fall through today.

So, tomorrow -- before we head for Oklahoma City -- we'll divert the 7 miles north to Okay, Oklahoma because after a rough day we're looking for someone to tell us that everything will be, well, "Okay."

May 18 - Day 18: Muskogee, OK - Oklahoma City, OK

We were sitting in a bank parking lot when one of the locals, Gary Armstrong, spotted us. He was, of course, attracted to the dogs and came over to learn our story. When he found out that we were riding to raise money and awareness for Assistance Dogs, he told us we had to meet Sue Harris. She worked at the Muskogee Chamber of Commerce, which was right next door. We

92

followed Gary into the Chamber to meet Sue. Sue's son was a recipient of an Assistance Dog from TheraPetics in Tulsa, so that is why he wanted us to meet her. She was fascinated by our story and came down to see the motorcycles and meet the dogs.

After chatting with them for a while, Gary invited us into his restaurant for a free lunch. He and his wife, Mary, were the owners of Club Lunch. We moved the motorcycles over in front of the restaurant and went in to enjoy the hospitality. It was a unique restaurant with antiques everywhere...on the walls, shelves, counters, just everywhere. Gary showed us around and gave the history of many of the collections. It felt like time travel back to the 50s or 60s as we looked at all the old telephones, bubble gum machines, metal advertising signs, coke machines, etc. It was fun to learn about the history behind them. Then, we were treated to delicious home-cooking and their hospitality. Yum!

After lunch, we left Muskogee and drove the 7 miles up to Okay, OK. We were always looking for interesting town names and how could you not visit a town called Okay? Especially after the tough day we had the previous day. We stopped in front of the Okay City Limits sign, which stated they were the Home of the Lady Mustangs State Volleyball Champions 1997. According to the 2000 census, the town of Okay had 597 people. Pretty impressive to have the State Volleyball Champions!

After finding out that everything was OK in Okay, we headed out to Oklahoma City for the evening. We stopped at a rest stop that had a sense of humor. They had a dog walk area that marked a stump with "Country Dogs" and a fire hydrant marked as "City Dogs". We laughed at their creativity!

May 19 - Day 19: Oklahoma City, OK - Tulsa, OK

Our day began with a visit to the Positive Tomorrows school. Their website describes them this way:

A Sanctuary of Hope; educating homeless children and their families for life. We provide private, free education that cares for the special needs of Oklahoma City homeless children, Kindergarten through 5th grade. Our teachers, social workers, and a host of volunteers nurture these children academically, socially and emotionally, preparing them for a seamless transition into public school as successful students and citizens.

We were intrigued by this interesting school and looked forward to letting them meet Max and Bailey and share our experiences with them. To make our visit more exciting, we had a representative from Paws With A Cause join us with one of their Assistance Dogs and one of their future Assistance Dogs, a black lab puppy. Both were a big hit with the students.

Since some students were fleeing domestic violence or seeking refuge from an abusive home life, we were not allowed to take pictures. To protect the identities of the students, they did not want pictures displayed on a website in case their location was discovered. That thought really brought it home to our hearts. It made us understand the tough situations many of the students were facing.

We had a great visit, and the students enjoyed the demonstration by our PAWS representative as well as visiting with Max and Bailey. They especially liked the time outside where they could visit with Max and Bailey in their sidecars.

After our wonderful school visit, we traveled the couple of miles to the Oklahoma City National Memorial. Luckily, we found a shaded parking place on the street and went to explore the memorial. As we approached the entranceway, we read the following words engraved above the entrance: "We come here to remember those who were killed, those who survived and those changed forever. May all who leave here know the impact of violence. May this memorial offer comfort, strength, peace, hope and serenity."

They did an outstanding job of making a symbolic memorial! Here is the description of the areas in the memorial as described on their website:

Gates of Time
These monumental twin gates frame the moment of destruction – 9:02 AM. – and mark the formal entrances to the Memorial. The 9:01 Gate represents the innocence before the attack. The 9:03 Gate symbolizes the moment healing began.

Reflecting Pool
The pool occupies what was once N.W. Fifth Street. Here, a shallow depth of gently flowing water helps soothe wounds, with calming sounds providing a peaceful setting for quiet thoughts. The placid surface shows the reflection of someone changed forever by their visit to the Memorial.

Field of Empty Chairs
The 168 Chairs represent those killed on April 19, 1995. They stand in nine rows, each representing a floor of the Federal Building where the field is now located. Each chair bears the name of someone killed on that floor. Nineteen smaller chairs stand for the children.

Survivor Wall
On the east end of the Memorial stand the only remaining walls from the Murrah Building. These walls remind us of those who survived the attack, many with serious injuries. Today, more than 600 names are inscribed on salvaged pieces of granite from the Federal Building lobby.

The Survivor Tree
The Survivor Tree, an American Elm, bore witness to the violence of April 19, 1995, and withstood the full force of the attack. Years later, it continues to stand as a living symbol of resilience. The circular promontory surrounding the tree offers a place for gathering and viewing the Memorial.

Rescuers' Orchard
Like the people who rushed in to help, this army of nut- and flower-bearing trees surrounds and protects the Survivor Tree. An inscription encircling the Survivor Tree facing the orchard reads: To the courageous and caring who responded from near and far, we offer our eternal gratitude, as a thank you to the thousands of rescuers and volunteers who helped.

Children's Area
In the aftermath of the blast, children from around the country and the world sent in their own expressions of encouragement and love. That care is immortalized today in a wall of tiles – each hand-painted by children and sent to Oklahoma City in 1995. In addition, buckets of chalk and chalkboards built into the ground of the Children's Area give children a place where they can continue to share their feelings – an important component of the healing process.

The Fence
The first Fence was installed to protect the site of the Federal Building. Almost immediately, people began to leave tokens of love and hope on the Fence. Tens of thousands of those items have been collected and preserved in our archives. Today, part of the original Fence gives people the opportunity to leave tokens of remembrance and hope.

We came through the entrance and felt the calming effect of the reflecting pool. Then the eerie effect of the Field of Empty Chairs hit us. It made the impact of the tragedy sink in. We could visualize all the people who were lost that day; it made it even more sorrowful to notice the smaller chairs representing the children lost. We paid homage to the lives lost and wandered back outside of the entrance.

The fence was the most heartbreaking. Nine years after this event and there were still thousands of tokens of hope, love and remembrance being left on the fence. One of the items hanging on the fence was a piece of wood painted green with one of the empty chairs painted on it and a little teddy bear painted next to the chair and the words "Remember the Children". Another item was the words God Bless America, made of wood and painted red, white, and blue. These items showed the pain and hope of those who left the items on the fence.

With heavy hearts, we went back to the motorcycles and headed towards Route 66 for our ride up to Tulsa. This was our first section of Route 66, and it did not look like what we were expecting. The road was not maintained very well, and it just looked like another countryside road.

May 20 - Day 20: Tulsa / Broken Arrow, OK

We started our day with a slow morning but went to visit Arrowhead Elementary School in Broken Arrow, OK in the early afternoon. They warned us they were having Silly Day at the school, so the kids would be dressed in silly hats, socks, and shoes. In honor of their Silly Day, Bailey put on his silly visor which was blue with white polka dots on the hat and red and white stripes on the visor. He fit right in. The children loved it! We had a fun visit.

After our school visit, we went to visit the Route 66 Harley-Davidson dealership. The staff was extremely friendly to us and the general manager, Jim Strickland, gave us two great Harley-Davidson T-shirts as souvenirs of our Route 66 trip. We gave him a Max and Bailey Hogs for Dogs T-shirt in return.

In the evening, we went to Outback for a cozy anniversary dinner. We splurged with steaks and a nice bottle of wine to celebrate our nine years of marriage. As we looked back at all the fun times that we had enjoyed with each other, we discussed our ride plans and were curious to see what we could accomplish together.

May 21 - Day 21: Tulsa, OK - Emporia, KS

The sun was just rising as we headed out onto Route 66. Today it was time to get our "kicks on Route 66". It was also going to be a long day for us, since our route would be 250 miles, one of our longest daily routes in mileage. Recommended in the Road Trip USA book, our first stop for the day was Ed Galloway's Totem Pole Park. How can you pass that up? It resided in Foyil, OK. Population in 2004 was 264. We arrived in Foyil and turned east onto Hwy 28A to find the park. We found it with ease in this small Oklahoma town and pulled in to do some exploring.

According to the sign at the park, the park was:

Built by Nathan Edward "Ed" Galloway 1937-1962 and listed on the National Register of Historic Places in 1999.

Ed Galloway (Born 1880, Died 1962) was a self-taught artist and craftsman. He retired from the Sand Springs (OK) Children's Home in 1937 when he and his wife moved to this site.

For the next 25 years, he worked seven days a week building the park and showing it to neighbors and tourists traveling U.S. Route 66 and Highway 28A.

The Totem Pole, built 1937-1948, is 90 feet tall. The base is 18 feet in diameter and 57 feet in circumference. There are 200 carved pictures on it, including 9-foot-tall images of Geronimo (Apache), Sitting Bull (Sioux), Joseph (Nez Perce'), and a Comanche chief.

The 11-sided Fiddle House, built 1948-1949, once housed 300 fiddles, each crafted from a different exotic wood, 90 inlaid wood pictures and inlaid tables - all made by Galloway.

Having fallen into disrepair, the totems were restored in the 1990s by the Kansas Grassroots Art Association. It was very interesting to wander around and look at all the unique structures. Hard to believe it was all constructed by one man. Before we left, we positioned the motorcycles to get a picture of the dogs in front of the 90-foot totem pole.

After exploring the unique park, it was time to head back out onto the road and find a little town for breakfast. Nine miles down the road, we saw a sign for Chelsea. Their claim to fame was that they were the site of Oklahoma's first oil well in August 1889. We saw this fact on a mural on the side of one of their buildings.

We turned on to the main street to see if we could find a little Mom and Pop diner for breakfast. We passed many abandoned buildings, but we were not disappointed since we stumbled across the Main Street Diner on one of the corners. We parked our motorcycles right up front near the door and left Max and Bailey outside to greet the Main Street's customers as they exited the quaint diner.

We had a nice relaxing breakfast and, of course, saved a couple of bites to reward Max and Bailey for being the greeters outside. We headed back out to Route 66 and up to Vinita, OK, home of the world's largest McDonald's. Yes, when we had these long rides, we looked for unique diversions such as these. I had seen it in the Road Trip USA book, and we took a detour to see if we could get a picture of it. Unfortunately, I did not realize it spanned across the Interstate, which was a toll road. We decided it would be too difficult to get a picture, so we turned around and headed onto US-60 on our way to Kansas. Thirty minutes later, we turned right onto US-169 and headed north. Around 10:30, we crossed over to our fifth state, Kansas. Once again, we made our obligatory stop in front of the Welcome to Kansas sign with a bright blue background and a big sunflower on it. We celebrated our 5th state and then climbed back on the bikes since we were not even halfway through our mileage for the day.

The road flattened out and the towns got farther apart. We went through Independence, KS, but could not find a sign where we could get a picture. This part of the ride was just downright boring! The entire way to Emporia was just flat and desolate land.

As we plodded along on the flatness, I heard Blaine in my ear relaying numbers to me. I flipped my radio station to those numbers and there it was..."Turn the Page" by Bob Seger. This is a phenomenal song and whenever one of us heard it on the radio, we would tell the other one which station it was on.

The song starts out with a single saxophone player playing a haunting tune which always gave me chills when I heard it. The accompanying guitar, drums, and piano play very low key, allowing the powerful lyrics to relay the loneliness of being on the road. After only 21 days on the road, we could already relate to the lyrics, riding endless miles that we just wished were through. I sang along, belting out the words, not worrying that anyone would hear me since we were alone on this empty stretch of road. As the lone saxophone closed the song, I realized I had tears running down my face, as I could feel the pain and loneliness of the lyrics. Some days on the road we WERE this song.

Emporia! It was rhyming with my emotion...euphoria, for finally stopping after that monotonous ride! Our hotel was easy to find, and we reveled in being able to relax for the evening.

The day reminded me that each day was going to be demanding. Sometimes it would be the weather, sometimes it would be the distance, sometimes it would be the exhaustion of daily travel. We knew we would be challenged daily but stepped up to that challenge and knew we could beat it!

May 22 - Day 22: Emporia, KS - Washington, KS

Unlike our ride the previous day with flat, undescriptive miles and miles of nothingness, our ride today had the green dotted line to show a scenic route. It was indeed scenic! We were greeted with rolling hills, farmlands, and cattle ranches. Heading up Hwy 177 and scooting over to Hwy 77 via roads 13 and 16, we took an 8-mile detour to visit Blaine, KS so that Blaine could get a picture of him in front of their town sign. We liked to find fun towns like that and get pictures in front of their signs...a fun diversion to keep our rides interesting. What we found was not much of a town any longer and we did not find the Blaine sign we were looking for. Oh well, back to our route.

As we headed back to our original route, we went to Randolph, where we had arranged to meet our escort. The Blackhawks Motorcycle Club from Marysville was going to escort us into Washington. We met up with the group and, of course, were overwhelmed with their support and generosity. They loved the dogs and gave us an excellent donation.

After introductions and lots of motorcycle camaraderie, we got onto our bikes and the club members escorted us to Washington. It was always fun to get a motorcycle escort to where we were going!

They brought us to the KSDS headquarters, one of our charity partners. KSDS was founded in 1990 and was the first organization in the U.S. to train both guide and service dogs. They set no age restrictions on their recipients.

Here are two of the dog stories from our website about their Assistance Dog recipients:

Secret Service

Often when I was out with Asics, my first service dog, I heard people comment, What a beautiful dog or What a good buddy or I'll bet he's a good companion or Bet he keeps you company. My usual response was then, and is now, "He's changed my life." He picks up things for me. He helps me transfer. He's the reason that I can be self sufficient enough to be on my own, which is an incredible miracle in itself. What people don't see and can never fully understand is how my service dog(s) changed my life. The "secret service" that he provides for me is not something that other people can see. It is in his eyes when we look at one another. It is in his presence when I hurt. Without words he understands what I need to get through a task or physical hurdle. He's there 24/7.

People no longer stare at me. Eyes are on my partner, not my spasticity. Eyes are on my beautiful dog, not my wheelchair. People no longer avoid looking me in the eye. They smile and speak. No longer do I hear from children, "Mommy, did that lady break her leg?" No longer do I see "Mommy" hush children and herd them the other way. Instead, children say, "Mommy, that lady has a dog." It is wonderful to hear mothers explain that the dog is helping me. When I go into a store, sales clerks no longer give me condescending smiles as they walk past me to offer help to another shopper. When eyes are off of me and my appearance and my disability, it allows me to be who I am — a unique person. One who laughs and cries. One who has responsibilities. One who has been entrusted to care for the beautiful dog who in turn cares for me. Pride wells up within me as I enter a crowded room and people turn to look, not to stare but to admire. I am not embarrassed. I do not feel like hiding in a corner because my wheelchair is noisy or my leg flies out at most inopportune times. I have confidence. I have that "secret service" that Asics gave me for ten years, and now Timon gives me as he carries on for Asics.

Often when I am out with Timon, my second service dog, I hear comments from people, What a beautiful dog . . . "Yes, and what a miracle," I think, as we smile secretly at one another.

Barbara Richards

Doppler Saved My Life

Doppler is my hero. Like most Labrador Retrievers, she has a very highly developed sense of humor and is not afraid to show it. Every day is a new adventure, and she greets the days with joy and enthusiasm, always wearing a big Lab grin. In addition to being my constant companion and best friend, Doppler is also my service dog. It was in this working capacity that she saved my life in the early morning hours of Tuesday, March 5, 2002.

Doppler and I became a working Assistance Dog team in June 1999 when we graduated from KSDS, Inc. in Washington, Kansas. As soon as we returned home after our two weeks of intensive team training, we continued to work and train for all the special skills I needed Doppler to help me with. One of these skills was for Doppler to be able to retrieve the portable phone and bring it to me from anywhere in my two-story townhome in case of an emergency, all the while hoping that we would never have an emergency where I would need her to do that! Well, all of our continued training really paid off.

I have rheumatoid arthritis and systemic lupus erythematosus. Both of these diseases are classified as autoimmune, which very simply put means that my immune system sees my own body cells as the "invaders" and attacks them, trying to destroy them. During the night of March 5, 2002, I had a severe flareup of my diseases, which means they were very active. The pattern for me is that these flares come on very quickly, and I have very little warning that they are going to happen. The inflammation and pain throughout my entire body is quite excruciating. It is difficult to describe, but needless to say, it is quite terrifying - especially because I live alone.

In a matter of 20-30 minutes, I could not walk or move because of the pain, and I was having difficulty breathing. I could not even roll over in bed to reach the phone that was only about 3 feet away. I knew that if I did not get medical help as soon as possible, I would be in real trouble. It was at this point that Doppler was able to go downstairs, get the portable phone and literally drop it on my chest so that I could start making some phone calls to get the help I needed. The paramedics arrived, and they were able to get me to the hospital so that treatment could be started. Do I believe that Doppler saved my life that night? Absolutely! If it were not for her I might not even be here, able to share her story with you.

Doppler and I have been partners for over five years now, and during this time she has brought me so much joy and laughter, in addition to the many things she assists me with in my daily living. My hope and prayer is that we will have many more years to work together as a team, and to be best friends. Thank you KSDS for making this partnership possible!!

Pam Soderholm

We were treated to a fantastic cookout with live bluegrass music. The community did an awesome job of coming out to support us. It was fun to meet so many interesting people, including staff, volunteers, clients, and service dogs.

When we met Phyllis, she was dressed as a clown. We had plans to stay with her for the evening. She had been gracious enough to open her house for us, but who were we really staying with? A clown? Ok, I was a little nervous there; I did not have the phobia of clowns, but really would have liked to meet the real person we would be staying with. We finally met Phyllis in person and her superb service dog, a black lab named Justice. We were able to stay at Phyllis' house and she relayed what Justice could do for her. She walked with a brace on one leg and Justice would help her walk. He was also there to pick up things off the floor for her.

Bailey and Justice hit it off right off the bat…Bailey was hooked! He stole her toys, and she would take them back. She was a service dog, so she was really smart! She knew how to get to Bailey's toys and even unzip the bag to get to them! Oh boy! Was I in trouble…how was I going to stop Justice from getting into everything? She could open doors and unzip bags. Bailey did not have a chance! But he still stole her toys, and she would steal his back. They were so cute together!

While Bailey and Justice fought over toys, Phyllis relayed what she had been through and how much Justice could do for her. Phyllis had a remarkable remission from Multiple Sclerosis (MS). She had spent 12 years in bed where she could not move. Can you even imagine 12 years not being able to get out of bed and to barely be able to move? 12 years! I admired her courage to finally be able to get out of bed and walk! She told us how the doctors had given up on her and how the one nurse who believed in her was losing hope. They had essentially written her off. She stated she anticipated neither death nor health. She just existed. After 12 long years, one day she finally had one small step that would lead her into a remission. Amazing! She has progressed and was now living a wonderful life with a leg brace and her supportive service dog, Justice.

May 23 - Day 23: Washington, KS

We started the day with a demo from Phyllis to show us the many tasks that Justice would do to help her. One of Justice's first tasks in the morning was to go into the kitchen, open the refrigerator, fetch a can of soda, close the refrigerator, and bring the soda to Phyllis while she was still in bed. This would help her start her day. It always astonished us at the diverse number of tasks that an Assistance Dog could complete.

After watching the cool things that Justice did for Phyllis each morning, we headed back to the KSDS headquarters for a delicious pancake breakfast. They were holding the breakfast as a fundraiser for us, and we were inspired with the fantastic support we got from this small town.

Karen Price, the director of KSDS, gave us a tour of their facility and told us about the fabulous things that they were doing. We learned KSDS trains and places approximately 20 dogs per year and had placed dogs with clients in 29 different states. That was impressive, since the entire town of Washington, Kansas, only had about 1200 residents.

After a very successful fundraiser breakfast, they took us on a tour of their small town. Later that day, we had dinner with the KSDS staff and Board of Directors. After dinner, we presented Karen with a $1,000 check as our initial payment that we were giving all our minor partners. This was followed by pictures of everyone gathered around Max and Bailey in their sidecars. Full of inspiration from the outstanding day, Blaine and I drove back to Phyllis's house for one more night.

May 24 - Day 24: Washington, KS - Kansas City, KS

After a couple of enjoyable nights with the hospitality of Phyllis and Justice, we had to head back out onto the road. As we started on our journey for the day, we went on our search for breakfast. We did not have to go very far when in Marysville, KS we found Carolyn's Kitchen Buffet. Blaine's journal entry of the day shows why we chose it:

Before we began this ride, we received some great advice from Jay Schwantes - our web designer and Executive Board Member. His advice: "Always eat at diners named after a woman and ALWAYS sit at the counter." So once again, we heeded his advice, eating at Carolyn's Kitchen Buffet (at the counter) and met some great folks. Our day was off to a great start.

We parked our bikes right out front and headed to the counter to enjoy breakfast. We had a splendid meal and chatted with some great people during our breakfast. It reminded us that the friendly small-town America still existed.

Our next stop was 140 miles down the road in Lawrenceville, KS. One of the puppy raisers for our charity partner, KSDS, was hosting a lunch for us with lots of the other KSDS puppy raisers. She was also thoughtful enough to get the newspaper and local TV station to come by for a visit to interview us.

When we got there, we were greeted with lots of fun people and KSDS puppies everywhere! Max and Bailey had a ball running around the yard with all the puppies. We had a fun lunch while we chatted with many of the puppy raisers.

Let me give you a little more background information about these incredible people. Puppy raisers are an integral part of service dog organizations. They take the puppies when they are very young and spend many months raising the puppies and training them with the basic obedience skills. They also spend many hours taking the puppies to as many places out in public to help socialize them. They give them very diverse scenarios to help the puppies get used to many people and many places. The puppies are allowed in all public areas just like a service dog is. Therefore, they take them into restaurants, stores, malls, movie theaters, etc. They bring them around all kinds of strange and loud noises to make sure they can handle anything with grace. Then, after many months of tireless training and socialization, they give them back to the service dog organization for the next level of training, so the dog can eventually be placed with the person with a disability who gets their independence through their partnership with the dog. It amazes me that these people can spend so much time with the dog and give them up. They are genuine heroes for their sacrifices. And we got to meet many of them today to say THANK YOU!

After we finished lunch, the newspaper and news crews came by, and we did our interviews. The news crew did a remarkable job filming us as we loaded our dogs into the sidecars and took action shots as we drove through the neighborhood several times. We then got pictures of us and all the puppies and puppy raisers in front of the motorcycles. We had a fantastic visit!

After a few hours of visits, lunch, and interviews, we headed back on the road for 40 more miles to our final destination for the night in Kansas City, KS.

May 25 - Day 25: Kansas City, KS - Jefferson City, MO

We awoke to a dark, rainy day. The forecast did not give us much hope…rain, rain, and more rain. The worst part of it was that we were still in the tornado prone areas, so the weather forecast had me worried. I continued to listen to a local radio channel, but, when they were giving tornado watches and warnings, they always just announced the county. They never said which cities they were near because I might have been able to recognize those. No, they used the counties. How in the world was I supposed to know which county I was in as we drove through numerous counties? I had not gone through my atlas that morning to list counties we were passing through for the day. I was frustrated with the lack of cities in danger mentioned in the warnings. Unfortunately, the rain and tornado threats continued for our entire ride. I feared each new watch and warning that I heard, and I just wanted to get to our destination for the night quickly!

Since we had stayed in Kansas City, Kansas, it was just a brief time before we crossed into Kansas City, Missouri, our 6th state. We plodded on through our rainy journey without the celebration of a new state. We truly wanted to finish our travels for the day and get out of the rain and scary tornado threats!

"Move to the right, move to the right!" I heard Blaine frantically screaming in my ear! He was yelling at me in a sudden panic via the CB. As his urgent message reverberated through my earpiece and into my brain, I looked around, trying to figure out why he was yelling at me and started to move right. Glancing in every direction, I saw nothing near me, so I was really confused. Why was he so adamant at making me move over? Suddenly, coming out of my blind spot on my left, I saw it, but it was too late! Panic engulfed me. I had a pickup truck right beside me within inches of my bike and he was moving into me! Terrified, I envisioned the wreck that was about to occur. I tightly gripped the handlebars to attempt to remain on the highway as the truck sideswiped me and then swerved to the left.

Blaine had seen this whole frightening episode pan out as he was following me. He saw the truck veer to the left, then veer to the right, and hit me as he suddenly scooted again to the left.

Moving in slow motion, it took me a minute to realize what happened and then I relayed it to Blaine. "He hit me!", I screamed to Blaine through the CB.

Blaine told me to move over and stop on the side of the road while he passed me and overtook this guy to make him stop. I slowed down and moved to the right and off the road when the truck also did the same thing. All three of us pulled off the road to survey the damages.

Blaine was eager to talk to this guy who may have just ended our 218-day charity ride. We were only 25 days into our ride, we had been riding in the rain all day, and now I had been hit by a truck! We were in the middle of nowhere, 50 miles from our destination of Jefferson City, MO and Blaine could not imagine me getting back on my motorcycle to get to our hotel, much less to finish our 7-month ride. His worst fear of the ride had become real!

As we came to a stop, Blaine hopped off his bike and raced to the truck to yell at the driver. The driver got out of his truck and immediately apologized. He did not realize that he had hit me! They both came back to see if I was OK. I was over at the sidecar hugging Bailey. The reality of the hit had just started to sink in with me. I started shaking but told both of them that I was alright. Then we immediately went to the left side of my bike and examined it to see what damage had occurred. The astounding thing was that Bailey and I were saved by a foot peg.

We had added foot pegs to the motorcycles as a last-minute addition before our trip. It gave us the ability to stretch our legs out straight and have something to rest our feet on. Important to us so we would not have to keep our legs bent the entire trip. More important to me now because it had probably just saved my life!

When he hit my motorcycle, he miraculously hit the foot peg. It got bent upward, but it was enough to get his attention and make him shift left again. We examined the peg, and it looked like with a little work and a couple of tools, we would be able to fix it.

The driver gave us all his info and said he would pay for any damages to the bike. He humbly apologized again. When we were satisfied, he got back into his truck and went on his way. Blaine and I stayed behind.

As the shock settled in even further, I began to shake and broke down in tears. I realized how close I had been to being in a serious accident! I was so thankful that Bailey and I were safe! Bailey had been my sweet, goofy pup since he was 8 weeks old. He was my baby and if anything had happened to him, then I would have been DONE. I continued to cry uncontrollably as it sunk in further. Blaine was terrified that I would not get back on the motorcycle. He expected my fear to overtake me and for me to give up on our ride. He assumed this was the end of our ride.

Blaine came over and held me as I cried. He comforted me and gave me time to calm down. Once my tears subsided, he asked me what I wanted to do. I paused for a few minutes as I contemplated our options. Eventually, I said we needed to get back on the bikes and get to our hotel. I did not want to stay out here in the rain all day. He was totally shocked at my response! He asked me if I was sure and ensured me I did not need to get back on if I was not comfortable. I was determined to continue.

Still shaking and petrified to continue, I hopped back on my bike. It took me a while to start my motorcycle. After several deep breaths to calm my nerves, I started my bike and eased back onto the highway. I reached deep down inside me for my inner strength to convince myself to get over my fears and tackled the final 50 miles to our hotel.

While I relaxed in the motel and cuddled with Bailey, Blaine went out to look at my foot peg. He found our tools and was able to take it off, fix it, and put it back on my bike so that I could use it once again. He came in and told me he had fixed it. I was ecstatic! It had now become a precious part of my motorcycle...not only as a footrest, but as a protector!

While reflecting on the day, Blaine told me he was astonished that I got back on the bike to ride to the hotel and that I was willing to continue with our trip. I told him I just had to overcome my fears and that the best thing for me was to just get back on the bike. It took every ounce of strength I had to be able to get enough courage to get back on that bike. I desperately wanted to quit! They say you must get right back on the horse when he throws you off, so I needed to do the same thing with the motorcycle. Also, there were too many people counting on us for this ride that I could not imagine disappointing them and giving up. Giving up is not in my nature!

For our journal entry that day, we decided not to tell the world that I had been hit. We debated at length on this topic. We did not want everyone to worry or start second guessing our decision to continue. We could not afford a negative influence to impact our decisions.

We also did not want any unpleasant publicity about our ride. Therefore, Blaine wrote the following journal entry:

Hey Toto, we're not in Kansas anymore. And, funny enough, we did not have to dodge tornadoes today, only rain. It was a wet ride from Kansas City, KS to Jefferson City, MO today. Max & Bailey enjoyed the ride in the comfort of their sidecars and rain covers. Janet and I were wishing we had rain covers, too.

Except for the usual additional solicitations for donations and mentioning a donation of the day, that was all he wrote. It was so short that I am surprised no one asked us what else we did.

We informed our board members and core volunteer team back home as well as our family, so they would know what we had been through that day.

Team,

Just so you do not hear it as a rumor, Janet was involved in an accident today just outside of Jefferson City. A small Isuzu truck swerved into her lane and clipped her highway foot-peg. She, Bailey, and the bike are unharmed -- only shaken and stirred a bit. We've decided that we'd like to keep this incident out of the news or public gossip, so please just share this among yourselves.

We have no idea what prompted him to swerve into her lane. Our best guess is that he nodded off at the wheel. He had just passed me (I ride behind Janet) when I saw him veer to the left and then start coming back to the right, into Janet's lane. I immediately warned Janet, and she started moving to the right even though the truck was in her blind spot, and she saw no danger -- she actually saw nothing at all until he clipped her bike while doing 60 mph.

It was a tense moment, but everyone is fine. She got right back on the bike, committed to this ride. We thank you for your own commitments.

All the best from Jefferson City (Jeff City to the locals)

May 26 - Day 26: Jefferson City, MO - St. Louis, MO

We awoke to another gloomy, rainy day. As I lay in bed, the events of the previous day swirled in my head. It had finally sunk in that someone had sideswiped me the previous day; Bailey and I were extremely lucky that we stayed on the road! The reality of how close we had come to having a severe motorcycle accident was creeping into my mind and that petrified me. I could not stand the thought of anything happening to Bailey. I was nauseous thinking about getting on my motorcycle again. I had to give myself a pep talk to convince myself that everything would be alright. I knew I could not let everyone down and just quit; I was stronger than that.

Blaine asked me how I was doing as he saw the worried look on my face. I told him how scared I was, but that I wanted to do my best to continue with our journey. I know Bailey could sense the fear in me as we loaded up the bikes, and I helped him into the sidecar. He bravely went into the sidecar and got buttoned up under his cozy rain cover. I desperately wished I could hide under that rain cover today. Instead, I took a deep breath, said a brief prayer, and headed out onto the open road.

Our route for the day was 109 miles along Hwy. 94. It was marked on the atlas with that green dotted line next to it, showing that it was a scenic highway, but I did not think we were going to enjoy the scenery. As we would have to do many days during our ride, we spent most of the day concentrating on those for which we were riding. To conquer my fears, I thought of the struggles that those with disabilities had and how strong they needed to be just to accomplish everyday tasks. I thought of Phyllis and how she spent 12 years not being able to move, much less live a normal life with everyday tasks. When remembering those everyday struggles, my task for the day seemed petty. We still had a message to deliver to the country, so I could not give up.

The skies did not lighten the entire day, and we kept a watchful eye out for anything that looked like a tornado. We again listened to the tornado watches and warnings on the radio as we continued our ride. Thankfully, at the end of this day, we were not destined for another motel. We had friends of my brother and sister-in-law that had offered hospitality at their house for the evening. One more gracious couple who opened their home to us without even knowing us. They knew my brother, heard what we were doing, and offered us a place to stay.

Thankfully, their house was on the western side of St. Louis, so we did not have to tackle the city traffic and roads in the rain. We maneuvered through their neighborhood and found their house. I heaved a loud sigh of relief as we parked our motorcycles. Blaine looked over and smiled. "I know it was a tough day for you, but you made it! Now let's go meet our new friends and relax!" I smiled back and wiped the tears of relief away from my eyes as I got off my motorcycle.

Our new hosts, Greg and Mary Bowles, warmly greeted us, helped us carry our gear inside, and showed us around their place. They poured us a glass of wine to take the edge off after our long, wet ride and told us to relax. The best part of staying at someone's house was the homemade meal! After eating out for so many nights, the homemade meal was an awesome treat! They made us feel so welcome, like we had known them for years.

May 27 - Day 27: St. Louis, MO - Salem, IL

The famous arch of St. Louis was a must-see since we were already going through the city. The Gateway Arch is 630 feet high and opened to the public on June 10, 1967. It is the world's tallest arch and was built as a monument to the westward expansion of the United States. There is a tram that will take visitors to the observation deck on top. Since I had a strong dislike of heights, I did not desire to make that trek. Blaine decided to forgo that trip as well. We got a great picture of the dogs in front of the arch. It was a challenge to get the dogs and the arch in one picture since the arch was so tall, but we finally succeeded.

One follower of our adventures, Debbie Dornfeld, was a caseworker for Senator Jim Talent. She had the day off and contacted us to meet us when we visited the arch. We coordinated the meeting, and she was able to see Max and Bailey. I found it interesting that people would track us down to meet the pups and see them in their sidecars.

As we weaved our way out of St. Louis, we crossed the Mississippi River once again and it was time for me to watch the road signs to make sure we entered the correct interstate. Our trip for the day took us on a brief stint on Interstate 64 and then we exited onto Hwy. 50. We traveled through little towns called Lebanon and Trenton...we had crossed into our 7th state, Illinois! We traveled through the beautiful countryside of small-town America, passing neighborhood service stations and houses with white picket fences. The day was beautiful as we traveled this outstanding country, but we knew our good fortune would not last all day. As we neared Salem, IL, the sky darkened, and we knew we were in for another storm filled night.

We found our home for the night, Super 8, as the wind picked up. We checked in and were told to park our bikes right out front. It was a great motorcycle parking area right in front of the hotel in plain sight from the front desk. Even better was that the overhang of the roof covered the bikes from the weather. We hurried to get everything stuffed into our hotel room and then went back out to cover the bikes and get them ready for the storm that was barreling upon us once again. We made sure we secured our bike covers for the increasing winds.

Here we were, once again, listening to the weather reports and praying a tornado did not hit our hotel or bikes. As we peered outside, we watched the torrential rains come down and listened to the high winds howl. We heard reports of large hail in many of the surrounding areas as we tried to go to sleep for the night.

May 28 - Day 28: Salem, IL - Louisville, KY

The day dawned bright for us, and we had weathered yet another storm in the Midwest. Despite the weather, we had enjoyed our stay at the motel. It was comfortable and clean...our room even had a nice recliner in it. The staff was wonderful as well. The general manager made a donation on behalf of the hotel. It was a pleasant surprise!

Our route for the day took us through 3 states...Illinois, Indiana, and Kentucky. I was excited to have routed us through French Lick, home of Boston Celtics star Larry Bird. This town fit my search for interesting names!

We continued down Hwy. 50 through Illinois and stopped in Lawrenceville, IL for lunch. According to my trusty Road Trip USA book, Lawrenceville was "named for U.S. Navy Capt. James Lawrence, best remembered for his dying words, 'Don't give up the ship', during the War of 1812". However, I am going to remember Lawrenceville, IL for its "24 Minute Parking" signs. Really? They could not give us the full 30 minutes?! I joked with Blaine as we parked the bikes and put up the dogs' umbrellas to give them shade. "Think we can eat in 24 minutes"? I even had him take a picture of that sign in case someone did not believe us!

As we came out after lunch, we were met by a reporter for the Lawrenceville Daily Record. We told her our story of our travels and mission to spread the news about Assistance Dogs. Another town in small town America, touched by our lovable dogs. As we wrapped up the interview, we continued on our way to French Lick. Eleven miles down the road, we crossed over into Indiana, our 8th state. Twenty-nine miles later, it was time for our next gas stop. With this stop, we noticed a remarkable difference than any of our other stops. With our huge motorcycles, leather jackets, and dogs in sidecars, we usually had a multitude of reactions at each of our stops. We always had the curious ones who would come up to us to ask about our Hogs for Dogs logos and to meet the dogs. Then you would have the ones who saw you and were curious but were too intimidated to come over to chat with us. And then you had those people that obviously saw you but pretended like they had not as they scurried on their way.

With our first gas stop in Indiana, we found that to be a different story. We stopped in Montgomery, IN at the Montgomery Mart gas station. EVERYONE stopped to chat with us or, if they were in a hurry, they would at least wave and say "Hi". Nobody ignored us. We spent close to an hour at our gas stop as we chatted with various people as they came to check us out. Even though many parts of the state had just been ravaged by tornados, they were all very generous towards our cause and we raised $50 at that one gas stop. Hooray for Indiana! We even had one little girl standing about 3 feet tall in a pretty pink dress give us a two-dollar donation. Her name was Bailey as well, but she was just too shy to come over for a picture with our Bailey and his sidecar. She was adorable!

Finally, we were off again in search of French Lick. As we approached the Hoosier National Forest, we saw a detour sign, "Local Traffic Only". Not knowing how far we had to go, we tried to continue in the same direction. When the flood waters covered the road, we decided it was time to turn around and try to follow that detour.

After backtracking a short distance, we followed the detour signs. I was ecstatic to have the GPS at this point! It, of course, automatically routed us time and again to our destination...no matter how many wrong turns we took. As we followed the detour, it became clear that we were being routed around French Lick. Darn! We continued on the detour and saw the horrible damage from the storms the previous night. Many areas were flooded, and we passed through Borden, IN which was devastated by a tornado! We said our prayers for the people we passed along our route who were cleaning up the destruction and counted our blessings that we had stayed out of the paths of these tornados.

As we crossed over into Kentucky, our 9th state, we navigated through Louisville to our home for the night, Red Roof Inn. We looked forward to our ride the next day through Kentucky and finally being out of the tornado prone areas! That was one area we dreaded the most. It was finally over and we were safe; we could feel the heavy weight of the stress slowly lifting off our shoulders.

May 29 - Day 29: Louisville, KY - Huntington, WV

We woke up to a beautiful day with plenty of warm sunshine! We had a long day ahead of us, 212 miles, but it was going to be a gorgeous day for the long ride, so we were looking forward to it. The people in Louisville had surprised us so far. With the city being in the middle of beautiful horse country with rolling hills of green grass and horses in the pastures, we expected the people to be a bit more laid back and relaxed. What we found during breakfast and our trip through the city to get out of town was the same hustle and bustle, gotta-get-to-work indifference that you get in most big cities. Nobody at breakfast was friendly, and we had to fight through traffic with no smiles to be found along the way. After a while, it became a contest between us to see who would be the first one to get a smile from a passing driver. "You got one yet?" "No, you?" "No...ooh, maybe, ah no, not a smile, a little interest, but no smile".

Eventually, we rode out of the city and began winding along the charming two-lane road through the countryside. The road wound through the beautiful horse farms with rolling green pastures and wooden fences setting off the perimeters. Occasionally, we would pass along a magnificent rock wall to set off the property from the road. It was absolutely stunning.

Following US-60 and then US-460 through the countryside, we ended up in Paris! Paris, Kentucky, that is. Their sign said Horses, History and Hospitality – Straight Ahead. Hmm, hospitality...maybe we should have waited and had breakfast here! But the small town fit our goal of interesting town names, so we stopped for a pit stop. The folks at the Shell station were friendly and the General Manager made a donation to us in honor of a friend of hers who is benefiting from a guide dog.

Continuing on the peaceful two-lane road, we found ourselves back on US-60 and went through a tiny town (pop. 342) called Salt Lick. We thought that was a very appropriate name for this section of the country!

Our ride was one of the most scenic of our trip so far. In our journal, Blaine described it this way:

It was one of those rides that we would not soon forget because the sights looked like an artist's painting. The smell of spring seemed more alive than normal, and the roads were left empty as though we requested them all for ourselves.

As we got closer to Huntington, we hopped onto Interstate 64 and then crossed into our 10th state, West Virginia! We headed into Huntington, took a wrong turn, and ended up in Ohio. Actually, we ended up in the wrong lane and could not get over in time, so we found ourselves crossing a bridge. We could not turn around mid-bridge, so we had to cross to the other side and there sat the sign...Welcome to Ohio. "That was quite the wrong turn," Blaine said, "you landed us in Ohio!" I turned us around and we headed back over the bridge to West Virginia. I did not think I could count that as our 11th state, since we stayed for about 30 seconds. We would be back another day via another route to say we visited that state.

Weaving around Huntington, we finally found our home for the night...yep, another Red Roof Inn. As we settled in for the evening, we discussed our excitement for the next day since we would rendezvous with some old friends and spend a couple of days riding with them.

Even though we would not be in Michigan for another two months, the Three Rivers Commercial-News ran an article about our ride and information about the planned events in Three Rivers.

May 30 - Day 30: Huntington, WV - Fayetteville, WV

Like a bad omen, we woke up to pouring rain and started dreading the ride for the day. We listened to the forecast, and it was a guessing game as to how much rain we would get for the day. We waited for lulls in the pouring rain to load our bikes and get all the rain covers on the luggage. With umbrellas over us, we uncovered each sidecar and installed the rain covers. The rain increased, so we went back into the motel to wait for another lull to get the dogs into their respective sidecars. The lull finally came, and we loaded up the dogs and headed down the road. As we headed out of Huntington, we left the rain behind and, even though it threatened more rain, it never came.

Our excitement started to bubble over as we anticipated meeting up with our board member, Jay. You may remember me talking about him during our pre-ride stage, helping with routes, website, motorcycle details, and, of course, our test ride out to the Outer Banks Bike Rally. I was doubly excited to be meeting up with him because he is the king of route planning. Therefore, I knew he would route us through awesome scenic roads. I would not have to fight with my GPS for 3 days! He had even emailed me a GPS file with our routes for the next 3 days, so I could follow along on my GPS if I so desired.

Preparing for our rendezvous, we stayed on Interstate 64 from Huntington to Charleston, WV and stayed on the interstate until we approached Charleston. So far, the roads had been straight and easy. Then we got off onto US-60 and the curves started!

Closing in on our final destination for the day, we still had not heard from Jay. We did a little sightseeing along the way and stopped by the Kanawha Falls area. It was a beautiful waterway along our route, and we let Max and Bailey out of their sidecars to stretch their legs. After a pleasant break, we continued on our way. We found a gorgeous waterfall cascading down next to the road, so we stopped for a photo op.

Knowing we needed to press on to find Jay, we continued along our route. Once we got close to our final motel destination, we finally passed Jay! Of course, since he was on two wheels, he immediately turned around and caught up to us.

Since we were just around the corner from our hotel for the night, we went and checked in and then went to the Dairy Queen next door for lunch. We asked where the other couple was that was supposed to be accompanying Jay for the ride. They had seen the supposedly torrential rains forecasted for the trip and decided to stay home. We were really disappointed, especially since we had ridden through so much just to make it to this point! Later we found out that they had changed their minds and wanted to join us…they would meet us later in the evening.

After lunch, Jay said he would take us for the tour of the area. He first took us to the New River Gorge Visitor Center, where we, of course, met lots of interesting people and sold a few T-shirts. Jay was starting to see our normal day-to-day routine. After spreading the word with the crowd, we headed back out onto the road. Jay stopped us for pictures of this impressive bridge, the longest single span east of the Big Muddy and tall enough to fit the Washington Monument and two Statue of Liberty statues on top of one another. He directed us to a little known one-lane, one-way road which winds down to the bottom of the gorge, across the old original bridge.

As we sat on the bottom of this route, we stopped by the railroad tracks and again caught the attention of a few tourists. While the train sped past us, we explained our charity ride and sold a few T-shirts for the cause.

We continued up the other side and stopped to get a few pictures near a waterfall on the way up. As we tried to leave, a couple from Greensboro, NC waved us over and asked us about our adventures. We again sold some T-shirts and spread the news of our cause. Jay realized we went nowhere fast, and we were interrupted everywhere we went.

Thankfully, we ended up at our motel before dark and went to the little restaurant inside called Elliot's. What a great stop for the night and we were already at our motel. We had a delicious dinner and then sat at the bar for a couple of beers. Blaine thanked Jay for the constant support as they touched base most days at the end of the day. With the extensive motorcycle rides that Jay had accomplished, he knew what we were experiencing. He was continuously giving Blaine encouragement, which Blaine then relayed to me.

Blaine and Jay reminisced about the old days and talked about their many hiking trips at Yellowstone. They made a pact on a bar napkin to take another hiking trip within the next two years.

Enjoying the music from a solo keyboardist/singer, we watched him for a bit and finally concluded that he was blind. But, boy, could he play that keyboard! Eventually, the other couple from North Carolina joined us.

May 31 - Day 31: Fayetteville, WV - Snowshoe, WV

I woke up knowing that today was going to be a great day, even if it rained like the weatherman was predicting. We were riding with great friends, eventually meeting up with more good friends, and the best part of all, I did not have to navigate for the day! Woohoo! Jay, the ultimate planner and tour guide, was leading the ride, so all I had to do was follow and enjoy the ride. I was psyched!

We went out to pack the bikes, and the sun was actually shining. Looking good so far! We met up with the others and set out to find breakfast. We decided on Tudor's Biscuits and munched on a little breakfast to start us off for the day. I told Jay that we desperately needed some dog food and if he ran across a Walmart on our ride today to please make a stop. Thankfully, as we rode through Summersville, we found the Walmart that I needed.

We parked our bikes at the curb in front of the nursery section and we just happened to be next to all the fresh, blooming flowers. There were several rows of these red and purple flowers in hanging baskets sitting by the curb. As I went to buy dog food, Max and Bailey enjoyed the view. We had to take a picture of them before we left because both pups had their noses stretched out towards the flowers. They were taking some time to smell the fresh flowers!

Unfortunately, I did not find the dog food that I wanted, so the search would continue.

Heading down Hwy. 39, we had an incredible ride through the picturesque countryside. Clouds occasionally would threaten us with rain, but we stayed dry. We found a quiet little roadside park and stopped to let the dogs out to explore the unfamiliar territory. There was a small footbridge over the river that had been flirting with us for the past few miles of our ride, so we wandered through the paths and over the bridge. We also found a water fountain with a spigot facing downward, so we let the water flow and Max and Bailey got a cool drink from the fresh running water. Ah, life was good!

A little further down our route, we stopped at the Hwy. 150 intersection to attempt to catch up via cell phone with our friends, Brad and Johnny. Jay's cell phone did not have any reception in this out of the way spot, so Blaine whipped out our satellite phone. We thought it might come in handy in some of the remote places we were traveling.

As expected, Jay gave us grief about always being prepared and asked what else we had on our bikes, but he was happy to use the satellite phone to make the call. Jay left a message for them and then tried to figure out what to do. He really wanted to take us onto the more scenic route, but he knew Brad and Johnny were riding along Hwy. 39 in the opposite direction until they ran across us. They were coming from Brad's place in Snowshoe, where they stayed the previous night and where we would all be staying at the end of the day. Since he did not get them, we continued on Hwy. 39 until we caught up with them. Just 10 miles into our ride, we saw their bikes outside of the Hillsboro General Store. They had stopped there to leave us a cell phone message. What luck! It was great to be reunited with more of our good friends!

We decided to backtrack a few miles so we could wander through a quaint little shop that caught our attention with a huge American flag painted on a sign outside. Since it was Memorial Day, it looked like an appropriate place to stop. We parked next to the flag and took a picture of Max in front of it. It was a magnificent symbol for our ride.

A menagerie of unique items surrounded the flag sign. They were even more unique as we wandered through the shop. All of us had a ball pointing out each interesting item we found amusing. We had a great chat with the owners, and they got a kick out of getting their pictures taken with Max and Bailey. Blaine found a wooden sign with Beware of Dog carved in it and a dog carved out of the top of it. We propped it up against Bailey's sidecar and he sat up in his sidecar with his goofy grin to get his picture taken. Not too ferocious looking of an expression to make that sign very convincing!

When we finished browsing and sharing, we backtracked a little more and hit Hwy. 150 to take the scenic route. It was absolutely breathtaking! Lush greenery, spectacular views, and a beautiful ride. And did I mention I did not have to lead this ride or even look at my GPS today? I was ecstatic! We approached a scenic overlook and pulled over to take a break. Max and Bailey were able to stretch their legs and had a ball running around in the fresh green grass. We all relaxed for a bit and enjoyed the camaraderie of our wonderful group of riders.

Jay is the ultimate tour guide when it comes to motorcycle rides, and he always knows where the pubs are! We stopped along the way in Marlinton at the B&B Roadhouse to enjoy a beer and catch up with everyone in our group.

After our refreshments, we headed out to find our last stop for the day. Brad owned a place at Snowshoe and had offered his place for our stay for the night. It was off season, so we had the entire place to ourselves. We unpacked the bikes, got Max and Bailey comfortable in the home for the night, and headed off to dinner at the only restaurant open. We kept them open until 1am and had an awesome time. And in Jay's words, we had to "adhere to the code of the rode...what happens on a bike trip stays on a bike trip!" My lips are sealed!

June

June 1 - Day 32: Snowshoe, WV - Charlottesville, VA

Gathered together in the parking lot, we packed all our stuff on the bikes and decided on getting a little breakfast at our first stop for the day. Brad had this great seat cushion he convinced me to try. He raved about how awesome it was, so I gave in and he slid it onto my seat. Our trip that morning took us down the mountain through many, many curves. I had a disadvantage to begin with since I had to physically steer around the curves versus lean through the curves like the rest of the two wheelers. I was also moving a little slow from our late night the previous night. As we started down the mountain, I realized too late that the great cushion that Brad had used would work great on a two-wheel motorcycle where you just sit on the seat. I, on the other hand, constantly shifted my weight on the bike through the curves to help me compensate for the three wheels. With this seat cushion, I could not slide left and right on my seat to shift my weight. I was also trying to keep up with the speed of the two-wheeled motorcycles in front of me, so with these two disadvantages, I was really struggling. Blaine was behind me and noticed that I was having trouble. As we swerved through the endless curves, I kept looking for a turnout area where I could pull over and pull this insane cushion from under my rump! There were no turnouts and no side shoulder. There was NO PLACE to pull over, and I did not know if I was going to make it down the mountain with this cushion. I was petrified that I was going to run off the road!

We finally made it to our first stop, and I leaped off the motorcycle, wanting to kiss the ground for finally making it there safely! Blaine yelled at me, "What the heck is going on with you? You nearly ran off the road several times!" I grabbed that cushion and shoved it back into Brad's face! "Here, take this thing," I cried! Shocked, he looked at my dismay over the cushion. I then explained to him how crucial it was to be able to shift my weight from side to side and that I could not do it with this cushion. I was afraid that I was going to shift my weight and the cushion would fall off and Blaine and Max would have an accident tumbling over

125

the cushion on the road. I was a wreck at having had to compensate for not being able to shift my weight and doing everything that I could to keep us on the road. We finally had a good laugh and Brad gladly took his lovely butt cushion back with him.

Our stop ended up being a quaint little spot. We were in Cass, WV, and our lunch stop (we started too late for breakfast) was at The Cass Country Store. The town was in the Cass Scenic Railroad State Park, and it had a neat little train that ran through it. We stopped in for lunch and while we were inside, it suddenly started raining. Brad was out by the bikes and did his best to keep Max and Bailey dry.

Continuing our ride to Warm Springs, VA, we entered our 11th state! We stopped at the Jefferson Pools to take a break and wander around the site. Blaine's journal entry summed up our feeling for this ride for the day:

I never knew such beautiful roads existed in this country. Joined by our friends and another board member, Brad Parker, we followed Jay Schwantes for 160 miles today through some of West Virginia and into Charlottesville, VA. Routes 66, 92, 39, 252, 56, Blue Ridge Parkway to 250 into Charlottesville. I may just use those route numbers for a lottery ticket. But then, I feel like we've already won with those numbers.

It came time to bid farewell to Brad and Johnny in a town called Steele's Tavern, and Jay was disappointed that there was no tavern in this town. Jay worked with Johnny on a route for them to get back home, and we continued to head to our destination for the night. Jay did not really want to go out to dinner, so he said he would buy dinner if we could just order delivery from Outback and eat outside at the hotel. It sounded like a perfect idea, so delivery it was! We had a lovely dinner at a little table by the pool and chatted the evening away. It was again another bittersweet night. We enjoyed the friendships and knew we would leave them again in the morning...just the four of us again. I did not want the evening to end, but alas, it had to, and we headed in for the night and prepared for the next day. Yes, I was again getting my route prepared...back to leading the pack.

June 2 - Day 33: Charlottesville, VA

I was happy to have very little routing responsibility for the day. We were staying in Charlottesville and meeting up with a couple of friends. Our old neighbors, from when we lived in Willow Spring, NC, outside of Raleigh, were now living in Charlottesville. We used to enjoy getting together with them because they were always so much fun. We missed our old neighbors!

While they were no longer married, we got to see both of them. We met Jim Walker for lunch, and it was great to catch up with him. Diana Mahle had invited us to stay at her house and we were looking forward to seeing her. Since she was working during the day, we found a quiet park nearby with a covered picnic area next to a serene river. It was a perfect afternoon work area where the dogs could relax in the shade of the picnic area and Blaine and I could catch up with our work.

After a couple hours of work, we headed over to see Diana. It was fantastic to see her again. After we got the bikes unpacked and the dogs settled, we sat down to enjoy a glass of wine with her. It reminded us of old times. Diana treated us to a delicious home-cooked meal, and we laughed throughout the evening as we reminisced.

June 3 - Day 34: Charlottesville, VA - Washington, D.C.

While it was hard to leave our dear friend's house, we were also excited about our ride this day...we were going to stay for a few days with our friends, Dave and Teresa Lee, who we had met while cruising on our sailboat.

I was nervous about our ride because we would enter the D.C. area with all the traffic. Thankfully, we were able to stay on back roads all day and had an enjoyable ride.

Blaine again had the perfect words to describe our ride into D.C.:

You would have thought that we were a Presidential motorcade as Max & Bailey made their way into the Washington, D.C. area. People honked their horns (pleasantly), waved, and gave us plenty of thumb's ups. Yes, Max & Bailey have taken the city by storm -- and we haven't even been downtown yet. That is Saturday's plan. I wonder if President Bush will wave from the White House.

As we drove through Fairfax, VA, we ran across Patriot Harley-Davidson and decided to stop. We enjoyed collecting shirts from different Harley dealerships, and I found one I liked with an American flag on the back. It represented our Harley ride around America.

Once we were done with our Harley shopping trip, we headed to Arlington. After safely maneuvering through the D.C. area, we made it to our friends' house, where they greeted us and welcomed us into their beautiful home. We were lucky to enjoy another delicious homemade meal and visit with our friends over a superb bottle of red wine.

June 4 - Day 35: Washington, D.C.

Today was one of our "no travel" days where it was time to catch up with paperwork, laundry, etc. It turned out to be a good thing because it ended up raining most of the day. Blaine attempted to wash our bikes. He washed his bike but ended up being rained on by the time he was finishing with mine.

Our hosts were at work for the day, so we had a nice, quiet house to continue our work. Max and Bailey were entertained by our hosts' precious black lab, Mischief. Bailey was having a blast playing with Mischief and all his stuffed toys! It was comforting to stay inside on this rainy day instead of being on the road again sitting in a puddle.

We checked in with our marketing firm to see if they had booked any spots for us on national TV and they had no success so far. We were less than a month out from being in New York, and we still did not have any media lined up. After four months, they had not produced anything for us, and they were not cheap! We knew that this was an election year so it would be harder to get on national TV, but if this marketing firm was as successful as they advertised, then we should have been able to get something from them so far. We decided to wait until we reached New York to see if we would keep them. They had been great at marketing themselves, but not so good at marketing us. They were too expensive to keep on if they were not providing us any benefits!

Our good news for the day was that we got a new sponsor at the Team Dog Level, $500. Terry Osburn was a Realtor Associate with Keller Williams Goldengate Realty in the San Francisco area and found out about our ride through some of our volunteers out there. Since she supports several pet-related charities each year, she was excited about becoming a sponsor for us. We were very excited to have her as a sponsor as well!

When David and Theresa got home, we took the evening off and enjoyed a delightful dinner with them. We reminisced about old times on the water when we had visited the Chesapeake on our boat. We had anchored near each other and enjoyed dinner and drinks in the cockpit on one of our boats each evening.

June 5 - Day 36: Washington, D.C.

We had been hoping to take one day to go sightseeing in Washington, D.C. When we woke up and saw another day of continuous rain, we were very frustrated! This was our last full day in the area, and we would not drag the dogs out in the rain for a sightseeing trip. We would not be able to get them out for pictures in front of all the neat monuments in our nation's capital.

We opted instead to take one bike and only Blaine and I would go out and run some errands. There were some things that we had to get done today, such as buying dog food before we ran out. Max and Bailey would not have been happy with us if we ran out!

We headed out to find a pet store and finally found one not too far away. Per Blaine's journal entry:

While picking up more dog food for our beloved duo, we were asked a great question, as only a young person can ask it. We thought it humorous enough to be worthy of sharing.

We were inside the pet store, wearing our rain gear, when in walked two young guys (maybe 9 or 10).

They both looked us over very carefully and then said, "What are you? Who do you work for in those suits?" Maybe we should have told them that we were Power Rangers or members of some secret society. We definitely looked like we were from outer space in all our rain gear and toting our helmets. But Janet spoke faster than me and gave them the truth. Maybe I'll get the chance to embellish the story next time.

Yes, I guess we could have had a little fun with these two young men, but I am too honest and told them what we were doing. We probably looked a little strange in our identical gray rain suits, carrying our motorcycle helmets, and being in the D.C. area with all the special government agencies.

After buying the dog food and the other items that we needed, we headed back to get into some dry clothes and hide from the rain once again. We were grateful for one more evening with our friends, relaxing over another delicious dinner.

June 6 - Day 37: Washington, D.C. - Annapolis, MD

After saying our difficult goodbyes, we again headed out onto the road. The rain finally looked like it would hold off for us, so we drove into D.C. to do a little sightseeing. The skies stayed cloudy, but we managed to stay dry as we visited the sites. As we were driving in, Blaine took a picture of Bailey and me riding down the road with the famous dome of the U.S. Capitol Building in front of us. We headed to the Washington Monument and took a picture of Max and Bailey on the green grass in front of it.

We were excited to visit the World War II Memorial, which had just opened two months earlier. My Dad had been in World War II, so this memorial was very special to me. It thrilled me to see that it was open!

According to their website, "The World War II Memorial honors the 16 million who served in the armed forces of the U.S., the more than 400,000 who died, and all who supported the war effort from home. Symbolic of the defining event of the 20th Century, the memorial is a monument to the spirit, sacrifice, and commitment of the American people."

Here is the description of the beauty and symbolism of the memorial taken from the Friends of the National WWII Memorial's website:

Plaza

The memorial plaza and Rainbow Pool are the principal design features of the memorial, unifying all other elements. Two flagpoles flying the American flag frame the ceremonial entrance at 17th Street. The bases of granite and bronze are adorned with the military service seals of the Army, Navy, Marine Corps, Army Air Forces, Coast Guard and Merchant Marine. Ceremonial steps and ramps lead from 17th Street into the plaza. A series of 24 bronze bas-relief panels along the ceremonial entrance balustrades depict America's war years, at home and overseas. Announcements of the memorial are located at the 17th Street ceremonial entrance.

Curvilinear ramps at the north and south approaches provide access to the plaza for visitors walking along the existing east-west pathways between the Lincoln Memorial and Washington Monument. These ramps provide a gentle entry to the plaza. Granite benches follow the curvilinear rampart walls.

Pavilions

Two 43-foot pavilions serve as markers and entries on the north and south ends of the plaza. Bronze baldacchinos are an integral part of the pavilion design. Four bronze columns support four American eagles that hold a suspended victory laurel to memorialize the victory of the WWII generation. Inlayed on the floor of the pavilions are the WWII victory medal surrounded by the years "1941-1945" and the words "Victory on Land," "Victory at Sea," and "Victory in the Air." These sculptural elements celebrate the victory won in the Atlantic and Pacific Theaters.

Pillars

Fifty-six granite pillars celebrate the unprecedented unity of the nation during WWII. The pillars are connected by a bronze sculpted rope that symbolizes the bonding of the nation. Each state and territory from that period and the District of Columbia is represented by a pillar adorned with oak and wheat bronze wreaths and inscribed with its name; the pillars are arranged in the order of entry into the Union, alternating south to north across the plaza beginning adjacent to the Field of Gold Stars. The 17-foot pillars are open in the center for greater transparency, and ample space between each allows viewing into and across the memorial.

Commemorative Area

Within a commemorative area at the western side of the memorial is recognized the sacrifice of America's WWII generation and the contribution of our allies. A field of 4,000 sculpted gold stars on the Freedom Wall commemorates the more than 400,000 Americans who gave their lives. During WWII, the gold star was the symbol of family sacrifice.

Rainbow Pool and Waterworks
The historic waterworks of the Rainbow Pool are completely restored and contribute to the celebratory nature of the memorial. The design provides seating along the pool circumference for visitors. Semi-circular fountains at the base of the two memorial pavilions and waterfalls flanking the Freedom Wall complement the waterworks in the Rainbow Pool.

Landscaping
Two-thirds of the 7.4-acre memorial site is landscaping and water, allowing the memorial to nestle comfortably within its park-like setting. The ceremonial entrance has three large lawn panels between the monumental steps. The elm trees have been restored to their original splendor, and a replanting plan replaced unhealthy trees. A landscaped contemplative area is located at the northwestern corner of the site. Canopies of flowering trees augment re-seeded lawns.

It was a beautiful memorial, and we loved the circular Rainbow Pool and the granite pillars encircling the pool. We walked around to find the North Carolina pillar, since that is the state that we called home. We took Max and Bailey's picture in front of that state pillar.

After looking at all the cool aspects of the memorial and taking Max and Bailey's pictures in front of it, we loaded the dogs in the bikes. Our next destination was the Vietnam Veterans Memorial to pay homage to those who gave all during the Vietnam War. The wall contains the names of the 58,318 men and women who gave their lives in service to our country. With respect to those Veterans, no pictures were taken here. The pups stayed in their sidecars, and I stayed with them as Blaine wandered along the wall of names, remembering those brave Americans.

We made one last stop to see the White House. While driving by it, we found an area where the crowds were small, and we could see the White House. We took the dogs out of their sidecars and took a picture of them with the White House behind them. Then we headed towards Annapolis, where we would be in our 12th state, Maryland.

Our decision to stay at the Loews Hotel in downtown Annapolis was for a couple of reasons. First, it was downtown and within walking distance of a lot of the places we liked to visit in Annapolis. Second, they are extremely pet friendly! They give your pets welcome gifts when you arrive and provide dog beds and other accessories as desired. They had given us a free stay when we were cruising with the dogs and Blaine had written an article about them in FIDO Friendly magazine. We gave them the business to thank them for the previous hospitality.

My Mom called to let us know that there was a follow-up article about our ride in the Goldsboro News-Argus. It was on the Opinions page. The reporter who had written our original article said that she had received a phone call from a gentleman asking about the latest news on our ride. Therefore, she wrote an update article about where we were and where we had recently visited. It was interesting to see how others had been following our ride.

We headed to one of our favorite pubs for dinner, the Rams Head Tavern, where they serve their locally brewed beer. Blaine and I each ordered a Copperhead Ale and settled in for a relaxing dinner.

June 7 - Day 38: Annapolis, MD - Rock Hall, MD

After all the rain the previous few days, it was thrilling to wake up to the beautiful sunshine.

We took a brisk half-mile walk to one of our favorite breakfast spots, Chick and Ruths Delly (and that is their name...it is not a typo). It was a fantastic nostalgic Mom and Pop restaurant where you got a lot of delicious food for an inexpensive price. They were unique in that they started out every morning by saying the Pledge of Allegiance, joined by all the patrons who stood up and recited it. What a magnificent symbol of America. We loved this place!

Our route for the day was only 60 miles, but would take us from the "western shore" of Maryland to the "eastern shore" of Maryland. The area we would travel was familiar territory and we would see some dear friends at the events planned for the day. I was extremely excited to be able to spend the next couple of days with great friends, but I was not looking forward to the several minutes of terror that I had to face in order to get there.

I had mentioned earlier that we owned a sailboat and had spent many years cruising on it. We had bought the boat at Gratitude Yachting Center in Rock Hall, MD and had traveled many times across the Bay Bridge and up through the eastern shore to Rock Hall. In all the previous trips across the Bay Bridge, I would always make Blaine drive across the bridge. As I told you earlier, when I had to drive across the Mississippi River that I had a great fear of driving over bridges.

The Bay Bridge is the one I feared crossing the most. It is 4.2 miles long and one of the longest over water structures in the world. I knew it would only take about 5 minutes to cross it, but I was terrified I would pass out during those 5 minutes!

We headed out of Annapolis and hopped onto US-50. I had several miles to drive while dread crept over me. I had to drive this monster rig over that bridge! As we approached the bridge, a sense of panic hit me hard, and I felt the sweat bead on my face.

We started driving across the bridge and I could smell the water. It reminded me of our peaceful times on the water aboard our sailboat. The air was fresh, and, as we entered familiar territory, my panic attack quickly faded away. Believe it or not, being out in the open on that motorcycle rig made me feel comfortable, and I again did not have the fear of crossing the bridge.

As we crossed over onto dry land, I felt a great sense of accomplishment! I had tackled that massive bridge! Now I was ready to greet the day with joy and look forward to spending the afternoon with our friends.

I had to put my elation aside and start our navigating again. We exited on to Hwy 301 and then, a few miles later, we turned on to Hwy. 213. We traveled through the little town of Centreville and then had a delightful ride through the countryside, passing the newly planted fields.

We crossed over the Chester river and headed into Chestertown, where we had spent many days when we were on our boat cruising. We always anchored out near the bridge over which we had just crossed. Blaine and I started reminiscing about our great times we had experienced here. We remembered a great jazz festival that we had attended one beautiful September day and our bicycle rides through town to get to the grocery store and to the McDonald's. When we cruised, we ate most meals on the boat, so that fast food was a pleasant treat for us back then. At this point in our motorcycle trip, we wished more for those great home-cooked meals we used to always enjoy on the boat.

Our route then squiggled through the smaller country roads another 12 miles to Betterton. This was absolutely beautiful country out here. I was in awe of the views, and it felt like the epitome of small-town America. We arrived in Betterton, and I started following my GPS a little closer and hoped it would get me to our final destination without running me across any dirt roads.

Thankfully, the GPS was good to me, and we found our next home for a few days with our dear friend, Michele Martinage. She had been our broker when we bought our new Island Packet 40 yacht and we had become dear friends in the process. When we arrived, she welcomed us with open arms into her small home and showed us around. Because it was so small, she was graciously giving over her house to us to stay in for the next couple of days, and she was staying with a friend of hers. She made sure we were comfortable and then headed out to allow us to get settled in and ready for the rest of the day. We planned to meet her at our first event of the day in Rock Hall.

After getting settled in for our stay, we headed back out on to the small back roads and weaved our way to Rock Hall, a quaint little waterfront town on the Eastern Shore of the Chesapeake Bay. Our event was being held in the parking lot of J&J's Seafood and was being sponsored by J&J Seafood, Gratitude Yachting Center, D. Lee Kraus, Styles Unlimited, Ace Hardware, and Maryland School of Sailing and Seamanship. Our good friend, Robin Kurowski of Gratitude Yachting Center, had coordinated it and she did a phenomenal job of organizing several events during the Rock Hall visit.

It was like a homecoming and the motorcycles kept rolling in. The word had spread, and friends of ours who were on their boats cruising through Maryland for the summer also stopped in to see us. The tunes were spinning, and we had a great time! The mayor of Rock Hall, Jay Jacobs, came on over the speaker and asked Blaine and me to come up for a special dedication. He then presented us with the first "Bone of the Town" to ever be given out. It was incredible! Akin to the "Key to the City", we were given a plaque in the shape of a bone dedicated to the four of us from the Town of Rock Hall. We were all so amazed at the uniqueness and creativeness of their Mayor! That was the most unique dedication we received from any town along our journey. We had a tremendous success at this event and raised over $1,000 from it. What a phenomenal amount for this small town on the Eastern Shore!

As the afternoon progressed, I was approached by a woman who introduced herself as the program director of the Kent County Medical Adult Daycare. She told me it was in Chestertown and asked us if we could come by the next day for a visit. It sounded like it would be a great visit, so I told her I needed to check on our schedule for the next day, but if we could fit it in, we would love to come for a visit.

The party finally died down, and we packed up for our trip through the countryside back to Betterton. It was nice to be going back to Michele's nice cozy house for the evening!

June 8 - Day 39: Rock Hall, MD

We awoke and grabbed a little breakfast before our busy day ahead. We could fit the Kent County Medical Adult Daycare into our schedule for the day, so they would be our first stop. This became one of my top three most memorable stops for our journey.

I programmed my GPS with the new destination, and we headed to Chestertown. As I mentioned earlier, Chestertown was one of our favorite places to visit when we were cruising, so we were excited about making this special visit. As we rode towards Chestertown, we again reminisced at all the great times we had in there when cruising and were so grateful to give back a little to their community with a visit from Max and Bailey.

We rolled into the parking lot of the Daycare and the program director greeted us. We discussed our strategy, and we decided to have the clients and staff come out to greet Max and Bailey while they were still in their sidecars. This way, they could all see our motorcycle rigs and the sidecars as the dogs relaxed in them. Then we would take the dogs out of their sidecars and continue our visit inside, where all the clients could spend some quality time visiting with the pups and learning about our journey.

As the clients came out, we welcomed them to come up to the sidecars to visit and pet Max and Bailey. We thrilled in their delight as they all came out joking and laughing at the sight of the dogs resting leisurely in their sidecars while wearing their goggles. It was a joyous time as each client greeted the dogs, but also heartbreaking to hear some of them tell us the last time they had petted a dog. Many posed for pictures next to the dogs. Two staff members from the Kent County News joined us, and they took pictures and gathered information for a newspaper article about our journey.

When everyone was finished visiting by the sidecars, we followed them inside to a large rec room area. They all sat in a large circle and Blaine told them about our journey and our cause. Next, Blaine and Max went one direction while Bailey and I went the other to make sure everyone could spend some quality time with at least one dog.

We thoroughly enjoyed our visit and there were many times when I was choking back tears as I was touched by the way the dogs made such a difference to those who had missed petting a dog. I had taken owning a dog for granted and did not realize the pain of not being able to enjoy the daily friendship of a furry friend. It tugged at my heartstrings to see the smiles as each person was able to pet and cuddle with Bailey or Max.

After a heartwarming visit, we headed out to load the dogs into the sidecars in order to go to our next event. As we were walking out, Blaine said, "I had the most incredible experience in there." He told me he was talking to a gentleman who had been there for years. As the man was petting Max, his eyes welled up with tears and he said thank you so much for bringing the dogs here for a visit. He stated that he used to have a dog which he could not bring into the Daycare, and he missed the dog tremendously. He said he did not think he would ever be able to pet a dog again and the visit with Max was so outstanding for him. At the end of this story, I could not hold my tears back any longer. After such an emotionally draining event, I finally broke down in tears. I could only act brave for so long.

With tears still streamed down my face, I loaded Bailey into his sidecar, got my gear on, and we headed back to Rock Hall. I was thankful for the 20-minute ride to regain my composure and stop the tears. As we approached Rock Hall, we noticed the Welcome to Rock Hall sign and tried to figure out how to get a picture of it with our motorcycles. We finally decided on taking a picture of the sign with one motorcycle in the background. Their welcome sign states "Nice People Live Here". We had to agree with the sign. This was a town of amazingly warm and friendly people. Yes, nice people do indeed live here!

Before our afternoon school visit, we stopped for a delicious lunch. Danny, the owner of J&J's Seafood, had invited us to come in for some Maryland crabs for lunch, so we headed over there. As we entered the restaurant, he greeted us and told us to bring Max and Bailey in to enjoy the air conditioning. Danny handed us a couple of Diet Pepsis and told us to have a seat and our lunch would be right out. We tucked Max and Bailey under the table, where they quickly relaxed in the cool air while Blaine and I guzzled down our first gulps of soda to quench our thirst. We were thankful to wind down a little and discuss our emotional visit we had just completed.

After a little while, we saw Danny coming out of the kitchen with a huge tray holding a dozen of his best piping hot steamed whole blue crabs, fresh from the Chesapeake Bay. We hungrily dug into them with expertise since we always bought or caught our own crabs whenever we cruised throughout the Chesapeake. Danny joined us at our table, and we told him about our heartwarming visit. I wiped away tears as we relayed how touched we were at seeing the reactions from all the clients.

The crabs were fantastic! As I picked out the succulent meat from the crabs, I put aside a few pieces so that Max and Bailey would have a treat when we were done. Danny saw what I was doing and said that they were mighty lucky dogs to get a nibble of crab at the end of lunch.

As we cracked open our last couple of crabs, our stomachs were full, and we were ready for the rest of our busy day. When we rose to leave, I gave Max and Bailey their treats for being so good at lunch. We thanked Danny for his exceptional hospitality and headed out to our motorcycles to pack up and motor off to our next scheduled visit for the day.

The next stop was at Rock Hall Middle School, where we parked outside under the trees for Blaine's two presentations. He did his presentations with the kids gathered around the motorcycles and sitting on the lush green grass. The presentations went well, and the kids enjoyed being able to visit and pet Max and Bailey before we had to head out again.

Our last event for the day was at a quaint little place in downtown Rock Hall called The Mainstay. We parked our motorcycles across the street from The Mainstay in the long line of motorcycles already parked there. We unloaded Max and Bailey and headed inside for our Meet and Greet. The support we received from this little town with a big heart again amazed us. It was the perfect example of the heart of America.

June 9 - Day 40: Rock Hall, MD - Souderton, PA

We said a tearful goodbye to our close friend Michele as we packed up the bikes and got ready to leave her house for another day of travel. She wanted to get a feel for being on the motorcycles, so she climbed on board mine. She looked right at home.

The forecast for the day was HOT, HOT, HOT, so we put Max and Bailey's cooling bandanas on and made sure our spray bottles were full. This was one day where our preparation came in handy. We had purchased bandanas that could be soaked in water and the gel in the bandanas stayed cool to cool down the pups. Each of us also had spray bottles within reach where we could easily spray our pup with water to help cool him down.

Our route would be a nice jaunt up the scenic Hwy 213 and then onto Hwy 40. We would take a quick hop onto Hwy 896 and then get onto I-95 to take us into Pennsylvania. Then we would get onto I-476 to loop us around the outskirts of Philadelphia and eventually we would run into the Pennsylvania Turnpike to take us to Souderton. We decided on taking mostly interstates to get us to our destination as quick as possible to get Max and Bailey out of the heat and into some pleasant air conditioning.

We headed out onto the back roads of the Eastern Shore of Maryland and found Hwy 213. It was a beautiful ride through the flat farmlands sparsely populated with houses. We commented as we crossed over the C&D canal that we wondered which of our cruising friends were getting ready to go through the canal heading north for the summer. We had traversed the canal on our sailboat a couple of years earlier.

A few miles later, we turned onto Hwy 40 and, shortly after that, we crossed into Delaware, our 13th state! We pulled over in front of the Welcome to Delaware sign to get our usual picture. We snapped our pictures and, while we were getting our gear back on, we saw a motorcycle come to a sudden stop a couple hundred feet behind us. Wondering why he stopped way back there, we saw him take off his helmet and store it away quickly and speed off. During our ride, we always wore our helmets for several reasons, so it took us a minute to realize that we had just come from a helmet-required state to a helmet-optional state. Therefore, he ditched that helmet as quickly as he could before resuming his ride. We kept our helmets on for safety reasons and also to promote the safety factors to any students following us.

After spraying Max and Bailey with our spray water bottles, we continued on. We took our road up to I-95 and buzzed north with all the other traffic, wishing for much cooler weather as we entered Pennsylvania, our 14th state. We turned onto I-476 and maneuvered our way around Philadelphia. It would have been nice to head downtown to explore the city, but with 100-degree weather, it was just way too hot! We finally made it to the Pennsylvania Turnpike and, thankfully, my trusty GPS routed us to our good friends' home.

We would stay the next few days with some amazing friends of ours, Hayden and Radeen Cochran, whom we had met while on our sailboat. As we pulled up to their house, Hayden welcomed us into their lovely home. He had snacks waiting for us and he laid them out on the coffee table and then showed us around the house before we sat down. Max and Bailey immediately went into relax mode as we got the tour.

While we were on the second floor of the house, Hayden realized that he had left all the food on the low coffee table with large Max and Bailey next to it. He figured he was going to come down to an empty table and was really surprised to see they had not touched any of it...even the nice plate of cheese, their favorite! He then mentioned his fear to us, and we had a good laugh. We were thankful we had taught them that they could not put their noses on the table; they were well-trained to not steal food off plates. They each earned a piece of cheese for being so disciplined!

June 10 - Day 41: Souderton, PA

After another great night's sleep, we awoke again to Hayden and Radeen's hospitality. We had a nice breakfast as we prepared for another busy day. It was very relaxing to stay with our dear friends. It felt more like home than our constant hotel visits. We were very grateful for this sweet hospitality.

We headed to Marlborough Elementary School in Green Lane, PA where Radeen was the librarian. She had set up four presentations for us. We were lucky to be joined by one recipient of a Seizure Alert Dog who had been trained by Canines Partners for Life, one of our charity partners. As we were getting ready for the presentation, Lindsey came with her mom and her service dog, Thorndyke. We chatted with them for a bit to make sure Lindsey was comfortable in assisting Blaine with his presentation. She said she wanted to help, but that she was also very nervous. She gave Blaine an explanation of the significant benefits that her Assistance Dog provided her.

Blaine put a chair in front facing the students for Lindsey to sit on. She sat on the chair and laid her helmet next to her, keeping it nearby in case she was alerted to an oncoming seizure. Her service dog laid down by the side of her chair.

This was a unique opportunity for us. Blaine usually just briefly mentioned that the Assistance Dogs could help someone who has seizures, but today he could expound on it. As he went through each presentation, he included Lindsey's story. Lindsey had had seizures since a very young age. At age 22, she was finally partnered with Thorndyke, who was trained to protect and assist Lindsey.

When a person has a seizure, they lose the ability to control their body as the seizure grips them with convulsions. They can still see and hear everything that is going on around them. Unfortunately, many people have been taken advantage of when they are in this incapacitated state. The person still knows what is going on around them and to them but cannot move. The seizure dog is trained to first protect the person during the seizure. The dog will walk around or lay down next to the person and will protect them from anyone else around them. They are also trained to assist the person when they come out of the seizure. They can help them steady themselves as they get back up or can retrieve whatever they need to help with recovery.

The amazing quality that cannot be trained, but often occurs with Seizure Alert Dogs, is that, after being partnered with their person, the dogs have the uncanny ability to alert the person of an oncoming seizure before they have it! This is the most tremendous benefit from the dog. That trait is not trainable, so it is not guaranteed that the dog will end up with it. The person must figure out what the alert signal is that the dog is giving them. For Lindsey's alert, Thorndyke would start circling her 20 minutes before her seizure would occur. If Thorndyke was not alerting her, then Lindsey had the comfort of knowing she had 20 more minutes of seizure-free time.

Before Thorndyke, Lindsey spent 24/7 with her mother at her side. She never knew when she would be knocked to the ground with a seizure. When she was in the bathroom taking a bath, she had to have her mother by her side. She always wore a helmet to protect her head against injury when she fell on the floor.

Now, with Thorndyke at her side, she could go out on her own and take a shower without her mother at her side. She finally could have a normal life!

After our presentations, we thanked Lindsey and asked if she would like to see Max and Bailey in their sidecars. She did, and we loaded them into their sidecars. Blaine then asked if she wanted to sit on one of the bikes and she enthusiastically accepted the invitation. We took Max out of his sidecar and put Thorndyke into the sidecar, where he laid down comfortably. Lindsey climbed onto Blaine's bike, and we took a sweet picture of the two of them on the sidecar rig.

That evening, we had a presentation at the Upper Perkiomen Valley Library. The local newspaper, The Hearthstone Town and Country, had posted an article a few days prior to invite the community to our evening presentation. Lindsey and Thorndyke again joined us.

The presentation started out as our other ones had, but then we were all alerted by Thorndyke as he circled Lindsey. Since it had not happened during our prior four presentations that day, Blaine asked Lindsey if this was her alert. She said it was. Blaine prepared the crowd with an explanation of what was about to happen and made sure Lindsey was alright with staying in front of the crowd. She bravely agreed and got prepared for her seizure. She put her helmet on, laid on the floor, and was joined by her mother at her side. Blaine continued with his presentation.

It was frightening to watch Lindsey as her seizure occurred. We saw Thorndyke protectively lay next to her and watched the uncontrollable jerking motions of Lindsey's body. After a couple of minutes, she started to come out of it. She slowly sat up on the floor to get herself oriented with the world again and then eventually resumed her position back in the chair. Blaine checked on her to make sure she was doing alright.

After Blaine was finished with the presentation, he gave the crowd an opportunity to ask questions. Unexpectedly, many attendees were assuming her seizure was a planned part of the presentation and they asked questions about it. We were caught off-guard at that claim and explained that it could not have been planned; seizures occurred randomly and unexpectedly. He explained to them that we did five presentations that day and that she was fine during the first four presentations. Eventually the seizure was going to occur, and it just so happened that it did while in the middle of Blaine's fifth presentation. The message really hit home to everybody in the audience, and we ended up with an entire room of supporters. Many bought T-shirts and made donations, but the empathy that they brought back in their heart was the most important gift of all. Hopefully, they would continue to support the service dog organizations.

June 11 - Day 42: Souderton, PA - Drexel Hill, PA - Souderton, PA

The school we visited this day gave us the most memorable entrance that we had in all the school visits that we did on our entire trip. We had begun the day with Hayden and Radeen again and would stay with them again that evening. It was raining, so we were thankful that we did not have to load our bikes with all our gear. We put Max and Bailey in their sidecars, fastened their rain enclosures, and then drove the 25 miles to Drexel Hill. We were scheduled to meet one of the teachers and her husband on their motorcycle at one of the exits. They were representing the Blue Knights Pennsylvania X Chapter. We stopped at the exit to meet them, and they gave Max and Bailey a wonderful surprise gift of two orange and black Harley-Davidson rope toys.

We were also surprised and excited to see that we were joined by the Delaware County Sheriff's Office and the Haverford Police Department who were also waiting for us. They were there to give us an escort to Hillcrest Elementary School, where the school children awaited Max and Bailey's arrival.

As we followed our police escort with their lights flashing, we rode onto the school property and could hear the band playing! We rounded the corner and finally saw the students. Even though it was raining, they were all lined up under a covered walkway, loudly cheering, waving, and holding signs they made that welcomed Max and Bailey to their school.

145

As we parked our motorcycles, they continued to cheer. Wow, it was just utterly breathtaking! There was so much fanfare you would have thought the president was coming for a visit. It was one of those moments where the impact of what we were doing really sank in. Those kids had been following Max and Bailey's progress for the past month and they were so excited to finally get a visit from them! This was a wonderful reminder for us of the impact that we were making.

As I got off my motorcycle, I went around to open Bailey's rain cover and a great cheer erupted, followed by laughter from the crowd as they got their first look at Bailey with his chin resting on the side of his sidecar. Blaine then uncovered Max, and another cheer went up! They continued to cheer, laugh, and applaud for quite a while until our host for the day came over to greet us.

They ushered the students into the auditorium as we got Max and Bailey out of their motorcycles. Blaine talked to the students about Max and Bailey's journey and the service dogs that they were helping. During his presentation, I kept Max and Bailey in the front next to the stage and a cute little red-headed girl came over to sit with them. Bailey was particularly soaking up all her attention as she petted him.

After the presentation, the students went back to their classrooms, and we were able to visit them in their individual classes. Max and Bailey enjoyed the attention they received from all the students. It was fun to see the excitement of these students as they could finally meet the dogs after a month of following their journey. We were honored to have lunch with one of the fifth-grade classrooms.

June 12 - Day 43: Souderton, PA - Cochranville, PA

Our goal for the day was to meet Canine Partners for Life (CPL), one of our charity partners for our ride. CPL was founded in 1989 by Darlene Sullivan, who perceived an urgent need for a quality service dog organization in the Northeast. They trained several types of dogs, including service dogs, seizure dogs, home companion dogs, and residential companion dogs. At the time, they were one of only a few organizations who would place a dog with a child under the age of 18 and were also one of the few to provide seizure alert dogs. They mainly placed dogs within 250 miles of their office. In 1996, they moved to a new

45-acre campus with a state-of-the-art kennel facility, training facility and office building.

We again started out from Hayden's and Radeen's place. Even though we would be somewhere else for the night, we would be back the following day, so we could leave a lot of our stuff there. What a blessing to pack light for the overnight trip.

We headed to Kennett Square, PA to join Canine Partners For Life in a booth at the Bikes and Blues rally. It was a great feeling to finally be able to join another of our charity partners in an event! It was interesting because even the toughest looking bikers could not resist coming over and meeting Max and Bailey and learning about our mission. As we spent our day in the booth, something even more incredible happened to us. Some friends of ours, the Gabor family, joined us. We had met while sailing on our sailboat and they lived in Kennett Square. Small world! It was so heartwarming to see them again. Very different atmosphere...on land versus cruising on a sailboat. It did not matter...they came and promoted us all day and it was like we had just seen them yesterday. The definition of genuine friends! The event was a tremendous hit, and we made $1,105 from donations and T-shirt sales.

After a successful event at the Bikes and Blues rally, we headed to the headquarters of Canine Partners for Life for a barbecue and to meet their staff and some of their clients. It was always such a fulfilling time when we got to visit our partners.

It was phenomenal to meet the staff who worked so hard towards their passion for providing service dogs and the clients who had benefitted from a service dog. It was always an emotional time for us. We enjoyed the relaxed atmosphere with the delicious barbecue dinner and new friends. As always, we were pleased to present our charity partner with a $1,000 check as a down-payment to hopefully a much larger final donation from our trip!

Here is one of the client stories from CPL that we posted on our Hogs for Dogs website:

Mandi and Phoenix Tackle High School Together

Phoenix knows that during math class, Mandi Burgess needs only her pencil, not her pen, and he makes sure to give her the correct writing utensil. Phoenix, a yellow Labrador retriever, has been Mandi's service dog for almost a year, and in that short amount of time he's been helping Mandi in her daily life of attending high school and spending time with friends, as well as giving her a new outlook on life.

Picking up things that Mandi drops, handing her books and notebooks during school, taking off her socks and shoes, and covering her when she needs a blanket are a few of the many things that Phoenix does for Mandi during the day. Mandi's mom, Susan, says that Mandi's morale has increased 100-fold since Phoenix and Mandi graduated from Canine Partners For Life. Mandi says that although she'll never join the military, she imagines that the service dog team-training program is much harder than military boot camp.

Now that Phoenix is in Mandi's life, Susan says that Mandi can go to the movies or to the mall with her friends and Susan knows Mandi will be okay, because Phoenix is there with her. Recently Mandi was able to experience spending the night at her best friend's house for the first time because of Phoenix, something that Mandi was not previously able to do because the family had no experience with disabilities. Mandi is also the only person with a disability in her high school, another experience that is improved by having Phoenix by her side.

Aside from his responsibilities as a service dog, Phoenix has served many other purposes in his and Mandi's life. Phoenix is often an icebreaker for kids that may feel uncomfortable approaching Mandi because of her inability to speak. Phoenix is very outgoing and becomes a topic of conversation, and an uncomfortable situation becomes much easier for Mandi and the other kids.

Susan says she knows that Phoenix has saved Mandi's life, because before he became part of Mandi's life, Mandi had been going through a depression and was actually hospitalized. Phoenix pulled Mandi out of her depression and helped her become more independent. For the first time in Mandi's life, she has someone for whom she is responsible and someone to take care of, instead of everyone taking care of her.

While she was looking for a service dog for her daughter, Susan said she researched many service dog organizations, but chose Canine Partners For Life because of the friendly, outgoing, and understanding environment. She also liked their pro-independence attitude.

After meeting so many great people and being overwhelmed by the stories from the recipients about how a service dog had changed their life, we headed to the home of our host for the night. Jennifer Kriesel, the Development Assistant for CPL, had been key in helping us set up the events and she offered to let us stay with them on their horse farm in Coatesville, PA. We enjoyed a great evening surrounded by dogs, horses, and nature.

June 13 - Day 44: Cochranville, PA - Souderton, PA

Waking up in a heartwarming house was always a blessing. We spent the morning walking around the lovely horse farm. Max and Bailey greeted the horses and Bailey did much better around the horses this time. We visited with their 10-hand pony and their horse in the barn. I loved petting the horses.

We enjoyed the novelty that one of their horses could give us a brilliant smile! Upon command, he tilted his head and gave us a very toothy grin. He was a cutie!

We enjoyed wandering through the fields and even saw a doe caring for her young fawn. It was awesome to experience the true blessings of nature! Everything was very green and fresh smelling. What a great feeling it was being out in the country.

We then headed to Hank's restaurant in Chadds Ford for a late breakfast. We again were delayed getting into the restaurant because we ended up chatting with a few people who wanted to know more about our cause. We finally got to catch up with our hosts to eat a relaxing breakfast. The food was delicious, and the staff was very friendly. We were pleasantly surprised when our hosts also picked up the tab for breakfast. The generosity of others always humbled us. So sweet!

Our next stop was at Hannum's Harley-Davidson to thank 'Bear' for his support of Canine Partners for Life and Hogs for Dogs. He had donated several items for our fundraising event, and we left him with a Hogs for Dogs T-shirt...and a great big thank you hug from me. We were grateful for the amazing support from people who did not know us but supported our worthy cause. Another reminder of the heart of America.

After a fun day of nature on the farm, breakfast at Hank's and socializing at Hannum's H-D, we headed back to Souderton for the evening. We were back at our friends' house for a relaxing evening. We were getting used to this! Could we just do day trips or short overnights from now on? Unfortunately, we could not hit the rest of the 48 states that way. Darn!

June 14 - Day 45: Souderton, PA - Worcester, PA - Souderton, PA

We were supposed to travel to York, PA to visit the Harley-Davidson Factory, but we got a call from the Bucks County H.O.G. chapter with a request that we could not refuse. We chose to delay our trip one day. We were asked to join the H.O.G. group for a visit to the Variety Club Camp in Worcester, PA. The camp was hosting their annual camp experience for children living with Muscular Dystrophy. We jumped at the chance and had a day with some of the best memories of our trip!

The camp was one week in duration and filled with interesting activities. The H.O.G. group had coordinated with the camp to have "Harley Day". We met a large group of Harley riders at Brian's Harley-Davidson in Langhorne, PA and then rode to the camp. I believe we had as much fun as the kids did! Of course, they absolutely LOVED Max and Bailey in their sidecars with their Doggles on. I believe every one of them came over to visit with the pups and to get their picture taken with them.

The Harley parked next to us had some awesome sounding tailpipes, and the owner was letting some of the campers come over and rev the engine to hear the pipes rumble. He would place their hand on the throttle with his hand over theirs and would help them turn the throttle as the engine revved loudly and strongly. Their eyes would light up at the powerful sound they had created. Their expressions were priceless!

The campers were having a treasure hunt as part of their visit. Some of them were looking for tattoos, which are pretty common in a Harley crowd, so I let them know Bailey had a tattoo. When he was neutered, he was tattooed with my driver's license number for ID purposes in case he got lost. They did this before the microchip became popular. It fascinated the kids that he had a tattoo!

After lots of visiting with the kids and the Harleys, we finally went inside to watch a little skit that the counselors had put together. They also had a bike contest with several different awards voted on by the campers. We all laughed as Bailey won the award for the best tattoo. Imagine that! Max and Blaine won the Most Leather award. But the best award came at the very end. Bailey and I won the Best Overall award! Bailey and I were so excited to go up on stage and receive this prestigious award. The award was a banner handmade by the campers. It was comprised of a roughly cut red cloth with the words "The Red Team Loves Harleys" and the word Harleys is surrounded by pasted-on red, white, and blue stars. The best part was that the cloth was signed by all the campers! That was such a heartwarming award to win! I was in tears as Bailey and I wandered back to our seats. "Look at all the signatures", I exclaimed to Blaine! It was a very special award.

After all the festivities, we rode back to our home for the night in Souderton with our hearts bursting with love and excitement from our uplifting day.

We had a plethora of amazing experiences on our 218-day journey, but these unexpected experiences, like this MDA camp visit, were our most memorable and this was rated in our top three.

June 15 - Day 46: Souderton, PA - York, PA

Our goal for the day was to make it to York, PA, so we could visit the Harley-Davidson Factory the following day. The MDA camp visit the previous day was well worth our small delay. We were still smiling ear to ear, remembering the expressions and smiles that we had brought to the MDA campers with Max and Bailey chilling in their sidecars. Their excitement was absolutely our delight, but ours was ten times greater!

Thankfully, we were not in a hurry because we ended up sitting in traffic for a couple of hours. It was a long, slow process to just make it a few miles. There had been an accident earlier in the day with two tractor trailers and several cars, but there were still very heavy delays even after they had the wreck cleaned up. The good news is that we made many people smile as they were stuck in this traffic. If you had to be in a traffic jam, what better way to pass your time than gazing over at a goofy dog hanging his head out of a sidecar?

We were elated when we finally made it to our motel, Red Roof Inn, and were able to use one of our free coupons. Blaine had contacted the corporate office for Red Roof Inns asking if they could sponsor us. They had sent a stack of coupons to our PO Box and JoLee had mailed them to Hayden and Radeen. It was nice to receive that package from JoLee, so we could finally start using those coupons. As we settled in for the evening, anticipation set in as we looked forward to our visit to the factory the following day.

June 16 - Day 47: York, PA - Souderton, PA

We finally made it to the Harley-Davidson factory! We parked Max and Bailey out front and put our brochure holders out. We loved that we could leave them out in the beautiful fresh air for an hour as we wandered through the factory. They loved being able to just chill in their sidecars for a bit and to continue to spread the word about our journey. We wished we could have had a hidden camera to videotape the expressions of the many Harley lovers coming into the factory. They definitely got more than they expected. Think of it…you love Harleys and are so excited to visit the factory to see how they were built. You have driven many miles and park in their lot and wander in when something catches your attention. It's a unique spectacle…a sidecar! But wait! Who is in the sidecar? Wow, a Golden Retriever! But wait again…it does not stop there…it keeps getting better because there is another hack rig with another Golden in it! Too cool!

While Max and Bailey were entertaining the crowds outside, we could enjoy our factory tour. At the tour center, we learned about the plant's history as well as the manufacturing and assembly processes that are done at the factory. We also sat on the demo bikes of the ones being made at the factory. Then we took a tour of the assembly facility where they assemble the Touring and Softtail models as well as limited production, factory-custom motorcycles. The facility also performed a variety of manufacturing operations, such as making parts like fuel tanks, frames, and fenders. It was so interesting to see the motorcycles being made and knowing they had assembled our bikes in the same factory.

After our educational tour, we headed back to Max and Bailey, who were still entertaining the factory visitors as they walked by. Actually, they were snoozing in their sidecars, waiting for our return. They were happy to see us, and we answered a few questions for some of the visitors entering the factory.

We were then off for a leisurely ride through the Pennsylvania countryside. To fit in with our rule of finding the interesting named towns, we rode through Bird in Hand and Goodville.

We also rode through the Amish country and passed many horses and buggies on the roads. Max and Bailey were a little confused about passing a horse on the road. It was a beautiful ride through the lush green scenery.

After returning to our home base for the evening, we had to pack all our things for our trip the next day. We were spoiled by being able to leave many things at our friends' house the past few days, so we did not have to haul everything on and off the bikes daily. We had a fun evening with our friends and were very melancholy for having to leave the next day. We had such an awesome visit and Hayden and Radeen were fantastic hosts.

June 17 - Day 48: Souderton, PA - Piscataway, NJ

It never got any easier. Even though we knew we would run into more friends and family along the way, it was always hard to say goodbye and head out with just the four of us to continue our journey. We had called Souderton home for 8 nights, even though we had traveled away for two of those nights. Most of our stuff had stayed there while we overnighted, and we knew we would head back the next day. Our friends had made us feel right at home.

Again, we had to throw the comfortable, down-home feelings out the door and head to places unknown. We packed up our bikes and my tears started before we could say goodbye to Hayden. Radeen was already at work, but Hayden stayed home until we left. Once more, it felt as if my heart was being ripped out and left behind, but I knew we had to continue our journey. We had a schedule to keep and many more people to see. We were only 48 days into our trip with 170 more to go! With tears streaming down my face, I gave Hayden a hug, thanked him for the hospitality, and climbed on my bike. The goodbyes were testing my strength!

On a positive note, The Hearthstone Town and Country newspaper included an article about our visit to the area the past few days. We also found out that we were on the front page of the Kent County News. I am not sure why they took so long to publish the article, but it was about our visit to the Kent County Adult Medical Daycare program on June 8th. We were told it was a well-written, informative article which was good to hear.

We only had 71 miles to travel, so we took part of the day for sightseeing to discover many of the fascinating covered bridges. My love of covered bridges came from my dad. We used to drive up from North Carolina to Massachusetts and the New England area over many summers and my dad was always looking for scenic views that he could take a picture of and eventually turn it into a beautiful painting. He loved to find covered bridges and would take many photographs, so I had time to explore them and enjoy their beauty. I was looking forward to sharing my excitement and passion about the covered bridges with Blaine.

In the 19th century, bridges were covered to protect them from the elements to help them survive longer. Most of them seem to be painted red, and historians believe the reason is to make the bridge look more like a barn to a horse. Since the

157

horses were skittish to cross high above moving water, this would help farmers and travelers cross with ease with their horses.

Pennsylvania is the state with the most covered bridges. During our recent travels, I had come across something that mentioned that Bucks County had many of the covered bridges, so I researched it further. We were traveling through Bucks County to get to our next stop for the night, so I decided to find these bridge locations and add them to my GPS maps. Since many of these were off the beaten path, I knew it would take a little searching to find them.

One of our Hogs for Dogs supporters had been following our journey and wanted to join us for part of our ride one day. We decided to meet up with him during our route for the day so he could join us on our search for covered bridges. We met up with him and his lovely daughter, who was riding on the back of his Harley Ultra Classic. I warned them that I had the bridges marked on the GPS, but they may be hard to find, so be ready for some U-turns. They were ready for the adventure.

We headed up Hwy. 113 and I followed my waypoints along the scenic road, eventually turning onto Hwy 116 and then Durham Road, which led to Dark Hollow Road. Turning onto Carversville Road, we ran across our first bridge, the Loux Covered Bridge, which was one of two covered bridges crossing over Cabin Run Creek. This bridge was constructed in 1874 and was 60-feet long and 15-feet wide. It was the second shortest bridge in the county and was the only one painted all white. We explored the bridge and were pleasantly surprised to see a deer walking along the shore next to a small waterfall below the bridge.

After a brief ride further down Dark Hollow Road, we dead ended into Covered Bridge Road, which led us to the Cabin Run Covered Bridge.

This bridge was built in 1871 and was painted red with white sides at the entranceway. It was 82-feet long, 15-feet wide, and had a vertical clearance of 11'10". It had no windows, and its inner and outer walls were made of vertical boards, so it was fairly dark as we walked into it. We then drove the bikes across the bridge, which was a little disconcerting considering it was made of wood. We made a U-turn and then drove back through so we could get a picture of us riding out of the bridge. It was very picturesque.

Just a few miles away, we pulled up to our third covered bridge called Frankenfield Covered Bridge, which crossed the Tinicum Creek. The sign on it said it was built in 1872 and was 130 feet in length with 11'3" in clearance. It had a great little pull out area for parking, so we parked our bikes and got off them to explore the bridge.

As we were pulling off our motorcycle gear, a huge bus pulled up next to us and a plethora of people started getting off the bus. We found out that they were from New Jersey and were taking a bus tour of Bucks County. The bus driver put our chance meeting into perspective; he said, "this was one attraction we had not planned for". Honestly, what are the chances of running into a bus load of people at a covered bridge in Bucks County, PA? They absolutely loved Max and Bailey and I believe that Max and Bailey stole the attention of most of them and they barely saw the bridge.

We spent plenty of time visiting with them and telling them about our journey. We handed out a lot of brochures and unexpectedly ended up with $115 in donations from them. All on a chance encounter at a covered bridge. Who would have figured!

After what seemed like an hour of chatting with the tour group, they loaded back onto the bus, and we managed to finally explore the bridge. It was painted like the Cabin's Run Bridge, red all over with white sides at the entrance. The outside consisted of vertical boards, but the inside was made of boards crisscrossing diagonally to make diamond shapes inside. Even though it was a lot longer than the previous bridge, the construction of the sides made it lighter inside.

Our last bridge was the Uhlerstown Covered Bridge. The sign on the bridge stated that it was built in 1832, but historians argue that it was actually built in 1856. It was 101 feet long with a clearance of 11'3" and crossed the Delaware Canal. It appeared to have the same colors and construction as the Frankenfield Covered Bridge, but it had a small rectangular window in the middle on both sides. It was interesting because the window was only on the outer construction, so you could see the diagonal boards in the inside wall.

This was our stopping point to say goodbye to our riding buddies for the day. As we crossed the bridge, we entered our 15th state, New Jersey! We started our 38-mile ride in Frenchtown and then traveled along Hwy 12 and Hwy 202, which eventually dumped us onto I-287 where we found our Motel 6 a few miles later in Piscataway. Since Motel 6 was owned by the same company as Red Roof Inn, we were able to use one of our free stay coupons for our evening. We were very grateful for these coupons!

After a fun day of sightseeing, we had to get caught up on phone messages and emails. While Blaine was listening to his voicemail messages, he began to dance! "What? What?", I excitedly asked him. He finally hung up and told me that our board member, Steve, had secured a spot for us on the CBS Early show on June 26 during our brief stay in New York City! Woohoo! I joined Blaine in his dance.

With this awesome news, it was time to take a serious look at our marketing company. We had been working with them for months and we were now only a few days away from being in New York City and they had not secured a spot on any of the morning shows. We were hoping to do the Today show, and they thought they would be able to arrange that, but they had had no luck. They had also requested a media packet nicely showcased with our Max and Bailey logo shirt as the cover and had sent this packet to the Tonight show with Jay Leno and had not been successful there either.

After seeing one of our board members secure a spot on a prime-time morning show with a little research and a lot of tenacity in just a short time, Blaine and I discussed letting the marketing company go. We were not seeing anything come out of their efforts, while at the same time we were getting events and media spots being set up by board members and friends. Plus, this company was expensive! We consulted our board members and made the final decision to let them go. Blaine sent our marketing company an email stating that they were fired.

June 18 - Day 49: Piscataway, NJ - Basking Ridge, NJ

We were only 14 miles from our school visit, so we could have a leisurely morning. We knew that this school was looking forward to our visit, so once we were on our way, we got excited. A few miles out, we met up with the PE teacher and several members of the Angels of Fire motorcycle club. They gave us a wonderful escort to the school. As we arrived at the Oak Street School, all the students were standing surrounding the parking lot. They erupted in a massive cheer when we drove in and many of the students were holding large signs and banners saying things like "Welcome Max and Bailey" and "Dogs wag their tails with their hearts!" They clapped, laughed, and continued to cheer as we parked and got off the bikes. It was an overwhelming welcome!

With a portable microphone, they welcomed us to their school...followed by another cheer from the students. We looked around and realized that the crowd not only included students and teachers, but many other members of the community had come out to greet us. Then one student read a touching story she had written about how Max and Bailey were heroes because of the charity ride to help people with disabilities. Next, the principal presented us with a check for $1,003.07...it was actually presented to us via one of those huge cardboard checks so big that two students carried it over to present it to us. It shocked us to have such a generous donation from their school.

A television crew was there filming our outside events, and they came over to interview us. In the middle of the interview, a lady ran over yelling at us about concerns for the safety of the dogs. I was startled and frightened, as I did not know what the lady's intentions were. The principal came over to attempt to interrupt the lady. As the cameras continued to roll, Blaine took a deep breath and exhaled; he remained calm as he answered the screaming woman's questions.

He addressed all the things that we had done to ensure that the dogs remained safe. First of all, our veterinarian had given the dogs a checkup to make sure they were healthy for the ride, and she had given us advice to keep them protected. The dogs wore comfortable harnesses that were attached to the sidecars to keep them from jumping out or flying out in the case of an accident. They had protective covers for their sidecars to keep them safe from all of nature's elements. Each sidecar had a comfortable, cushioned bed for them to lie on during the rides. Both pups always wore their Doggles when riding to protect their eyes. The television crew and the principal nodded their heads as Blaine explained that the dogs' safety was our number one priority. Blaine finally de-escalated the scene, and the lady backed down.

After all the outdoor excitement, we unloaded Max and Bailey out of the sidecars to join the students inside. We had a wonderful lunch with them and then Blaine gave two presentations to all the students.

When we were done with the presentations and went to load Max and Bailey onto the bikes, we were invited to join one of the families for dinner. We went to get settled into our hotel before we went back out for dinner. The hotel had been reserved for us by one of the volunteers and was more expensive than we usually paid for hotels, but that was what they reserved for us and there really was not anything else in the area. Actually, it was nice to splurge on a nicer hotel, but we felt guilty for staying in a more expensive place.

We joined the family for dinner, and they had many other neighbors join us. The dogs were able to run around outside with many other neighborhood dogs and they had a ball playing with them. They were happy to have some time to just be dogs! We had an absolutely wonderful time. It was relaxing and everyone was so friendly, and they made us feel right at home. They were also interested in our T-shirts and logo gear, so we sold much of that as well. Then they presented us with a donation to pay for our hotel. That eradicated our guilt for staying in that nice hotel. Wow, this community was amazing! Blaine and I were truly touched by this wonderful community's generosity and heart!

June 19 - Day 50: Basking Ridge, NJ

It was time for another down day to catch up on paperwork and emails. Max and Bailey enjoyed the day off from riding. By mid-afternoon, Blaine and I needed a break, and we decided ice cream was just the ticket. So off we went in search of ice cream. We had no success in Basking Ridge, so I used my trusty GPS to find the closest ice cream shop. Thankfully, it was only a few miles away in Millington, so off we went. We found the well-hidden Baskin Robbins store and savored our waffle cones, while Max and Bailey each enjoyed a cup of vanilla. After 50 days on the road, we savored this small treat!

We found Bailey on the front page of the Courier News with a picture taken at the Oak Street School. Unfortunately, there was no article to go with the pictures and they did not mention our website either, which was not very good publicity for our ride.

June 20 - Day 51: Basking Ridge, NJ - Goshen, NY

Our route was a mere 68 miles, so we could easily forgo the Interstate and take the more scenic ride up Hwy. 206 and Hwy 94. It was a beautiful ride through the country, and we took our time and enjoyed the scenery. As we passed into New York, we celebrated crossing over into our 16th state. We were a third of the way (in number of states) through our 48-state adventure. Woohoo!

We were headed to the Silent Farm Bed and Breakfast where the owners, John and Mary Quick, were hosting us for a few nights. We were a little nervous since we did not know our hosts, but were thankful for the generous donation of the complimentary stay with them.

Once we arrived and got settled into our room, they gave us a tour of their picturesque place. We received a tour of their house and then we walked to the stables and around the luscious green fields of their horse farm. Max and Bailey enjoyed being able to run around with no leashes. Blaine and I enjoyed the peacefulness of the area.

After our tour was complete, John and Mary welcomed us with a delicious cookout. Wow, we were thoroughly enjoying ourselves as we viewed the beautiful peaceful scenery and grazing horses while munching on burgers right off the grill. This certainly beat hanging out in a chain motel with a delivery pizza for dinner! We were looking forward to the next couple of nights in this oasis.

Later that afternoon, we loaded Max and Bailey onto the bikes for a rendezvous at the ice cream shop. Lucky dogs...Max and Bailey were bound for ice cream again! Mary had made arrangements to meet the True Colors motorcycle club at the Twin Cones Custard Stand in Bloomingburg. Blaine asked Mary if she wanted to ride there in the passenger seat on his bike and she jumped at the chance. We put Blaine's extra helmet on her and off we went! Since Mary knew the way, Bailey and I followed them, and I got to enjoy my ride instead of navigating; it was quite a pleasure for me.

We rode up into the ice cream shop and were greeted by the motorcycle club. They enjoyed meeting Max and Bailey and we savored our ice cream, compliments of the motorcycle club. Free ice cream is the best! Max and Bailey were ecstatic to get ice cream two days in a row. I helped Max enjoy his cup of ice cream and Mary had a ball feeding Bailey his vanilla ice cream with his enormous tongue lapping it off the spoon. After a great visit, we headed back to the B&B to relax for the evening.

June 21 - Day 52: Goshen, NY

Our morning started with Blaine on the phone with Chad Austin on WRWD 107.3, a country music station in Poughkeepsie, NY. He was recording the conversation about our charity ride to be broadcast the following day. After Blaine was done with the interview and we had a chance to munch on some breakfast, we headed to the Raymond C. Cramer school to meet with their special needs classes. Unlike some of our other school presentations, there was no need to explain the challenges facing individuals living with physical disabilities; these students were living with these challenges every day. So, instead, Blaine talked about dignity, independence and how an Assistance Dog could enhance their lives.

The students then got a chance to see Max and Bailey in their sidecars and exchange pets for wet doggy kisses. A few of the teachers bought T-shirts and one student presented us with a huge glass jar of coins, totaling $63, that all the students had contributed towards. It was a very touching visit for us.

Next, we stopped in New Paltz to chat with a freelance writer about our journey and then made a stop in Newburgh to check in with Moroney's Harley-Davidson. We ended our busy day with a visit to the home of our volunteer, Gail Nozell, who had arranged many of the events and school visits in this area. She and her family made us feel very welcome as we joined them for a lovely dinner.

June 22 - Day 53: Goshen, NY

We started off the day with a visit to Montgomery Elementary school where Blaine did several presentations. We did not have permission to bring the dogs into the school but could do several presentations outside under a tent that they provided. It threatened rain on us again, so we were happy to finish all the presentations with only a few sprinkles. Blaine was a little hoarse by the time he was done giving so many presentations, but with the large number of students we educated about Assistance Dogs, he felt it was worth it.

We had an afternoon outing at a park where we could enjoy some time outside and meet many of our supporters. We also met a couple of recipients of Assistance Dogs. One of them was a young lady who was a tall, slim brunette. She was sitting in a wheelchair and had a yellow lab for an Assistance Dog. We enjoyed our chat with her, learning about her Assistance Dog.

When we were done, we headed to Copperfield's Cafe since the owner had invited us down for dinner. Since we enjoyed the company of a few people with whom we had spent the afternoon, we asked them to join us. When we got there, we faced an issue that people in wheelchairs face quite often. There was no handicapped ramp to get into the restaurant. Actually, there was really no way to get the wheelchair through the front door of the restaurant.

One guest we invited was the young lady in the wheelchair. Upon seeing the lack of accessibility, she said she would just not join us for dinner and that it was fine. We would not hear of that! We were determined to have her join us or we

165

would go somewhere else! As we discussed different options, such as picking her up out of her chair and carrying her into the restaurant, the owner said we could dine in the back room of the restaurant and there was a back entrance...down some stairs. Our crew was determined to get her in there for dinner with us. Blaine and one of the other guests picked up the wheelchair and carried her in her wheelchair down the stairs. She was able to get to our new table, and we had the pleasure of having her delightful company for dinner! Where there is a will, there is a way! We were not taking "No" for an answer. But it opened our eyes to yet another hurdle faced even after gaining independence with an Assistance Dog.

June 23 - Day 54: Goshen, NY - Poughkeepsie, NY - Goshen, NY

Early mornings had never been my favorite, and we had to drive an hour to get to our morning radio show. We were excited to be on another show, so we loaded up the pups early and headed for the hour drive to Poughkeepsie. We were going to be on the Karlson and McKenzie show on WPDH 101.5 FM.

They welcomed the four of us into the studio and we put on Max and Bailey's Doggles to give them a preview of our ride. We had a great interview with them, and they made it fun. Later in the day, we were stopped by one of their listeners to let us know they heard our interview and loved what we were doing. It was exciting when you knew your message was heard!

Next, we headed another 40 miles in a different direction to make a stop at Outback Choppers in Tuxedo, NY. The owner, Paul Maloney, had heard about our ride and invited us to visit his shop. Yes, he is from the "Land Down Under," thus the name Outback Choppers. We enjoyed our visit and got some pictures with their cute mascot, Chopperoo, the motorcycle riding kangaroo. We traded T-shirts...Max and Bailey shirts for a couple Outback Chopper T-shirts. While we were there, a gentleman who had been following our ride came to meet us. He rode many miles to come meet Max and Bailey. It still was profound that someone would drive a long distance just to meet us!

After a full day of events, we drove the 29 miles back to Silent Farm to relax for the evening. We had planned to stay somewhere at a hotel and Mary and John had gratuitously extended our stay with them. We were pleased to stay one more night with our awesome hosts.

As I planned our route for the next day, I finally got to the point where all the maps would not download to the GPS. It was too large of a download and the GPS ran out of space. After two hours of waiting for it, the download failed. Frustrated, I sat down and cried! How was I going to lead us into New York City? I had been struggling for over a month and a half with this nightly download, often having to attempt the download multiple times, and tonight it failed. Of course, it was for the place where I needed it most!

I pulled out my trusty paper atlas and figured out the route up to the city limits. I wrote my route down until I got into the city and then mapped that city route in my GPS. I planned to put blue painters tape on my gas tank in the morning and write down the route to get to New York City where my GPS would finally take over. My brother had given me the idea of using painters tape on the gas tank for routing instructions and that idea finally came in handy. Thank you, Den, for that ingenious idea!

June 24 - Day 55: Goshen, NY - New York City, NY

This was one of those days where I wanted to stay under the covers. We had just spent four excellent nights at this cozy bed and breakfast with fantastic hosts, and we had to say goodbye again. Plus, we were going to be traveling into downtown New York City! I was a nervous wreck about driving in that crazy big-city traffic. Some days I hated the fact that I was the Navigator! I was terrified of driving in this huge city!

While we packed our bikes and got ready to go, our hosts greeted us with a tremendous surprise. We knew that our first couple of nights were free, compliments of our gracious hosts, but when we decided to stay for a couple more days, we expected to pay for those days. As we got ready to settle up, the generosity of our hosts surprised us, as they said they were covering all four nights. We were humbled by their tremendous gift! It never ceased to amaze us with the power of strangers becoming friends on this journey.

Next, Mary helped me once again. Remember that big jar of coins that we received from the Raymond C. Cramer school? Mary saw me trying to figure out where I was going to store this heavy glass jar full of coins and said she would trade me the jar of coins for the value of the coins in paper bills; much easier to carry! Her thoughtfulness was greatly appreciated!

I must have done well with the big city driving because Blaine made the following entry into our daily journal:

I normally highlight Max & Bailey's adventures in these few paragraphs, but today Janet gets top billing. For a woman who stands only 5'3" tall and just learned to ride a motorcycle in October 2003, she rode into Manhattan like she owned the place. She pushed her way left and right through taxis and limos, stood toe-to-toe with the bumper-to-bumper traffic and led the Hogs For Dogs team right to the front door of our hotel. Sure, having Max & Bailey helped us ease our way into traffic, but I was so proud of the way she handled that bike today that I wanted to share it with you.

I was in tears when I read his journal entry that evening. I was proud to have tackled my fears and the New York City traffic successfully and to realize that he appreciated the feat. Of course, it was also helpful that the cab drivers loved Max and Bailey so much that they eased up around us and let me squeeze in front of them. Go Max and Bailey!

Blaine and I used some of our hotel points to stay at the upscale Westin Hotel at Times Square. As we pulled up behind a couple of limos outside the hotel, there were crowds of very tall guys and lots of television cameras filming them. Blaine and I wondered what all the hoopla was about. Once the media got sight of our pups, all cameras swung over to them. Seems we had arrived at the same hotel where all the guys in the NBA draft were staying. Some of the NBA players came over to greet Max and Bailey. As I unloaded Bailey, I felt extremely short at 5'3" next to all these players over 6 feet tall.

Max and Bailey usually adapt well to all experiences, but this hotel tested both of them. After all our extensive travel together, we ran into two situations that were brand new to them. First was the escalator which led to the check-in counter on the second floor. We had to be very careful not to get any fur or paws stuck in it. Bailey looked nervously at the moving stairs and was trying to figure out how to get on them. I finally coaxed him, making sure he safely stepped on the stairs. He did not like them at all and moonwalked back down the stairs. Since they were moving forward and he was moving backwards, we ended up staying in one place. I found this so humorous that I ended up in tears, laughing at him.

Once I regained my composure, I convinced him to move forward, and we finally made it up to the second floor to check in to our room. I stood there wiping away the tears from my eyes as I was so tickled at his usual goofy self!

While Bailey and I were tackling the escalator, Blaine was still down on the first floor chatting with one of the basketball players. They were laughing at Bailey's antics. The basketball player relayed that it had been a lot of work to get to the NBA draft, and he never expected to be upstaged by a couple of dogs. He loved the idea of our charity and gave Blaine a donation. Blaine wished him well in the draft.

Next was Max's test. He did not like the glass walls. On the second floor, there was a glass wall overlooking the first floor and he would not get near it. He pulled back the opposite way. Then we walked into the glass elevator to go up to our room. He really was not happy about that idea. After that trip up, we found a back elevator that was enclosed and nowhere near the glass walls overlooking the first floor. For all subsequent trips with the dogs, we took that back elevator all the way to the first floor...no glass walls and no escalators. For dogs who rode motorcycles and had cruised on a sailboat, who would have guessed that they would have issues with glass walls and moving steps!

After getting the dogs settled into our hotel room, we went to park the motorcycles in the designated hotel parking garage. We went in and started our normal parking procedure. Blaine would always back his motorcycle into the parking space and then I would move mine in front of his, stopping inches away from his motorcycle. Each sidecar would be inches away from the opposite bike's front tire. That way, we easily fit into one parking space.

The parking attendant came over and told us we needed to be in separate parking spaces. He wanted to charge us for two parking spaces instead of just one. The dogs were not in their sidecars and could not provide that bridge of laughter. Therefore, we were just two more motorcyclists in the vast New York City. After a lot of convincing, and a little arguing, we were able to leave our bikes in that one space.

Since we could not see our motorcycles from our hotel, we took out the thick chain and heavy-duty lock we had packed when we started our journey. We intertwined our chain through both bikes and secured them with the lock. We had come prepared for times like this. We checked to make sure that all compartments and the sidecar backs were locked. We emptied all compartments that could not be locked and hoped our bikes would be safe. As we walked away, the grouchy security guy was still giving us the evil eye.

June 25 - Day 56: New York City, NY - Brooklyn, NY - New York City, NY

It was Blaine's 40th birthday and a day to celebrate! We had a very busy day ahead of us...starting out super early in the morning for a Jimmy Buffett concert! Buffett was playing out on the plaza for the Today Show, so we got up at 5:00 to head on out to get a spot to enjoy the concert. Yes, I said 5:00 AM. I have never been too alive at that time of the morning. It was already crowded when we got there, but we were able to still get a decent spot to watch the show. We were trying to meet up again with Hayden and Radeen, since they were in New York City too. They were a bit later than us and tried to inch their way towards us as the concert began.

We enjoyed an excellent Buffett concert which made us miss our boat and cruising lifestyle. We met a fantastic group of people from North Carolina, and they sang Happy Birthday to Blaine, so we had a good start to the day. Nothing like friendly North Carolina people!

Next up for the day was a trip to the Brooklyn Harley-Davidson dealership for yet another event. From Manhattan to Long Island, we traveled through the Brooklyn Battery Tunnel. We again approached the dealership with our normal trepidation, never knowing how the event would pan out...especially here in Brooklyn. They gave us a warm welcome, and we set up our bikes for display with Max and Bailey in the sidecars enticing people to come visit.

Inside, the food started to pile up. We had an anonymous donor bring the food to us and it was quite a spread! Awesome Italian hospitality! We had a huge spread of sandwiches and pasta and it never disappeared throughout our entire stay at the dealership.

Outside, we had our normal display of Hogs for Dogs T-shirts for sale. Our gracious hosts were helping us sell T-shirts with a very convincing, heavy-handed sales tactic. You would hear them call out passersby in their heavy Brooklyn accents, "So, how many T-shirts you want today...looks like you need three T-shirts...what sizes do you need? No, do not think two will do...definitely need three. So, what sizes do you need? Yep...definitely need three...what were those sizes again?"

How did you turn away that marketing blitz? If you did not buy all three T-shirts, what were the consequences going to be? We laughed as we watched; I figured I could learn a few things from their sales pitch. T-shirts were flying off the table! Everyone walked away with an extra T-shirt. The organizers pulled off a very successful event. We loved this dealership.

We also had great representation from our major partner, Paws With A Cause. One of their reps showed up with her service dog along with one of the field trainers with a PAWS foster puppy.

As our day wound down, we packed up our gear and prepared to head back to our hotel in Manhattan. We made $1350 in T-shirt sales and donations and were ecstatic about our event! We still had a night ahead of us to celebrate Blaine's 40th birthday. Hayden and Radeen were planning on joining us for the evening. As we headed back to West 43rd Street to the Westin to shower and dress for the evening, the rains started coming down. Our trip back from Brooklyn was WET! Our elation from our event faded, and the rain continued. The traffic was also extremely heavy, so we did not make the great time that we had expected. By the time we got back to the hotel, we were both exhausted and soaked and just wanted to go to bed. But we still had a celebration to attend!

We phoned our friends when we got back and told them we still wanted to go out but needed a shower and were running behind schedule. They easily worked with us, and we decided to just meet up at the Mexican restaurant in the hotel. After showers and feeling refreshed, we headed to the restaurant and to a fun dinner with our friends. After lots of food and margaritas, the restaurant staff brought Blaine a HUGE sombrero to wear, and we all sang Happy Birthday to bring in the new year for him. Hayden and Radeen offered to take the sombrero home with them to hold until we could get it on our next visit with them, since we were short of storage on our bikes for this trip and that certainly would not fit.

June 26 - Day 57: New York City, NY - Danbury, CT

We had another brutally early morning as we got up at 4:30 to get ready for our television appearance. These early mornings were killing me! The elephants were back in my stomach as I thought about our impending interview. This was the day that we were being interviewed by CBS's The Saturday Early Show's weatherman, Ira Joe Fisher, live on national TV. Finally, we could get our message out on a major news channel!

With sweaty palms, we anxiously rode the one mile through the city traffic as we mentally prepared ourselves to be on a news show that would be broadcast across America. I was grateful that it was a Saturday, so the traffic was much lighter, allowing us to arrive with time to spare. The taxis were again gracious in helping us into the traffic. One of them even paced next to us on our right side, next to the sidecars, to let his passengers get a good view of Max and Bailey.

At 6:00, we drove up to the plaza and parked in front of the General Motors building. After we got settled, we realized our sidecars were facing the plaza, with the street behind us. We figured they would want us to have the sidecars facing out with the building behind us, so we timed ourselves with the traffic and streetlights and turned around to face the other direction. We also figured out that there was a small area at the crosswalk that was a ramp from the street up to the curb so we could drive onto the plaza.

Just as we got ourselves positioned again, the show's staff came out and asked us to turn around. So, once again, we timed it with the traffic to find a lull to turn ourselves around for a third try. Thankfully, we had one of our board members, JoLee, there to assist us, especially with the timing of the traffic. Their staff directed us as we positioned our bikes to be staggered, where my motorcycle was ahead of and to the right of Blaine's motorcycle. It would allow Ira Joe to stand between our two bikes and the Hogs for Dogs website on the back of the tour pack on my bike would be very visible during the broadcast.

Next, the staff gave us our microphones with the usual instructions of attaching the box to your belt in the back and snaking the microphone up through your shirt and attaching it onto the front collar of your shirt. This was tricky to do while you are standing on the street in downtown New York City! I had to get a little help in snaking it through my shirt without flashing the city.

Once we were settled, Ira Joe came down, met the dogs, and introduced himself. He was down to earth and absolutely loved the dogs! We chatted a little about our ride to help him set up some questions for us and we got ready for the segment. We also introduced him to our representatives of Paws With A Cause who had joined us the previous day at the event in Brooklyn. They had their service dogs with them, so we thought it would be nice to show the service dogs on the segment.

We were surprisingly pleased with our time on the air. Ira Joe asked us some outstanding questions, allowing us to give plenty of information about our ride and to explain the benefits of Assistance Dogs. The interview was fun; it was humorous, but still conveyed the importance of service dogs. He stretched our segment longer than expected because we kept seeing the show's staff give the "wrap it up" signal and Ira Joe kept on chatting with us. We could tell he was enjoying the dogs and our unique story.

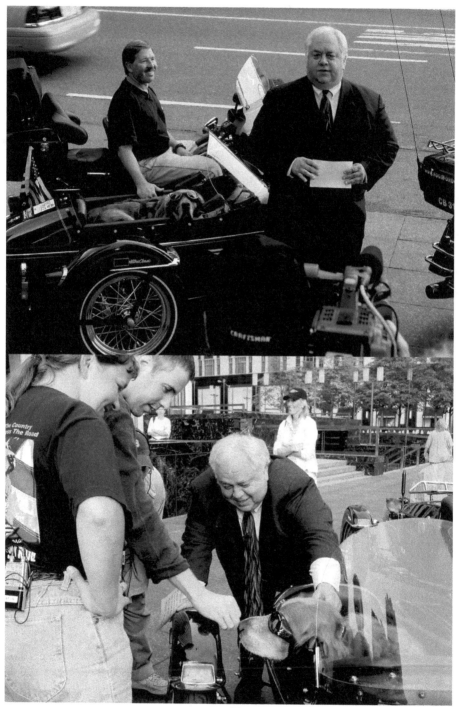

After we were off-the-air, Ira Joe continued to chat with us and gave Max and Bailey lots of attention. He loved the dogs! He also chatted with our Paws With A Cause representatives, but we were disappointed that they did not show the actual service dogs on air. We never saw the videotape of the show, but we got good feedback that it ended up being an awesome segment.

After the CBS staff went back inside, we met a gentleman by the name of David who worked for Applause, the toy company. He worked in marketing, and we discussed several different media and product opportunities with him. He was very interested in our cause and enticed us to go over to the NBC building to see if we could attract the attention of the Today Show. We sat outside of the Today Show building and chatted more with David about different fundraising opportunities. He gave Max and Bailey several stuffed animals to cuddle with on our ride. Even though we sat outside of the NBC news studios for a long time, we were unsuccessful in attracting any attention.

After a long morning, we headed out of New York around 2PM and headed to Connecticut, our 17th state. We were heading to an event at the infamous Marcus Dairy Bar. The Marcus family started a dairy farm in 1913 and, in 1948, they opened a small diner to sell good food and their Marcus Dairy ice cream. By the early 70s, it had become a famous motorcycle destination. It was a perfect destination for a Sunday morning motorcycle ride on Route 84 or Route 7; it provided a delicious breakfast with a parking lot full of motorcycles where you could hang out and browse. They also had Super Sunday events where they would have contests and vendors selling motorcycle related goods to raise money for various charities.

We were invited to stop there for a Cruise-In Car Show, where many gathered with their cool vintage cars. We set up our bikes and received loads of attention as many people came to meet Max and Bailey. Many had seen us on TV that morning on the Early Show. We had a fun time relaying our message as we had a comradery with the car enthusiasts and our fellow motorcyclists.

Bailey was so exhausted from our long day that at one point he stretched out his paw to hang over the edge of the sidecar and put his head hanging next to it over the edge and fell deeply asleep! After being up since 4:30 in the morning, I totally agreed with Bailey and wanted to crawl up into his sidecar and join him in a nap!

We finally were to the point where the show was breaking up and we felt that we had let everybody out there know about our cause, so we packed up our stuff and headed to the Holiday Inn for the night.

June 27 - Day 58: Danbury, CT

Yet again, we woke up early and headed to Marcus Dairy for their famous Sunday Biker's Breakfast. We arrived and found a perfect spot to set up our bikes with our T-shirts for sale and information readily available. Once there, Blaine headed into the restaurant to buy breakfast for us. In the usual style, we bought breakfast, but ended up spending an hour eating our breakfast sandwich as we spent time in between each bite to tell each visitor about our trip and why we were out there. Max and Bailey were a colossal hit among their approximately 1,000 riders who visited them that morning.

I loved Blaine's journal entry that day explaining the reaction of one biker:

And, like everywhere else we've been, the bikers were extremely supportive of Max &
Bailey's 2004 Ride Across America. Max & Bailey were a REALLY big hit with one rider
who rode in on a beautiful custom chopper. He was smiling, pointing, and screaming as he
parked his bike. "I saw those dogs on TV yesterday," he yelled. Before long, we were
surrounded. I never got his name, but his enthusiasm was contagious. So, if you know
him, please pass along our thanks for his help.

We also had visits from a couple of different families from Raleigh, NC who helped us spread the word. It was so nice to get a helping hand from our home state of North Carolina. After another very full morning, we headed back to our hotel to relax. As part of my daily routine, I counted our donations and T-shirt sales. We had made $1,300 on our two-day visit to Marcus Dairy, which was a great success!

June 28 - Day 59: Danbury, CT - Yorktown Heights, CT - Cheshire, CT

We headed out of Danbury, CT to make a lunch time visit with one of our charity partners. Guiding Eyes for the Blind was our only partner who trained guide dogs for the blind. They started in 1954 and provided their guide dogs free of charge to their recipients. Guide dogs were more well-known than other types of Assistance Dogs, so this organization had become more successful with their fundraising. The other Assistance Dogs organizations were still trying to get the word out of what service dogs could do for someone with a disability other than blindness.

We traveled to Patterson, NY to their breeding center. As we arrived, we were enthusiastically greeted by their staff and volunteers who were very welcoming and loved seeing Max and Bailey in their sidecars! They had been following our journey for the past two months and were excited to meet us.

As we took pictures of their staff and volunteers with our Hogs for Dogs team on our bikes, we noticed Max and Bailey's noses in the air as they smelled the food cooking on the grills out back. It smelled yummy! They ushered us in and treated us to a tremendous barbecue lunch of hamburgers, chicken, and ribs. This was a pleasant surprise!

We were able to do our normal presentation about our ride and give them the initial $1,000 donation from the ride's proceeds. We were then presented with Guiding Eyes polo shirts and were asked to cut the beautiful cake with "Welcome Max and Bailey" written on it.

Next, they gave us a tour of the facility. Part of the tour involved puppies! They had several puppies that were part of their breeding program, and we were able to meet them. OMG! Puppies! That made my day. I was in heaven! We were very impressed with their breeding facility and their processes.

Before we left, many asked about our Hogs for Dogs gear we had for sale. After a frenzy of T-shirt and hat buying, we had sold almost $1,000 in our logo gear!

We also had the pleasure of meeting a couple from Florida who had been following our ride. They were nearby visiting family and had been exchanging emails with Blaine for a few weeks. After finding out when we would visit Guiding Eyes for the Blind, they made a special trip to come meet us. After meeting Max and Bailey, they too purchased some logo gear and made a $100 donation to Hogs for Dogs. It was always amazing to see the support we received from people we did not know that were following along with us on our journey!

After the fun and educational site visit and the delicious lunch, we headed to my cousin's house. We were super excited to stay with my cousin, Steve Kulpa, and his family for the next two nights! I had not seen my cousin in years, and I was eager to visit with him.

June 29 - Day 60: Cheshire, CT

Today was one of our down days. Unfortunately, we were so swamped with emails, finances, and paperwork that we could not really enjoy the day. I would have loved to have been able to spend more of the day with my cousin, but there was just so much that we needed to get done. I was truly disappointed

Thankfully, by the end of the day, we had almost caught up with everything and could enjoy a very nice home-cooked meal and the hospitality of my cousin and his family.

June 30 - Day 61: Cheshire, CT - Newport, RI

We were disappointed to leave my cousin's house since we did not get much time to visit with him and his family. Unfortunately, we had a schedule to keep, which was the biggest downside of our trip.

We booked a much-needed service appointment at Gengras Harley-Davidson. All six of our motorcycle tires were starting to bald, and both motorcycles needed the 10,000-mile service. We were grateful that, after hearing our story, they squeezed us into their busy service day. We traveled the 26 miles up to the dealership in East Hartford for our appointment.

Blaine's journal entry for that day explains how gracious the dealership was to our cause:

Gengras Harley-Davidson did us a HUGE favor by squeezing us in to replace our six balding tires and complete our 10,000-mile service on both bikes. Rob Ruggiero not only made room for us, he gave us a discounted price as their contribution to Max & Bailey's ride. When we got our bill at the end of the day, we also found that one of the techs working on the bikes had donated some parts at his cost, too!

Needless to say, Rob and our two techs (known as Tim A & Tim B) get the Max & Bailey's Five Paw Rating for customer service. If you live in, or near, East Hartford and need a recommendation on a Harley-Davidson dealership -- look no farther than Gengras H-D. Tell them Max & Bailey sent you.

When the bikes were ready, we headed towards Newport. We took the back roads and drove through beautiful Mystic, CT. Soon we were entering Rhode Island, our 18th state!

As we crossed the bridge into Newport, we breathed in the sea air and saw all the sailboats dancing on their anchors. It felt like home. While cruising on our sailboat, we had visited Newport, and the scenery of all the sailboats reminded us of our cruising days. We were excited to visit this beautiful town on our motorcycles.

July

July 1 - Day 62: Newport, RI

We started off the day by riding near the anchorage and reminiscing about the times we had anchored our sailboat in this very anchorage.

After finding out that two of our cruising friends were anchored in Bristol, we took the day off to go visit them. We loaded Max and Bailey into their sidecars and hit the road for the 24-mile drive up to Bristol.

As we headed into the town of Bristol, we loved their patriotic spirit. Not only did they have their flags flying everywhere, but they even had their center line on the road painted red, white, and blue! Now that is getting into the spirit of the 4th of July!

We met our friends, Randy and Sheri Schneider, along with their sweet black lab. Max and Bailey were delighted to see Pepper since they had run around with Pepper during our cruising days. The four of us decided on a nice little pub for lunch so we could catch up with each other. We reminisced about all the fun times that we had when we had ended up in the same anchorages while cruising. We missed the cruising community, and it was very special for us to spend the afternoon with our dear friends.

July 2 - Day 63: Newport, RI

We had a change in our schedule, so it gave us a chance to stay in Newport for one more day and again catch up on our work. It was exhausting to continue to ride each day, attend events and school visits, and keep up with the daily tasks that were needed to run the organization. Blaine continued handling the daily emails, event planning coordination and the daily journal for our website while I continued the daily struggle of creating the route for the next day, downloading it to our GPS, and keeping our financials in order.

Even when we got discouraged with all the work that this ride involved, we would always be reminded of the reason that we were dedicated to the ride. Blaine's journal entry for this day gave true meaning to why we were on this ride:

The entire country is looking forward to another holiday weekend. This Fourth of July marks America's 228th year of independence. That's certainly something to celebrate.

For some, however, independence has a different meaning than the freedoms we've enjoyed for the last two centuries. To some, their Declaration of Independence is signed by more names than just those of our forefathers. It is a made up of the signatures of millions of their fellow Americans all waiting for a service dog of their own. Their independence is still years away because the waiting lists - their Declaration of Independence - are longer than the services currently available.

Max, Bailey and the Hogs For Dogs team will be celebrating this Independence Day with those thoughts in mind. Your donations have already provided the funding necessary for three individuals to have a service dog of their own. You've given them the gift of independence. But there is much more work to be done.

July 3 - Day 64: Newport, RI - Holland, MA

It was time to get back on the road. As we traveled the 80 miles to our destination for the night, we crossed into Massachusetts, our 19th state! We had been graciously invited to stay at Restful Paws Bed and Breakfast. Our journal entry for that day describes it well:

The B & B, run by Raymond and Barbara Korny, is a place where pets aren't only tolerated, they're treated like celebrities. And Max & Bailey always enjoy the celebrity treatment. Maria, the Korny's teenage daughter, made sure that the dogs were spoiled rotten and had plenty of love during their stay.

The rooms are beautiful, and the common areas are spacious and dog friendly. There is even a bone-shaped pool under construction to give the pooches a place to relax and unwind with their owners. This place is sure to have a bright future and we're thankful to the Korny's for hosting Max & Bailey for the night. And if you need a cool indoor place to run and play, try out the downstairs area called the Hounds' Lounge.

After we got settled into our room, we took Max and Bailey outside to roam through the lush, wooded trail behind the B&B. Maria joined us and the pups loved being able to run around and explore off their leashes. They were in heaven!

This was a lovely place to stay, and the rooms were very quaint. We relaxed for the rest of the day to get ready for the next couple of busy days.

July 4 - Day 65: Holland, MA - Boston, MA

Our destination for the day was in the Boston area. While we were staying in Braintree, we had been invited to a cookout in a nearby town. The invitation was from a well-known family who was friends with one of our board members. We accepted their invitation with the agreement that we would not mention them in our journal.

We had a fun time enjoying the cookout and seeing the cool toys, aka expensive cars, that they owned. Blaine ran across a unicycle while we were there, and he finally proved to me that he could actually ride one. Max and Bailey ran around their back yard and had some fun as well. It ended up being a nice way to spend the Fourth of July holiday.

July 5 - Day 66: Boston, MA - Needham, MA - Stamford, VT

Our event for the day was the Needham Exchange Club's Country Fair Days Parade in Needham, MA. Before the parade, we had been invited to the community pancake breakfast. It was always nice to eat a meal that did not come from a restaurant, so we thoroughly enjoyed the pancakes and bacon. Max and Bailey, sitting in their sidecars, soaked up all the attention.

The gentleman who had invited us to join him in the parade also had a sidecar rig and his German Shepherd rode in the sidecar. Blaine's journal entry describes our parade adventure well:

After breakfast, we made our way to the parade assembly area, led by our escort Joe and his German Shepherd, Cody, in their Harley-Davidson sidecar rig. Then, just as the parade was about to begin, the skies opened up with light showers followed by heavier rains. Too late to bail out of the parade, so we put a cover over the dogs and rolled on. Joe and Cody led the way, with Janet on one side of the road and me riding in reverse so both sides of the parade could see the dogs in sidecars. It was a big hit with everyone except the police -- they were not so crazy about me riding backwards for the three-mile route, but they let us finish the parade.

After the parade was over, Joe invited us over to his house so we could put on some dry clothes before leaving for western Massachusetts. His hospitality was very welcome, as we both felt like drowned rats from the rain.

We headed through the mountains of Massachusetts, and I couldn't contain my excitement about showing Blaine the famous Mohawk trail and the town, Adams, where my parents grew up. As we continued through the mountains, I sensed a strange feeling on my bike. The sounds were unfamiliar, and it felt like a rougher ride. The road surface had changed recently, so I chalked it up to road noise and feeling from the different surface. We finally changed surfaces again and my issues were not going away.

Finally, I decided I needed to bring up my concerns with Blaine to see if he was noticing the same things. As I stated what I was feeling, he looked at my bike and noticed a huge wobble. He told me to pull over immediately!

Since we were in the mountains with few places to pull over, I had to continue a ways further until I found a small gravel road on our right side. I pulled over, and we looked again at my bike. Blaine laid on the ground and finally said "Aha". He saw that the spokes on my rear tire were breaking. We were out in the middle of nowhere! We also knew our route to our home for the night included many mountains, endless curves, and the famous hairpin turn of the Mohawk trail. It was too dangerous for me to continue with my motorcycle.

Blaine took out our cell phone, and we had no cell coverage. We were very thankful that we had come prepared and had a satellite phone with us. Unfortunately, the tree cover was extreme, so Blaine had to work hard to get a signal and stand in one spot once he got connected.

He called our Harley-Davidson emergency service number and reported our problem. They filled out our problem report and said they would call us back when they had a tow truck on the way. Blaine repeatedly told them it needed to be a truck that could hold a huge motorcycle with a sidecar and a normal motorcycle trailer would not hold my bike/sidecar outfit. He also got their number in case they could not get through as they called in to our satellite phone. He explained our predicament, and they understood our communication problems.

Thankfully, they finally called us back and said that there was a tow truck on its way. We attempted to explain where we were, but since we really did not know exactly where we were, all we could do was explain where we had been and to look for the little side road. As luck would have it, it started to rain as we waited for the tow truck.

We put the rain covers up over the dogs on the sidecars and climbed into our rain gear. I threw up an umbrella to help us stay dry, and we waited on the side of the road for what seemed an eternity. We did not know if they could contact us via the satellite phone and we did not know if the tow truck would be able to figure out our location with our directions to the emergency service company. Again, my frustrations mounted as we waited and waited...and waited.

Finally, we got a call into our satellite phone from the towing company. He could not find us, and we relayed the areas we had passed and where we thought we were located. He eventually found us, and a bit of relief crept over me. Another plus was that he was equipped to haul a car, so my sidecar rig could easily fit onto his platform. I looked on as he connected my motorcycle and I watched it get hauled onto the tow truck.

We called my cousin, Jean Kurpiel, who we were staying with for the next couple of nights and she agreed to find us on our little gravel road and pick up me and Bailey. We watched the tow truck head off with my motorcycle and a feeling of abandonment swept over me as we waited for my cousin. Bailey and I stood next to all the gear that we had to take off the motorcycle…luggage, saddlebag of dog stuff, bin of dog food, laptop bag, etc. and prayed that it would not rain again and that my cousin could find us.

With delight, we saw my cousin pull into the side road. We loaded my stuff into her vehicle, and Bailey and I climbed in. We headed out, and Blaine followed behind.

Jean lived in the small town of Stamford, Vermont, just north of the Massachusetts state line. So, for Blaine, he crossed over into his 20th state with his motorcycle. While Bailey and I had physically entered Vermont, it did not feel like I could really count it, since my motorcycle did not come with us. We kind of sat in an unusual situation where Blaine and Max had hit another milestone on the journey, while Bailey and I still needed to accomplish that task.

Once we stopped and had a landline phone available, we called the dealership that received my bike and told them how urgent it was that we get back on the road as soon as possible. We settled in for an unknown number of days.

July 6 - Day 67: Stamford, VT - Adams, MA - Stamford, VT

We got the update from the Harley-Davidson dealership that they needed to order a replacement wheel for my motorcycle, and they gave us two options. We could continue with another rear wheel with spokes or change the type to a solid wheel. We decided with all the extra weight on our rigs that it made more sense to put the solid wheel on instead of the same spoked wheel.

We had planned to go visit my aunt and uncle, Ed and Lil Kulpa, in Adams, MA but we had hoped to bring both of our bikes, so they could see Max and Bailey in their sidecars. Instead, we had to settle for riding only one motorcycle with no dog in tow. We still had a pleasant visit with my aunt and uncle, but were very disappointed that my motorcycle was not available for the visit. I got a chance to show Blaine the small town of Adams where my mom and dad had grown up.

July 7 - Day 68: Stamford, VT

Finally, we got the call that we had been anticipating. My bike was fixed and ready to be picked up! We headed out to Aldo's Harley-Davidson in Bernardston, MA to get my beloved bike back. Aldo's did a fantastic job of getting my bike fixed quickly so we could stay on our schedule.

Once the bike was back at my cousin's house, I got busy putting all the stuff back into it. Thankfully, after being on the road for 68 days, I knew where everything went to fit it all in the motorcycle and sidecar, so it did not take me long to pack it. I felt complete again, having my motorcycle back and being ready to continue our route.

We enjoyed one last evening with Jean and her husband, Mike. Jean hosted a wonderful dinner with my aunt, another cousin of mine, and Jean's children attending. I was happy to be able to see more relatives while we were there.

July 8 - Day 69: Stamford, VT - Dover, NH

Yet again, it was time to say goodbye to family. Even though we were going through a difficult time with the motorcycle repairs, we had a fun time staying with my cousin and being able to visit with other relatives while we were there. It was always so difficult to leave family or friends behind to head out to the great unknown again.

I was excited to have my motorcycle back and to finally be back on the road with it. It was nice to have everything back in its place on the bike, load Bailey into the sidecar, and climb back onto my hack rig. Since we did not have the chance to enjoy it when we arrived and I did not get to ride it on my bike versus in a car, we headed back through the Mohawk Trail.

Wikipedia describes it this way:

The Mohawk Trail began as a Native American trade route which connected Atlantic tribes with tribes in Upstate New York and beyond. It followed the Millers River, Deerfield River and crossed the Hoosac Range. Today, the Mohawk Trail is part of Massachusetts Route 2, which was created as one of the United States' first scenic highways. It follows much of the original Indian trail, from Orange, Massachusetts to Williamstown, Massachusetts, for about 65 miles through the Berkshire mountains. The Mohawk Trail was added to the National Register of Historic Places on April 03, 1973.

191

This is the area where my parents grew up and we visited every summer. The most prominent feature I remember is the famous hairpin turn. Therefore, I was eager to get on the road and share this beautiful ride with Blaine. Our ride for the day would be 178 miles, so a long drive for us, especially having to drive more slowly through the curves of the mountains. But it was also going to be very scenic, so we were both looking forward to it. We would start by heading through the Mohawk Trail on Route 2, take a small stretch of I-91 into New Hampshire, and then Route 9 the rest of the way to Dover.

It was indeed a beautiful ride. It was foggy when we started out, which made it an even more breathtaking journey through the lush green mountains. We inched our way through the hairpin turn and our arms got a workout as we twisted and turned through all the curves in the road.

We, of course, had to stop at the Big Indian souvenir shop. Who could resist with the teepee and large Indian statue greeting you? I love Jamie Jensen's description of this stop in Road Trip USA. He stated, "There are also some enticingly kitschy old Indian Trading Posts, packed full of postcards, plastic tomahawks, and moccasins; my personal favorite is the Big Indian, fronted by a historically inaccurate, politically incorrect, and photogenically irresistible 35-foot-tall statue of a Plains Indian." He describes it well. Naturally, we had to get a picture of the bikes in front of the huge Indian statue.

We continued on and headed up I-91 into Vermont. Even though we had stayed just over the state line in Vermont at my cousin's house, we finally took a picture of us in front of a Vermont sign, and I felt that we officially had crossed Vermont off our list of states to visit...our 20th state. We had pulled into the visitor's center and parked right in front of it near the "Welcome to Vermont" sign engraved in the marble block. It took a while to get our pictures because interested tourists surrounded us once again.

After we got pictures of just us and the bikes in front of the sign, we headed back onto the road. Just a few miles further and we turned onto Hwy. 9, crossed the Connecticut River, and into our 21st state, New Hampshire. I could not believe that we had been through 21 states in just over two months!

The rest of our ride was pretty uneventful, but we enjoyed the scenic drive and were grateful for the relaxing trip that day. We arrived in Dover and my trusty GPS brought us to our motel for the night.

Blaine's journal entry aptly describes our evening:

When we arrived at the hotel in Dover, our noses detected some delicious seafood being cooked just next door at the Fish Shanty Restaurant on Central Avenue. Little did we know that while we were checking in, the restaurant staff was pinned against their windows admiring Max & Bailey.

We settled into our room, answered about 100 emails and then remembered that seafood smell. Soon after we entered the Fish Shanty, we were recognized as the people with those cute, motorcycle dogs. Annie and the entire restaurant staff treated us remarkably well, even buying us drinks. We returned the favor by leaving behind several photos and brochures. By the end of the evening, our stomachs, and our hearts, were full. These are good people serving even better food. Stop by and see them if you ever visit Dover.

July 9 - Day 70: Dover, NH - Sebec Lake, ME

We were really excited about our trip today. We would meander through the back roads of New Hampshire and Maine and end the day at a friend's cabin, where we would spend the next couple of days. As we woke up and got ready to go, our excitement dwindled. The forecast for the day was more rain, and it did not look like we were going to get away from it today.

It would be a long day ahead of us. Our route was 194 miles. It took us up NH-4, which turned into ME-4, then onto Hwy 202 up to Dover-Foxcroft, and then a little further to our final destination. About 5 miles into our ride, we crossed a small waterway and saw the Maine State Line sign. Since we did not see a Welcome to Maine sign, we crossed back over the bridge and made a U-turn. Thankfully, there was an extra lane on the bridge, so we could stop in the middle of the bridge and get a quick picture of Bailey and me next to the Maine State Line sign. We briefly celebrated our 22nd state and then we were off again.

Thankfully, we made it through some of the day with only the threat of rain and we were able to make a quick lunch stop before the rains came. But then they came hard. We stopped for fuel and a break from the rain when the bottom fell out. The cashier was so nice. She came out to see Max and Bailey and told us to just stay there at the gas pumps under the cover until the rain let up. She essentially said that nobody is coming out in the rain, so just stay there until it lets up. As I look back at the picture, I have to laugh. Bailey got tired of the rain cover and whittled his nose through the velcroed areas so he could stick his nose out and get some fresh air. We did not even open Max's rain cover, and he was perfectly content to stay nice and cozy inside. You cannot even see Max in the picture we took…he is hiding undercover.

When the rain finally let up, we thanked the cashier and continued on our way. We finally made it to Dover-Foxcroft and scouted out a grocery store where we could come back for groceries for a few days. We had been to the cabin before and I was worried that we would have a difficult time getting to the cabin on the dirt road leading up to it, since we had all that rain. As we approached, we had to be very careful and dodge the potholes, but we made it to the cabin safely.

Our friend, Don Bitting, had offered his place to stay when he heard about our ride. We had met Don via some of our sailing friends, but then Blaine later learned that he was the owner of the electric company that Blaine worked with when he worked at Glaxo. It was a small world.

After we parked near his house, we went looking for the hidden key. He had told us where to look for it, but we were not having any luck. We were thinking we were going to have to find another place to stay for the evening. Yikes! Finally, we got in touch with our friend, and he talked us through the path to find the beloved key.

Our friend who owned the cabin on the lake called it a "camp". When we had first come up to the "camp" one summer while we were in Maine on our boat, I was expecting a tiny, primitive dwelling. Well, the "camp" consisted of a main building with two bedrooms and two baths and a nice kitchen and living area, plus a wonderful, enclosed deck overlooking the beautiful lake. Then there was a garage and guest building with another bedroom, bathroom, and a small kitchen. So much for a "camp"!

After we got unpacked, Blaine and I headed into town to get some groceries for the next few days. It was time for a little down time for us and we were looking forward to not going anywhere for a couple of days.

We found the little grocery store and bought our groceries. We knew there was a grill, and we had not had steaks in a long time, so we splurged on a couple of steaks and a nice bottle of cabernet for dinner that evening.

This was indeed a slice of heaven. Sitting overlooking the beautiful lake, we enjoyed juicy steaks fresh off the grill. Perfect!

July 10 - Day 71: Sebec Lake, ME

Well, this was supposed to be some well-deserved time off, but I found I was way behind in my accounting! After all our events in Pennsylvania, New Jersey, New York and Connecticut, I had receipts stuffed everywhere and donations to record, so I spent most of my day catching up on the accounting. Blaine was thoroughly burned out and just needed a little R&R, so he relaxed and read most of the day.

I knew that if I did not catch up with the finances that I would fall far behind and would probably never get caught up. Therefore, I continued to work while Blaine relaxed. I envied his ability to relax while I continued to work. As the day wore on, my envy turned to fury as I was exhausted from this constant bookkeeping, and he sat nearby lounging and relaxing.

By the end of the day, I was finally caught up, but I had to discuss my frustration with Blaine. I knew I was acting like a child having a temper tantrum, but I just could not release my anger. Thankfully, after living in close quarters on our boat, we had learned to patiently talk things out when one of us was frustrated or angry, so we could understand each other's perspective. Blaine let me vent my resentment and gave me a hug to comfort me. He reminded me of Edmond and Phyllis, and I knew how important our ride was for people still waiting for their service dogs. That calmed me down. He offered to cook dinner to give me a chance to unwind after working through finances all day.

July 11 - Day 72: Sebec Lake, ME

It was a beautiful sunny day, so we spent some time out at the lake to let Max and Bailey enjoy a refreshing swim. They had a blast! Blaine and I enjoyed the sunshine and fresh air. We tossed tennis balls into the lake and Max and Bailey galloped in to retrieve them. Bailey preferred to find the biggest stick (or should I say log) and haul that around, so we ended up tossing tennis balls and sticks into the lake and they happily retrieved it all. They also loved taking breaks and relaxing in the warm sun to chew on one of the huge sticks.

Eventually, the fun came to an end, and it was bath time! Not a favorite time for either Max or Bailey. They absolutely LOVED the water when they could splash and swim in it, but hated the water when it came time for a little scrub. Even though they were not crazy about it, they lay waiting for their turn and stood nicely as they got washed. Just like washing a car, except that they liked to shake when they were most full of water to see how wet they could get us too.

We all sat on the back deck in the sun to dry off and enjoy the warm sunshine. I was finally a happy camper, as I got a day to relax instead of doing anything related to the ride. Some days, I really just needed a break from it all!

July 12 - Day 73: Sebec Lake, ME - Mexico, ME

Our route for the day took us down Hwy 150 and US-2 into Mexico. Not the country of Mexico, but the town of Mexico, Maine. We were very disappointed in not finding a plethora of Mexican restaurants throughout the town. We were looking forward to large margaritas and Mexican food, but we had to settle for something different.

We found a super Walmart in this small town, so we stopped there for a few items. I headed in to make more copies of our promotional postcard picture we used for advertising, and Blaine went to visit with the group of RVs parked in the parking lot. He hoped to tell the group of our journey and find someone who wanted to experience our journey with us and become our chase vehicle. Unfortunately, he only got incredible tours of the RVs, but nobody was willing to follow behind us. Darn! We would continue to have to pack everything on our bikes.

After checking into the Madison Resort Inn and unpacking our bikes, we went searching for a car wash to wash our rigs. Since we had been in so much rain lately, along with riding the dirt driveway to the camp, our bikes were filthy. We found a car wash, unloaded the dogs, and Blaine washed the bikes while I walked the pups around on their leashes.

After arriving back at the hotel, we found a wide-open grassy field behind the hotel, so we took Max and Bailey out there for some exercise. They enjoyed rolling around in the grass and playing fetch with a couple of tennis balls. It was a nice way to unwind from the ride.

As we settled into our normal evening activities, Blaine gave me an update on our Erie, PA plans. A while back, we had received an email about a special lady, Virginia Paine, who was in the Veterans Administration (VA) Hospital in Erie. The email was from a friend of a friend, and she asked us to visit Virginia when we were in the Erie area for our events. This is what the email said about Virginia:

Not only is she a WWII Vet, but she has also served as a VFW Commander (the 1st woman) and Chaplain. She is just an amazing woman. And her dog involvement is tremendous. She bred, raised, showed, and judged golden retrievers; wrote the book on English Toy Spaniels and had Goldens and bloodhounds trained for tracking and assisting the local police. The list goes on and on. So, you can see why she would be so excited about the adventure the 4 of you are on!! Virginia is 82 years old now, forgotten more than most will ever know but unfortunately cancer is taking a toll on her. I really hope you can make this visit happen.

Virginia was suffering from cancer, and we did not know if we would make it in time because her health had been deteriorating daily.

Kathy Everden was the volunteer who was organizing all the events in Erie, along with the visit to the VA Hospital. She had been keeping us updated on Virginia's health and it was good to hear Blaine read the update from Kathy that, even though Virginia was not doing well, she was in high spirits and was excited about meeting us.

July 13 - Day 74: Mexico, ME - Burlington, VT

Our ride took us through the incredible White Mountain National Forest, giving us astounding views of lush, green mountain vistas. The highlight was a beautiful stretch of road on Hwy 112 called the Kancamagus Highway, or the "Kanc" for short. It had magnificent scenery! While the sky threatened rain all day, to our delight it held off, giving us an enjoyable dry ride along the winding two-lane roads up and down the mountainsides.

We passed a sign that said, "Brake for moose," so we kept a vigilant lookout for them. We certainly did not want to collide with a moose!

After such an enjoyable ride, we were dismayed with the rest of our day once we reached Burlington. Blaine's journal entry explains our experience:

Unfortunately, the day - and our euphoric mood - were quickly erased when we arrived at our hotel for the night. After checking in to our reserved room (and unpacking), we were told that we would have to move from our preferred non-smoking room to a smoking room because of the dogs. So, we packed up all our stuff and moved to our new 'pet tolerant' room. The air conditioner does not work. There were used towels hanging in the bathroom, and a huge stain decorating the drab carpet. Oh, and the desk chair seat was not (still is not) attached to the chair. I discovered that last bit of information when I fell through the chair. Oh - and we even got to pay extra for all these privileges. So, where are we staying? Not some dive hotel on the wrong side of town. We're at the Days Inn Hotel in Burlington, VT.

If your plans bring you (and your dog) to Burlington, we'd suggest you not submit yourself to the less-than-friendly atmosphere here. And yes, we'll be chatting with the manager in the morning. They would not speak to us today.

I normally would not rant about a service on this website, but this experience is one that nobody else should have to live through. Not even for charity.

It appalled us that they would make us move after we had unpacked everything into the room that they had assigned us. Then, to move us into a smoking room when I had reserved a non-smoking room was insulting! After everything else that went wrong with the room, we had called the front desk and asked to speak with a manager. They refused to connect us to a manager! If we were not so tired, we would have packed up the bikes and gone searching for someplace else to stay. We were mortified!

So far on our ride, we had been extremely lucky with finding pleasant hotels that were dog friendly. It was always a challenge to find a hotel to stay where they accepted dogs and I spent a lot of time each evening researching different websites to find dog-friendly options in our next destination. Since it was hard to find much information on the different locations, sometimes we just had to take our chances. This was one of those days where we just had to suck it up and endure a horrible hotel. We had to remember it was only one night of misery.

Thankfully, after we got settled in, we received some good news to brighten our day. JoLee had been sending emails to update us on what we had received in the mail on a regular basis. We were pleasantly surprised that we had received a letter from PAWS where we were copied on a thank-you letter to the Raleigh HOGS group for their $2,000 donation. It was wonderful to see that our ride was indeed making a difference!

July 14 - Day 75: Burlington, VT - Utica, NY

We headed down Route 7 in search of breakfast. We were in luck that day because we found the local Mom and Pop diner, Burdick's Country Kitchen in Ferrisburgh, VT. We parked right in front of the door and headed inside for a delicious breakfast. They again fit the local Americana style of friendly local people and we had a great time chatting with everyone about our journey.

After our stomachs were satisfied, we headed back onto Route 7, hopped onto Route 17, and were back in New York. We then followed Route 8 the rest of the day. It was another scenic drive, and we went through the Adirondacks, but the skies threatened rain the entire day, so we did not spend a lot of time sightseeing. We wanted to get to the motel before it poured on us. We were not so lucky. Once again, the rains found us and we spent the last 50 miles curving through the mountains and being drenched by rain.

We finally made it to the motel, and we unloaded our bikes and the dogs. Bailey and Max were unloaded first and brought into the motel room. Our daily routine was to park near the room and make trips back and forth, unloading the bikes and bringing our gear into the room. While this occurred, Bailey knew he could not wander outside, but would instead sit just inside the door guarding the room. This day we took a picture of him standing guard at the door, sitting with his red, white, and blue dog toy in front of him. It became one of my favorite pictures of him.

We were sitting in the motel, looking out at the rain, and dreading having to go back out in it for dinner. As we were discussing our options, Blaine got an email from one of our board member's friends. He and his wife were keeping up with our ride and saw that we were in their town for the night. They offered to come pick us up and take us out to dinner. Awesome! Of course, we accepted.

Before we left for dinner, the couple and their young daughter came in to meet Max and Bailey. The rain had let up enough that we managed to get the dogs outside and get a picture of this family with the two dogs and one of our motorcycles. Then they took us to dinner. We had a lovely evening chatting with our new friends, and, at the end of the evening, he picked up the check and refused to let us pay. They also bought a couple of Max and Bailey T-shirts and made a donation to our organization.

They totally made our day. After a long afternoon in the rain, it was so nice to have a dry ride to dinner, a fun meal with new friends, and great conversation. Topping that off with support for our organization, they were a true example of the heart of America!

As we settled in for the evening, Blaine said he received another update from Kathy. Here is what it said:

I have to stress that Virginia is not doing well at all. We are hoping that she is able to get out of bed on Saturday, but that may not happen. Since the VA is a government building, there are strict regulations concerning visitors, but we have received special permission to enter the hospital and go up on a couple of the floors to see Virginia and the other patients. (Just so you know, the last time this happened, Lassie came to visit!!) Originally, they had just planned on us being outside in the pavilion.

Wow! We were honored to have Max and Bailey fit into the Lassie classification and that we would now be able to go into the hospital for visits versus just being outside in the pavilion. However, we were still very concerned that we would be too late for our visit with Virginia. Hold on, Virginia!

July 15 - Day 76: Utica, NY - Buffalo, NY

This was one of those days where the goal for the day was just to get from Point A to Point B. We had another day of rain...all day long. We also had a long ride...196 miles on I-90. Since it was going to rain all day and we just wanted to get to our destination as fast as we could, we stuck to the interstate for the day.

We stopped for fuel twice. I think it was more for the escape from the rain for a few minutes than really needing fuel. Once we got to our motel, we were happy to be staying at a Motel 6. They "leave the light on for you" and with this dark, dismal day, it was a joyful sight. We just hoped for a day without rain finally for our visit to Niagara Falls the following day.

We received another email from Kathy stating that the activities director at the VA continued to keep Virginia updated on our ride and she was still very excited about our visit. However, her health was continuing to decline, and our anxiety increased as we worried about whether we would arrive in time to meet Virginia.

July 16 - Day 77: Buffalo, NY - Dunkirk, NY

We took a detour and went to Niagara Falls. I had been there with my parents when I was very young, but Blaine had never been. The only way up there was on the interstate, so that was how we approached the park. When we got near the exit, the traffic slowed and then eventually stopped. We sat in traffic for a quite a while, not moving at all. We saw the emergency vehicles go by and the people in the surrounding cars started getting out of their cars. We finally got word from one trucker that there was a vehicle overturned on the bridge. Seemed like we would be there for a while. We took the opportunity to visit everyone who ventured from their cars and came over to visit with Max and Bailey. We again gave out brochures. It was interesting to see the scenarios where we ended up meeting people and telling them about our journey!

Finally, the word came that the accident was cleared, and everyone started getting back into their cars. Looked like we could see Niagara Falls after all. We followed the traffic onto the next exit and into the park. After settling into a nice parking spot in the parking lot, we prepared Max and Bailey for their walk. We realized we could take the dogs into the park in certain areas, so they directed us to the correct gate and off we went. We were excited to take them with us!

We enjoyed looking at the majestic falls as the water crashed over them leaving sprays of mist in the air. It felt like we walked for miles to see the different angles of the falls in order to see both the American and Canadian (also known as the Horseshoe) Falls. The Niagara Falls are the most powerful waterfalls in North America. Almost 4 million cubic feet of water falls over the crest line every minute, increasing to 6 million cubic feet per minute during high flow. Hard to imagine anyone attempting to go over them in a barrel! Truly amazing that so many people have actually survived that fall.

We were able to get the dogs' pictures in front of the falls. One more American iconic destination that we visited with the pups.

July 17 - Day 78: Dunkirk, NY - Erie, PA

Our primary mission for the day was to go visit the VA Hospital in Erie, PA to meet Virginia. As we arrived at the hospital, we were met by Kathy, who informed us that Virginia was having a very tough day, so we would visit her in her hospital bed. Kathy had made sure we were cleared to enter the hospital and a staff member checked our therapy dog badges as we entered. We were honored to visit this VA hospital. Blaine had served in the Air Force in the TACP unit with a supporting role with the Army at Ft. Bragg. My Dad had been on a Navy ship in WWII while my brother, Den, had been in the Army during Vietnam and my other brother, Paul, had been on a Navy submarine during the latter years of the Vietnam War. Therefore, we deeply supported our Veterans.

This was another day that we were grateful that we had gone through the therapy dog training. Having the therapy dog certifications allowed us to be cleared into the hospital. Kathy then led us up to Virginia's room. While we were ecstatic that we made it here in time, I am not sure any of us were prepared as we entered Virginia's room. It became obvious that her days were coming to an end. Her breathing was labored, and her skin was a deep jaundiced yellow.

Since she was having one of her rougher days, they had laid one of our Max and Bailey T-shirts over her because she was too weak to put it on. As Bailey and I approached her bed, my sweet, goofy Bailey climbed right into bed with her. I am not sure what prompted him to do it, but he somehow knew that was what he needed to do. Thankfully, he figured out how to be gentle with her and he laid with her during our visit.

Emotionally, this was one of my hardest days of the trip. I fought back my tears to remain strong during our visit with Virginia, but it was extremely difficult. I laughed at Bailey's silly behavior, but my heart broke knowing that cancer was winning the battle, and this was most likely the last time she could have a visit from a dog. It was so hard not to break down into tears; I honestly do not know how I had the strength to keep a brave face on.

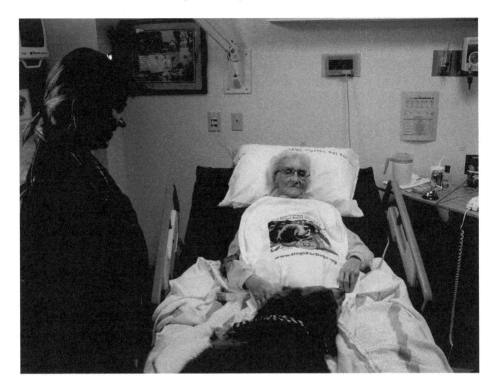

When our time was up, we left her room and I had to take a quick break to regain my composure before we went to more rooms to visit with the other patients. Choking back tears, I asked our escort for a few minutes so I could take some deep breaths and get my brave face back on. Then we were off to visit the other patients. Remember, this was a VA hospital, so we were meeting these wonderful veterans who had served our country. We were honored to bring a little joy into their life during their hospital stay.

They escorted us around to many other rooms and we also met many patients as we passed them in the hall. It tickled most of them to meet Max and Bailey and get a chance to hear about our journey and see the pups with their Doggles on. It was a special day for them but was absolutely one of our top three most memorable days of our trip.

After we were through with the visits, we loaded up the pups and headed to our next event. I was not sure how I was going to make it to that event because I was emotionally depleted! Blaine and I were extremely grateful to Rick Hairston for recommending that we get the dogs certified as therapy dogs. I know we would not have been able to go into the VA for that heart-wrenching visit without those certifications. Thank you, Rick!

We followed our escort out to a motorcycle shop called Precision Bikeworks, where the owner hosted our team to spread the word about our trip and sell a few T-shirts. We even got a visit by the local TV station and did an interview with them.

July 18 - Day 79: Erie, PA - Cleveland, OH

We took a leisurely morning to recover from our emotionally stressful day the day before. Our afternoon event was as Jr's On The Bay restaurant, home of the Sloppy Duck Saloon! The owner, Jr, was fabulous to us.

Blaine's journal entry of the day gave a great overview of our afternoon:

The Hogs For Dogs team spent the afternoon dodging rain showers during our fundraising event at Jr.'s On The Bay in Erie. I really am beginning to think that Mother Nature has something against Hogs For Dogs' events with all the rain she has thrown our way. And we are beginning to take it personally because it only rained until our event was over. Then the sun came out as we drove away from Jr.'s on our way towards Cleveland.

But the rain did not keep everyone away and Jr. was gracious enough to let Max & Bailey hang out inside while the rain cleansed the bikes. Jr. also bought enough shirts to outfit his entire staff in Hogs For Dogs T-shirts. Everywhere we looked, Max & Bailey were looking back at us from the back of all those shirts. I may be biased, but I thought they all looked great!

We also had several special visitors come out to the event, including Christine, her service dog Chelsea, and a service dog in training, Blake. They were joined by some of the volunteers from New Hope Assistance Dogs in Warren, PA. Once again, we were reminded just why we are making this ride - rain or not.

We thoroughly enjoyed our time with our special visitors and savored a splendid meal during our huge rain shower. Max and Bailey soaked up the attention as they hung out inside and it was so cool to see all the staff running around in Max and Bailey T-shirts! The hospitality and generosity of our hosts never ceased to amaze me!

Our volunteer, Kathy, was an excellent example of the power of our volunteers. She wanted to make a difference, and she did. She organized a very memorable visit to the VA hospital and two fundraisers that allowed us to raise $1,420 in just two days! Who said one person cannot make a difference? The heart of America was alive in Erie!

After another successful event, it was time for us to hit the road because we still had a 110-mile ride to get to our next city. Our volunteer rode out of town with us a short ways and then we again had to say our goodbyes and head out on the road alone. I cannot say all these goodbyes ever got any easier.

We stayed on the interstate for our entire trip so we could make it to our destination quickly. As we entered Ohio, we celebrated our 23rd state! We found our motel and settled in for the evening, knowing we had a very early morning the next day.

July 19 - Day 80: Cleveland, OH

Our day started with an early morning interview and the journal entry perfectly describes it:

Our morning began with a 6:50 a.m.interview with WAKR Radio's Ray Horner. We've done a lot of these radio spots and I have to say that Ray's was one of the best; he asked good questions and led us to important facts for his listeners.

The dogs were already in the bikes while I was on the air with Ray, waiting for us to dash off to Cleveland's Fox 8 Studios. So, as soon as I hung up with Ray, we climbed on the bikes and headed for the studio--only this time our bikes sounded a little louder than usual. The reason for all the noise was quickly spotted; the Fox 8 News helicopter was circling over the Motel 6 waiting for our departure. Somehow, I was left feeling like a certain football player, driving a white Ford Bronco and wearing gloves that did not fit as we made our way down the highway. In case the question comes up--I'm innocent and the gloves do not fit, too.

Yes, we felt like that "certain football player" as the helicopter followed us from our hotel to the Fox 8 News station. We knew the station would be following us. They had asked us where we were staying and the time we would be leaving the hotel to ride to the station, so the traffic helicopter would be able to find and track us. Track us they did! They followed us the entire way to the station. It was a bit intimidating to have a helicopter following you! I was really nervous about following my GPS. I was hoping it would not be one of those days that it routed us through some odd area or gave me a street name instead of a highway number. I did not want to get lost with the helicopter following me and them saying to their viewers, "Where are they going?" How embarrassing would that be? I stressed and sweated the entire way. Luckily, the GPS was cooperative that day and I followed it directly to the news station with no problems.

We drove up to the station and found out that they wanted to do the interview outside of the news station with us on our motorcycles and the dogs in their sidecars. We ended up with several minutes of interview coverage on the news that morning and they asked some excellent questions. We were able to really highlight the real reason for the ride and what awesome things a service dog could do to help a person with a disability gain independence. We were really excited about our interview!

Once the interview was over, we had plenty of day left to do a little sightseeing and run a couple errands. We headed to the Rock and Roll Hall of Fame but could not find parking we liked to be able to go inside and leave the dogs with the bikes. Instead, we parked the bikes towards the front and snapped a few pics of the dogs both in and outside of the bikes in front of the unique guitars that lined the front of the building.

Next, we tried to eat lunch at the Hard Rock Cafe, but the wait was so long we decided to find another place for a quick bite. We were not having much luck so far. After finding another place for lunch, we headed to PetSmart for some dog food. Bailey was ecstatic about this visit since he always picked out a new toy when he got to wander in PetSmart!

As we were coming out of PetSmart, we ran into two friendly ladies in the parking lot. They were both in wheelchairs and were looking at our bikes. They were curious about our cause. We told them what Assistance Dogs could do for them and they were excited about the opportunities. We chatted with them for quite a while and one of them even bought a couple of Max and Bailey T-shirts from us. We hoped they eventually applied for service dogs for themselves. We never knew the eventual impact our ride would have.

Next, we went to visit the South East Harley-Davidson dealership. We loved visiting all the Harley dealers along our journey. We hung out there for a while until it was time to meet a new friend for dinner.

Sgt. Tim McLeod from the Akron Police Department had invited us to dinner. He was instrumental in getting us in touch with all the media in the Cleveland/Akron area and we were extremely grateful for that! During dinner, we laughed as we replayed the scene of the helicopter following us to the Fox 8 news station. We had a delightful dinner with our new friend who had made a difference by connecting us with local new stations. We loved the small-town America feel in this big city! He even surprised us by picking up the dinner tab. Our volunteers and supporters rocked!

We had an unexpected donation that came in that day, too. While we were out on the road, sometimes we would get a trucker to chat with us on the CB. We had our CB channel on the back of the bikes just for this reason. We had chatted with one of these guys when he saw us on the road and then he went to our website (also on our bikes) and donated to our organization! It was amazing to see that he loved our story relayed via CB and took the time to make a donation to our cause. The heart of America existed in our truckers as well!

Even though we had a fabulous day with the media and a fun dinner with a new friend, our journal entry for the day ended on a somber note:

Now, for some sad news. If you've been following our travels, you know that Ms. Virginia Paine, a WWII vet, requested that we visit her in the Erie VA Hospital where she was battling cancer. Max & Bailey arrived on Saturday to grant her wish. Bailey even climbed into bed with Virginia and gave her lots of love. I'm sorry to report that Virginia passed away Sunday evening at 10:30 p.m. So, while we hit home runs with the media today, our dugout was full of many tears.

Here is where I would normally hype our limited-edition Max & Bailey shirts or ask you to consider making a donation. Today, I'll just ask you to hug someone close to you. I think the world could use a few more of those. They're free, so give as many as you want.

After a great day, we came back to our motel and received the email with that news. As Blaine read it aloud, I sat down and just sobbed. She passed away the day after our visit! These emotional times were taking a toll on me. We were both devastated!

I was not the only one in tears as we relived the visit with her. Blaine broke down in tears as well. Our day with her had been so emotional, and we knew she was just hanging on by a thread. It appeared that she was hanging on just long enough for Max and Bailey's visit. We were so blessed to have been able to meet her and let the pups visit with her on her next-to-last day on this earth. When we started our ride, I never imagined the powerful events that we would encounter on this journey.

July 20 - Day 81: Cleveland, OH - Toledo, OH

Our ride was 119 miles, skirting around Lake Erie from Cleveland to Toledo. We rode along the water on US-6 until it ran into Hwy 2, which we followed into Toledo. We had no pre-planned school visits or events for the day, so it was time to see what Toledo would bring us.

We found our home for the night, Red Roof Inn, which was another one of our free nights donated to us. The only thing I knew about Toledo was it was famous for its industry and from the TV series M*A*S*H. For those of you who remember that beloved series, you remember Corporal Klinger always talking about Toledo. The actor who played Klinger, Jamie Farr, was from Toledo and they made his character from Toledo as well. He always talked about Toledo and those famous hotdogs from Tony Packo's. I remember an episode where they called Tony Packo's and had them ship some of their hotdogs to Korea. So, of course, the one thing we had to do in Toledo was to find this famous restaurant and try those world-famous hotdogs!

While Max and Bailey got settled in for the evening, I got online and searched for the famous hotdog place in Toledo. With a search of M*A*S*H and hot dogs, I, of course, found Tony Packo's website. They had several locations, so we chose the original location on Front Street. I put the address into our GPS, and we headed downtown for dinner.

The restaurant is famous for its M*A*S*H connections, as well as another tradition. It seems that the daughter of Tony Packo was able to get Burt Reynolds to visit the restaurant when he was in town playing "The Rainmaker" at the local auditorium. She wanted his autograph, and he decided to sign one of their hotdog buns. That started a tradition which includes buns autographed by scores of celebrities and many presidential candidates. The tradition started off with the signing of original buns, but eventually they changed to plastic hot dog buns to gather those famous signatures.

We found the iconic restaurant and discovered a nice little parking place tucked away, so we parked and went in. After being seated, we scoured the menu to see what we wanted alongside the famous hot dog. I decided to just add some fries with it, while Blaine got the combo number one which included the world-famous hot dog, a side, and a bowl of their world-famous chili! How fun! This was another slice of Americana that we were grateful to experience. As we ate our hotdogs, we imagined being in the scenario from M*A*S*H and getting the hotdogs delivered overseas in a war zone. What a great story!

July 21 - Day 82: Toledo, OH - Brooklyn, MI

We headed out for our journey, which was going to be fairly short. The route for the day only covered 72 miles, so we could make a leisurely trip and we looked forward to it. It was rare to have such a quick route for the day. We crossed over into Michigan, which was a major milestone on our journey. While we were nowhere near the halfway point in terms of days or miles, we had reached our halfway point in terms of states. Michigan was our 24th state! We were ecstatic! It was also mind-boggling that we had already been through 24 states.

We looked forward to our stop for the evening. We were fortunate to have a house stay donated to us by yet one more volunteer. This volunteer had a house that was a retreat for them, and they were not currently staying there. How awesome was that! We were grateful to have a nice, quiet overnight stay to get accounting, emails, and planning accomplished.

Our route was taking us to Brooklyn again, but this time it was Brooklyn, MI, not Brooklyn, NY. The house was located about 30 miles southwest of Ann Arbor, MI. It was surrounded by trees and had a lake behind it, so it was very peaceful. After unpacking our bikes, we settled in for the afternoon and evening, both of us working on our laptops.

Blaine had been noticing an issue with his laptop's hard drive for a few days, and, as he started working on emails, it was noticeably worse. Since we were going to be in Elgin, IL for several days, we decided it was finally time to order a new one, so it could be sent there. He started browsing the web for a new laptop and placed his order. We hoped it would get delivered in time for us to receive it in Elgin.

When Blaine switched over to checking his email, we found out from Tom Molter that his local newspaper, the Sturgis Journal, wrote an article promoting our events that were coming up in Three Rivers, Michigan. We were getting excited about those events.

Knowing the busy days we had ahead of us, we enjoyed the quiet, relaxing evening.

July 22 - Day 83: Brooklyn, MI - Lansing, MI

This day was a day to celebrate! The plans that I had been working on for the past month finally fell into place. Our route was constantly changing as new events and school visit opportunities came up. I had a basic route set up when we started the ride, knowing which states we would be in during each month. However, the exact route, cities, and towns we would visit were constantly changing as we got closer to them.

A month earlier, as I was continuing to plan our route, it looked like we would be in South Dakota during the time of the Sturgis Motorcycle Rally, which is one of the biggest motorcycle rallies in the world! We were thrilled at the timing, but we did not know if we could find a place to stay within a decent driving distance. To make the search for a hotel even harder, it had to be dog friendly.

I had spent the past month searching each evening for a place for us to stay. I had broadened the search to places that were an hour or more drive from the rally, but these hotels and motels had been fully booked. People booked accommodations for the rally up to a year in advance. I had become doubtful that we were going to have a chance to attend because I was not being successful in my nightly search.

Finally, the search was over! I booked a hotel that was dog friendly and was only 20 minutes away from the rally. YES! I was ecstatic! I had been searching for the availability of that hotel for a month with no luck, so there probably was a cancellation and I snagged the available room. The odds of us being near Sturgis at the time of the rally and then actually being able to find a hotel nearby were extremely small, but I had accomplished it!

Blaine saw me get up from my laptop and do a victory dance. He laughed at me and asked me what I was up to. He knew I had been working on the Sturgis reservations for a long time, so all I needed to exclaim was "I got Sturgis!" and he knew what I was talking about. He responded, "Woohoo!" and did a victory dance with me.

With a successful morning of planning under our belts, we headed to Lansing, MI where we were meeting several of the PAWS puppy raisers along with their puppies-in-training. After a short jaunt west on US-12, we turned onto US-127 for the rest of our short 65-mile drive to Lansing.

One of the puppy raisers had volunteered their house for not only the gathering but also for dinner and as accommodations for the evening. We had a fun time that evening, and Max and Bailey played with the puppies in training, including Harley from the Hogs for Dogs Dirty Dozen litter (which I will explain shortly.) We enjoyed getting to know these remarkable people who spend so much time raising and training puppies that they eventually give back to PAWS. That must be extremely difficult to give the puppy back after months of training and love, but also extremely rewarding to see the trained dog paired with someone with a disability who gains independence because of that dog.

July 23 - Day 84: Lansing, MI - Grand Rapids, MI

After a fun evening with the PAWS puppy raisers, we were looking forward to seeing them at our exciting meeting with Representative Rick Shaffer at the Michigan Capitol Building.

As we rolled up to the east steps of the Michigan State Capitol, they greeted us with a crowd of not only the PAWS puppy raisers but also others who had gathered to hear Rep. Shaffer. Deb Davis, who we had met at our original Paws With A Cause visit, was there to greet us. It was wonderful to see Deb again. We also finally got a chance to meet Tom Molter, who was a puppy raiser for PAWS and had organized events for us in Three Rivers, MI where we would head after Grand Rapids.

There was a podium set up at the bottom of the steps, and the organizers directed us to park our bikes on both sides of the podium. The dogs received a lot of attention as everyone came over to greet them.

There was a Paws With A Cause banner behind the podium and we hung our Hogs for Dogs ride banner under it. We took our T-shirts out of our packs to sell and put them on the table they had set up for them.

Shortly before 10:00, Rep. Shaffer came over to greet Max and Bailey. He gave a brief speech declaring his support for Assistance Dogs organizations and, specifically, for Paws With A Cause. Blaine was able to speak as well, and he talked about our journey and the importance of puppy raisers in the industry's formula for success.

Next, we presented Rep. Shaffer with a Hogs for Dogs T-shirt and a plaque that had been created by one of the Paws With A Cause supporters. There were several newspaper and TV reporters who interviewed Rep. Shaffer and Blaine.

After the speech and presentation, they invited us for a tour of the Michigan State Capitol Building. A volunteer took care of Max and Bailey while we entered the tour, along with the puppy raisers and their dogs in training.

The Capital Building holds a place in history for one of the first state capitals to be topped by a lofty cast-iron dome. They designated it as a National Historic Landmark in 1992. As we entered the dome area with its floor made of squares of glass, we looked up to see the magnificent ceiling with spokes of gold and a turquoise circle in the center with gold stars on it. We were told the best way to view it was to lie on the floor, so all of us laid on the floor to admire the beauty. It was quite a sight to see all the puppy raisers laying on the floor with all the service puppies in training next to them.

Once our tour was complete, we loaded the dogs into their sidecars and drove to our lunch stop at The Barn Tavern. Max and Bailey, along with the puppies in training (and their handlers), were all invited inside, and we had a fun lunch as we shared stories from the road. Some of the staff bought T-shirts, and we ended up with a free lunch. It was a welcomed break after the festivities of the morning.

With full stomachs, we drove to the Baymont Inn and Suites in Wayland, MI to unpack the bikes and relax for a while. We were grateful that the Baymont Inn and Suites had donated the night's stay. As we were unpacking our bikes, we realized the amount of stuff that we unpacked every single day. We had a picture taken of us with one of those large luggage carts that are available at hotels. It was packed all the way up to the top bar. We had two tour packs of T-shirts, two rolling luggage bags of clothes, two roll bags with toiletries, two laptop bags, one saddlebag liner with dog supplies, my leather planner binder, a refreshment bag, my purse, and our two helmets attached to the top bar. It was eye-opening to see how much we packed and unpacked every day.

Everything had its place on our bikes. The two rectangular tour pack bags of T-shirts rode on our luggage racks on the back of the bikes. Our rolling luggage bags rode in our passenger seats with the toiletry roll bags attached to the tops. All of our dog supplies (bowls, toys, food for the night, etc.) were in a liner bag that fit in one of my saddlebags on the side of my bike. The laptop bags fit inside the tour packs on the back of our bikes. We stored our refreshment bag behind the seat of one of our sidecars. I stored my planner and purse in another saddle bag.

Obviously, our helmets were worn whenever we were riding. That was a lot of gear!

After a little time to relax, we headed back out to the Wayland Summerfest to allow the crowds to meet Max and Bailey and to continue to spread the word about Assistance Dogs.

At the end of the day, we crawled into bed with smiles on our faces, remembering the fantastic day.

July 24 - Day 85: Grand Rapids, MI - Three Rivers, MI

After the long day the previous day, we were moving a little slowly as we got ready for our day. We knew we had another big day ahead of us as we visited the headquarters of Paws With A Cause and then traveled down to Three Rivers for more events.

As we loaded Max and Bailey into their sidecars, we were met by ten bikes from the Gold Wing Riders Association. They were there to escort us to the PAWS headquarters. They accompanied us with flashing lights and fancy horns. As we approached PAWS, we were greeted by a crowd of people who were on the street awaiting our arrival. You could hear everyone cheer as we rolled onto the grass in front of the Paws With A Cause sign.

We started off with some photo opportunities with all of us still on our bikes, followed by meet and greets with everyone that had gathered to meet us. The media was there to interview us and take pictures. As Blaine and I wandered around chatting with people, Max and Bailey chilled in their sidecars as they adored all the attention and pets that they were receiving. We met many of the recipients of the PAWS Assistance Dogs to hear of the impressive things that their service dogs could do for them and the independence that it had brought to them. These are the stories that inspired us to continue our ride each day. As Blaine stated in our journal entry for the day, "their stories are heartwarming and always filled with joy and genuine appreciation for the work that PAWS, and similar organizations, have done on their behalf."

Once Max and Bailey were unloaded from their sidecars, they were presented with a sweet bouquet of dog treats that were made of dog biscuits in the shapes of motorcycles and dogs. Max, our food hound, found it even more exciting than all the attention and pets!

They ushered us into the building where the festivities continued. Many of the puppy raisers were there with their puppies-in-training and some of the puppies-in-training were even dressed up in black leather to embrace the motorcycle theme. There were several activities along with lunch, and then the PAWS crew presented us with some fantastic gifts to commemorate our visit and our ride. They gave us a framed picture, which included individual pictures of the dirty dozen, each labeled with their name. It included our logo and the PAWS logo. The dirty dozen was a litter of twelve yellow lab puppies that were named in honor of Max and Bailey and our Hogs for Dogs ride. Their names were Bailey, Carley, Chopper, Cruiser, Harley, Journey, Max, Norton (type of motorcycle), Price (after our starting point and sponsor, Ray Price Harley-Davidson), Rider, Scooter, and Tarrin (tearing it up?). We were so honored to get this picture with all their pictures on it in memory of all these future service dogs! Max and Bailey's legacy would live on!

Bailey Carley Chopper Cruiser Harley Journey

Paws With A Cause
Hogs For Dogs Litter
June 2004

Max Norton Price Rider Scooter Tarrin

They told us the story of the naming process for that Dirty Dozen. One day they all sat in a circle throwing out names that were related to motorcycles, riding, or anything dealing with our ride. They usually did not name any of the dogs with human names, but, of course, the names Max and Bailey were the exception. The other challenge was they could not use names that were used before with other service dogs. The brainstorming continued until they named all twelve pups.

They also presented us with two wooden laser-inscribed plaques: one with our logo on it and one with Max and Bailey's picture carved in it. They were beautiful! Blaine was asked to say a few words about our ride, which he did eloquently as usual. Then we presented Mike Sapp, the PAWS CEO, with a check for $5,000 as our initial donation to our major partner from our ride.

We also had time to catch up with Deb Davis. Blaine had been calling her on her toll-free work phone number a few times per week, but we did not realize the impact that it was making. Deb said she looked forward to those frequent update phone calls and would often sit at her desk at the end of the day waiting for those calls. She was tracking our progress daily. She was also sending this progress report out to various entities on a scheduled timeframe. She emailed the CEO, PAWS staff, and PAWS managers on a weekly basis. The stakeholders and donors received monthly updates. She kept the field reps updated with emails 2-3 times a week with an update of where we were yesterday, where we were today, and our plans for the next couple of days. She notified volunteers, clients, and field reps when we would be in their area. This allowed us to get demo dogs and client/dog teams at many of our events and school visits.

After all the presentations, it was time for a ride to our next destination. The Gold Wing Riders again escorted us out of the PAWS headquarters and there were about 15-20 bikes along for the escort down to Three Rivers, MI. As we neared Three Rivers, our escort grew even larger with more bikes joining us along with the St. Joseph County Sheriff's Department and the Three Rivers Police Department leading the way. They delivered us to Scidmore Park, which was the destination for our next event. They directed us to parking spots on the grass with signs marking the spaces for Max and Bailey.

As Blaine stated in our journal, "it was an emotional arrival for the Hogs for Dogs crew. People surrounded the bikes, loved the dogs, shook our hands and made generous donations." A representative from the Chamber of Commerce was the master of ceremonies for the afternoon with presentations by the mayor, our hosts Tom and Linda Molter, and Bob Komenski with his Assistance Dog, Weaver. The Molters had been the foster puppy raisers for Weaver, so he was well known in the Three Rivers area. Bob was in a wheelchair, and he told the crowd about all the awesome things that Weaver could do for him, such as pulling his wheelchair, opening and closing doors, picking up things as small as a dime (reducing the risk that he will fall out of his wheelchair while attempting to retrieve dropped objects) and getting help if Bob was injured.

Susan Stewart also spoke about her service dog, Sable. Some of the tasks that Sable performed for Susan were assisting Susan in getting up each morning, bringing her a soda from the refrigerator, getting the phone for her, getting clothes out of the dryer, and picking up items around the house. Susan also demonstrated some of those things by having Sable retrieve a phone and pick up a dropped towel.

Blaine was also asked to speak again about our ride. After all the speeches, there were not many dry eyes in the crowd, and we were again reminded of why we were doing this ride, which sparked our desire to keep going.

The day ended with a quiet dinner at the house of Tom and Linda Molter. Tom was the key person who set up all the events in Michigan. We were very grateful for all the effort and hard work he put in to make our Michigan events such a success! Our donations were over $800 for the events during the day, which was a cause for celebration. We were also on the front page of the Three Rivers Commercial-News newspaper with an article about our visit to the Capitol in Lansing the previous day. We were overwhelmed by Tom's generosity, which included him and his wife hosting us for the night accompanied by a lovely dinner. By the end of the evening, we felt like we were with old friends.

When we set off on this trip, we never realized how many friendships that we would make along the way. It was remarkable how many people opened their homes to our crew of four and made us feel welcome and right at home with them.

July 25 - Day 86: Three Rivers, MI - Michigan City, IN

Our day started down at the Fire Hall, where our volunteers were cooking up a scrumptious pancake breakfast. When we drove up, Max and Bailey were again surrounded by everyone who had come down for the breakfast to support our cause. The two pups were loving the attention and being in so many photographs. Once the crowd dissipated, we walked in to enjoy some breakfast. As we entered the Fire Hall, we smelled the aroma of blueberry pancakes and sausages sizzling on the large griddle. After another round of greetings and chatting, we finally got to sit down and enjoy the breakfast that we had been anticipating. We had a few quiet minutes to savor our breakfast before heading back into the crowd.

Along with the breakfast, the organizers also had games and prizes. Dan Davis, Deb's husband, ended up winning the chipping contest to see who could get the closest to the pin by chipping a golf ball over a water hazard. He graciously donated his winnings to our charity. I won the 50/50 raffle, and I also donated the winnings back to Hogs for Dogs. The fundraiser was not only a lot of fun for everyone, but it raised a lot of funds for our cause. The people in Three Rivers were awesome in their support for us!

A little before 1:00 in the afternoon, the festivities had ended, and it was time to head towards Chicago for our next set of events. Once again, we would have to say another tearful goodbye; at least we could enjoy a great escort to the Indiana border. We had around 20 motorcycles that lined up to escort us.

We pulled out behind our escort a little after 1:00 and began our exit ride out of Michigan. The Three Rivers police department led us through town as police cars with flashing lights escorted us and stopped traffic at all the stoplights. It was always exciting to get such special treatment like a police escort! I enjoyed following the lead bike through the countryside and not worrying about my GPS for a while. We made a stop at a gas station along the way to take a break. It was bittersweet to chat with all the riders who came to visit with Max and Bailey as we enjoyed the camaraderie while knowing we would leave them at the next stop. After everyone was back on their motorcycles, we continued to the Indiana border.

When we reached Niles, MI which was just north of the Indiana border, everyone pulled into our last stop to say goodbye. I took a few deep breaths to rein in my emotions. Goodbyes were always so hard. We took a group picture of all the riders next to their motorcycles and another one of them all gathered around our two motorcycles with the dogs in their sidecars. After the pictures, we hugged, said our goodbyes to everyone, and pulled out back onto the road for our 41-mile drive to the Red Roof Inn in Michigan City, IN.

As we rolled towards our destination for the night, the tears rolled down my face and I already missed the dear friends that we had known for only a couple of days. The goodbyes were getting harder as we forged on alone, leaving our newly found support group behind.

After we got settled in for the evening, I worked on catching up with finances after the events from the previous couple of days, while Blaine started to back up his files from his failing laptop onto compact discs. After all the events over the past few days, we were a bit melancholy.

July 26 - Day 87: Michigan City, IN - Elgin, IL

We went into breakfast and immediately started having people coming over to ask us about the dogs. Everyone was extremely friendly and did not mind coming over to chat with us. After hearing our story, many of them made donations to our charity. It was encouraging to have so many people approach us and then make a donation! We were stunned.

As we were heading back to our bikes, a thought occurred to me. I looked over at Blaine and said, "you do realize what state we are in, don't you?" Blaine said, "Indiana". I then said "Exactly! Remember the stop at the gas station in southern Indiana where absolutely everyone said hi and most came over to visit us? That was Indiana! This has got to be the friendliest state in the U.S." Blaine said "Oh yea! I remember that stop. Yep, after that stop and this one, it is definitely the friendliest state. I do not know if any other state can beat them!"

After breakfast, we continued to Elgin, IL which was about 40 miles west-northwest of Chicago. We were driving through Chicago on the way there, so I was concerned about the traffic. Thankfully, our ride was uneventful, and we arrived at our destination, which was where we would stay for the next few days.

Our hosts, Scott and Heidi Heifetz, were related to my sister-in-law, Debbie. Scott is Debbie's brother and, when Debbie told him about our trip, he and Heidi immediately volunteered their house for us to stay when in the Chicago area. When we arrived, they greeted us and showed us around their house. There was a nice, comfortable area where Blaine and I could work, and Max and Bailey could relax. We were excited to unpack our motorcycles and not have to pack them again for a few days.

As we briefly checked our emails, we found out from Tom Molter that we had again been on the front page of the Three Rivers Commercial-News about our events in Three Rivers. He said it was an excellent article that explained the wonderful tasks that Assistance Dogs could perform. We were excited to have made it to the front page of their newspaper for the second time that week.

After we got settled in, we relaxed and enjoyed dinner with Scott and Heidi. We told them about Blaine's laptop issue and that a replacement laptop would arrive soon at their house. The rest of the evening was spent relaying stories from the road and hearing sweet stories about my brother and sister-in-law. Even though this was the first time we had met them, Scott and Heidi made us feel at home. These were the times we treasured on our journey!

July 27 - Day 88: Elgin, IL

This was a very disappointing day for me! We were supposed to ride up to Oconomowoc, WI where I was born so we could go sightseeing. There were no events involved...just a pleasant day trip to see the town where I first existed. Instead, we stayed in Elgin awaiting Blaine's laptop. Blaine spent the day trying to back up as much data as he could from his quickly failing laptop. The new laptop was supposed to be delivered this day, but as the day wore on, we got word of the delay in delivery. It was a very frustrating day where we felt we could have accomplished so much more had we not been pacing while waiting for this important delivery. While we had survived the threat of tornados, the impact of a motorcycle sideswipe, and the stress of the constant travel, we were thinking the delay of a laptop delivery was going to cancel the entire trip!

July 28 - Day 89: Elgin, IL

I honestly do not know how we survived this day! Blaine was so frustrated with the delay of the laptop and lack of ability to respond to all the emails for events and school stops, that he was unbearable to live with. I literally had to sit at the opposite end of the house for the day! I was extremely happy that we were staying in a house and not stuck together in one hotel room. If I had been in the same room as he was, then we would have ended our trip that day. He was being extremely irrational about his laptop, and I really could not talk any sense into him. I knew it was not the end of the world, but, in his eyes, there was nothing that could survive this. Finally, by the end of the day, he realized it was not the end of the world and wrote this journal entry:

We are often asked how we remain so upbeat while dealing with fatigue and the long hours associated with Max & Bailey's Ride Across America. After all, this is a long ride; 218 days, to be exact. We left on May 1st from Raleigh, North Carolina and we'll return to Raleigh on Saturday, December 4th. Our schedule has us riding rain or shine, hot or cold. And there are days, like the last two, that we find ourselves struggling to remember why we're out here. Today, I even muttered a few choice words about just quitting and going home because one thing after another kept going wrong - very wrong.

Topping the list was my laptop's fatal crash. The hard drive now sputters and whirls, but often gives nothing but errors in return. I spent all day yesterday recovering as much data as possible instead of our planned visit to Oconomowoc, Wisconsin. Fortunately, I was able to recover almost all my data except for my Outlook Express Inbox, which was open when the drive crashed. In that inbox were many emails with important information about upcoming events and the addresses where I was to send logo gear for this week's events. All lost. It looked like a Chinese fire drill here today as we made phone calls trying to resurrect enough information to save the events.

Janet and I were at each other's throats so badly over issues that we had to sit at opposite ends of the house to save our personal relationship. More than once, we came to verbal blows over things that we would normally resolve peacefully. It seemed everywhere we turned we were faced with a brick wall. I was about to throw up my arms and admit defeat.

Then I remembered the story of Edmond, who used to struggle for hours, dragging himself across the floor if he fell out of his wheelchair. And the story of Lindsey, who could not be alone for the first 22 years of her life because of her unpredictable seizures. Phyliss spent twelve bed-ridden years fighting the incapacities associated with her Muscular Sclerosis. And there was the tough-looking biker at the Outer Banks Rally that gave me a $10 donation with tears in his eyes, hoping this year would be the year - after many years of waiting - that his disabled father would receive an Assistance Dog. These people and millions just like them overcome incredible obstacles every day, many with the newfound help of their Assistance Dogs. Suddenly, my problems seemed insignificant and silly.

It's for them that Janet and I are out here. It's for them that we often work 16- or 18-hour days. It's for them we ride, rain or shine. It's for them that we find creative ways to solve difficult problems while maintaining our constant movement. And it was their stories that put me back on track today. They have always been the ones that kept us going before, but I lost sight of that today, for just a moment.

So, we may be limping along with a dead laptop computer for a few more days and struggling to keep our events going with the absence of some lost data, but with their stories to inspire us, more than 300 volunteers to keep us on track, and your support to fuel our success, we'll get through this tough time. And we'll ride for them today, we'll ride for them tomorrow and we'll ride for them each of the next 129 days until we return home.

This may not be the uplifting 'News From The Road' that you came here looking for, but every now and again, a little reality from the road is worth sharing. This trip is exciting and personally rewarding, but there are pitfalls now and again. If I did not mention those pitfalls, I might never be able to explain how important all our volunteers, board members and supporters are on a daily basis. A phone call from a good friend just reminded me that we are not out here alone. He and many of you ride with us every day.

That, my friends, is how we stay upbeat in trying times. We cannot afford to fail.

July 29 - Day 90: Elgin, IL

Our day started out with a visit to the Larkin Center in Elgin. The center helped kids ages 8-18 who were having emotional or behavioral issues. To protect the identity of these kids, we were not allowed to take pictures, and we respected their request. We found the staff and students to be very gracious. They seemed truly interested in Max & Bailey's adventure as Blaine stood before them talking about our trip and teaching them about Assistance Dogs. We had a very enjoyable visit and the kids had fun with Max and Bailey.

The rest of the day we were at the house where I continued to work on routing and accounting and Blaine tried to work without the use of his computer. We hoped that the new laptop would arrive, but by the end of the day, we were still awaiting its arrival. Thankfully, in the evening, we went to Scott's and Debbie's sister's house for dinner, so it was nice to have the distraction without concentrating on the missing laptop.

July 30 - Day 91: Elgin, IL

We were excited to have an afternoon event at a place called Huggable Hounds up in Crystal Lake, IL. It was a dog bakery and boutique. The sky was overcast when we left, and we were nervous that our event would be rained out. As we drove the 24 miles, the sky cleared, and the weather turned out to be beautiful. They were fantastic hosts and even had a cake for Max and Bailey with peanut butter icing. We had fun meeting everyone who stopped by and even raised a few hundred dollars for the cause. Blaine's laptop finally arrived late in the day, so he spent the evening setting it up.

July 31 - Day 92: Elgin, IL - Milwaukee, WI - Chicago, IL - Elgin, IL

This was one of our longest days on the trip! We started out the day with a 121-mile trip up to House of Harley in Milwaukee, Wisconsin, crossing into our 25th state. We were invited to the Open House that was part of the Wisconsin H.O.G. Rally. The House of Harley staff was wonderful and one of the local PAWS field instructors made sure we had a perfect spot for us with two tents to park our bikes under so the dogs would be in the shade all day. We hung one of our T-shirts up, put out the donation bin and began greeting the crowds that came over to see Max and Bailey. The event was a tremendous success, and we raised almost $1,000 in donations and logo gear sales!

During the event, we watched the clock because we knew we had to leave at 4:00 to head down into Chicago. At 4:00 sharp, we had our bags packed up, and we headed on the road for another 88 miles into the heart of Chicago. I was nervous routing us through another big city full of traffic! We were heading to the Tribune Tower downtown to meet with WGN's Steve Dale on his weekly talk show, Pet Central. As we neared our destination, we ran into a snag, and I panicked. The area was closed because they were filming the next Batman movie under the Tribune Tower. Knowing the tower was our destination, we wandered around a bit to find another parking garage in which to park. We were getting very nervous that we would miss our radio interview. With only a few minutes to spare, we found a parking spot and quickly headed for our interview.

Blaine had been calling into Steve Dale's show once a month, so his listeners were familiar with our ride. It was fun to be in the studio in person instead of being on the phone, and Steve Dale was finally able to meet Max and Bailey. After the radio show, we took pictures with Steve and then headed back to our bikes.

It was late, and we had a 50-mile drive back to Scott's and Heidi's house. We were hyped up from the radio interview and all the day's events, so we chatted via our CB radios to help get us through the long, late-night ride.

August

August 1 - Day 93: Elgin, IL - Letts, IA

After several days of staying in the same place, it felt a little strange to pack up all of our stuff onto the bikes again. But since we had done it so many times before, it did not take us long to get packed. Our destination for the day would be Iowa. That is a state you hear little about...what exactly is in Iowa?

Our route for the day would be around 200 miles. The first half of the trip we were on our own. We headed down Hwy 47 and then hopped onto I-88 for the rest of the trip. In Rock Falls, IL, we met a few riders from the group, Abate from Iowa, District 15. There were about 15 bikes that met us at that rendezvous point. We had time to meet them, but again headed down the road to our next rendezvous point, Ducky's Lagoon, a local biker hangout in Andalusia, IL just across the Mississippi River from Iowa. Here we picked up about 35 more bikes for our escort into Muscatine and our 26th state, Iowa.

They escorted us across the river and into a memorable event. I found out what was in Iowa...amazing people! One of our volunteers, who was a KSDS puppy raiser, Jennifer Blair, had coordinated this event for us. With the support of the Muscatine community and businesses, they had put together an incredible outdoor benefit dinner and a live auction. We had a wonderful time as we mingled with the bikers that had escorted us into town and the amazing people who lived in Muscatine. There was also wholehearted support from many other puppy raisers for KSDS and some of their clients. We were speechless to see the outpouring of support from them. After a fun time and lots of mingling, they ended up raising around $5,000 for our organization! Wow, phenomenal! One single volunteer with a vision rallied an entire town to support us and look at what they accomplished!

Then, after all the hoopla was over, our wonderful volunteer who initiated this event had planned for us to stay with her and her family the couple of days that we were in town. We followed her back to her house and were welcomed in like family. We felt right at home. Yes, indeed, we were discovering the incredible generosity of America!

This story about her puppy raising experience was one of the dog stories on our website:

The Many 'Tails' Of A Puppy Raiser

My name is Jennifer Blair and I have been a puppy raiser for KSDS, Inc., located in Washington, Kansas, since 1996. KSDS trains labs and golden retrievers for assistance work. I am currently raising Crash a male yellow lab, my sixth KSDS puppy. I tell people that I waited longer to get my first chance at puppy raising than I waited for my children! Now, I have both two and four-legged children and am permanently addicted to 'puppy breath.'

My first puppy was Snickers. She was part of the 'Sweet' litter of puppies, with all the puppy names being a part of that theme. She was an easygoing, hardworking doll baby. Snickers is a working guide dog in Nebraska. Snickers being my first taught me many lessons. She acknowledged that she remembered me with her tail thumping against the wall. But those beautiful brown eyes were no longer focused on me. I saw the trust and love for someone that she learned through our relationship intent on her partner. As Snickers skillfully guided her new partner away from KSDS into their new life tears of pride rolled down my face. Snickers saved the most important lesson for last.

Molly, from the KSDS 'Orphan Annie' litter, was my second pup. Her motto was always "where there is a will, there is a way". Her work ethic made her a challenge to raise. Her favorite way to get my attention while I was busy was to bring my dirty laundry to me, knowing full well that the laundry was off limits, but retrieving was good. It worked for her every time. How do you ignore a dog presenting you with underwear in front of a client? Molly is now using her creative work ethic as a service dog in Kansas.

You learn as a puppy raiser to somewhat guard your heart, knowing you'll be giving the puppy back. But there was no way to guard my heart from Angus, our third puppy who received his name from a KSDS donor. He was laid back, pliable and an easy to raise pup. He fit into our family and stole everyone's hearts right from the beginning. Unfortunately, Angus was released from the training program for problems with his hips. Our family voted unanimously to adopt him as a permanent member of the family. He is now a four-legged puppy raiser and my daughter's trophy winning 4-H project.

I took on a special KSDS project with our fourth puppy, CeCe, from the 'Double C' litter. CeCe was a year old when KSDS requested that I work with her. She had not been well socialized and needed some additional tender loving care (TLC) if she was going to graduate from the program. CeCe was a sweet girl with a good heart, but ultimately wasn't cut out for assistance work. She was placed with a loving family as a pet by KSDS.

My fifth puppy, Lightning, came from the 'Storm litter' and is currently training in the intermediate program at the Topeka correctional facility. Lightning was an absolute dream to work with: smart, willing, happy and self-confident. He was everything it takes to be an Assistance Dog wrapped up in a strikingly beautiful boy. I hope that he will soon pass his physicals and change someone's life.

Which brings us to my latest protégé, Crash, the half-brother of Lightning and Molly's nephew. At only 3 ½ months old, Crash looks like another winner in the making.

I am very proud to be a KSDS volunteer puppy raiser. I have traveled places, found treasured friendships, and done things that I never would have done before becoming a puppy raiser. People often comment, "I could never do what you do, it would just be too hard to give them up." It is hard to give them up. Being a puppy raiser is a nonstop roller coaster of emotions. With every puppy, I bring a new adorable bundle of potential into our home and the hearts of my family. But adorable only gets you so far. Housebreaking, obedience classes, and socializing them in public can be a trying process. Our home and our hearts bear multiple scars from my puppies. The process is definitely a labor of love.

When the recall letter arrives, I find myself on the vertical climb of the puppy raiser roller coaster. I often ask myself, "If I don't open it, would I still have to give my puppy up?" Maybe I could go underground, change my name and escape with my baby. I have learned that this is the time to keep my thoughts on the end result. KSDS reminds us that this is not about the dogs, it is about the team. Sometimes as a puppy raiser I need to be reminded of this.

These puppies that we have loved and trained for 18 months, or longer, have more important things to do. I tell people who say they couldn't give them up that I have learned that I can raise a puppy and give it up if someone else can learn to live without the full use of their eyes, arms, or legs. My raising a puppy is just one piece of the puzzle that helps others live more independent lives. That, by itself, makes puppy raising worth all the work.

If timing is on my side, when I return one puppy, I come home with a new bundle of potential, sniffing puppy breath all the way.

These puppy raisers were our heroes! They sacrificed so much to provide the needed training for these Assistance Dogs. I did not know how they did it!

We learned that the Grand Ledge Independent newspaper included an article about us and our visit to the Barn Tavern several days prior. We wished they had printed these articles the following day so that we would have been able to see them.

August 2 - Day 94: Letts, IA

We woke up to a leisurely day with no official events planned. However, it was a very special day; it was my birthday!

We were invited to go to an afternoon cookout at the house of one of the KSDS puppy raisers. Max and Bailey had some fun and ran around the yard with many of the foster puppies and a few of the clients' Assistance Dogs. All the dogs got a day off that day! We enjoyed our burgers and hotdogs and lots of comfortable conversation and relaxation. They surprised me with a birthday cake and a bright orange Big Dogs shirt, which they had decorated with the paw prints of many of the KSDS foster puppies in training. They also gave Blaine a Big Dogs shirt for his birthday back in June. It was a fun time.

Next, one of the puppy raisers treated Max and Bailey to a complimentary grooming. He had brought his table, and we first put Max and then Bailey up there for a special grooming. Blaine's journal entry tells of the special gift we received at the end:

Ed Maynard spent about an hour sprucing up Max & Bailey's appearance on Monday. Then, as Ed was cleaning up his tools, he and his wife Nancy asked to speak with us in private. Ed looked very somber, and I was worried that Ed saw something while grooming Max or Bailey that we had not noticed. By the time our conversation was over, we were all crying because Ed and Nancy offered us a free Golden Retriever puppy from their breeding stock when the time came to let Max & Bailey go on to chase Frisbees in the sky. The same beautiful Golden Retriever breeding stock that they use for the puppies that they donate to KSDS for Service Dogs. Their dogs are priceless.

Max & Bailey have many good years left and could never be replaced. But, knowing there is a Golden Retriever puppy waiting to cheer us up when Max & Bailey's time comes is a gift that only comes from the heart, and we were left with no words to appropriately say thank you. It will be a birthday present that Janet, nor I, will ever forget.

We were in tears after learning of their tremendous gift to us. It never ceased to amaze us of the big hearts of the people we were meeting on this journey. I was having a very memorable birthday!

After a fun cookout, we headed back to the Blair residence and had a relaxing evening getting to know our phenomenal volunteer and her family. Iowa was turning out to be an unforgettable state, and we still had one more stop in Iowa the following day.

August 3 - Day 95: Letts, IA - Shell Rock, IA

Our route for the day was 143 miles through the farmlands of Iowa, so we hit the road before 10:00 after we said our goodbyes to Jennifer Blair. We expressed our appreciation for the excellent fundraising event, the afternoon cookout with the puppy raisers, and the birthday celebration for me. It had been an incredible stop.

We enjoyed our ride through the green pastures and farms leading to our next destination. Our hosts for the night were more puppy raisers for KSDS, Hank and Rita Wilson. I had their address in my GPS, but as we approached, I was nervous about finding it. There was not much out there except miles and miles of farmland. Thankfully, my GPS routed us there with no problems and we drove up to a warm Iowa welcome!

Rita retrieved cold drinks for us and gave us a quick itinerary of the day just before the newspaper reporter/photographer got there. We were used to the interviews by now and knew how to steer the questions to where we needed them to be to give the info on our journey, charity partners, and purpose for the trip. We also knew which things to clarify to make sure they reported the facts correctly in their story. The difference this time was that this photographer would go the extra mile (or two) for just the right picture!

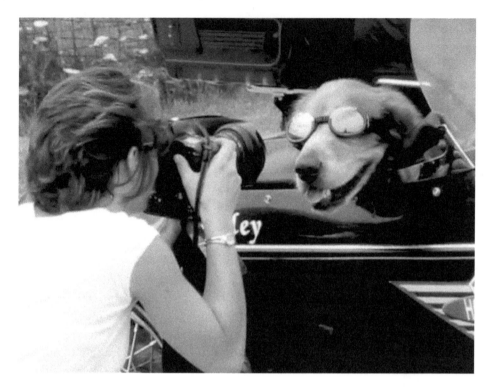

She took some close-ups of the dogs in their sidecars, but she wanted some action shots as well. She asked us to go back out onto the road and she would be out in the field taking pictures as we passed by. Thankfully, it was a very quiet back road, so we did not encounter any traffic. We followed her lead as we slowly drove up and down the road a few times. We would pass by her and then see her run down the embankment and across the road to the other side to prepare for our return trip. She did this several times until she was satisfied and told us to head back to the Wilsons'. When we got back, we learned that in her zealous to get the best pictures, she was trying to race from one side of the road to the other when her shoe got stuck in the mud. She continued without it to get the pictures and then went back to look for it. She never found that other shoe. Thankfully, she came prepared and had a spare pair of shoes in the car. Sounded like it was not the first time she lost her shoe!

Rita and Hank ended the evening hosting a fun dinner with friends, family, and KSDS clients and we sat around listening to all the stories from the farmers. We had a fun time, and their generosity raised several hundred dollars for our organization.

August 4 - Day 96: Shell Rock, IA - Minneapolis, MN

As we headed out of Shell Rock, we found a gas station where we could get a copy of The Courier to see the news article from our interview and awesome photo shoot from the previous day. While our article did not make the front page, there was a picture of Bailey in the upper right corner with the caption "Dogs on Hogs: Cycle ride provides dogs for the disabled". We made the front page of the Metro section. Thankfully, it was well written with all the facts straight. We were happy for another successful article.

The route for the day was 197 miles and took us up I-35 into Minneapolis, MN, our 27th state! Our destination for the night was with a couple who volunteered a stay at their house and Blaine's journal entry explained connecting with them finally:

I am sure you have heard the saying that "timing is everything." Well, it was never truer than for our arrival in Minneapolis. Months ago, Todd and Rene Norton had invited us to

241

stay with them when they learned about Max & Bailey's Ride; I said we'd call when we got closer, then our computer crashed, and I lost their info for a while. I finally caught up with these guys on Tuesday night, less than 24 hours before our arrival. No sweat. Todd was very calm on the phone and said, "we'll see you tomorrow."

Well, these two were anything but calm. They immediately began an all-out media blitz for Max & Bailey's arrival, began working on some local appearances to maximize exposure and loaded up the house with food. (side story - Rene called friends to ask, "What do you think people from North Carolina will eat?") We arrived late on Wednesday to big hugs, fajitas for dinner and small (calm) talk about the next day's plans.

When we arrived, Todd and Rene welcomed us into their house, introduced us to their dogs, and helped us unpack our motorcycles. We did not know this couple at all, but we immediately felt at home. They were so welcoming and fun! After a couple of hours chatting with them over a fajita dinner and margaritas, we felt like we had known them for years! It was truly a wonderful evening, and we knew we would have a ball with them the next day with the itinerary they had planned.

August 5 - Day 97: Minneapolis, MN

We had an incredible day and Blaine's journal for the day does an excellent job of describing it:

When the phone started ringing at 6:00 am the next morning, we knew that could not be normal. The radio stations were broadcasting Max & Bailey's arrival, local friends were checking in with their progress around the city and the local NBC affiliate KARE 11 was on the phone asking what time they could come shoot some video. And all that was before 9:00 am! Todd and Rene were turning the city upside down, shaking loose every possible opportunity.

Later in the day, a small band of riders joined us as we made our way down to The Joint, one of Minneapolis' best biker hangouts. We were greeted by the owner, fed and watered, and invited to hang out our 'wares' to raise a little awareness as bikes rolled in and out. But it was still early, and this was the first Thursday of the month: bike night at Dulono's Pizza. So, we followed Todd and Rene's taillights to Dulono's where there must have been 1,000 bikes parked in a two-block area. So where do you park?

Rene jumps off her bike, parts the crowd with her charming personality, and makes a hole for us right up front in the middle of the pack. We sold shirts, we passed out brochures, and we made friends. Then it was back to The Joint to close up the night - but not until we had the chance to ride through the downtown lights of Minneapolis on the way.

A great day and a great night with great people. Maybe it was just the timing, but we happen to believe that Todd and Rene just ROCKED the city until they woke up for Max & Bailey's arrival. They showed us just how successful a local media blitz can be.

August 6 - Day 98: Minneapolis, MN

There is no better compliment on a host/hostess than telling them they made you feel right at home, and we'd like to stay another day. We were so comfortable at Todd and Rene's home and enjoyed their company so much that we took them up on their offer and stretched our visit to one more day! We rearranged our schedule for the next couple of days so we could spend the day catching up on emails and paperwork for the trip and then take a much-needed quiet night with our new friends! We agreed to go out for dinner and a movie.

Todd and Rene took us to one of their favorite local Italian restaurants, and we had an excellent meal. They graciously picked up the tab for us. With our hectic schedule and constant traveling, it was so nice to sit down and enjoy a meal with great friends...I mean REALLY enjoy the relaxing meal. Then off to a movie instead of rushing home to paperwork! And Rene knew how to top off my evening...smuggling a bottle of wine for us into the theater! Maybe I should have been passing my wine over to Blaine, since he sat next to a very loud and obnoxious cynical man. Sometimes you just want to give some people a reality check...I'm sure if we told that man about all the people we were riding for and what they battled each day, then he would have a better outlook on life!

August 7 - Day 99: Minneapolis, MN - Fargo, ND

After three awesome days in Minneapolis with our terrific hosts, we reluctantly packed our stuff back on the bikes and got prepared for our journey to Fargo, ND. Todd and Rene decided to escort us out of town with a short detour to the Mall of America for a picture. We got the dogs loaded up and took our last picture with our new friends.

To continue with our theme of visiting as many national icons as possible, we had to stop by for a picture in front of the famous Mall of America, the nation's largest retail and entertainment complex. The mall boasts 4.2 million square feet of gross building area and 40 million visitors annually, which is more than the combined populations of North Dakota, South Dakota, Iowa, and Canada! It contains 520+ stores, an aquarium, movie theaters and an entertainment complex including an indoor roller coaster!

We arrived at the Mall of America and found the entrance with a huge Mall of America sign. Now to find the perfect place to park to get a picture of us in front of the sign...hmm, it looked like it was going to be on the sidewalk. With mall security riding around us on bicycles, we made our plan...quickly get up on the sidewalk, arrange our bikes, pose while Todd took our picture and Rene kept lookout duty. Ready, set, GO! We rode up, positioned ourselves (thankfully the dogs were chilling naturally with their heads hanging out of the sidecars), smiled for the pics, and then jumped on our bikes and road quickly out of the parking area...with Rene yelling "Hurry" and a security guy chasing us off on his bicycle! Thankfully, he could not keep up with our motorcycles and we quickly lost him! Whew! We laughed as we cruised beyond his reach.

We rendezvoused with Todd and Rene at the end of the parking area to get our gear on for the ride and to say our last farewells. Another goodbye! Our sailing adventures with our daily "nice to meet you" and "farewell 'til we meet another day" lifestyle had prepared me for this, but it was still difficult! We hugged them tightly and thanked them for their endless hospitality, generosity and friendship and got on our bikes for the long ride ahead. With tears rolling down my face, I followed Todd and Rene for the first short leg of our trip. As they arrived at their turnaround point, I saw Todd hold his arm up and circle his finger as the usual motorcycle "turning around" signal and knew they were heading back home. We waved and bid another farewell to our phenomenal new friends! Goodbye to the security of their home and off into the unknown again, but I was grateful for the wonderful days of hospitality with this inspiring couple!

We continued our 243-mile day on Interstate I-94 up to Fargo, North Dakota, our 28th state! I was looking forward to seeing Fargo…how many people can say they have been to Fargo, North Dakota! We met a few people at our rest stops that had seen us on Minneapolis' NBC affiliate KARE11 and on CNN the previous weekend, so we knew our media coverage was getting the word out about our ride and our cause. We were not sure how our ride was covered on CNN, but we were excited about the national coverage! The rest of our ride was uneventful, and we checked into our home for the night, Holiday Inn Fargo.

Next, it was that famous time of day…what's for dinner? Remember that commercial: "Beef…It's what's for dinner." Yep, that was what's for dinner! Being Fargo, North Dakota, we decided on a rustic little restaurant called the Timber Lodge Steakhouse. They had a pleasant atmosphere and friendly staff, so we were ready for a nice, relaxing dinner. Unfortunately, mine started off a little wet…after our waiter dumped a glass of water all over the table…and me. Well, I am used to getting wet on this ride, but I really thought I was safe from a soaking by being inside…guess not. Oh well, the waiter was really apologetic and got the table cleaned up while I tidied up in the ladies' room best I could. We still had a wonderful dinner, and they discounted our bill as compensation. Even though we were only spending the one evening there in Fargo since we had no events planned there, we still got to experience the friendliness of the people there.

August 8 - Day 100: Fargo, ND - Sioux Falls, SD

Our route for the day had us heading 241 miles down Interstate 29 and into our 29th state, South Dakota.

The journal entry sums up our adventures for the day:

With a weather report that sounded like nothing but rain, we left Fargo, North Dakota, completely confused and surrounded by beautiful sunshine. Just to be safe, we stopped only once in North Dakota for an obligatory photo. Today's photo... could have been taken anywhere along the route. Unfortunately, it all looked the same: flat & corn mixed with hay fields.

South Dakota, to the south (of course) teased us with verdant rolling hills that seemed to take forever to reach - even at 70 mph. I know we do not normally take interstates, but all the other roads we looked at ended (or began) with loose gravel, so we stayed on the highway for the 240 miles. Our efforts were rewarded with a quick crossing of the North/South Dakota border and some very friendly folks at a gas stop.

If you haven't traveled these parts before - and we haven't - I'll set the scene for you. The highway is bordered by rolling fields (more corn, grain, and hay) and only rarely is the highway intersected by other roads. So, with our bikes running on fumes, we were quick to exit at the Hwy 12 exit off of I-29. Looking for fuel and a bite to eat, we pulled into the Conoco Coffee Cup Fuel Stop, an oasis in a cornfield desert. That's where we met Wendy.

Wendy, one of the Coffee Cup's employees and a professed dog lover, came out to see Max & Bailey as soon as we arrived. We got her permission to pull the sidecars up onto the sidewalk so we could chomp on a slice (or four) of pizza. While we ate, Max & Bailey used their charms on the Cup's customers and staff alike. As we were leaving, Wendy told us that Max & Bailey's photo was going up on their Wall of Fame - the same wall where they keep the photos of all the famous people who've stopped at this little oasis. If you're ever on I-29 in South Dakota - tell Wendy we said hello. She - and everyone else - treated us nicely.

We really enjoyed our lunch stop and experienced the friendly people of Summit, SD. With full stomachs, full fuel tanks, and cheerful dogs from all the attention, we headed down I-29 to Sioux Falls, SD. We laughed as we talked about our stop. Max and Bailey's picture was now on their Wall of Fame next to Montgomery Gentry, Trick Pony, and Poison. They were the new celebrities of South Dakota!

We arrived in Sioux Falls and found our home for the night...what has become our home away from home, Red Roof Inn. They were inexpensive yet friendly hotels, and this one met up to our expectations. When we arrived, we met Victoria, who became very enthusiastic about our ride. Seems this cause was dear to her heart. She had a 4-year-old son, Caleb, who suffered a medical accident that left him with a spinal injury shortly after birth. Caleb had a service dog, which helped him greatly. Unfortunately, Victoria had to pay $10,000 to another "charitable organization" to get this service dog for Caleb. It broke our hearts to know that, with all the medical bills she endured, she also had to pay for Caleb's service dog. It gave more meaning to our ride to know that we were bringing awareness and raising funds to help others get Assistance Dogs that were free or inexpensive to those that truly needed them!

August 9 - Day 101: Sioux Falls, SD - Chamberlain, SD

Chamberlain, SD was our destination for the day with only 141 miles to cover. We could not leave Sioux Falls without going to see the falls for which they named the town. I planned our route for the day to detour to Falls Park, where we took an enjoyable walk and saw the beautiful falls of the Big Sioux River flowing over the pink quartzite. It was very relaxing to hear the water flowing over the gray and pink craggy rocks of the park. Max and Bailey posed for their required "landmark" pictures.

We headed to our next stop, J&L Harley-Davidson; of course, we had to stop at the Harley shop! After buying another pin to add to my leather Harley vest to show that I rode my Harley in South Dakota, we were off to put some miles under our tires for the day.

The word for the day...WIND! We rode down Interstate 90 with the torrential winds in excess of 20-25 miles per hour blowing sideways across us for the entire trip! This was one of those days that we were both extremely thankful for having three wheels. I cannot imagine riding in those winds with only two wheels! To compensate for the wear and tear we were getting from the wind, we stopped often to rest. Therefore, when I saw the sign for Mitchell's Corn Palace, we just had to detour!

Believe it or not, this unique structure in Mitchell, SD attracts half a million visitors annually and is decorated completely by naturally colored corn and other grains and native grasses. Each year, they strip the murals at the end of August, and they complete new murals by the first of October. The building itself is used for festivals, exhibits, graduations, and basketball tournaments.

We rode around the building a couple times to look at all the murals, see this spectacle, and find the perfect spot for the obligatory picture. Ironically, the mural Bailey and I posed in front of was a tribute to the Lewis and Clark Expedition.

We continued our battle against the winds with a lunch stop and a well-deserved break at a rest stop. The travelers we met along our stops surprised us by saying they saw us in the local newspaper in Waterloo, IA or on KARE 11 out of Minneapolis. Max and Bailey were definitely spreading the word about our trip and our cause! Our most unique group we met were five very handsome motorcycle riders from Quebec, Canada, heading to Sturgis for the rally. They were fun to meet and three of them bought Max and Bailey ride T-shirts as souvenirs! They all surrounded Max and his motorcycle for the obligatory photo.

Eventually, we had to get back out on the road and into the wind. As we continued our relentless battle with the winds, I began thinking about our ride. We were very close to being halfway through with the ride. Looking back at our days, I realized it was like our days on the boat. We either had really awesome days or really challenging days, but nothing in between.

On the boat, we had days that tested our every ounce of strength. We would spend a day battling the weather, hoping our boat would not end up on the rocks, struggling for our very existence. Then the next day we would be anchored all by ourselves in the most beautiful harbor surrounded with white sandy beaches and watching the sky turn phenomenal shades of reds, oranges, purples, and blues while drinking a rum punch with a little freshly grated nutmeg sprinkled on top. There never seemed to be days when you were just existing.

Our ride was proving to be the same way. We had days when we battled the weather all day long or worked through the hassles of a bike breakdown. Days when our emotions seemed to pull out our soul, holding it in a tight grip. Then we would have the opposite extreme with cheering crowds excited to see Max and Bailey after months of waiting. We would be ecstatic that we could get another great donation or attend another remarkable fundraiser. Days when we would be so grateful to bring a little joy to someone in a nursing home. Our ride was an emotional roller coaster. The winds had been brutal the whole day, and it seemed it must have taken a toll on Max and Bailey as they stretched out on the bed snoozing that evening.

August 10 - Day 102: Chamberlain, SD - Valentine, NE

We awoke to sunny skies and were dancing with joy for the fantastic ride ahead of us. After being on the interstates for the past few days, we could get back to the small-town roads of America. It was a unique ride where we switched time zones twice. We switched from Central Time to Mountain Time and then back to Central Time again. By the end of the day, we did not know what time it was supposed to be.

We had an excellent ride as we crossed into our 30th state, Nebraska, and I cannot describe it any better than Blaine did in our journal for the day:

I've sat here for a few minutes trying to find the right words to describe the landscape we traveled today....but today's ride was different. It was both featureless and full of contrasts. It was long rolling plains, and then it was hills and valleys right out of some old western movies. It was corn fields with new tassels waving in the wind and sunflowers standing at attention. It was farmers in their John Deere tractors, wiping their brows and waving as we passed by in a blur. In a word, it was America. At least the picture of America that I had in my mind as a child when my classmates and I would sing America the Beautiful before classes each morning.

We ended up at the Trade Winds Lodge for the night and met some wonderful motorcycle riders from Franklin, NC. It is a small world when you can be so far from home and end up next to someone from our home state who understood our current experiences. It was nice to chat with them about North Carolina...a bit of a warm fuzzy. They even bought two Max and Bailey T-shirts to support our ride. We wound down the evening with a quaint dinner at the Bunkhouse Restaurant. I guess I expected something a little different in a town called Valentine, but it was a normal stop in small town America.

August 11 - Day 103: Valentine, NE - Chadron, NE

Our route for the day was only 138 miles, so I looked at my trusty Walmart Rand McNally Atlas and saw that we could detour for some sightseeing. We left Valentine, NE with grand plans to do just that...sightseeing! We planned on visiting Snake Falls and the Merritt Reservoir State Recreation Center, then heading through the beautiful Samuel R. McKelvie National Forest. Even though my GPS route said to take Hwy 20 the entire way, we detoured down State Road

97 to find Snake Falls. Our journal entry for that day perfectly described our adventures:

Our first stop was supposed to be the Snake Falls on the Snake River. Well, we turned left where the sign said to turn and were immediately greeted with a deeply rutted dirt road with overgrown vegetation on both sides of the narrow lane. Could this be right?

At the end of the road was a small structure that read, "Snake Falls Sportsman's Club." Again, we asked ourselves, 'could this be right?' We decided that this road and this structure could not possibly be the state-run tourist site. So, we pulled out and went looking for the official state park stop. Well folks, that rutted road and run-down building WAS the right place. We decided (actually, our kidney's decided for us) not to return down that road to see the falls. Next stop was the Merritt Reservoir State Recreation Center.

The roads were in much better shape, but we needed to purchase an all-day permit if we wanted to take a much-needed 15-minute break. Again, we passed and rode to the next stop: a relaxing ride through the Samuel R. McKelvie National Forest. That sounds like a good plan, doesn't it?

Well, see our photo #3 in our Photo-of-the-Day section and see if you can tell what's wrong with that picture (besides being a little blurred). I'll give you a small hint: THERE ARE NO TREES IN THE NATIONAL FOREST! Samuel R. McKelvie must have been the logging legend that cleaned out the forest or he had a great sense of humor.

So much for our sightseeing. No falls, no recreation center, and no trees in our forest! What is that old saying..."Cannot see the forest for the trees"...well, we did not see the forest OR the trees. The picture is not really a great one to share, just a blurry picture of Bailey and me on our bike sitting next to the Samuel R. McKelvie National Forest sign with nothing but grassy fields behind us...not one tree in sight, not even one! I truly believe the picture of Bailey and me next to that sign is blurry because Blaine was behind the camera laughing about the forest...or lack thereof!

After our frustrations of trying so hard to do some sightseeing and being beaten down all morning, we decided just to head for Chadron. We took Road S16F (yes, that is the correct naming of the road...who names these roads?) and headed back up to Hwy. 20 towards Chadron. We passed through the small towns of Cody, Merriman, Gordon, Clinton, Rushville, and Hay Springs and even though the map showed that we should have a scenic drive starting in Gordon, we mainly rode through desolate prairie land. We were thankful to finally get to Chadron and check into our Super 8 for the night.

August 12 - Day 104: Chadron, NE

We could not move up to the Sturgis area yet, so we stayed another day in Chadron. We were supposed to head out to Alliance, NE to see Carhenge, but after our fiasco at sightseeing the previous day, our hearts were not in it, and we postponed the trip for another day. Instead, we took a down day to catch up on our finances, emails, etc. We went to dinner at the rustic Old Main Street Inn. It was relaxing and enjoyable as they made us feel welcome and peppered us with questions about our unique adventure across America.

August 13 - Day 105: Chadron, NE - Mount Rushmore - Rapid City, SD

While the highlight of the day was going to be Mount Rushmore, our drive took us through the scenic route in the Black Hills National Forest and up the Needles Highway in Custer State Park. The custerresorts.com website describes it this way:

The Needles Highway is more than a 14-mile road—it is a spectacular drive through pine and spruce forests, meadows surrounded by birch and aspen, and rugged granite mountains. The road's name comes from the needlelike granite formations that seem to pierce the horizon along the highway.

The roadway was carefully planned by former South Dakota Governor Peter Norbeck, who marked the entire course on foot and by horseback. Construction was completed in 1922.

Our first stretch of our route took us through rolling meadows where we encountered our first buffalo jam. That was where a herd of buffalo gathered on or near the road and everyone stopped for pictures of them. Thankfully, they stayed far enough off the road where I felt safe, and Blaine was able to click a picture of Max in his sidecar with a herd of buffalo behind him.

The route through the Needles Highway was a spectacular drive through the narrow winding road and was a bit of a challenge going through the two narrow tunnels which were 8'9" wide and approximately 10 feet high. The scenery was stunning as we wound around the granite spikes.

Next up was the iconic Mt. Rushmore! Thankfully, we had a persistent volunteer who worked during the summer as a Mt. Rushmore employee and was also a PAWS Field Representative. After a lot of persuasion, she got permission for us to take Max and Bailey up to the viewing platform where we could get some unique pictures of them with the four presidents close behind. We stood in awe over the iconic faces carved into the mountainside.

On our way to Rapid City for the night, we detoured through the downtown roads of Sturgis to get a glimpse of what our next day would look like...motorcycles, motorcycles, and more motorcycles with lots of leather thrown in. We looked forward to introducing Max and Bailey to that crowd the next day.

August 14 - Day 106: Rapid City, SD (Sturgis)

The word for the day was "Sturgis". This is the motorcycle rally of all rallies! One of the most popular questions from bikers to bikers...is "Have you done Sturgis"? That is all you have to say, and they know exactly what you are talking about.

The Sturgis Motorcycle Rally website states that the rally started on August 14, 1938 with a race of 9 participants and a small audience. It was started by Clarence "Pappy" Hoel who owned the Indian Motorcycle Franchise in Sturgis. In 1949, for the first time, they blocked off the Sturgis Main Street for a 2-hour awards ceremony. In 1964, one block of Main Street was officially closed for motorcycle parking over the course of the 3-day event. In 1965, the Rally moved to a 5-day event. In 1975, it evolved to a 7-day event.

The City of Sturgis started allowing temporary vendor licenses in 1979 and they had 9 vendors. In 1988, that number grew to 188! In 2000, they reached their highest attendance ever...over 633,000 people! It has become so popular that many of the attendees were bringing their children and driving campers with their bikes on trailers, riding their motorcycle in the last few miles. This has prompted many of the attendees to wear T-shirts or patches stating, "I Rode Mine to Sturgis"...meaning they rode their motorcycle the entire distance from their home without the trailer...to imply they are a "real biker"!

The rally is known for the rowdy crowds, to include drinking and nudity. We laughed about all the comments on the lack of nudity...we only saw a couple of topless women and that was it. Why? Because the weather was too COLD! Yep...seemed the girls wanted to cover up in that weather.

The city closes a large section of Main Street, and it is popular to park your bike on that street or to cruise up and down it. Attendees park up against the curb near the stores and also in a strip, two bikes deep, down the center of the road which allowed bikes to cruise up one side and down the other.

David Vance was an old friend of our board member, Jay, and he guided us to the perfect spot for the day. He knew we needed shade for the dogs and had been coming to this rally for years. His expert advice to us was to meet him early in the day in front of Buddha's Tattooing and Piercing. Why? No, not because he wanted to get us the "I was at Sturgis" tattoo...but because it was one of the tallest buildings and would provide us shade most of the day. He knew Max and Bailey's requirements. By 9:30, we were in the shade and enjoyed our day chatting with all the bikers passing by and asking about Max and Bailey's adventures. Since we did not have a $700 vendor permit, we did not sell T-shirts...just gave out brochures about our cause and allowed everyone to enjoy Max and Bailey's uniqueness!

We were quite a hit as all the experienced bikers and wannabee bikers wandered the streets. Everyone stopped by to see the dogs in their sidecars and took pictures of them. They were indeed unique in this sea of motorcycles. There were two young guys who stopped in front of Max and Bailey and kept making non-flattering comments about the pups. I quickly grew tired of their derogatory comments and was frustrated at their arrogance. I hit my breaking point and spouted, "my dog has more miles on his bike than you two combined"! As they contemplated my statement, I told them the miles that Bailey had already ridden, and they immediately quieted as they realized my statement was true. Beaten in Harley miles by a dog! Ha! I glanced over to see Blaine silently laughing as he watched me hold my own as a biker chick and defend my riding buddy. Bailey and I totally rocked our Harley expertise! I was proud of myself knowing everything I had already accomplished.

The press found us, and we were interviewed by a TV station while we were hanging out on the strip. A quote from Blaine's journal entry that day shows just how popular Max and Bailey were:

But I will say that on one occasion, Max & Bailey stole the show from a young lady who was posing on a bike for a large group of photographers. When we rode by, all cameras were turned on us and not her.

By late afternoon, we were ready to head back to the hotel for some rest. We had a 30-minute ride back to our hotel. As we were heading out of Sturgis in the stop and go traffic of the rally, I felt a difference in my bike. It did not seem to stop with the normal ease. As we got close to exiting the town and hitting Interstate 90 back to our hotel, I realized the problem. My rear brakes on the bike did not seem to work well. The fundamental problem with that...they also controlled my brakes on the sidecar.

Now let's look at that problem...three sections of brakes...front, rear and sidecar. Big rig...really needing all three sets to stop it safely. Now I was down to one set...front. The ride back to the hotel was going to be interesting! To compensate for the loss of brakes, I had to make sure I was a great distance from any vehicle ahead of me and had to use downshifting to be my primary source of braking.

I drove very carefully back to our hotel and worried about getting this recent problem fixed. Was this going to delay our trip? Thankfully, my motorcycle class gave me the knowledge to maneuver this bike with my limited brakes and I brought it safely to the hotel...Bailey was safe for the day! Blaine checked it out when we arrived, and I appeared to have a severed brake line. We called the local Harley dealer, Black Hills Harley-Davidson, and they were open special hours for the rally...this was Saturday afternoon, and they were scheduled to be open on Sunday. Boy, were we in luck! Blaine and I made plans to ride both bikes (sans dogs) to the dealership in the evening, so I could drop mine off and I could ride back on Blaine's bike. They promised us to get it fixed in the morning and get us on our way...what a deal!

August 15 - Day 107: Rapid City, SD - Alliance, NE

We arrived at the Harley dealer the next morning, eager to pick up my bike. To our great relief, the bike was ready when we got there, but upon checkout we realized they did not give me the bike key back. They questioned whether I had left a key and I assured them I did. The key is not a requirement when dropping off a bike like it would be for a car. I am so used to locking the bike each night and setting the alarm that I automatically gave them the key when I checked in. Well, the key was certainly not with the bike.

We checked out, got the bike ready to leave, and waited while they looked for the key. They had to find every person who had contact with the bike in the past two days. We stood waiting as they brought several keys out to try. This one?

Click click. No. How about this one? Click click. No. Maybe it is this one. Click click. No. Well, you get the idea.

After about 45 minutes of questions and research, the key finally appeared. Yay, we could get back on the road. Note to self...if you give up your bike key again to a Harley dealer, mark it so it is noticeable. Ever realize how many Harley keys are at the dealer and they all look the same? They rarely have a unique key chain attached like a car key would have. Just a black key FOB and the bike key...all looking the same! From now on, my key would have a pink ribbon attached...or at least something making it unique and unable to be lost.

I was mentally calculating our distance and agenda for the day and trying to figure out if we were going to be able to see everything as we scooted back to the hotel to pick up Max and Bailey. I had planned to take us down the Iron Mountain Road, through the Wildlife Loop Road in Custer State Park and then all the way to Alliance, NE with a stop at the famous Carhenge. We were excited that the Harley dealer could get us out of the dealership by 11:00 on a Sunday, but were not excited about the delay with my key.

We packed up the bikes along with the pups and began our sightseeing trip for the day. Our first leg took us down Highway 16 to Keystone, where we connected with Highway 16A, aka Iron Mountain Road, also developed by Peter Norbeck. This magnificent road included three single lane granite tunnels and three wooden pigtail bridges where the road curls and passes over itself. The purpose of the pigtail bridge is to navigate sharp changes in elevation in a small amount of space. Therefore, the road crosses over the bridge and curves around and underneath the same bridge, forming a corkscrew effect, thus being nicknamed a pigtail bridge.

The ride on Iron Mountain Road was spectacular! This was one of those rides where I longed to have only two wheels. The road contained 314 curves and 14 switchbacks to excite even the most experienced motorcycle rider. For the two of us riding three wheels, it was another exercise for the arms. But today I did not notice the extra arm strength needed in the turns because I was awed by the breathtaking views! As we headed through one tunnel, we saw the stunning site of Mount Rushmore framed by a "V" shape of trees. Of course, we had to stop at the turnout at the opening of the tunnel for a picture or two.

We continued in delight through the beautiful wilderness and quiet roads down to Custer State Park. Along the way, we found a quaint, rustic-looking general store to stop for a soda for Blaine and me and a cool drink of water for Max and Bailey. There was a nice little sitting area out front where we could enjoy our refreshments and the perfect sunny, cool weather.

Next detour was through the Wildlife Loop Road. We had to watch carefully, so we did not miss the entrance to this pleasant stretch of road that forms an eighteen-mile-long semi-circle around the southern end of the park. It is a beautiful landscape of rolling prairies and pine-covered hills with an abundance of wildlife that includes bison, prairie dogs, elk, white-tailed deer, mountain goats, big horn sheep, antelope, and begging wild burros. This was a bit unnerving since there was so much wildlife wandering around and here we were on our motorcycles with no cover to protect us. Hope those bison kept their distance!

It was a remarkable ride up close to that much wildlife. We watched as antelope and hundreds of bison grazed across the prairies. The burros wandered unafraid into the roads and were so brazen that they would come up to the car windows begging for food. The adorable prairie dogs were so cute as they sat up on their hind legs to watch us ride by. Thankfully, we got to see plenty of wildlife up close, but not too close!

We continued to Hwy 87 and then Hwy 385 through wide open country to gently rolling hills and large groups of bison grazing along the way. We headed through Hot Springs and into Nebraska, passing through Chadron onto our final destination of Alliance. We hoped we would get to see Carhenge before it got dark.

We plodded on for another hour through the northwest section of Nebraska, passing no towns along the way. As dusk approached, we finally reached the famous Carhenge! Carhenge is a giant size replica of Stonehenge made entirely of cars from the 1950s and 1960s. They planted the cars trunk down with other cars stacked on top of them.

There are also plenty of other artistic displays of cars, such as the four Ford cars painted green, yellow, pink, and white called the "Fourd Seasons." According to its website, this creation was inspired by Vivaldi's Four Seasons and is supposed to represent "the Nebraska landscape's seasonal changes as wheat is planted, grows, matures, and the field lies barren during a windy winter."

I wandered around with Max and Bailey while Blaine took artistic pictures of all the structures. We watched the sunset as the sky turned beautiful shades of oranges, pinks, and purples.

When it became too dark to enjoy the art structures, we hopped on our bikes and rode into Alliance to our hotel for the night. As we checked into our hotel, we learned of a tornado that was spotted in the area which had produced softball sized hail! At that point, we were very thankful for our late departure with my failed brake line. Had we left at our intended time, we would have been driving into Alliance during that hailstorm. We were certainly counting our blessings for the unexpected departure delay at the dealership.

August 16 - Day 108: Alliance, NE - Cheyenne, WY

We crossed over into Wyoming, our 31st state, during our ride, and were met by the Cheyenne ABATE group for an escort into Cheyenne. We arrived at the Plains Hotel and were greeted by our hosts, Bob and Jill Jensen, the owners of the hotel. Jill learned about us from one of our charity partners, KSDS, because she had a service dog provided by them. They had special parking places reserved for us right in front of the hotel and immediately came to welcome us as we arrived.

After everyone took pictures with the dogs in their sidecars, we were escorted into the hotel and given a tour of the magnificent historic hotel. The décor was stunning, and it was much fancier than we were used to staying in. They made us feel at home with the lovely room they had donated for our stay and invited us to join them and others for a very special dinner.

August 17 - Day 109: Cheyenne, WY

While we were really excited for all the media attention we got in this town for our visit, the 4:00am visit to their CBS affiliate was really pushing it! I am not a morning person…especially at 4am…and not when I have to be perky about our cause at that time of the morning. However, we made it to the TV station in time for our interview.

Later that day, the Plains Hotel and the Union Pacific Depot Museum held an event for us on the Depot Plaza, which was right across the street from the hotel. The local radio station, KRRR, was there doing a live remote to promote the event. We were pleasantly surprised when we were joined by the mayor, and he read the following proclamation.

City of Cheyenne Proclamation:

Whereas, *approximately 54 million Americans (nearly 20 percent of the overall U.S. population) are living with some form of physical disability in the U.S., and*

Whereas, *Hogs for Dogs will travel through all 48 states of America raising public awareness and resources for people with disabilities and Assistance Dog organizations that support them, and*

Whereas, *Hogs for Dogs is a volunteer-based charity dedicated to supporting canine not-for-profit organizations, and*

Whereas, *by partnering with schools and students, Hogs for Dogs plants the seed for future generations of civic-minded individuals in the hope that supporting charities and actively helping those in need will become a priority in their lives; and*

Whereas, *the City of Cheyenne is proud to be included on the tour route to help support aide to individuals who need guide or Assistance Dogs.*

Now Therefore I, Jack R. Spiker, Mayor of the City of Cheyenne, do hereby proclaim

August 17th, 2004
Hogs for Dogs Day

in Cheyenne and urge all our citizens to join in recognizing the importance of supporting charities and actively helping those in need.

It was a fabulous event and was the perfect way to celebrate our 109th day on the road. We had reached our halfway point in the number of days we would be on the road! I could not believe that we had achieved that milestone. What a tremendous accomplishment! It did not feel like we had been on the road that long.

August 18 - Day 110: Cheyenne, WY - Steamboat Springs, CO

Our route began on I-80 and went through Laramie, where we ran across Laramie Harley-Davidson. Since it was raining and was not a pleasant ride, we took a break and browsed the Harley shop. Blaine found a T-shirt to buy.

We had been looking forward to the scenery in Colorado, but all we saw was rain, mist, and low-hanging clouds. We pulled off the road in front of the small "Welcome to Colorful Colorado" sign and took a couple of pictures. We had just entered our 32nd state, but you can barely tell it is Bailey and me in the pictures. Bailey was behind his rain cover, and I was bundled up from the rain and cold with my helmet, sunglasses, and neck warmer pulled up over my chin. It was a very quick stop for the obligatory picture entering the state, but we were miserable in the rain and not very joyous for this next milestone. This was one of those days where we had to concentrate on our purpose to get us through the day.

We slogged on to our Super 8 for the night and unpacked the bikes, glad to finally get to a warm, dry place to relax. We found the Old Town Pub for dinner to get a little comfort food after the unpleasant ride for the day.

August 19 - Day 111: Steamboat Springs, CO - Rock Springs, WY

The weather forecast said it was going to clear up, but we sloshed through rain for the rest of our ride in Colorado. After entering again into Wyoming, we ran across a sign that said Continental Divide. This is the line which divides the watershed that drains into the Atlantic from the watershed that drains into the Pacific. We were three states away from reaching the Pacific Ocean and having successfully crossed the country from east to west. Our anticipation increased as we thought of that milestone!

The sun was coming out, and we stopped to shed our rain gear. We met a couple from England who were driving their rented RV to Yellowstone, and they came over to take pictures of the dogs. We told them about our ride, and they went back to their RV to get a donation for us. It was always interesting to see how Max and Bailey's ride turned into donations for our cause.

On our way to dinner, we found another Harley dealer, Flaming Gorge, since it was near the restaurant. We ran across the new Harley model, the Deluxe, and we both really liked it. It was definitely a model that I could see myself riding in the future.

After riding every day, sometimes the simplest things meant a lot to us. We would ride thinking about our upcoming stop and a lot of times we thought about dinner. It was something to look forward to at the end of our long days on the road. This evening, for our dinner delight, we went simple and visited a Chinese restaurant. We had not eaten Chinese food in a long time, so we were really looking forward to it. Now, I had been to hundreds of Chinese restaurants, and they were usually all quite similar. If you ordered sesame chicken or General Tso's chicken, you pretty much knew what you were getting. It could be a little sweeter or spicier than the competition, but were always very close. Of course, there is an exception to every rule....and this restaurant was the exception to Chinese restaurants.

Without a doubt, this was the worst Chinese food that I had ever had. Do not get me wrong here. It is not like I just ordered my normal General Tso's chicken, and it was not good. This was a BUFFET, and it was all bad. There were some sort of meatballs that I swear did not have any meat in them. The egg rolls were bland and tasteless. The sesame and General Tso's chicken tasted very different...and not in a good way. We just had to laugh, because every time we sampled another item from the buffet, we were not disappointed with the unusualness of it. After looking forward to a delicious Chinese food dinner, it was extremely disappointing to have a dinner where you could not find one tasty item...even with all those selections!

August 20 - Day 112: Rock Springs, WY - Jackson, WY

We started our day with brunch at Sonic and it ended up being a profitable stop for our charity. Blaine gave kudos to them in the "Donor of the Day" section of our journal:

Barbara and the team at the Rock Springs Sonic get top honors today. We stopped in for a quick bite before hitting the road to Jackson. As we were about to leave, she came out to see the dogs. She learned our story and made a personal donation which was followed by almost everyone on her staff - most on roller skates - coming by to offer their support and donations.

Blaine's journal entry for the day also described our change in scenery and the crazy weather we experienced:

For the first 100 miles from Rock Springs to Pinedale, WY, I thought we were in the deserts of the southwest. Long, flat, sandy plains held together with tuffs of sagebrush and the occasional flowering weed were all you saw for miles. But off in the distance, the Rocky Mountains loomed large. At least when we could see them through the rain and dark clouds.

As we arrived in Pinedale, the oddest thing happened. We had rain to our left, lightning in the mountains to our right and sunshine directly above us. So, where did the dime size hail come from that was hitting us in the face? It was time for fuel anyway, so we pulled in for cover. If you did not know before, hail really stings when you're on a motorcycle.

The good news is that during our stop in Pinedale, we met some wonderful folks, one of which called the local newspaper - The Pinedale Roundup. They came out, took photos, chased us down the road, took more photos and a short story will appear in today's Roundup.

I loved how a simple stop could turn into a media opportunity! Max and Bailey had once again spun their magic and created another chance to teach more people about Assistance Dogs. We were grateful for more media attention, hoping it would bring in more donations to help our cause.

Our last seventy-five miles of the day brought off and on rains, making us do the dance of constant donning and removal of rain gear to stay comfortable. Finally, the sun came out, giving us stunning views of the Rocky Mountains as we weaved our way up to Jackson.

August 21 - Day 113: Jackson, WY

You know the word is getting out about your cause when the park ranger greets you with "So these are the two famous dogs that I have been hearing about". Evidently, everyone who had passed us at our last stop was already talking about us.

We spent the day exploring Grand Teton National Park along with its amazing scenery. We drove up U.S. 191 to Colter Bay and then circled back to our Motel 6 via Teton Park Road. The majestic mountains were met at the bottom by sparkling lakes and beautiful wildflowers. It was breathtaking!

While it was a sightseeing day with a plethora of scenic pictures taken, we met plenty of people from all over the country and passed out loads of brochures, so we felt it was a very productive day.

August 22 - Day 114: Jackson, WY - Idaho Falls, ID

For breakfast, we thought we would make a quick stop at a McDonalds, but by now we should have known no stop would be quick. Max and Bailey again drew lots of attention and people stopped to talk to us as soon as we arrived in the parking lot. We shared our story and received two $100 cash donations within just a few minutes! It is funny that the only other $100 cash donation we received during breakfast was again in a McDonald's parking lot. Who knew the Golden Arches would be so profitable for our charity?

Our first goal for the day was to get Max and Bailey's picture under Jackson's trademark antler arch. We had tried a couple of times in the past two days, but either the weather was not cooperating or there were too many people crowding around the area. Of course, whenever we drove the dogs to a crowded area, we were swarmed with people wanting to meet the dogs and get a picture of them in their sidecars. We finally got the crowds to allow us to get Max and Bailey out of the sidecars for a couple of pictures along well-known areas in the town.

With a bit of luck, we snapped a picture of Max and Bailey under the famous antler archway with no crowds around them.

Next, we brought them over to the huge stuffed buffalo that was in front of one of the stores. We could not get Bailey within 20 feet of that massive buffalo. He thought it was alive and was not going anywhere near it! Max, who is usually the calm one of the two, was brave enough to go sit near it for a picture. We noticed when he sat near it that he was leaning away from it, instead of having the straight posture he usually has when sitting. Even he was not too sure about that intimidating buffalo!

After our photo shoot in Jackson Hole, we headed west through the rain and thunderstorms and into Idaho, our 33rd state, where the rains held off long enough for us to get our obligatory photo shoot in front of the colorful "Welcome to Idaho" sign. Blaine even picked a few purple wildflowers for me for one picture which went well with the purple mountains on the welcome sign.

August 23 - Day 115: Idaho Falls, ID - Craters of the Moon National Monument

Our mission for the day was to go out to visit Craters of the Moon National Monument and Preserve. It was another idea from the Road Trip USA book and was included in our National Parks Pass. The Road Trip USA book quotes Washington Irving describing the park as a place "where nothing meets the eye but a desolate and awful waste, where no grass grows nor water runs, and where nothing is to be seen but lava."

Blaine describes it in our journal entry for the day:

I think every little boy wants to be an astronaut when they grow up. I was no different. I remember my grandfather giving me a poster of the moon out of a National Geographic magazine and how I stared at it for hours wondering what it would be like to be Neil Armstrong, to actually travel to the moon. My grandfather and my dreams of becoming an astronaut are both gone now, but I had the chance to relive a little of that dream today at the Craters of the Moon National Monument.

The land for the monument was set aside in 1924 and protects a very rare volcanic landscape that has been formed by lava flows that began some 15,000 years ago and recurs every 2000 years - give or take 100. And it looks very much like how I would imagine the moon's surface, minus all the scrub vegetation that has tried to get a foothold where dirt has settled in the cracks and crevices.

This was an interesting place. It really looked like we were traveling on the moon. There was very little vegetation, only a little scrub brush here and there. Massive amounts of lava rock were strewn around the landscape. The Inferno Cone was a massive hill that looked like it consisted of red-brown sand and gravel. No vegetation at all! The wind was howling, but we took the dogs out of their sidecars for a few cool pictures, making them look like they were venturing on the moon.

On our way back to Idaho Falls, we stopped in a little town called Arco for a gas stop. We gazed up at the mountain nearby and saw various numbers painted randomly on it. As we drove on, we wondered what they meant. We ended up finding a little place for lunch and Blaine did a wonderful job in describing our stop in our daily journal:

The surprise of the day was our stop in Arco, Idaho for lunch on the way back to Idaho Falls. We stopped for gas about the same time our stomachs sent up a flag saying, "FEED US." But Arco struck me as a town with little in the way of food possibilities, until we found Pickle's Place. We got some good advice in the parking lot: "Try the fried pickles."

Now, I'm not from around here - as they say - but fried pickles did not sound like the kind of appetizer a man would order in a strange town. I was wrong. Not only were the fried pickles delicious, the locals were extremely friendly. I even learned what all the numbers painted on the side of the mountain stood for. It seems that every graduating class since 1927 has climbed the mountain, lowered a poor soul down on a rope and painted the year of their graduating class into the hills. You can see the numbers for miles away. Once again, my first impressions were wrong: Arco is not a small town, it is a town with a huge heart.

August 24 - Day 116: Idaho Falls, ID - Colter Bay, WY

I was excited as we headed out for the day because we were heading back into Grand Teton National Park to Colter Bay for the night. Again, the scenery was spectacular as we drove through the Park. We saw lots of wildlife along the way…stopping to view the moose in the fields near us. It was fantastic!

We stopped for the night at one of the Jackson Hole Homestead cabins in Colter Bay Village. Before we headed to the cabin, we stopped in the General Store. This is where my girl scout, "always be prepared" mentality came in handy. Since we were pretty much in the middle of nowhere, we purchased our dinner at the General Store. A bit of cheese, a little meat, some crackers, and a bottle of wine, and we had dinner for the night. I already had plates, cups, knives, a wine opener, etc., so I was prepared for our picnic. We headed to our cute log cabin for the evening. It was quite rustic…one bedroom with a private bath attached and no Wi-Fi or TV. The dogs enjoyed being able to run around outside since there was nothing around us…nothing but trees. We had a great picnic dinner and were thankful we had brought books to read with us to settle us in for the evening since there was no internet available.

August 25 - Day 117: Colter Bay, WY - Gardiner, MT

This was definitely one of the toughest days of the entire trip! First, we had to leave this cozy little cabin in the woods after snuggling in the warm bed while listening to the rain on the tin roof. Second, it was an intense, pouring rain! And third, it was REALLY cold! We packed our bikes up in the rain and tried to wait for a lull in the rain to get Max and Bailey in their sidecars. We eventually gave up on the lull and just made a run for it.

I'm not sure exactly how I was able to drive my motorcycle. I had so many layers on that I looked like the Michelin tire man. I could barely move my head with the neck warmer up so high to cover as much of my face as possible. Max and Bailey were completely enclosed in their sidecars with their rain covers around them. I was wondering how much heat they could generate and keep inside. I was considering joining Bailey and trying to recruit someone to be the driver for us.

I had been looking forward to this day for a long time. Blaine had spent many vacations hiking Yellowstone. He and our board member, Jay, had been talking about their Yellowstone adventures for years. This was supposed to be one of the highlights of our journey. Instead, it lived up to its "Christmas in August" legacy.

This was August 25th, Christmas in August in Yellowstone. According to local legend, in the early part of the twentieth century, a freak blizzard stranded visitors and their stagecoach at the Old Faithful Inn. Rather than lament the fact that they were snowbound in a hotel, the guests celebrated Christmas, since it looked like Christmas outside.

As we approached the entrance to the park, I was wondering if this event was going to be re-enacted! We stopped at the Yellowstone National Park sign for our obligatory pictures. We quickly posed and snapped the pictures, so we could hurry on our way. Blaine wanted a picture of him next to the Yellowstone National Park sign, but he had to wade through a massive puddle of water in the bone-chilling weather to get there.

On our approach to the park gate, we got something even worse than snow...HAIL! Our journal entry for the day shows how miserable the ride was:

Today was so cold and miserable that I actually considered leaving Janet for a younger woman. Caitlyn - that was this young woman's name - is the National Parks employee that greeted us as we entered Yellowstone Park. And though she was attractive, that was not why I considered leaving Janet for her. It was the dry heat coming from her little booth that I yearned for with all my heart. But alas (don't you just love the word 'alas') I came to my senses and climbed back on my bike -- the one covered with hailstones -- and followed Janet into the frozen tundra of Yellowstone.

Now, for those of you who want to recreate this journey at home, here's what you do. First, change into three layers of warm clothes enclosed in a rain suit. Add a neck warmer and a tight-fitting helmet so that you can barely turn your head side-to-side. If you feel like the Michelin Tire man, you've done it right.

Next, fill the bathtub with two inches of cold water and add ice. Sit down in the tub, turn on the shower full blast with cold water. And when you can no longer feel your fingers or toes, have your spouse, significant other or friend hurl dry ice at your face to simulate hail at 45 mph.

When you think you've had enough, remember that you're going through all that discomfort to help others; specifically, to help those living with physical disabilities achieve greater independence through the assistance of a service dog. It won't make you any warmer, but you may begin to understand why we do it.

If you climb out before your lips turn blue - or if you refuse to do it all - you have to make a donation. Those are the rules; climb in the tub or open your wallet. Which will it be?

Honestly, with those two options, I would have been making a HUGE donation! I was ready to donate to anybody who would have taken my place. We drove through the park in agony, wishing we could be at our destination immediately. We finally got to the Old Faithful Inn for a rest stop. Boy, I wished this was our stop for the night! Blaine showed me around the Inn, and we bought some hot chocolate to warm up. Sipping hot chocolate next to a fireplace helped to thaw me out. Unfortunately, it was short-lived, and we had to head back out to the freezing weather to make it to our stop for the evening.

We exited the park and crossed into Montana, our 34th state! We were so excited to finally be at our hotel for the night. I cannot honestly say I have visited Yellowstone, since it only entailed driving madly in the hail and rain in order to get to our destination for the night. This definitely rated as one of the worst days of the trip!

August 26 - Day 118: Gardiner, MT - Billings, MT

We awoke to a little brighter sky than the previous day, but it was still cold and overcast. Our day's plan was to go on the steep and beautiful climb through Beartooth Pass and on to Red Lodge for the night. This route would also include many hairpin turns as we curved through the mountainsides. I had two routes entered into my GPS, but we needed to see if Beartooth Pass was open. With the wintry-like weather, we were afraid it would be closed due to snow. We entered Yellowstone and asked the rangers about the Pass. We were told it was closed and that we would need to find an alternate route.

Thankfully, I was prepared with the alternate route in the GPS, but our route just went from 121 miles to 177 miles. It would probably take the same amount of time since our alternative route would be mainly on an interstate and the other route included numerous hairpin turns and switchbacks. With our hack rigs, it would have been a strenuous ride, but we were still sorry to miss the beauty of that scenic route. We debated on our alternative route and were concerned with the section of road between the interstate and Red Lodge. Changing our minds, we went directly to Billings, MT where we had an appointment the next day to get our bikes serviced.

Before we started our trek to Billings, we explored a bit of Yellowstone. Since we had entered the park's north entrance, we found Mammoth Hot Springs Terraces, which looked like frozen terrain layered like stair steps. Yellowstone National Park's website describes how they are formed:

The step-like terraces form as heated water moves along the Morris-Mammoth Fault. The hot water carries dissolved calcium and bicarbonate to the surface of the terraces where pressure lessens. Carbon dioxide then escapes as gas and the carbonate combines with calcium to precipitate as travertine.

Their website also explains the different colors:

The Mammoth Terraces are constantly changing shape and color. Springs, which were active one to five years ago, may be dry and lifeless now, yet activity may later resume. Along with changes of thermal activity come changes in color. Fresh travertine is bright white in color and as it weathers, it changes to gray. Bright colored cyanobacteria and algae mats which were dependent upon a stable temperature and a flow of water also change as the microorganisms die creating a stark, bleak landscape.

We saw that the Minerva Terrace was a bright white with intermingled shades of light gray, making it look like it was formed of ice in that cold weather; other terraces were dark gray. One area was active as hot water cascaded down the terrace. It was beautiful as steam rose from the hot waters into the cold air and the terrace showed shades of yellows and browns. There was also a 40-foot-high cone of travertine, which they called the Liberty Cap. It was astounding to see the formations that Mother Nature could form.

Our travels through the park also brought us to the rugged, brown wooden sign with its white lettering marking the "45th parallel of latitude, halfway between the equator and North Pole". Of course, we had to park our motorcycles in front of the sign and take a picture of Max and Bailey at the 45th parallel!

Before starting our 170-mile trek to Billings, we filled our gas tanks. After the tanks were full, we headed onto the interstate. I had spilled a little fuel on my gloves, and I smelled gas when we took off. It stayed with me a few miles, but then it went away. I figured that I just had it spilled on me and that was the cause. When we entered Billings, we refilled our tanks, so we would be ready for our ride after the bikes were serviced. Upon refilling my tank, I smelled fuel again on our ride to the hotel. When we stopped, we realized my gas tank was leaking! It had been leaking for most of our ride and had been leaking onto hot exhaust pipes. Yikes! I was fortunate that the bike did not catch on fire!

We pulled the motorcycle to the far end of the parking lot, so we would not be dripping fuel near the building. We tried to figure out where the leak was coming from but could not figure it out. It appeared to be leaking from somewhere underneath the tank, but it was in an area that we could not see. Therefore, we could not find a way to stop the leak temporarily. We had just filled the tank, so I had a very full tank! We could not let it continue to leak fuel overnight, so we decided we had to figure out how to siphon the fuel out of the tank.

Blaine hopped on his bike and roared off to find a store nearby. I sat next to my bike and cried. I was so thankful that I had not been in the middle of Beartooth Pass when we found the leak, but I was also so tired of having problems with my bike. It was always mine and not Blaine's. First the spokes of the tire in the mountains of Massachusetts, then the brakes in Sturgis, and now the fuel tank had a leak! I was dreading to find out how long it would take them to replace a fuel tank! What was this going to do for our ride schedule? I also started second guessing myself...why didn't I notice it was leaking sooner? Why didn't I pull over when I originally smelled gas? Why didn't I question it when we were refilling our tanks? It was only making me feel worse.

Then the shock of the situation really set in. The fuel was leaking on hot exhaust pipes all day! What if we had caught fire along the way?! We would have been on the interstate in the middle of nowhere. Could I have gotten Bailey out of the sidecar in time? Could I have gotten anything else off the bike? Could the gas tank have ignited and exploded? I could have lost the entire hack rig today! As I sat by my bike waiting for Blaine to return, the realization of what could have happened set in, and I sat there in tears and shock.

After what felt like an eternity, Blaine came back into the parking lot, but he was not thrilled with what he found. He ended up with a small gas container and a cheap siphon kit. He started working on the siphon kit to see if we could get this fuel out into the container instead of dripping all over the parking lot.

Blaine worked for an hour trying to get the siphon kit to work. There was not anything I could do but sit beside him and worry. Using his previous experience with our boating projects, he knew he somehow needed to prime it. By sucking into the tube, he was able to get the flow going and the siphon finally worked. He eventually got the fuel down to a level where it was not leaking. At last, we could relax for the evening.

When Blaine went inside to wash his hands of the fuel, he was reminded that there were worse issues that we could be dealing with. His journal entry for the day explains:

When I came back inside to wash all the gasoline from my hands, I found this confused little bird outside our hotel room door. It was on the second floor, disoriented and scared. My first attempt to rescue the bird only succeeded in chasing it farther into the hotel. I tracked the little bugger down again, this time at the end of the hall. After a short discussion (with the bird), I motioned him (or her?) towards the lobby door. Silly bird flew right into a window and fell to the floor, allowing me to gently pick it up and carry it outside. It turned to look me in the eye and then flew away towards the sunset. A good omen, I hope.

It reminded me that our problems were not as great as they could be. We were not fighting for our lives like the little bird trapped indoors. Maybe Mother Nature will give us a few good days of weather for my good deed.

August 27 - Day 119: Billings, MT

The folks at Beartooth Harley-Davidson were expecting us to come in for a servicing and to get new rear tires put on the bikes. They were not expecting the leaking fuel tank that I came in with! We waited impatiently as they looked at my fuel tank for a diagnosis. We were afraid that the tank would have to be replaced and were wondering how long it would take to get a fuel tank shipped in. What did the future hold for our schedule?

The technician finally came out to give us the bad news. Two stainless steel cables had worn a hole through the steel gas tank. They did not have a gas tank in stock, so they were calling around town to see if they could find someone to weld it. Thankfully, a place called Sprockets agreed to weld it and pressure test it. They ran the tank over to get it fixed while we prayed that this would fix the problem and allow us to stay on schedule.

We spent some time wandering through the store and it was my day to find a T-shirt that I liked. That T-shirt was always going to remind me of how they saved our ride by getting my gas tank welded!

Five hours later, with a sigh of relief, we headed out the door with two motorcycles with new fluids and rear tires and one with a newly repaired gas tank. These guys were so fantastic to squeeze our fuel tank issue into their busy day and find a solution to keep us on track with our schedule. Now that was exceptional customer service! We were ecstatic for the gas tank repair to be completed in one day! Max and Bailey gave them a HUGE paws up for getting our bikes ready for the next day!

August 28 - Day 120: Billing, MT - White Sulphur Springs, MT

It was that time of day when we again needed to figure out where we were going to eat. After 120 days on the road, no restaurant seemed exciting or appetizing. Early on in our ride, I realized that I could not eat three large meals out at restaurants for 218 days. I would gain so much weight that I would not fit on my motorcycle anymore; Bailey was not about to give up his sidecar for me. Therefore, many days we decided on brunch so we could get some miles behind us before eating or get a late start to squeeze a little more rest into our demanding schedules.

This day, we again opted for brunch. We picked one of our favorite restaurants to give us each the selection we wanted. Blaine's favorite meal was breakfast. He could eat a large breakfast every morning. I loved breakfast too, but I liked to splurge once a week on bacon and eggs, not several times a week. After only a few days on the road, I was tired of eggs. Yuck! Blaine would be all excited over another big breakfast with eggs, sausage or bacon, toast, hash browns or maybe pancakes with it. I started dreading another breakfast. Therefore, we found our new favorite brunch stop...Denny's!

After living together in a small boat, we had learned how to talk things out and make compromises, so this was the perfect compromise. No more fighting over breakfast or lunch decisions. It allowed Blaine to order breakfast and me to order lunch ANY time of the day. Blaine would get his favorite, Moons over My Hammy...a ham and scrambled egg sandwich with Swiss and American cheese on grilled sourdough, served with a choice of hash browns or grits. He would always get the hash browns. While he was eating breakfast, I could eat my Denny's favorite, the Club Sandwich...thinly sliced turkey breast, crisp bacon, lettuce, tomato, and mayonnaise on toasted white bread served with a mound of French fries or hash browns. I would always choose the fries and ditch the tomato.

After brunch, I gave Max and Bailey their obligatory two bites of people food from our breakfast as a treat for waiting patiently for us in their sidecars. As we prepared to get on the road, another reporter stopped us. This one was from the Billings Gazette. We spread our news about our trip and let him take a couple of pictures; then out on the road we headed. We made it into the newspaper the next day, but there was only one picture with a caption about our ride...and, again, they did not include our website to direct people to obtain more information. They did not even mention the Hogs for Dogs name. We were frustrated at the missed opportunity to spread the word about our ride.

Our destination for the night would be the small town of White Sulphur Springs, MT. I had found a Super 8 motel that was dog-friendly there, so we headed west on Interstate 90 and turned north on Hwy. 89. We had powerful winds against us the entire trip! As usual, I was in front and gave Blaine and Max a little relief from the strong winds. We only had miles and miles of plains around us, so there were no trees to block the winds from us. The winds were so strong that I just could not keep my speed up. "You going that slow on purpose?" Blaine eventually asked me. "I can't go any faster!" I exclaimed, "The wind is blowing too hard for me to reach the speed limit." We continued to struggle against the demanding winds when I started to worry about fuel. We seemed to be out in the middle of nowhere and I was not getting my usual gas mileage with the fight against the winds. Getting really nervous, I said, "Hey, Blaine, can you lead for a while? I'm getting low on fuel and need to follow you for a while until we find a gas station! Getting scared that I will run out." "Sure," he replied as he headed around me. Throughout our trip, we had noticed that the person in front got worse gas mileage than the follower. The person in the back could get a "lift" by drafting behind the front vehicle. Therefore, we agreed to switch positions, so Blaine could take the brunt of the winds until we could find a gas station.

We continued to look for a gas station and I was praying we would find one BEFORE I ran out of fuel in the desolate terrain, one of my greatest fears. That would require us to have to split up; one person staying with the bike with no fuel and the other person going to find fuel. At long last, we spotted a gas station and stopped to fill up. Yay! One less stress on the road...finally a full gas tank! What a wonderful feeling that was!

We headed back out onto Hwy. 89, still battling the strong winds, but I was back out in the lead. The atlas had shown this road as one of those green dotted scenic roads. I was not seeing too much out here that was scenic. Blaine summed it up well in his journal entry:

The ride was fairly unremarkable in terms of land features, so there are no new photos today. Just imagine long (very long) stretches of open field punctuated by the Rocky Mountains and the Crazy Mountain Ranges to the very distant east and west. We had one opportunity for a photo stop. There was, however, a fully loaded 18-wheeler sneering at me from behind. So, a quick stop did not seem like the right thing to do if we did not want to get squished like a bug.

When we stopped for the evening, we were greeted with info from Summerville, SC. Small town America at its finest shown via Blaine's journal entry:

I wanted to share some good news from Summerville, SC. My parents, along with lots of their friends and local radio station (WSC FM94.3), held a community yard sale yesterday to benefit Hogs For Dogs. People came from all over the area to donate items for sale. The yard sale was truncated in the afternoon by rain, but they still managed to raise $453.00. All the leftover items were donated to the local Goodwill, so two charities benefited from their efforts.

August 29 - Day 121: White Sulphur Springs, MT - Conrad, MT

Our route for the day took us 160 miles up Hwy. 89 and through the Lewis and Clark National Forest. As I mentioned before, my ancestry ties back to members of the Lewis and Clark expedition, so we were excited to travel in the shadow of these two famous explorers. We were especially excited to see that this national forest actually had trees in it! The view was absolutely breathtaking.

We found a nice little place to pull off the road and enjoy nature for a while. It was perfect. When I used to travel with my parents, we often would pull over next to what we called a babbling brook, essentially a vivid stream with water running over large rocks and making a peaceful rushing water sound. As we pulled over, I saw the comforting, babbling brook. The only problem with this stop was that it was windy, overcast, and COLD. Blaine was enjoying the surroundings, so he went wandering off for a bit to take some pictures of the fantastic scenery. I sat perched against my bike, enjoying the sounds of the rustling water and trying to stay warm. Unbeknownst to me, Blaine was down the stream bank looking up at me and snapping my picture. The only part of my head that you can see is the top of my forehead. You can see a little of my sunglasses and the rest of my entire head is covered in my neck warmer. I look like I am about to rob a bank, but at least I was staying warm.

This was a great little spot to let Max and Bailey stretch their legs without their leashes, so we had gotten them out of their sidecars for a little exploration; this was the Lewis and Clark National Forest, so exploration was a must! The sun finally came out for a visit, and we basked in the warmth. Max knew how to enjoy it as he lay in the nice, warm grass and sunlight. Bailey, our adventurer, was too busy sniffing and exploring everything to realize the sun was even out.

Blaine did a wonderful job summing up our day:

Temperatures were all over the scale today. We were warm, then cold, then freezing before it turned warm again. It was a comedy of constant clothing changes as we clicked off the miles to Conrad, Montana - tonight's stop.

299

Conrad is a blue-collar whistle-stop town that just pops up as you are traveling through all the wheat and cattle farms along I-15. To put it in perspective, our hotel for the night (Super 8) has a 60' tall sign out front that screams Gas-Diesel-Motel-Casino. The railroad tracks are just behind the motel and the entire town seems to be in the casino at the moment. I spotted a large grain mill with an old General Mills 'G' logo on it, but can't confirm if it's still in operation.

The folks here are extremely friendly, and I normally have a very open mind to new places. I just can't seem to find the charm in this one, however, and I'm sorry for that. It appears to simply be a place that is halfway between somewhere south and somewhere north of here, and this is just a place where folks rest until they move on the next day. People like us.

When we settled in for the night, we had a major catastrophe; well, at least for Bailey it was. One of his beloved toys, Dinosaur, split and the stuffing was coming out. Bailey absolutely LOVED his toys, and he played with all of them enthusiastically. When I took it from him, he looked devastated! I could not just throw Dinosaur away, so I knew I needed to fix him. I had packed a little sewing kit with me, so I sat down to mend the toy. Bailey promptly sat right next to me touching the toy with his nose every few minutes to make sure Dinosaur was being taken care of. He seemed to be saying, "Are you done? Can I play with him now?" Once I had finished, I handed it to him, and he pranced around the room, throwing it around and chasing after it. That was his favorite toy for the rest of the evening. I had saved the day! (At least for Bailey.)

August 30 - Day 122: Conrad, MT - Kalispell, MT

We woke up excited to start the day. Today was going to be an awesome day! We planned on riding the Going To The Sun Road in Glacier National Park! We headed out early and after a quick jaunt on I-15, we turned onto Hwy. 44 and then once again were on Hwy. 89 on the way to the park. We traveled through the Blackfeet Indian Reservation and arrived in St. Mary's at the eastern end of Going To The Sun Road. We grabbed a quick bite to eat to get us through our afternoon adventure. After lunch, we headed across the street to get our obligatory pictures in front of the Glacier National Park sign.

The Federal Highway Association website describes the park and its history:

Going-to-the-Sun Road in Montana's Glacier National Park attracts millions of visitors each year to enjoy a drive through its beautiful scenery of lakes, streams, mountains, and facilities. Established as the tenth park in the Nation on May 11, 1910, Glacier National Park covers more than 1 million acres, including 175 mountains and 26 glaciers, with the Continental Divide essentially cutting the park in half. The 50-mile Going-to-the-Sun Road runs along and over these steep mountains. The elevation at Logan Pass, located in the midsection of the road and the highest point accessible by car, reaches 6,646 feet.

Going-to-the-Sun Road was one of the first National Park Service (NPS) roadways specifically intended to accommodate the automobile tourist. The 51-mile road passes alongside the glacial lakes, alpine forests, and huge sheer cliffs of Glacier National Park in Montana. The road had a significant impact on road design policy throughout the National Park System and is an excellent example of the National Park Service's sensitive response to topography and scenic features. Bridges, retaining walls, and guardrails were specified to be made of native materials. Rock excavated from adjacent mountainsides during construction was used to build most of the structures alongside the road. Large blasts of explosives were not allowed since it would cause too much destruction to the landscape. As a result, only small blasts of explosives were used.

Going-to-the-Sun Road was a great feat of engineering because of the many obstacles faced by engineers and laborers during the construction of the winding road. Sheer cliffs, short construction seasons, 60-foot snowdrifts and tons of solid rock made road building across the Continental Divide a unique challenge. The road is an early example of the collaboration between NPS and the Bureau of Public Roads.

Blaine's journal entry describes our experience:

In his book, Road Trip USA, Jamie Jensen describes the 50-mile-long Going To The Sun Road as "a magnificent serpentine highway that is arguably the most scenic route on this planet." After experiencing that ribbon of road through Glacier National Park yesterday, we completely agree.

At every bend and around every corner, there was something more spectacular to see. Fortunately, there are a sufficient number of turnouts and pull-offs where you can stop your vehicle to take in the scenery. The trick was to pull off BEFORE you got caught up in the scenery and went off the road. I almost made that mistake as I was transfixed by the most beautiful waterfall spraying water on Max & me as we turned a corner. I quickly learned my lesson and pulled over for future viewing opportunities. The 50-mile route took us nearly 6 hours to complete - if that gives you any idea of how often we stopped.

We entered the park and, within the first mile, were awed by the spectacular scenery! There were beautiful lakes and waterfalls throughout the entire park. The forests were lush with green trees and babbling brooks scattered the scenery. The mountains and glaciers were amazing; some were still capped with snow. We stopped often just drinking in the magnificent views. It was very interesting to see the tree line; this was the area where trees could no longer grow because they could not tolerate the environmental conditions. You could view the lush green trees growing up to a certain high elevation and then they would just disappear and all you could see at the top of the enormous mountains were the striped sedimentary rock formations. Each new scene, with every turn of the road, was just like a postcard. Our pictures were spectacular, but I do not think you could take a terrible picture with all that incredible scenery. That park was my favorite place we visited on the entire trip.

At one turnout, there was a stone wall with a lovely field behind it. The wall was about shoulder high and the field behind it was the same level as the top of the wall. The field was beautiful, with green grass dotted with little white flowers and large gray rocks scattered throughout. While I was enjoying the view, an adorable squirrel came out to look at me. He was a Columbian ground squirrel, and he had come out of his burrow to visit. They hibernate for 7-8 months of the year, so he was out looking for more food to fatten him up for the hibernating months. He was so cute with a gray back and tail, reddish brown face, reddish brown tints on his underbody and long, black claws on his precious little paws.

He cautiously wandered through the field toward me. Then he crept along the stone wall and came up to me for a visit. Even though I was not supposed to feed him, I could not resist giving him a Triscuit cracker...it's wheat, right? He took the piece of cracker in his tiny paws and, sitting up on his hind feet, held the cracker while he nibbled on it. He sat there less than 2 feet from me and nibbled on his gift. He was absolutely precious! After giving him the rest of the Triscuit pieces, we decided we needed to continue on our way. It was such a beautiful area with fun creatures of nature to watch. I could have sat there for hours, but we still had many miles to go.

As we were coming out of one tunnel and starting down the mountain, I went to downshift and felt nothing. I'd been on the road for 122 days and felt pretty confident with my shifting capabilities, so why wasn't I finding the shifter? When I looked down, I realized the shifter was not in the appropriate place. It had broken off the linkage. Why was it always on a mountain that I had bike trouble? I relayed my problem to Blaine, and we pulled to the side of the road. Luckily, this was one area that actually had a place to pull over.

Blaine looked at my shifter and found that all the parts were still there. The linkage had just slipped off a spindle. We spent about 30 minutes on the side of the road while Blaine fixed my bike. Surprisingly, we had a multitude of motorcycles pass us by and none of them stopped. We could not believe that nobody stopped to see if we needed any help. Was everybody too busy being a tourist that they forgot the friendliness of small-town America? Evidently so.

August 31 - Day 123: Kalispell, MT - Sandpoint, ID

Our route was 171 miles long and took us into a new time zone, the Pacific time zone. It was not a very scenic ride, but we had time to stop at the Kootenai Falls in Libby, Montana. The falls were named after the Kootenai Indians, who once inhabited the area and viewed the site as sacred.

We took Max and Bailey out of their sidecars and wandered alongside the falls. The views of the falls were spectacular! The white water from the falls splashed along with the green color of the water. The sound of the rushing water was soothing, and we enjoyed the diversion.

There was also a swinging bridge sitting high above the falls, and we walked up to explore it. I am not a fan of heights, so I was reluctant to walk onto it. The bridge was made of wood planking and the side rails were made of brown wooden posts and green chain-link fence material. Blaine quickly walked out onto it and we took the leashes off of Max and Bailey so they could wander the bridge with Blaine. He took some cool pictures of the pups on the bridge.

I finally summoned up the courage to walk on the bridge very carefully by myself so nobody else would make it swing. Blaine got a picture of me on the bridge before I scurried off again.

After a satisfying, scenic break, we loaded the pups back into their sidecars and continued on to Sandpoint, ID. While Blaine had fixed my shifter, I felt that there were other issues with my motorcycle. There was a Harley dealer in Spokane, so we decided to see how it was doing tomorrow on our ride there.

September

September 1 - Day 124: Sandpoint, ID - Spokane, WA

Our journal entry for the day included the following:

Today is Bailey's birthday. He turns ten today and we plan to celebrate with vanilla ice cream (his favorite), maybe a little cake and a small gift or two. We can only carry so many things on the motorcycles and his toy bag now has 8 different stuffed toys. Of course, like a small child, if you try to throw one away, he grabs it and runs. Anyway -- we hope you'll join us in singing happy birthday to Bailey.

I was looking forward to our celebration that evening to honor Bailey's day of birth. I always enjoyed watching Max and Bailey's enthusiasm as they slurped down ice cream. I was also anticipating finding a PetSmart or Petco to let Bailey wander the aisles and pick out another toy as his birthday present. My excitement was short-lived.

Our route for the day was only 65 miles, so we spent our morning working from the hotel to catch up on emails and accounting. We made sure we were packed up by checkout time and headed out for some lunch. With full stomachs, we headed down U.S. 95 and then Hwy 53 towards Spokane. Each time we approached a town and had to slow down and speed back up, my shifting capabilities continued to decline, and my mood declined with it. I cringed with every shift of my gears and the reality of my mechanical degradation sunk into my brain.

I was frustrated also at the possibility of disappointing Max and Bailey. I had started the day singing a rendition of Happy Birthday to Bailey and told him we would give them ice cream that evening to celebrate. Now I realized that we may not be able to do that. Some of you may think that it should be no big deal...the dog would not understand or remember that promise. I, on the other hand, truly believed they not only understood the ice cream at the end of the day but were looking forward to it.

We crossed over into Washington and pulled in front of the Welcome to Washington State sign for the obligatory picture. This was our 35th state. Unfortunately, I was not in much of a mood to celebrate, so we took our pictures and moved on. This eastern section was not what I expected. I was expecting rugged wilderness with forests, and we were surrounded by massive fields of farms and greenery over flat terrain. Despite my foul mood, I had to admit that it was a beautiful countryside!

Gratefully, we found another Motel 6 near the Harley-Davidson dealer in Spokane, so we planned to take my motorcycle in first thing in the morning. I was at my wit's end as I limped into Spokane and cautiously routed us to our hotel. I mentally ran through my previous problems: broken kickstand (self-fix), broken spokes (towed and fixed with 2-day delay), severed brake line (fixed overnight), leaking gas tank (fixed in one day), lost gear shifter (self-fix on the side of a mountain). I was so tired of my motorcycle breaking down and was not looking forward to yet another visit with a Harley-Davidson service shop. Do not get me wrong; the Harley-Davidson service departments that we had visited had been excellent to us, but I did not want to visit EVERY Harley-Davidson service department in the U.S.!

We unpacked our motorcycles and then Blaine took another look at my bike, including a test ride around the block. He realized how desperate my situation had become and we debated on what to do for dinner. I really wanted to take the dogs with us to dinner and get Bailey's celebratory ice cream afterwards. The smart way to go would have been for me to ride on the back of Blaine's bike to dinner and forgo the ice cream for the day. I was heartbroken because I wanted to celebrate my beloved Bailey's birthday, and I was determined to make it work. This is where my hard-headedness came into the argument. Since I really could not shift beyond second gear (and that was with some difficulty), we decided to only ride around the corner to a nearby Chinese restaurant and take the dogs with us. I literally stayed in first gear the whole way. It was slow going, but I was enthusiastic because we were going to celebrate Bailey's birthday, despite my current predicament.

We had a flavorful dinner at a gourmet Chinese restaurant with superb fresh ingredients. It was a truly enjoyable meal after such a frustrating day and my tense shoulders finally relaxed. After a lovely dinner, we went next door to buy some ice cream for Max and Bailey. My spirits lifted as I briefly forgot about my problems and watched the pups slurp up their vanilla ice cream. Happy 10th Birthday Bailey!

September 2 - Day 125: Spokane, WA (Janet), Spokane, WA - Moses Lake, WA (Blaine)

We were at the Harley-Davidson dealership as they opened their doors. I brought in my motorcycle and explained my issues as well as my usual spiel about our journey, our obligations, and the extreme importance of being back on the road as quick as possible. They promised to do their best, and we went back to the hotel to wait for the verdict. After a couple hours, the dreaded call came in and they were going to need to order parts. Blaine and I discussed our next course of action with this latest wrench thrown into our plans.

The day progressed to be one of the most difficult days of our trip for me, since Bailey and I were going to have to split up with Blaine and Max. We decided that since I needed to wait in Spokane for parts for my bike and we did not want to disappoint the schools waiting for our visit, Blaine and Max would go on without us. Depending on how long it took for the parts to arrive, Bailey and I would just have to catch up when the repairs were done. For the first time on this trip, we would travel by ourselves through the state of Washington and possibly other states, depending on the speed of the repairs.

My stomach was in knots as we made our plans and figured out what things we needed to swap or split to go our separate ways. We had to split dog food, dog bowls, and dog supplements. Since Blaine had the only cell phone, I took the satellite phone in case of an emergency on the road. With no GPS on his motorcycle, I gave him detailed directions written on wide blue painters tape and taped it onto his gas tank as his navigator for the day. The feeling of dread increased with each item we swapped or split. The camera went with him so he could document the school visits that Bailey and I would be missing.

With tears in my eyes and legs feeling like they would collapse under me at any time, I helped Blaine pack up his bike and get Max ready to go. As the tears spilled over my cheeks, I gave Blaine a hug, told him to drive safely and to call me when they arrived. I took the camera and snapped a picture of them ready to travel for the day. I handed the camera back to Blaine and then watched them drive off to their next stop. I turned and headed back to our hotel room with acute anxiety. This was the first time in our journey that I was truly petrified at what lay ahead. I did not know how long the repairs would take and how far I would need to travel to catch up with Blaine and Max. My only comfort that I had was my wonderful buddy, Bailey, to keep me company and protect me on our next leg of travel.

Blaine stopped at the Wellpinit School on the Spokane Indian Reservation to continue with our school visits to teach the kids about service dogs. Since I was not there to take pictures of the visit, one student volunteered to take pictures and sent them to Blaine.

After the visit, Blaine headed to Moses Lake for the night. As he was riding along I-90, he realized he was getting very low on fuel and was not sure how much further he could go, so he started a search for a gas station. He exited into a small town called Ritzville and wandered around looking for a gas station. Having no luck, he stopped at the post office to ask for directions. After a brief hesitation, the post office worker picked up the phone and called someone about fuel. After she hung up, she told Blaine about a gentleman who lived nearby and had a 55-gallon drum of gasoline where he could pick up a gallon or two. Taken aback by the instructions, he hesitated, but then thanked her for the help.

Blaine followed the instructions and approached the house that he was directed to. An older gentleman came out and Blaine prayed that he had the correct house! He relayed the instructions given to him by the postal worker, and the guy hesitated to respond. Just as Blaine was getting nervous that he was in the wrong area and was not sure how this guy would react, the guy responded with "Yup". Relieved, Blaine explained what our charity was about and the fact that he had to leave me behind with bike repairs. After getting a couple of gallons of fuel in the tank, Blaine asked to pay the gentleman, but he refused. Blaine traded him a Hogs for Dogs T-shirt and thanked him for his generosity.

Blaine called me at the hotel when he finally made it to Moses Lake. He relayed his adventures of the day, and I was beyond thankful that he had made it there safely!

September 3 - Day 126: Spokane, WA (Janet), Moses Lake, WA (Blaine)

Blaine continued with the school visits by visiting the 5th grade class at the Monument School in Quincy. He was supposed to visit one more school that day, but due to some confusion, it was cancelled. Therefore, he stepped next door and was able to spend time with another class as well.

I, on the other hand, could not get the butterflies to quit fluttering in my stomach. I attempted to catch up on accounting and continue to plan the next few days of our journey. With no vehicle and no stores nearby, I was stuck in my hotel room all day. Finally, late in the afternoon, I got an update that my part would be in by 10:00 in the morning and I would hopefully be on my way by noon. I did a little celebratory dance and told Bailey that we would be back with Blaine and

Max the next day. Bailey gave me a big tail wag and a sloppy, wet kiss as a thank you for the good news. I called Blaine and gave him the good news and he did a celebratory dance as well. Tomorrow we would be back as a team!

September 4 - Day 127: Spokane, WA - Moses Lake, WA (Janet)

I packed up all our stuff and checked out of the hotel as I waited to be picked up by the Harley-Davidson dealership. They were kind enough to send one of their technicians to pick us both up and take us to the dealership. We settled into the customer waiting area as they worked on my motorcycle. The part had come in that morning, so it was just a matter of time for the repairs to be completed and we could head out on our way.

The time stretched on, and it was past noon. I found a snack machine and grabbed some crackers and a soda for my lunch and tried to be patient, but my anxiety mounted. Thankfully, everyone was friendly to Bailey as he laid at my side and waited with me.

Finally, the good news came! My bike was fixed and ready for the ride to Quincy. Thankfully, we had purchased an extended warranty and my repairs were again covered at no cost to us and the charity.

I packed our stuff onto the motorcycle and got ready for our journey. We had 111 miles to travel, and the good news was that it was on the much-traveled interstate the whole time. The bad news was that there was really no major town in between if we ran into a problem.

We headed out, and I filled up our tank with gas so we would have no trouble making it to our destination. As we headed out of town, I smelled something funny, so I pulled over to look at my bike again. I saw a small puddle of green fluid on one part of my bike, but I saw nothing dripping onto the ground. I wrongly assumed that it was just left over when they refilled my transmission fluid after they replaced my part. I debated on heading back to the dealership to have them look at it but assumed they had done the fix properly and decided to continue on our way. I got back onto the bike and headed out onto the interstate, excited to be reunited with Blaine and Max.

I was enthusiastic about our destination for the day, but I could not get the butterflies to subside as we headed down the interstate. I knew that I had Bailey for protection, and this comforted me as we headed down the road alone. If we ran into problems, nobody would dare attack me with a huge dog at my side. Yet I still prayed for no more problems and a safe trip to be back with Blaine and Max as a team.

312

I tried to concentrate on the beauty of the countryside as we traveled along the interstate, but my mind would not relax in order for me to do that. I played the mental game to keep me calm as we barreled down the interstate as quick as possible. As we approached our exit, I again smelled the same smell and realized I did indeed have a leak. I continued to our hotel and greeted Blaine with some good news and bad news.

We were all very grateful to be back together again, but our excitement waned quickly as we confronted my leaking transmission. My puddle that I had cleaned at my last stop had returned and it had continued to leak down the side of my bike and burn on my tailpipe, giving it a highly tarnished look. To make matters worse, it was Saturday night. We went into Blaine's hotel room and looked on the internet for nearby auto parts stores. It was after 5:00 and everything was closed for the evening; not only closed for the evening, but closed until Monday morning.

My emotions were again on a roller coaster ride. I was ecstatic to be back with Blaine and Max and devastated to know that my bike was still not fixed. I did not know what to do, how serious it was, and if we were stuck in this small town for two more days.

We were supposed to head to Seattle the next day for a couple of days off. It was time for a couple days of rest and relaxation with a little time to explore Seattle. Blaine had never been, and I was excited to show him the sites I had loved the last time I had visited.

After wandering through town and finding all the auto stores closed, we headed to dinner to discuss our options and get our heads back on straight. We enjoyed the food, but it really was not a pleasant dinner as the possibility of another delay was thrown in our face. I wrestled with my decision and figured that I should have heeded my doubts and gone back to the dealership to have them look at my bike again. Then I realized that I would have been another day or two in Spokane without Blaine and Max and I leaned towards my initial decision, happy to be a team again.

We eventually called my brother to discuss our options and get his opinion on me driving the bike to Seattle to get it fixed there without a refill of transmission fluid on the way. He discussed the rate at which we figured it was leaking and decided that I should be alright to ride it to Seattle to be fixed. We felt a little better as we headed back to the hotel for the night and the anxious ride to Seattle the next day.

September 5 - Day 128: Quincy, WA - Seattle, WA

We woke the next morning with our dreaded ride ahead of us. We called the Spokane dealership and told them of our problems. They gave us two options. We could head back to Spokane to get it fixed or we could go forward to Seattle and have the Seattle dealership look at the problem. The Spokane dealership agreed to pay the Seattle dealership for any repairs that they did. We opted to move forward to Seattle.

Again, we were riding through another section of interstate with almost no towns to speak of on our route. We were heading through the Snoqualmie Pass with high altitudes and a few stops. We did not know if my bike would make it all the way to Seattle, so we said our prayers and headed out onto the interstate.

The scenery was beautiful, and I attempted to take my mind off my bike troubles and enjoy nature. It was not really working, as I prayed constantly to get me safely to Seattle. We stopped for lunch and a rest stop and looked at my bike again. It appeared to be doing alright, so we forged ahead to the Seattle dealership.

I was ecstatic to make it into Seattle, and we fought the big city traffic around the south side to the dealership.

Our journal entry describes our dealership experience:

Janet has a little bell attached to her front fork for good luck. Well, I'm beginning to believe that the little bell is broken because we spent all day Sunday limping her bike from Moses Lake to Seattle so that Seattle's Downtown Harley-Davidson could find and fix the leak from Janet's newly rebuilt transmission.

Richie - the assistant service manager - had been warned by the Spokane dealership (did the transmission work the first time) that we were coming. So, when we arrived, they immediately had Janet's bike on the rack and were pulling things apart to find the leak. Thirty minutes later, Herb (today's technician) asked me to come back and look at what he'd found.

The gasket used to seal the top cover on the transmission had changed recently. The Spokane dealership used the old gasket (easy mistake) which meant that it could never seal properly. Herb quickly replaced the gasket with the correct one and did a thorough inspection of other parts as he put the bike back together. He found three loose magnets in our magneto, replaced them, and continued looking for problems. I think he solved two or three other issues before his work was finished. I wonder if Herb would want to follow us the rest of the way around the country?

We don't hold any grudges against the Spokane dealer. It was an honest mistake, and they worked hard to help get us back on the road, paid all the bills at the Seattle dealership and were very nice to Bailey when he and Janet had to hang out there all day.

After they completed the bike repairs, we were able to go explore Seattle. We were ready for a break, so we headed to check into our hotel. This was another time when we wanted to splurge a bit, so we used some of our hotel points to pay for a couple days at the W hotel.

Blaine went in ahead of us to check us in and then came back out with a cart for our stuff. As I followed him back in with the dogs, I was wondering why he was taking us into the bar; we had the dogs with us! It took me a minute to realize the candle lit area was not the bar, but the lobby and registration area. We soon found that this would be the norm for the entire hotel, and Max was not a fan of the dimly lit halls and stairways.

After we got all our stuff unpacked from the bikes and got the dogs settled in the room, we headed out to look for a dinner spot. Not too far away, we found a Mexican restaurant. Perfect! After a nail-biting day of riding and hoping we would make it to Seattle, we needed a good margarita!

September 6 - Day 129: Seattle, WA

This was one of the few days that we took off on the trip. Actually, no day was really off. It was just that we were not riding to another destination. Instead, we were catching up on our emails, accounting, routing, and planning. It was a pleasant change to sit in a plush bed as I worked on my laptop. I was thrilled we had used some of our hotel points to splurge for a couple of days.

In the afternoon, we took some time off to enjoy a bit of Seattle. Blaine and I went out to the World-Famous Pike Place Fish Market and enjoyed watching them throw the fish around. I smelled all the beautiful flowers for sale in the market. It was fun browsing through the shops.

Next, we walked down by the waterfront. It was nice to be by the water again! We wandered down to Pier 62/63 and Waterfront Park. We stumbled across a Red Robin, and it was burgers for dinner! YUM!

September 7 - Day 130: Seattle, WA - Vancouver, WA

Our first stop of the day was at the Space Needle on our bikes to get some pictures of the dogs in front of it. The Space Needle was built for the World's Fair held in 1962 and it is 605 feet high. Now think about putting the bikes and the dogs in front of the Space Needle and trying to get pictures. Yea...not too easy to fit everyone into the picture!

We continued heading south and, as we passed through Tacoma, we ran across Destination Harley-Davidson and decided to make a rest stop there. As the dogs were being greeted by other motorcyclists, Blaine and I wandered through the T-shirt section. Today it was a win for Blaine as he found a T-shirt that he liked. It was probably good that we both didn't find T-shirts we liked at every dealership or we would have been shipping a lot of T-shirts home!

On our route down to Vancouver, WA we would pass Mt. Rainier to our east. It was something we just had to detour and see! We made it a rule to stay under 200 miles in a day because it takes so long for our stops with the dogs. Today, instead of going 164 straight to our destination, we were going to detour to explore Mt. Rainier and our route would be 228 miles.

Blaine described our route through the park:

Because of our timing, and our ultimate route to the south, we entered the Park through the southwestern Nisqually Entrance, made our way east to the base of Mount Rainier at Paradise and then exited the Park at the southeastern Ohanapecosh exit. Based on that experience, we would suggest skipping most of that route west of Paradise and entering the opposite way (through Ohanapecosh) and traveling towards Paradise. The views and pull-offs are much more dramatic from that direction - even when the peak is shrouded in clouds as it was for our visit.

We had fun taking our time through the park and stopping in the various pull-offs for the views. The dogs enjoyed the ride, and we took their pictures as they sat surrounded by wildflowers in front of the snow-capped Mount Rainier.

The scenery was amazing, with mountains, a lake, wildflowers, and waterfalls. I had fun walking across two gigantic trees that crossed over a rocky shore and rushing waters. They had been sawed off to make the top flat and a sturdy wooden handrail was attached to them. It was nice to get off the bikes to stretch our legs and enjoy the fresh air and scenery.

After spending the entire day sightseeing, we maneuvered our way to Vancouver to stay with Trey and Kris Casebar who were close friends with my brother. Den & Trey had known each other since 7th grade and went to school together. After Den was in the Army for three years, they reunited and lived in a bachelor pad "mansion" with about five other guys. All the guys who lived there rode motorcycles back then and have remained good friends ever since.

When Trey heard about our motorcycle trip, he quickly offered us a place to stay when we were out in Oregon. He still rode a motorcycle, so he was very interested in our trip. It was fun to spend the evening getting to know Trey and Kris and to finally meet one of Den's dear friends.

September 8 - Day 131: Vancouver, WA

We got a vacation day scheduled for this beautiful part of the country. Trey was our tour guide for the day, and we spent it touring the Columbia River Gorge. It was absolutely breathtaking! I was happy to follow Trey and just enjoy the scenery with no worries about routes. He took us up one side of the river and then down the other. We saw spectacular views of the river, pausing to see many waterfalls. We stopped to take a lunch break and then had to cross the river, which was the excitement for the day because the bridge was just made of metal grating. I was so very grateful for having three wheels going over that bridge! Trey, on two wheels, was thrilled to be across it as well. It was a relaxing day of sightseeing, and Trey and Kris were gracious hosts.

September 9 - Day 132: Vancouver, WA - Waldport, OR

After a great couple of days with our new friends, we headed west again until we were skirting the coastline. We crossed into Oregon, our 36th state! Again, the scenery was impressive. We stopped many times along the coastline to take pictures and just enjoy the magnificent vistas.

We arrived in Yachats just in time for the Barbecue fundraiser that they were holding for us. We parked under a covered area where they were already grilling, and Max and Bailey's noses went up with the delicious smells. We had a marvelous time visiting, grabbed a hot dog, and enjoyed the event. They raised $251 for us, and we sold $372 in logo gear. Now that was a productive barbecue!

September 10 - Day 133: Waldport, OR - Golds Beach, OR

Our day started out with a visit to Waldport Elementary School, where Blaine talked to around 300 children about Max and Bailey's adventure and what Assistance Dogs could do. The students were very attentive at that young age and asked a lot of questions. They enjoyed being able to pet Max and Bailey in their sidecars. It was a great way to start our day!

After our visit, we started our 160-mile trek down US101 as it snaked along the coastline. The views were out of this world! The trip took us much longer as we stopped often to take pictures and enjoy the ocean views. Since I grew up on the East Coast, I was used to flat terrain meeting the ocean. This landscape was just the opposite. It was a very rocky coastline with enormous boulders jutting out of the beautiful blue ocean. We stopped to take pictures of a lighthouse sitting on the edge of a mountain with gigantic rock outcroppings in front of it. The lighthouse and its surrounding buildings were white with red roofs, which was a striking contrast to the green mountain and blue ocean.

At one point we were down at sea level, so we found a place to stop and walk along the beach. It was cool to see horses being ridden on the beach. We enjoyed a relaxing ride as we slowly made our way down those 160 miles.

September 11 - Day 134: Golds Beach, OR - Redcrest, CA

Our morning started with breakfast at a small diner in Golds Beach. While we were eating, a couple stopped by our table to chat about the dogs; we told them about our charity ride and gave them a brochure. When we were ready to leave, we were pleasantly surprised that our bill had been paid by that couple. They had already left, so we did not get a chance to thank them. It was a pleasant reminder that the kindness of small-town America still existed out there.

It was another day of relaxing rides along US101 overlooking the Pacific Ocean. We started out with foggy weather, but it finally cleared up to give us a sunny ride. Early in our ride, we crossed into California, our 37th state! Our route took us through the Avenue of the Giants, where we rode among the tall, powerful redwoods. We stopped in the Trees of Mystery park where there was a 49-foot statue of Paul Bunyan and 35-foot statue of Babe the Blue Ox beside him. Of course, we just had to park our bikes in front of the famous statues and take a picture of Max and Bailey with them. Boy, these dogs got to see more in a year than many people do in a lifetime!

For lunch, I had already made plans to visit the Samoa Cookhouse. It was recommended in Jensen's Road Trip USA book, and I could not wait to try it out. The logging cookhouse was built in 1890 by the Louisiana Pacific lumber company and is packed with logging memorabilia. Jensen wrote "take a seat at one of the 20-foot-long tables (redwood, of course, covered in checkered oilcloth) and dig into the family-style feast."

We went inside and sat down at one of the long tables. There were no menus; instead, you received family-style platters of food on the table with whatever they were serving that day. The items rotated daily with selections like fried chicken, pork steaks, pot roast, spaghetti, beef stroganoff, chicken parmesan, and meatloaf. Lunch came with soup, salad, bread, a vegetable, a starchy food (potatoes, rice, noodles), and dessert. It was an all-you-can-eat feast, and everything was delicious. Afterwards, we wandered around looking at all the logging memorabilia. It was a fun lunch stop.

Next, we entered the Humboldt Redwoods State Park and stopped to look at the gigantic redwood trees. It made us feel small standing under these majestic giants. We took Max and Bailey through the walk thru tree where a sign stated that it was approximately 900 years old and was burned in a 1930s forest fire.

Next, we drove through the Shrine Drive-Thru Tree. It was 5,000 years old, 275 feet tall, 21 feet in diameter, and 64 feet in circumference. It was impressive! We stopped in the middle of it with our sidecar rigs and took pictures of us. It was great to take the day to do some sightseeing, but we also got a lot of attention for Max and Bailey, which resulted in many donations for the day.

We were lucky enough to stay in one of the cabins at the Redcrest Resort in the middle of these giant redwoods. It was a quaint resort, and we were grateful for such a marvelous day to enjoy the sights after so many days of racing through the rain!

It was the anniversary of 9/11 and Blaine wrote this in our journal to end the day:

It seemed very fitting for Max & Bailey to travel down the Avenue of the Giants today, the anniversary of the attacks on the World Trade Center Towers and the Pentagon. Today's giants were redwood trees, some 18-feet in diameter and over 2000 years old, that stretched their limbs to the sky. But I was also thinking of the large number of ordinary citizens who made extraordinary sacrifices three years ago, and of the families who lost their loved ones on that black day in American history. Those individuals are also giants in my book, and I took my moment of silence while in awe of the giant redwoods. I hope you took your own opportunity to reflect.

I am going to keep this update short because I do not believe my words should compete with the thoughts and prayers of those remembering 9/11 in their own way.

September 12 - Day 135: Redcrest, CA - Williams, CA

We continued our southernly route down Hwy. 101 and, after about 12 miles, we ran across a little Mom and Pop diner called Knight's restaurant. Its sign had a figure of a knight in armor riding a horse. We loved Mom and Pop diners, so we stopped for breakfast. I ordered the short stack of pancakes, which was different for me. I usually went for eggs versus something sweet. When it came out, I told the waitress that I had ordered the short stack and she told me that WAS the short stack. It was the largest stack of pancakes I had ever seen! I shared some with Blaine and I still had more than half of it left when I was finished. The waitress was extremely friendly, and she even packed three slices of ham in a to-go container for Max and Bailey. That is why we love Mom and Pop diners. Cannot beat the hospitality!

We continued to ride through the amazing redwoods and ran across another drive-thru tree. The Chandelier Tree was 315 feet high, had a diameter of 21 feet, and had a maximum age of 2400 years.

Our ride took us through the two extremes on the temperature chart. We started off in the morning under the shady redwoods bundled in many layers. As we continued riding east, the terrain changed, as did the temperatures. As soon as we crossed the mountains from the coastal region to the desert valley, we started unzipping all the vents in our leather jackets and then unzipping most of the front of our jackets. Then I was unbuttoning the buttons on my denim shirt underneath the leather jacket. I finally had to tell Blaine that we needed to pull over to strip multiple layers off to be comfortable. We ended our ride with the least amount of clothes that we could get away with and were spritzing Max and Bailey with their water sprayers to keep them cool in the dry, desert-like heat. Wow, were we ever thankful to get to our Motel 6, get out of the heat, and enjoy the air conditioning for the rest of the day!

September 13 - Day 136: Williams, CA - Sacramento, CA

Our route took us down I-5 and then I-80 over to the Del Paso Elementary School in Sacramento. We were joined there by our special guest Jackie Post who was a Field Trainer for Paws With A Cause. Jackie brought a PAWS demo dog, Libby, with her to demonstrate many of the commands that were taught to the service dogs. While we could talk about the amazing things that a service dog could do, it was much more powerful for the students to see a service dog in action.

Libby was a dark red Golden Retriever like Max and Bailey, only more petite. The kids enjoyed watching Libby pick up dropped items off the floor, turn on a light switch, and fetch a phone. It was a large crowd of students, and the demo was definitely appreciated as well as the visit with Max and Bailey afterwards.

September 14 - Day 137: Sacramento, CA - Fresno, CA

Our route was 161 miles, and we stayed mainly on Hwy 99, so it was nice to be off the interstates. It was an uneventful ride, but we were happy to get to our destination. We were staying with Greg and Susan Sims, who graciously volunteered a stay at their house for a couple of days. As previously stated, Susan was the creator/editor of FIDO Friendly magazine. Even though Blaine had been a contributing writer for them for a few years, we had not met Susan in person before. It was great to meet her and Greg and to enjoy their hospitality.

Susan had been following our adventure from the beginning, so she told us she had shivers as she saw us rumbling down the street towards her house. We were all thrilled to finally meet each other. After writing about dogs for many years, Susan said Max and Bailey were the coolest dogs as they relaxed in their sidecars and enjoyed the ride.

September 15 - Day 138: Fresno, CA

Our school visit with St. Helen's Catholic School was only a short 12-mile drive from the Sims' house. The students, dressed in their uniforms of white polo shirts and blue shorts, were waiting for us outside as Max and Bailey pulled in. It was always so much fun to see the excitement of the students when Max and Bailey pulled up in their sidecars! The entire school was there to enthusiastically greet them.

It was a beautiful, sunny day, and they held the presentation outside. Blaine talked to the students about service dogs as Max and Bailey snoozed in their sidecars nearby. While the students were very attentive to Blaine as he talked, they also enjoyed watching the dogs. After the presentation, the principal surprised us with a $100 donation to our charity from their school.

At the end of the day, we were treated to a delicious dinner hosted by the Sims and attended by other contributing writers of FIDO Friendly. It was a fun dinner, and we were again grateful for the hospitality!

September 16 - Day 139: Fresno, CA - San Francisco, CA

Spending the past couple of days with the Sims had been a lot of fun, so we were sad to have to again say our goodbyes. After a leisurely morning, we hugged Greg and Susan goodbye and headed out on our 152-mile trip to Campbell Middle School for our next presentation.

Our friend, Sheila Walters, who was the vice-principal, met us at the door as we arrived. We presented to a small group of students, but they were very attentive and asked a lot of good questions. Jackie Post and Libby were able to join us again to give the students a demo, and Libby was a big hit.

After the presentation was over and the students got a chance to meet Max and Bailey, we were whisked away by a 10-motorcycle escort by the Mt. Diablo H.O.G. members. I got the pleasure of following the escort and not having to worry about the routing to our next stop. It was so enjoyable to have a no-stress ride following along behind for our 58-mile ride to Pacheco.

We were thankful that we would stay at the home of Terry Osburn in Pacheco, who was a sponsor of our ride. They greeted us with a BBQ dinner that evening for us, our escorts, and many of the volunteers for the following days' events. While we were enjoying the delicious dinner, our board member, Jay, rode up on his rented Harley. He flew out from North Carolina to join us for the few days that we had events in the Contra Costa County area. He was a sight for sore eyes! I gave him a tight hug and told him how good it was to see him. We spent an entertaining evening catching up with him.

September 17 - Day 140: San Francisco, CA

We started off our San Francisco area events with a corporate-sponsored event at the Wells Fargo Corporate Offices in Concord, CA. We were escorted into the event by members of the Mt. Diablo H.O.G chapter, who also helped coordinate the activities. They held the event out in the courtyard of their main office complex and throughout the day we had employees and visitors come by for a visit. Tracey Stevens-Martin from the Contra Costa County Animal Services organization, a co-sponsor, did an amazing job overseeing all the activities and presentations to make sure it ran smoothly.

The day included clowns, face paintings, snow cones, glass blowing, a dunk tank, and representatives from our major partner, Paws With A Cause. We had a tremendous show of support as Max and Bailey had a constant string of visitors throughout the entire event. Blaine made a presentation where he talked about our ride. Next, the glass blower handed Blaine a blown glass figurine of us riding on our motorcycles with the sidecars. We were honored to receive that special gift. It was an incredible piece, and we were in awe of the detail! The event ended up being an enormous success and raised over $5000 for our organization.

In the afternoon we went to the Contra Costa County Animal Services offices to visit with the staff there who had been key in helping organize our festivities for our San Francisco events. A group of girl scouts were there who had helped raise supplies for the shelter. They loved meeting the dogs and Bailey enjoyed the tummy rubs from them.

September 18 - Day 141: San Francisco, CA

Our second San Francisco event was at the Grand Opening Open House celebration at Mike McGuire's new Devil Mountain Harley-Davidson. There was a massive turnout at the event, and we were busy all day talking about Max and Bailey's ride. Our event coordinators had several booths selling our Hogs for Dogs logo gear, a silent auction with gift baskets donated by local businesses, a dunk tank run by the Dirty Dogs Motorcycle Club, food, drinks, face paintings, and other activities. It was a phenomenal event! We were blown away by all the activities supporting our ride. Tracey and her team had outdone themselves!

Blaine and I were pleasantly surprised when we were able to visit with a couple of our dear friends. Aaron Sherrill, who used to work for Blaine at Cisco, stopped by to visit us. He had spent time with us on our boat a couple of years earlier and we had not seen him since then. It was great to see him.

Then Kathy Celestre surprised us with a visit. I had known her since before I was in kindergarten, and I could not count the number of years since I had last seen her. She lived nearby in Walnut Creek, CA, and it was really special that she came over for a visit with us.

We even had a couple of the Hells Angels come by our booth to visit the dogs. It does not matter their reputation...nobody can resist Max and Bailey in their sidecars with their Doggles on. Therefore, we got lots of smiles and laughs from them and Max and Bailey got free pets as well.

We were exhausted by the end of the day but were on an adrenaline high from all the great publicity and fundraising. Our first task was to tally up all the donations from the event. Thankfully, there was a lot to count. Blaine and Tracey sat down to count the cash donations, and I worked on the other donations. I was always amazed at how generous and supportive the motorcycle world was to charities. We ended the evening with a nice, quiet dinner with Jay, Tracey, and Tracey's family.

September 19 - Day 142: San Francisco, CA - Campbell, CA

Rain again plagued us as we awoke to the sounds of raindrops on the roof. Our day was to start out at Dudley Perkins Harley-Davidson followed by a fundraising ride along a scenic route, including the Bay Bridge, ending at the famous Alice's Restaurant. The dark clouds and steady rain were a stab in our heart, as we knew the rain would discourage riders from joining us on our fundraising ride.

The rains had let up by the time we left Pacheco and the sun came out as we headed to San Francisco. We gathered at Dudley Perkins and a couple of TV news stations had come out to interview us. We even had a special visit from Michela Alioto-Pier, a member of the San Francisco Board of Supervisors, welcoming us to the city.

Before we left on our ride, Blaine presented Jay with a special gift. Jay had recently gotten a new Chihuahua, and he was considering creating a seat on the gas tank for him. Blaine had found a small pink T-shirt that would fit the

Chihuahua that said, "If you can read this, the bitch fell off." He gotcha Jay! We all laughed while Jay grumbled over the gift.

Even though the sun had come out, we only had around 15 motorcycles that came out to ride with us. I was happy again that I could just follow along without worrying about the route. I had never been to San Francisco, so I could enjoy the scenery. We made a stop near the Golden Gate bridge and snapped a few iconic pictures of us, the dogs, and our hack rigs in front of the bridge.

We snaked our way along the coastline, and it was thrilling to watch the waves crash along the beach as we rode. Eventually, we ended up at Alice's restaurant. It was a fun afternoon, and the dogs got a lot of attention as we ate lunch. After a relaxing lunch, we again had to say goodbye to Jay as he was heading home on a redeye flight that evening. It was another difficult goodbye.

September 20 - Day 143: Campbell, CA - Spreckels, CA

Our route for the day was only 65 miles. We would stay with one of Blaine's old high school friends for the evening in Spreckels, CA. This was near Monterey and Blaine had been talking about how great the Monterey Aquarium was ever since he visited there many years prior on a business trip. Since we could not spend an entire day in Monterey so both of us could enjoy the aquarium, Blaine offered to let me go in by myself.

We headed down Hwy. 101 and detoured over to Monterey for my aquarium adventure. We found a nice parking garage where Blaine and the pups could chill, and I headed to the aquarium. As Blaine was outside catching up on emails, I headed inside to the sea life. I wandered through the aquarium and had a ball watching the sharks, rays, eels, penguins, and sea otters. The beautiful tropical fish and jelly fish against the blue background made for some awesome photos and I tried to catch the only Great White Shark in captivity on camera but was not as successful with him. It was an exceptional aquarium! I wished I could have spent more time in there and had Blaine along with me, but since he and the pups were outside waiting, I cut my time shorter than I would have liked. Maybe someday I would be back to spend a leisurely visit there.

We loaded up the pups and headed out, but the GPS would not load in the parking garage, so it took a few minutes for us to get our bearings and figure out how to get out of Monterey. We eventually made our way out and rode the short distance to Blaine's friend's house.

Blaine had lost contact with his high school buddy, Peter Sisson, for 23 years. He said it took him 19 years to finally find him again. (Remember these were times before Internet and the boom of social media.) He was so excited to meet up with him in person. Peter offered us a place to stay at his house and the two of them caught up with each other. Peter suggested going out to one of their favorite Italian restaurants, Gino's, which sounded excellent to us.

We spent the evening thoroughly enjoying the scrumptious Italian food and superb wine as Blaine and Peter caught up with each other. I enjoyed meeting him and his family since Blaine had been talking about him for a long time. We cherished special evenings like this.

September 21 - Day 144: Spreckels, CA - Santa Maria, CA

Our day started out with a school visit to Marina del Mar Elementary. Peter joined us for the school visit, so he could continue to ride with us for a portion of our journey for the day. The students were outside waiting for us when we arrived. Once we were safely parked, they all came over to greet Max and Bailey. A couple of students even had Harley-Davidson shirts on. Once everyone had time to say "Hello" and pet the pups, we went inside for the presentation. It was one of the more challenging ones since we had issues with the projector and Max and Bailey were unusually restless, but it was still an informative presentation which the students seemed to enjoy. Before we left, we were pleasantly surprised with a $105 donation made from teacher and student donations!

With Peter following behind our two bikes, we headed out on our 174-mile journey for the day. Our route took us along the scenic Hwy 1, which snaked along the rugged California coast. Our trip took us up and down the mountainous terrain and overlooked the ocean. The colors of the ocean were a mixture of sea-foam green, turquoise, aqua, and deep blue and were scattered with large boulders. The shore alternated from beautiful sandy white beaches to sheer walls of rock meeting the water. The views were breathtaking!

The road was curvy, so it was a challenging ride for us with our sidecar rigs. These were the days where we wished we were on two wheels. But then we would not have had our sweet pups beside us. Max and Bailey had their noses in the air, smelling the fresh breezes from the ocean. We stopped at several overlooks to enjoy the beautiful scenery and take pictures. Peter stayed with us for over half our route and then it was time to say goodbye again. I know it was harder for Blaine to not be able to spend more time with his longtime friend, but I also hated to say goodbye since I had really enjoyed getting to know Peter. Yet another difficult goodbye.

As we were swerving along the magnificent roads winding along the edges of the steep cliffs overlooking the coastline, Blaine was feeling a small wobble. He soon realized that his rear wheel was popping spokes. The same problem that I had in the mountains of Massachusetts. Why did it always have to pick a time where we were winding along steep inclines to start losing spokes?

This may sound a little mean, but today I was glad that Blaine's motorcycle was having problems. I was not glad that we had more problems, but I was very happy that it was finally HIS motorcycle that was having the issues and not mine!

We pulled over to look at the wheel and figure out what we were going to do. Blaine verified that his assumption was correct. He was starting to pop spokes on his rear wheel. We were nervous to have him continue riding as the roads were winding along the edge of the cliffs. We had already covered more than half of our route and as we looked at the GPS, we noticed that the last quarter of the route turned inward, away from the ocean. After discussing our options, Blaine decided he thought he could make it to the hotel on this tire. We would just have to take it slow and easy. We both took a deep breath and continued down the road. Thankfully, the mountainous road turned into a gentle ride at sea-level and we felt more encouraged that we would make it safely to our destination. Our tensions released as we rode into the parking lot of our hotel in Santa Maria for the evening.

Once we had checked into our hotel, Blaine researched and found that there was a local Harley dealer in town. He called them up and pleaded with them for assistance to help us get back on the road quickly. They called around and found a tire in Santa Barbara and said they would see what they could do to get it up to them. We prayed we could get it fixed in the morning and still make our afternoon event at Pomona Valley Harley-Davidson. After our stressful afternoon wondering if we were going to make it to the hotel, we decided to go out, relax and enjoy a Mexican dinner…margaritas were definitely part of that plan!

While we normally got donations on a daily basis, we ended our evening with a unique donation, which made our day a little better. Blaine described it in our journal:

We had several donations of note today, but I'd like to highlight one that was made in honor of 'Louie the Dog'. Louie was a 4-year-old Blood Hound that passed away suddenly after ingesting something harmful to his body. He is best remembered for his recent act of bravery in protecting the family home from burglars whom he not only chased out of the yard, but then tracked them for several miles afterwards. To honor Louie's heroic memory, a $100 donation was made by a friend of Louie's family - a donation in honor of one canine hero in the hopes of providing the necessary financial support to provide other canine heroes to people living with disabilities.

September 22 - Day 145: Santa Maria, CA

When we checked in with the Harley dealer, they reported they could not get the tire up to them in the morning, so Blaine decided to take my motorcycle down to Santa Barbara to pick up the tire. Since they would not fix it until the afternoon, we called and canceled our event at Pomona Valley Harley-Davidson. We were so disappointed because this was the first event in 145 days that we had to cancel. Our hearts were heavy knowing there were people who had organized an event for us and people looking forward to meeting Max and Bailey and we would let them down. It was beyond our control, but it still hurt.

Blaine took my bike with Bailey in his sidecar and rode down to Santa Barbara to pick up the new tire which they strapped onto the Tour-Pak luggage rack of my bike. After the 180-mile trip, Blaine dropped off the tire with Santa Maria Harley-Davidson and they agreed to put it on the bike that afternoon. By the end of the day, we had Blaine's bike back and were ready to continue on our journey; thankfully, only missing one day out of our trip.

I did not even bother to attempt to download the route for the day. With the massive road structure in LA, I knew our route would never download to my GPS. Instead, I prepped the major stretch via blue painters tape instructions and only downloaded the instructions to get us to our final destination. After 145 days on the road, I knew when it was a moot point to try to download GPS maps.

September 23 - Day 146: Santa Maria, CA - Los Angeles, CA

Our distance for the day was 187 miles. This would be another long ride and we wanted to make it to LA before the traffic got too bad. It was a race against the clock. We almost succeeded, but traffic started getting thick the last half hour of our ride. This definitely beat our other cities as having the most lanes of traffic. At one point we were sitting in six lanes of traffic and all of them were slow! The heat was baring down on us, so we were eager to get to our hotel. The folks of LA may be used to unusual things out there, but it is not every day that you see two Golden Retrievers in sidecars. Needless to say, even in the heavy traffic, Max and Bailey were a tremendous hit with the LA drivers.

With a sigh of relief, we finally made it to our hotel and got settled in. Blaine went out to Pomona Valley Harley-Davidson. He met the event coordinator for the event we had to cancel and gave him our apologies in person. Blaine then coordinated with the dealership to have them ship all the T-shirts from that event to one of our next events.

Later that evening, we met up with a couple of people from one of our minor charity partners. They had connections with people at Disneyland and they had coordinated a school visit as well as a visit to Disneyland the next day, so we met them for a late dinner.

September 24 - Day 147: Los Angeles, CA

Our day started out at Ball Junior High School where their motto is "Believe, Achieve, Succeed!" That was very appropriate, since we were going to spend our afternoon at Disneyland. Our presentation was to a group of eighth graders who would be involved in Community Service projects when they entered high school the following year. Therefore, it was thrilling to share with them our journey to assist people with physical disabilities in getting service dogs. We also were fortunate that we had a representative from one of our charity partners to demonstrate commands that a service dog can perform.

We were excited about our afternoon visit to Disneyland. The President of Disneyland Resorts made special arrangements for us to come onto the property with Max and Bailey in their sidecars and get pictures in front of the Mickey Mouse statue.

They also gave us Winnie the Pooh ears and Eeyore ears, which Max and Bailey wore, respectively. Max looked so cute in his Pooh ears with his orange lensed Doggles on him. Bailey could not quite pull off an Eeyore look-alike, since he still had his goofy smile on his face. No gloomy look for Eeyore.

Bailey

Next, they surprised us by presenting us with a $500 check signed by Mickey Mouse. They presented the check on behalf of the Disneyland Resort cast through their Guide Dogs Recycling Fund, a program where all the proceeds from bottle and can recycling went to Guide and Assistance Dog programs. It was a magical afternoon for us.

September 25 - Day 148: Los Angeles, CA - Barstow, NV

Another milestone was in the works for the day. During our day's journey, we would start heading east again! After spending almost the entire month of September on the west coast, we would finally make that easterly turn and start our home stretch across the country. But before we headed east, we turned our attention north once more...to another American landmark, the Hollywood sign. We could not come all this way without taking a little time to find the Hollywood sign! Now finding it would be a bit of a challenge since there was no address to go to in order to get to the Hollywood sign. You had to find a place that was away from the sign, but where the sign was actually visible. Therefore, I set my GPS to find Griffith Park where I was hoping we could get a picture of us with the sign in the background.

We traveled 38 miles to go back up to find the sign. We were lucky enough to find it, but finding a place to pull over in order to get a picture proved to be a challenge. We finally found a place to pull over and were able to get the obligatory pictures with the Hollywood sign behind us. Yet one more American landmark checked off our list.

Next, we were off to Barstow, which would give us a good hopping off point to cross the Mohave Desert. Because we knew it would start getting hot in the afternoon, we hopped onto I-215 and then onto I-15 to get to Barstow as quick as possible. We got there in the early afternoon, and we hid away in one of our sponsor hotels, Red Roof Inn, for the afternoon. During our ride, we entered Nevada, which was our 38th state!

September 26 - Day 149: Barstow, NV - Hoover Dam - Las Vegas, NV

The annoying alarm rang at 4:00 AM. We both looked at the clock and then at each other and said, "Are we insane?" We had to head through the Mojave National Preserve for the day. We knew we would be in the desert for many hours, so we were going through it at the best temperature of the day...early morning. I was nervous about this part of our ride with fears about having a bike break down in the middle of the desert in the scorching heat! First stop of the day was definitely a nutritious breakfast to get us started.

Denny's was our choice for this early morning breakfast stop. Thankfully, they are open at 5:00 in the morning. Remember my desire for lunch food versus breakfast? Yes, I ordered the club sandwich with fries at 5:30 in the morning. Yum! And you guessed it...Blaine ordered his usual Moons Over My Hammy. We then headed out on our desert adventure. It was actually cold at this time of the morning, and we were bundled in our leathers.

"I feel really ridiculous riding into the desert with five layers of clothing on, but it is freezing out here this morning", I said to Blaine over our CB. He agreed, then said "But you know it will heat up quickly, so this is our best time to go!"

Knowing it would be 100 plus degrees for the day, we enjoyed the cool weather and raced across the desert. As we visited one of the Visitor's Centers, we found the dog walk area with a sign reading "Caution: Rattlesnake Crossing". I hated snakes and was ready to get out of the desert area! Where was that beloved civilization? We continued on to Hoover Dam and arrived there mid-morning when the day was heating up quickly. Being rushed to get Max and Bailey out of the heat, we hurriedly saw the dam and took our gratuitous pictures with the dogs.

As we arrived in Las Vegas, we went directly to our hotel to get the dogs out of the heat.

We were not in one of the fancy hotels on the strip, but off the beaten path at yet another dog friendly Red Roof Inn. Unfortunately, our room was not ready, so we found a fast-food restaurant that gave us some shade for the dogs and a nice lunch stop for us. The shade and the dry heat made it bearable for us until our hotel was ready. Finally, we could check in and Max and Bailey chilled out in the refreshing air conditioning. We let the dogs rest for the afternoon since we planned to hit the strip in the evening to give onlookers the chance to see Max and Bailey in their sidecars. Priceless!

Since this was my first visit to Vegas, I was looking forward to experiencing "Vegas". Blaine and I started with visits to some of the casinos on the strip, followed by dinner. As we entered our first casino, it was a sensory overload! There were bells dinging everywhere, along with flashing lights. There was an air of excitement through the crowds. Neither of us were gamblers, but we played a few slots machines for fun.

After a while, the smoky atmosphere was too much for me and we decided to walk along the strip. It was fascinating to see so many street performers doing different performances; there were musicians, singers, jugglers, magic shows, and those dressed up in costumes like Elvis, Marilyn Monroe, showgirls, superheroes, etc. It turned all the sidewalks into one big party! It was fun walking around and seeing all the different themes of the hotels. We saw the free pirate show in front of the Treasure Island hotel with all of its sexy sirens and pirates, along with pyrotechnics simulating cannons firing.

Since the evening had cooled off, we headed back to pick up the dogs to cruise the strip. With the dogs in tow, we turned onto the strip. It was like daylight, as all the hotels were dazzling with lights. The traffic was stop and go at a snail's pace, but it gave us plenty of time to attract the attention of the Vegas crowds. It was an eclectic crowd with evening attire ranging from casual to dressy to formal with a lot of "what were you thinking" mixed in. No matter how they were dressed, Max and Bailey caught their attention, brought smiles to their faces, and gave them a memory of Vegas that they would not forget!

September 27 - Day 150: Las Vegas, NV

Max and Bailey hung out at the hotel for the day while we went to get our motorcycles serviced at the Las Vegas Harley-Davidson dealership. We hung out at the Harley dealership while they performed the oil change and put new tires on our bikes. It allowed us to catch up on emails, accounting, and routing. After our bikes were ready for many more miles, we headed down to the Vegas strip to watch the sights and eat dinner at the Harley-Davidson Cafe.

September 28 - Day 151: Las Vegas, NV

While we had been very lucky for most of our events, some days we were not so lucky. Unfortunately, the event for the day was cancelled, and we ended up having a down day to continue to catch up with emails, planning, and accounting.

September 29 - Day 152: Las Vegas, NV

We were invited to visit the Henderson District Public Library to meet some of their volunteers. The staff at the library had worked hard to get the media's support for Max and Bailey, but they cited "breaking news" for the reason they did not show up. Instead, we spent our time visiting the wonderful volunteers and their therapy dogs. They had an awesome Reading for Rover program where the children were able to come in and read to the dogs, thereby encouraging the children to read. The children were so excited to be reading to the dogs, and this led to a tremendous boost in their reading skills.

After our visit to the library, we had a gracious offer from one of the therapy dog volunteers to join her and her pups in their swimming pool at their house. Therefore, Max and Bailey got to spend the afternoon splashing and leaping into her pool, chasing tennis balls, and playing with the other pups. They had a blast, and it certainly was a great way for them to cool off from the Las Vegas heat!

As the evening set in, we took one last ride down the strip.

September 30 - Day 153: Las Vegas, NV - Cedar City, UT

Our 176-mile ride started out with the flatness of the Nevada desert, but soon became mountainous with huge red cliffs. We briefly crossed through a small section of Arizona, but since we did not stop there at all, we did not count that in our number of states visited. As we entered Utah, it became our 39th state! We were now down to the single digits in the count for the number of states remaining. It was amazing to think about the number of states we had already visited and the adventures that we had experienced.

As we headed to Cedar City, the landscape changed, and the temperatures began to drop. Blaine described the stunning scenery best with his journal entry for the day:

The high desert geography is also much more scenic, with dramatic cliffs and sunset-colored canyons. It was a real feast for our eyes after the barren, low lying Mohave landscapes.

We had been invited to visit with the students at Southern Utah University and were greeted by Dr. Genell Harris, who taught elementary education at the university. As we rolled up behind the library, we quickly attracted attention from all the students. We enjoyed our visit with them and were then invited over to a welcoming dinner at Dr. Harris's house.

October

October 1 - Day 154: Cedar City, UT

Our morning started with a gathering at Park Discovery for special education students so we could teach them about Max and Bailey's Ride Across America. We spoke with a news reporter about our ride and were featured on the front page of the People and Places section of The Spectrum newspaper in St. George, UT a few days later. Thankfully, it was well-written, and it included our website.

Next, we went to Fiddler Elementary School, where Blaine spoke to a large group of future teachers from Southern Utah University. Last, he spoke to a group of second graders at Fiddler Elementary. The local newspaper, the University Journal, was there, and they posted a picture of Blaine and Max during his presentation, but again did not add our website to the picture.

We had some time left in the afternoon, so we headed up to Cedar Breaks Park, elevation 10,400, for a little sightseeing. As we headed up the mountain, I felt something stinging my face and realized it was freezing rain! Ouch! I told Blaine that I wanted to pull over to put my face shield onto my helmet and he agreed. We found a spot to pull over and got our face shields on and continued up the mountain. Much better with the shield on, but, boy, was it getting cold! We continued to head higher, and the freezing rain turned into snow! In less than a week we'd gone from the extreme heat of the desert to freezing rain and snow!

The scenery on the way up was stunning. We passed many forests of white birch trees topped with brilliant yellow leaves. The snow kept coming down, and we kept heading up. We finally got to a lookout point, and it just took our breaths away! It was like a mini Grand Canyon with many hues of orange.

As the snow continued to come down, I found enough to make a couple snowballs to throw at Blaine when he was not looking!

October 2 - Day 155: Cedar City, UT - Page, AZ

We had a fantastic ride and Blaine's journal entry described our scenery for the day:

I cannot remember a day when we have seen such a variety of landscapes in a single day's ride. From high desert plains to sandstone cliffs reaching thousands of feet into the sky to deep canyons painted by eons of exposure to the elements. It was an amazing day to be a tourist with a camera.

We rode through Zion National Park and saw the picturesque sandstone cliffs in colors of cream, pink, and red.

As we continued on to Page, I suddenly felt something sting my leg and I swatted a huge insect off me. It really hurt and tears sprung to my eyes; my heart started to race. My mind leaped off the deep end and thought about the worst-case scenarios. I'm usually not allergic to any type of bug, but what if this one was an exception? I threw rational thoughts out to the wind and my "What Ifs" kept coming. I started reprimanding myself for forgetting to pack our EpiPen for these types of incidents. I looked at the GPS and realized how far away we were from the closest town. My throat felt like it was closing. I started to have trouble breathing!

Then I had to set my mind over matter. I took a few deep breaths and threw the "What Ifs" into the wind. I realized I was imagining these symptoms and that the sting was going away, and I was going to be fine.

At the end of the day, we crossed over into Arizona, our 40th state! Only 8 states to go!

October 3 - Day 156: Page, AZ - Grand Canyon, AZ

Our route was not extremely long at 116 miles, but it seemed to take forever as we headed towards the Grand Canyon. I was excited to see the Grand Canyon for the first time and my expectancy made the miles crawl by.

Finally, we arrived at the park and took the obligatory pictures at the park entrance sign.

This was the first time Blaine and I had been to the Grand Canyon and the views were phenomenal. You could see ribbons of colors in the mountains down through the deep canyon. We hauled the dogs out of their sidecars and took pictures of them in front of the majestic canyon. I am scared of heights, so I stayed far from the edge, but Blaine sat down on the edge of the cliff and I kept my distance and took his picture with the Max and Bailey logo on the back of his shirt.

Blaine's journal entry describes his endeavor and also cheers on our faithful volunteers back home that were making our school visits and events possible.

Small. That's how I felt with my feet dangling over the edge of a sheer cliff after a very strenuous climb down, up and over some challenging terrain to get there. Janet and about twenty other onlookers cheered when I finally arrived at that point, but my heart was cheering on its own. I had finally arrived at the Grand Canyon! And after coming this far, I simply had to look over the edge, swallow my fear of falling and take in the Canyon's enormity. I felt very alive at that moment - but small.

Rather than bore you with more words about today's ride, I wanted to take a moment to highlight the efforts of some very special people working behind the scenes on our behalf. Unless you have planned an event for us in your area, you may never have heard of April Fort or Annette Rowan. These two ladies are on our board of directors and have been working their tails off to coordinate with volunteers from around the country to make our events possible. I thank them often but can never repay them for their relentless dedication to this ride.

If you are an educator, you've probably spoken to Beth Cassels on more than one occasion. Beth, also on our board of directors, has worked tirelessly to help organize the hundreds of school requests we've received since leaving home. If we arrived at your school on time and on the right day, Beth is the reason why.

Now, how about the website? Do you enjoy your visits here? Do you find your way around the site with ease? If so, please join me in thanking Jay Schwantes, my long-time friend, mentor and now our website/media guru. Jay has been a pillar of support for this ride since the idea's conception over a year ago. He helped with motorcycle and equipment selection. He helped organize our ideas into realistic goals. He masterminded the route we've taken for Max & Bailey's Ride. And he's done it all for the sum price of a handshake and a few cold beers.

October 4 - Day 157: Grand Canyon, AZ

We spent the morning catching up again on routes, finances, emails, and planning; then we took the afternoon for ourselves to see the west rim of the Grand Canyon. Blaine's journal entry explains our disappointing visit:

Yesterday's ride around the east rim of the Grand Canyon was spectacular and personally moving. Today, we took half a day for ourselves and visited the west rim. The big difference is that the west rim has blocked all vehicle traffic except for the shuttle buses. So, you stop where they let you stop, and you see what they want you to see. Somehow the wild nature and grandeur of the Grand Canyon was not so, well, wild or grand.

October 5 - Day 158: Grand Canyon, AZ - Sedona, AZ

The destination for the day was Sedona, a 110-mile journey. We had hoped to stop for more photo opportunities but found all the parks and parking areas came with a fee. We did not want to have to pay for our brief stops. We were missing all the free parks that were available in our home state of North Carolina. There were a couple of photo opportunities when we ran across an area with striking birch trees with their snow-white tree trunks and another stop near a stream in the Red Rock area. We were disappointed that we did not get to stop more often due to all the parking fees.

October 6 - Day 159: Sedona, AZ - Phoenix, AZ

I was looking forward to our destination today since we would be visiting with my cousin, Nancy Walter, and her husband, Jim. We were cousins on my dad's side, as her dad and my dad were brothers. I had not seen her in many years and was looking forward to the visit. They lived in Fountain Hills, a suburb of Phoenix.

Our 121-mile trip was HOT! We had been used to the cool, dry air in the upper desert regions, but were not prepared for running into the heat again.

We ran across the Chapel of the Holy Cross, which is a Catholic church sitting amid the red rocks of Sedona. From the road, you can see an enormous cross where the base of the cross is in between two gigantic stacks of red rocks and the rest of the cross towers over them. The cross stands out a little while the church building sits behind it with its width only as wide as the width of the arms of the cross. It was striking how it looked like it had just grown out of the massive rocks. We were lucky to pull onto the side of the road and take a picture of the amazing church with the bikes in front of it.

After the extremely hot ride, we were grateful to finally make it to my cousin's house. It was a sweet reunion, and we had a fun time spending the evening in their welcoming home.

October 7 - Day 160: Phoenix, AZ

Our route for the day was 87 miles out to Arlington Elementary School. We scooted through Phoenix and out into the desert. This was one of those days where I was cussing the GPS! It had been a while since it got us lost, but today was one of those lost days. When we neared the area for the school, the GPS routed us right into a section of impassable dirt roads. So frustrating! We did not want to go bumping along some dusty dirt road, so we discussed where we had come from and looked around the desert for another route to try. It seemed that every paved road dumped us onto another dirt road. We eventually found our way and found the school. Finally! Our host met us at the door, and we entered to set up our presentation. Not out of the woods (or desert) yet, we then had technical difficulties to overcome. At last, we were up and running and could give their great group of students a presentation about our ride along with a little modeling with Max and his Doggles!

On our way back, we took a break and found some shade to hide under for a bit. This is where I finally understood the saying "but it's a dry heat". The heat is just as hot as on the east coast, but the difference here was that when you got into the shade, you did not have all the humidity keeping you hot and sweaty, so it felt cooler in the shade. We welcomed our shade break and then continued on back to my cousin's house for the night.

October 8 - Day 161: Phoenix, AZ

It was not a fun afternoon for me and Blaine explained it well in our journal entry for the day:

I lost my voice during our school presentation on Thursday and have sounded like a 13-year-old going through puberty ever since. So, with our school cancellation today, I spent the day trying to rest, fill up on vitamin C and recover before tomorrow's events in Tucson. Though frustrating, I cannot complain too loudly since this is my first real bout with illness on the trip.

Janet, however, complained plenty because I left her with her least favorite tasks today: talking with the media, both radio and newspaper reporters. With my voice shot, Janet rose to the occasion and promoted our Tucson event on KVOI-AM 690 at noon today and quickly followed with an interview for the local Fountain Hills Times. We are always grateful for the media's help in spreading our message, but Janet prefers to let me do the public speaking. So, today I owe her a big hug for filling my shoes while my voice was left squeaking and squawking.

Yes, I definitely complained dearly! I swore up and down that Blaine could talk and just wanted to throw me into the spotlight. I despised public speaking, which is why Blaine did all the talks and speeches at all schools and public events. Now, he was saying he could not talk enough for the radio and newspaper, so it was up to me. Newspaper I could semi-handle, but radio? UGH! But I had no choice. I could not deny the radio station an interview, so I stepped up and talked to the radio on-air personalities and promoted our Tucson event, then told them about our ride and our cause. I followed up with an interview with the local Fountain Hill Times, which was not nearly as frightful as the radio interview! Then I turned to Blaine and told him he HAD to get his voice back to normal. This was not my cup of tea; I did not sign up for this and he needed to get better and step back up to the plate! Thankfully, after a day of quiet, he was back to normal. Whew!

The town of Fountain Hills where we were staying is known for its fountain, which was the world's tallest when it was built in 1970. It held that record for a decade. It spews a tall plume of water from a concrete water lily structure in the middle of a man-made lake. The plume of water rises to a powerful 560 feet in the air!

Since part of our journey was to see unique sights like this, it was a must for us to visit it. Early in the evening, my cousin Nancy led us out to the fountain, and we were able to take a perfect picture of Max and Bailey in front of the tall plume of water. It was impressive!

October 9 - Day 162: Phoenix, AZ - Tucson, AZ

While it was hard to leave my cousin's house, we were headed to Tucson, AZ where we would stay with friends of ours who used to be our neighbors when we lived in Willow Springs, NC. We were excited to see them.

Our ride was another long one at 154 miles and we scooted along down I-10 as quick as we could. It was great to see our hosts, Brad and Barbara Brock, along with their two boys, when we arrived at their house. After unpacking our bikes, we sat down to catch up with each other and it was like a homecoming. We did not get to chat too long because we had a spaghetti dinner fundraiser to attend at the Desert Gardens Cumberland Presbyterian Church. Brad had enlisted the support of the Triple S & E 4-H club, Boy Scout Troup 141, the local Lion's Club, and many more church members and volunteers. Pastor Mike McNeese was kind enough to offer us the use of the church for the event.

Not only did the town come out to support us, but we got a chance to meet Joe Nowak, who drove almost an hour to meet Max and Bailey, enjoy a delicious spaghetti dinner, and buy a Max and Bailey T-shirt. We were excited to meet him since he was the father of Pat Nowak, who worked with Carolina Canines for Service.

Everyone enjoyed the tasty spaghetti dinner, as well as meeting Max and Bailey. They also showed their support by purchasing some of our logo gear. We were humbled by the excellent turnout for the dinner and, as the dust settled from the event, they raised $886.50 for our cause.

October 10 - Day 163: Tucson, AZ - Deming, NM

We woke to the mouthwatering aroma of bacon. Our friends had made breakfast to get us started for the day. We were very grateful for the home-cooked meal. After a very tearful goodbye, we headed out to our next adventure. We visited the Saguaro National Park in Tucson before leaving the city. As I mentioned earlier, I expected to see the "Snoopy" cactus all over the deserts. Since we had not seen much of them, we could not miss this whole National Park full of them! We headed into the park and there they were..."Snoopy Cactus"! How could you call them "Saguaro" cactus when you could easily call them "Snoopy" Cactus? Yes, they were all over the place. So many, with so many different shapes. We spent quite a time trying to find one that had the best shape and the best place to get the dogs out to get a picture of them without getting their tails full of cacti spines, the large needle-like structures on the cacti. Eventually, we got the dogs out at another national landmark to get their mugs taken in front of the cactus. Priceless!

Then on to our next stop for the night, Deming, NM. I found we were passing Tombstone, AZ on our way, so, of course, we had to detour the 24 miles to visit this interesting town. Who hasn't heard of Wyatt Earp and Doc Holliday and the infamous shootout at the OK Corral? After entering Tombstone, AZ, we parked the bikes and wandered the city to see all the neat attractions. We visited the ice cream shop to get an afternoon treat and explored the interesting saloons and history of this great little town.

Of course, we had to visit the "Hawg Corral", the local motorcycle shop! On our way there, we stopped at an intersection and ran across a crowd of locals dressed for the events (1800s garb with dresses and boas for the women and guns and cowboy garb for the men...cowboys and bar girls). How cool! As we gawked at them crossing the street in their notorious clothing, they began to gawk at our two dogs in sidecars. We both were loving each other's uniqueness! They all came over to greet us (as we were at a stop sign). They gathered around and Blaine took a picture of them all crowding Bailey and me. What a fun stop!

We decided we needed to head out and get to our motel, since the weather did not look like it was going to cooperate with us. We had 187 miles to get to our stop for the night in Deming, so we raced down I-10 trying to beat the storm. After 82 miles, we crossed over into our 41st state of our journey and stopped in front of the Welcome to New Mexico sign for some pictures. For Blaine it was especially sweet, since this marked his 50th state he had visited. He had lived in Hawaii and had visited Alaska during his time in the military, so this was the last state he needed to complete all 50! He parked his motorcycle in front of the sign and made the number "50" with his hands to commemorate his accomplishment.

Huge streaks of lightning were constantly flashing to our left, and I prayed that they stayed away from us until we stopped for the night. They were REALLY intense, and I was extremely nervous that we would end up in the middle of a tremendous storm. We raced many a train along the way as the tracks paralleled the interstate. Thankfully, we beat them all, but were disappointed that none of them blew their horns at us as we passed them by.

We finally got to our destination with no rain on us. Thankfully, we beat the storm. Yes! I could not believe we made it there safely with no rain after all that lightning. Another challenge, another success! We headed out for dinner to celebrate. That could have been a majorly ugly day, yet it turned out to be really fun! After we returned from dinner, the bottom fell out; it was a major rainstorm. Boy, did we get lucky to miss that rain and be safe inside when it finally caught up to us!

October 11 - Day 164: Deming, NM - El Paso, TX

Our route for the day was 170 miles. We did not have many back road options out in this area, so we had to stay on I-10 all day. It was a quick, very uneventful trip. Our accomplishment for the day was entering our 42nd state! Texas! With that achievement, we knew it would be awhile before we would cross into state number 43 since Texas was so big! We stopped at the Welcome Center and took our picture in front of the big Texas sign with the vast state of Texas on it.

We entered El Paso and were finally in a place where we could use one of our LaQuinta free stays. Jay had a friend who worked at LaQuinta, and they had donated a few free stay coupons to us. This was the first time since we started our ride that there was a LaQuinta in our destination city. We were excited to finally stay at one.

After getting settled into our hotel, we went on a search for a nice Mexican restaurant. We figured El Paso would have an authentic one. Boy, were we wrong. We wandered around up and down an exit or two and just could not find a Mexican restaurant for dinner. Really?! We were in El Paso, and we could not find a Mexican restaurant? This just seemed so very wrong! Disappointed, we finally gave up and just grabbed some fast food for dinner, so we could get back to our hotel and get some work done.

October 12 - Day 165: El Paso, TX - Van Horn, TX

Our morning started out at the El Paso Community College where we were invited to speak about our journey and cause. It was a pleasant visit and some of the staff bought logo gear, so we were happy that we had the opportunity to visit there.

After grabbing some lunch, we rode the 112-miles to our next Texas town. It was a very uneventful and boring ride.

Our biggest achievement of the day was hearing from our accountant and board member, Terry O'Malley, that our 501 (c)(3) determination letter was received in the mail! Woohoo! It had been a very long process, but we finally were a tax-deductible organization.

The IRS had received our application and cashed our check on Feb. 20th. We had some glitches, such as a problem with our Amended Articles of Incorporation not being processed after they were filed with the Texas Secretary of State. It took a couple months to get that resolved, and I finally had to call them and beg to get a copy faxed to me at our hotel in order to get the IRS moving along with the application.

This was a tremendous success since it made all previous donations to Hogs for Dogs tax-deductible as well. The approval was retroactive back to our incorporation date. This was tremendous for our non-profit organization!

October 13 - Day 166: Van Horn, TX - Midland, TX

We spent another day trying to cross the vast state of Texas. Our route was a long 182 miles with very little scenery. We were riding on the interstate in order to get to our destination as quick as possible and there was really nothing to see out there, which made for a very boring ride. The only exciting thing was that we would stay at a LaQuinta for the evening, and they were usually quite nice. We had to appreciate the small things on boring rides like this.

October 14 - Day 167: Midland, TX - Abilene, TX

It was day 3 of crossing through Texas on our way to Dallas. We drove another 156 miles on the boring interstate. Again, there were no unique stops with photo opportunities. We were more than ready to reach Dallas!

October 15 - Day 168: Abilene, TX - Dallas, TX

It excited us to know that at the end of the day we would finally be in Dallas. We drove 76 miles along the interstate and took a brief detour to visit Strawn, TX. We had been invited to speak at a school visit with Strawn Elementary, Junior High and High School students. The first presentation Blaine gave was to the elementary students. Bailey must have thought that the kids were getting bored mid-way through the presentation because he rolled on his back with all four paws up and played dead, which he had never done before. The students were chuckling at Bailey. I took a picture of his goofy pose and then tried to get him to lie down properly so that the students could concentrate on Blaine again.

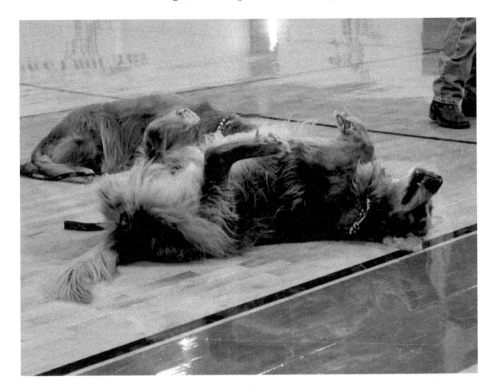

Luckily, PAWS representative Karen Vass joined us with her demo dog, Rock. It was always a special addition to our presentations when we could have a demo dog demonstrate many tasks that service dogs can do.

For the next presentation, the basketball bleachers were filled with Junior High and High School students. Blaine learned that the Strawn High School football team - the Greyhounds - were the State 6-man football champs from the previous season. After explaining what an Assistance Dog could do for someone with a disability, Blaine asked the students who their quarterback was. A tall, lanky student with short, black hair stood up. Blaine asked him to sit in a chair beside him and to pretend that he was disabled and sitting in a wheelchair. Blaine laid down an item near him on the floor and asked him to pick it up without moving his legs. Blaine used this scenario often to help the audience realize how difficult small things were to someone living in a wheelchair. After several failed attempts, Blaine then explained how an Assistance Dog could have helped him. It was always a great way to have the message really hit home. It was also beneficial to have the demo dog then demonstrate how he could pick up that item off the floor.

After the successful school visits, we headed back out on the road and to the interstate for our last leg into Dallas. Blaine's transmission had been failing like mine had done and as we headed toward the interstate, the transmission finally gave up. Why did this always happen when we were in the middle of nowhere?! We were still on the small road leading from Strawn to the interstate, so we had to again call a tow truck. On a positive note, we had experience calling into the Harley-Davidson service number to request a tow truck for our hack rig. We were also grateful that Karen had been at the school with us and was not far away. After a call to her to let her know about our motorcycle breakdown, she came back and picked up Blaine and Max to take them to our hotel.

October 16 - Day 169: Dallas, TX

Our event for the day was at the Texas Motor Speedway, so we were bummed that Blaine and Max had to arrive there in a rental car. However, it was our only way to get our entire team to the Speedway. We were meeting up with PAWS representatives next to the "Racing for Independence" simulator sponsored by Terry Cook and the Ford Power Stroke Diesel by the International racing team. It was an excellent partnership where they were raising money and awareness for Paws With A Cause. Since we were also raising money and awareness for PAWS, we were invited to join them at the Speedway for their racing event.

Terry and his team were super gracious to our Hogs for Dogs team, and we had fun being in the middle of such a large NASCAR event!

After the event was done, Blaine returned his rental car and went to pick up his motorcycle at Ft. Worth Harley-Davidson.

When we got back to our hotel, we sat down to continue to look through our pictures, which we had done the past few evenings. We decided we wanted to create a calendar of pictures of Max and Bailey on their adventure to sell for the charity. Two of our volunteers were supposed to be selecting the pictures for the calendar, but they could not narrow down the ones they liked the best…they said all the pictures were great. Therefore, Blaine and I decided we would need to whittle down the pictures. Even the two of us had a difficult time, but Jay, our board member who was designing the calendar, said that we could put two pictures per month, so we picked out 24 of our favorite pictures. We were happy to have completed the task as we were running out of time to get it designed and printed for the end of the year sales.

October 17 - Day 170: Dallas, TX

Our event for the day was a poker run hosted by PAWS representatives and volunteers along with Sneaky Pete's in Lewisville, TX. A poker run is a motorcycle event where they stop at five different locations and draw a playing card at each stop. At the end of the event, the person with the best hand wins.

The last stop at our event was at Sneaky Pete's. While we did not get the turnout that we had hoped for, we still had a great event. The winner of the poker run had a Jack-high straight and the runner-up had three 9s. Our raffle winner was not present, but they had left their tickets with a friend and instructed them that, if they won, the money was to be donated back to our charity. We were blessed to again have a raffle drawing donated back to us! The PAWS representatives and volunteers were also able to promote their organization to everyone at the restaurant as well. All in all, we felt like it was another successful event, and we were grateful for everyone who organized it and volunteered.

October 18 - Day 171: Dallas, TX

Our day started with a brief ride over to Holy Trinity Catholic School in Grapevine, TX. We met the middle school students in their uniforms of white or blue shirt and tan shorts/pants. It was a great group of students. We were lucky enough to have Karen there again with her demo dog.

After our first school visit, we had time for a quick lunch before our next school visit. We were able to join Karen and her fiancé, Bob, for lunch. In the following excerpt from our journal for the day, Blaine does an excellent job in describing this touching story:

Let me return to that quick lunch I mentioned. It was during lunch that we received what may be one of the most unique, thoughtful, and touching gifts we've ever received. Bob, Karen's fiancé, works with canine search and rescue. In that capacity, he was one of the many who helped search through the World Trade Center debris after 9/11. Bob shared with us just how grueling and emotionally draining it was to be there during that time. Children would often hold up photos of their loved ones as he made his way to work, pleading for Bob and his dog to help find them among the rubble. Bob was in tears as he recounted the story, and we were in tears listening to it. Then he shared the gift.

He said that he had returned back to their hotel room after an extremely difficult day and found a small package lying on his bed. When he opened the box, he found it full of dog booties made to protect the dogs' feet while they searched the rubble. And on each bootie, school children from a school in Michigan had colored inspirational pictures or messages. Bob picked up each bootie, one at a time, to examine their messages. By the time he was finished, his spirits were markedly lifted. These students from Michigan had sent him just the support he needed. The booties, however, were too slippery to use on the dogs' feet - but they were just what the teams needed to keep them focused on the difficult job in front of them.

Well, Bob saved those booties and continues to use them for inspiration every time he and his dogs get called to a scene. His gift to us was two of those highly treasured booties to help remind us that we're not out here alone - that people around the country care about our welfare, are supportive of our goals, and are quietly cheering for us to push on - regardless of the difficulties we face. Those booties, sent to Bob nearly three years ago, are still inspiring people around the country. Thank you, Bob, for sharing such a meaningful gift with us. We consider them priceless.

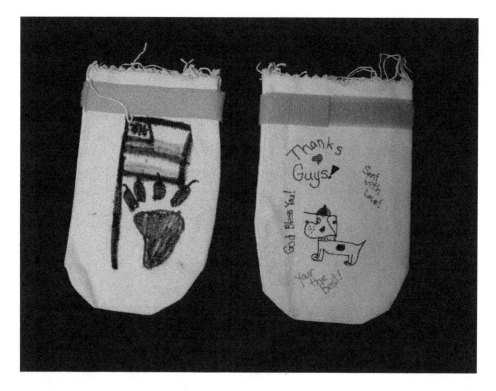

Tears were streaming down our faces as he gave us those booties. They gave him a boost during the searches of 9/11, and he was passing on this precious gift. After 172 days on the road, it meant so much to us to receive this heartwarming gift and to know people were behind us every day as we hit the pavement for another town. Many of our days had been grueling and this reminder that we had many people who were cheering us on meant the world to us. We were all choked up as we left for our next school visit.

We headed out to our afternoon school visit at Robert Muller Center For Living Ethics in Fairview, TX. The students' ages ranged from pre-school to elementary, so it was difficult for Blaine to keep the younger students engaged in the presentation. Thankfully they had a projector, so Blaine could share our route and some pictures from our ride to keep them interested. It was a small group of students and a couple of them came over to sit next to Max and Bailey to pet them while listening to Blaine. Again, after the presentation, the students got to pet the dogs in their sidecars. By the end of the day, Bailey was exhausted and just laid down in his sidecar with his goggles still on and fell asleep. I wished I could have joined him!

After such a long emotional day, we decided to just pick up a pizza and dine in for the evening. We had taught the next generation about service dogs and, in return, we had received a priceless gift that told us we were not alone on the road as we finished our journey. This was another treasure from the heart of America.

October 19 - Day 172: Dallas, TX - Georgetown, TX

It was time to leave Dallas and head to the Austin area. Before we left the Dallas area, we went to the Richardson, TX Comcast studio, where we filmed a 30-minute segment for a show called Insight Out. We were excited to once again be able to get more media coverage for our cause!

Once completed, we headed to Georgetown, TX which was outside of Austin. We were looking forward to staying with a friend of ours who used to work for Blaine when he was at Cisco Systems in the Research Triangle Park, NC. Larry Russell now lived in Georgetown and offered to let us stay with his family while we were in the Austin area. It was wonderful to again stay with friends. It was fun to catch up with them and have a relaxing evening.

Our charity partner, Canines Partners for Life, had contacted us a few days earlier and asked us to name one of their new puppies. We were honored to name a future service dog. After batting around several names, Blaine and I named the puppy April, after one of our most hardworking volunteers. Blaine announced the new puppy's name in his journal entry for the day.

That evening, it thrilled us to receive pictures of the first few pages of our calendar, and Jay was doing a phenomenal job of designing it. It was fascinating to see our idea become a reality with an incredible calendar layout.

October 20 - Day 173: Georgetown, TX

We were happy to have a leisurely morning where we enjoyed a relaxing breakfast and again chatted with our friends. After 172 days on the road, we were grateful to not be in another restaurant. No rushing and no interruptions from people asking about our ride. We savored the food while it was hot and were not multitasking with marketing our charity ride.

My cousin, Nancy, informed me we had made it into their local newspaper, the Fountain Hills Times. Our article and pictures took up the entire front page of the Inside Fountain Hills section. She said it was a good article, and they even included our website so everyone could follow our adventures.

In the early afternoon, we went to Knowles Elementary School, where we did another presentation.

Later in the afternoon, we were excited for another television interview where the local CBS affiliate, KEYE, came out to our friend's house and interviewed us about our ride.

October 21 - Day 174: Georgetown, TX

The day started out with an exciting interview...Blaine was on the national Bob and Tom radio show! We were ecstatic to be featured on this national radio morning program. While the interview was at 7AM, they had already been talking about our charity and sharing our website, so we started seeing an increase in traffic. The interview with them went very well and by the end of the day, we saw almost 360,000 hits on our website. Now that was an awesome way to get the news out about our charity ride! It amazed us at the tremendous response that we got from that one radio spot!

Our first school visit of the day was to the Texas School for the Deaf. We had been a little nervous about this visit since these students were living every day with a disability. What we found with our visit there was that we ended up being the ones with the disability for the day. Even though the students there could not hear, they all knew sign language. Therefore, they could talk to each other with ease and usually could read our lips and understand what we were saying. It was the two of us who could not read the sign language. We had to have an interpreter.

The presentation that Blaine did was very well received. They had put a person up on stage next to him to sign everything he was saying. We both noticed that they ended up switching the person doing the signing. Blaine was quick to figure out why. He had been telling the story of our journey and was verbally mapping out our journey. His description included many state names..."we started in North Carolina, went west to Oklahoma, up one state to Kansas, back east to West Virginia, up to Maine, west to Washington, down the Pacific coast to California and then east to Texas". He looked over to the interpreter after they changed and said, "you have to spell every state name, don't you?" The answer was "yes" and we all laughed as he had completely worn out the first interpreter!

Our next stop was another school visit at Bowie High School, where we sat outside under an oak tree and talked to their special needs students about service dogs. The next to last stop for the day was at Dogstuff in Austin. The news station, KVUE-TV, caught up with us there where they interviewed us for their evening news.

The final event for the day was at the Legendary Hill's Cafe and was co-sponsored by Austin Harley-Davidson. The Austin HD group saved us a spot right up front near their booth. Blaine even got invited up on stage between Doak Short and The Dirty Dogs to introduce the audience to our ride and cause.

It was an extremely long and eventful day, but we were happy to have had wonderful school visits, fun events, and amazing press coverage! We climbed into bed well past 11pm, exhausted, yet ecstatic on a very successful day.

October 22 - Day 175: Georgetown, TX - Houston, TX

After such a busy day the previous day, we really did not want to crawl out of bed to start our long day. Our route was going to be a long one, 182 miles, plus we had to say goodbye to our friends yet again!

The ride was on the highway the entire time, with no good photo opportunities along the way. When we arrived in Houston, we headed to the downtown studios of KHOU-TV for an interview. Blaine headed into the studios to let them know we had arrived, and the receptionist picked up the phone and announced, "We have dogs!" in an animated voice. A couple minutes later, we were greeted with many of the staff who came out to visit with Max and Bailey. Our story aired on the 5pm and 10pm newscasts, so we were already a hit in Houston.

October 23 - Day 176: Houston, TX

After so many days of riding through the desert areas, we had gotten used to the sunshine. We had not gotten used to the blazing heat, but we were liking all the sunshine. Then along came Houston. We woke to pouring rains with high winds. With no break in the rain, we decided we had to cancel our radio interview, which was the first media event that we had to cancel. We ended up hanging out at the hotel, looking out the window wishing the rain would ease up.

It finally stopped for a few hours before our afternoon event, but it came back with a vengeance once we got Max and Bailey in their sidecars. Since we were already loaded up, we headed on over to the event at The Ice House. We were definitely a grumbling pair as we sloshed our way over to the event. Like a couple of drowned rats, we wandered into the event. The rain eventually subsided, and we ended up meeting some really nice people and were happy that we trudged through the rain to get there.

October 24 - Day 177: Houston, TX - Beaumont, TX

The day turned out to be sunny, and we did not have an event to rush towards, so we took a 12-mile detour off our route to go to the Waterford Harbor Marina in Kemah, TX to visit some cruising friends. After many days of events and fourteen days spent in one state, we enjoyed our leisurely day heading to our last stop in the big state of Texas!

October 25 - Day 178: Beaumont, TX - Lafayette, LA

We finally crossed into our 43rd state! YAY! Only 5 more to go! Wow, I could not believe we were so close! Unfortunately, we ended up crossing into Louisiana on a bridge, so we did not get a chance to take a picture at the state line. Darn! Therefore, our first Louisiana pictures were taken at the rest area. We got lovely pictures of the swampland, and a very unique spider. Wonderful...my favorite...spiders! Ick! "Can you find something a little more attractive than a spider for our Louisiana pictures?" I ask Blaine. "He was really unique...and made an awesome picture!" he exclaimed. "Great", I thought. Nice photography of a spider? Not looking very positive for the introduction to the state...I despised spiders! Spiders and swampland may not have been a good start, but New Orleans was not far away! I started thinking about Bourbon Street and Beignets (excellent doughnuts famous in New Orleans).

Until that day, Oklahoma had the honor of being the state with the worst roads. Well, Louisiana had just won that honor! We road on Interstate 10 into Louisiana. We noticed the road surface change at the border. We immediately went into a hypnotic bump, bump, bump mode. The road was built in 20-foot pieces and not attached to each other very well. Therefore, we spent MANY miles with this maddening bump, bump, bump feeling as we headed over the highway pieces. "OK, this has definitely won the prize for worst road!", I groaned to Blaine. "Absolutely!" he replied. How many more miles did we need to ride on this insane road? Thump, thump, thump, thump, thump, thump, thump. OK, how long could we stand this before we went insane?! Thump, thump, thump, thump, thump, thump, thump. I really could not imagine the rest of our miles like this. How many more miles did we have? 70ish? Oh boy! After about 20 miles of this thumping, we decided we needed lunch and a break for our kidneys, who had not enjoyed this incessant thumping. We pulled off and found a nice little Sonic that offered welcoming shade and friendly clientele.

Thankfully, shortly after we got back onto the Interstate, the road went back to normal with no more thumping. We were extremely relieved! It was uneventful until we arrived at our hotel. First, we had no internet and Blaine had to finally go down and help them reset the wireless router. Later that evening, our toilet overflowed. The hotel decided it would just be best to move us to another room. While after 177 days of unpacking our bikes with our huge amount of gear (luggage, T-shirt cases, laptops, dog stuff, etc.), we really did not appreciate having to move all that stuff twice for the evening! While we were grateful that we were using one of our free coupons and were not paying for this room, it was a test of our patience when we just wanted to be settled for the night.

October 26 - Day 179: Lafayette, LA - Cut Off, LA

Our route was 137 miles for the day; first on US-90 and then along LA-1. It was a flat road that took us through many small towns. While stopped at a gas station, I overheard a gentleman talking about going to the Bayou. I knew then that we were in Louisiana. As we rode down the small road of LA-1, there was a canal that paralleled the road and we saw many docks with working boats tied up to them. I was not sure where the Bayou was, but I felt like we were there. After missing being on our boat, it was a comfort to be along the water again. We stayed at a little motel in Galliano, LA since we had a school visit the next day in Cut Off, LA.

October 27 - Day 180: Cut Off, LA - Lutcher, LA

The fifth-grade teacher at Cut-Off Elementary had contacted us back in April and asked us to visit with them on our way through Louisiana. In preparation for our visit, the students and parents held a Pickles and Sweets event to raise money for Max and Bailey's ride. They presented us with a check for $443.68. It surprised us with what this small town had raised for our ride and our cause. We were honored to also have the parents join us for our presentation and to meet Max and Bailey. Their generosity again humbled us.

On our way to Lutcher, we passed a shrimp boat docked in the canal and stopped for a photo op. It was white, trimmed in weathered pale pastel green with rusting rigging. We felt like we were home since we were used to seeing all the shrimp boats in our home waters of North Carolina. We parked the bikes next to it and Blaine set up the miniature tripod, snapping a picture of us next to this comforting remembrance of home.

October 28 - Day 181: Lutcher, LA - New Orleans, LA

We headed off to another really out of the way school for the day, Lutcher High School, 45 miles outside of New Orleans. We headed out on Interstate 10 with my trusty GPS mapping our route...hoping it could find its way when we got to the small country roads. We had been told we may get a police escort, but had gotten no word on where to meet them, so we assumed it would not happen. My trusty GPS stated to go 28.2 miles to exit 194. We got to the exit and took a left onto Hwy. 641. I prayed that the GPS was right because we were really in the middle of nowhere...just us and a whole bunch of swampland. It was a bit eerie.

After about a mile on this road, we had a motorcycle policeman pull in front of us and motion us to pull over. "I hope this is our police escort!" I exclaimed to Blaine through the CB. "Because if it is not, I believe we will be in a lot of trouble out here." The officer stepped off his motorcycle and came to talk to us. He was young and attractive but appeared gruff as he had a serious look on his face and was not smiling, so, boy, was I nervous! Of course, since I was the lead bike, he walked up to talk to me; I was starting to sweat! He introduced himself as Officer

Travis Lawless of the St. James Parish Sheriff's motorcycle division. Ugh! We were in the middle of nowhere in the swampland of Louisiana and we got pulled over by Officer "Lawless"...how ironic! This was looking a little scary! Thankfully, he then stated that he was our escort into Lutcher. "Whew"; I breathed out an enormous sigh of relief! It would have just been nice if he would have smiled, so we would have known he was on our side.

He did a fine job in escorting us all the way to Lutcher High School, where we had another awesome reception by hundreds of students and staff. We had an attentive audience as Blaine used one of their star football players to put in the imaginary wheelchair to show how his life would change with just the right hit to him in a game to make him paralyzed and dependent on that chair. It hit home with the students again.

After our presentation, we were presented with another check for our charity and Max and Bailey were blessed with gifts for them too: two gigantic rawhide bones dressed in purple and gold ribbon...their school colors, of course! We headed out to the motorcycles to let the students pet Max and Bailey after we loaded them in their sidecars. Many staff and students bought Max and Bailey T-shirts. Officer Lawless finally gave us a smile and bought a T-shirt from us as well. Even with the gruff, "boy, you are in deep trouble" exterior, he was indeed a really nice guy who was supportive of our charity. Another splendid story of small-town America. What an excellent morning!

We spent the afternoon at Harley-Davidson of New Orleans at their kickoff event before the Steel Pony Express event started the next day. Afterwards, we headed to the house of one of our volunteers who was instrumental in organizing our Steel Pony events. Carolyn Kerner was a Paws With A Cause field trainer and our gracious host for the next four nights.

October 29 - Day 182: New Orleans, LA

Our event for the next three days, the Steel Pony Express motorcycle rally and music festival, was in its seventh year and had an attendance of over 50,000. Their bands included Big and Rich, Lynyrd Skynyrd, and Blood Sweat and Tears. There were motorcycle manufacturers there showing off their custom motorcycles and fancy choppers. It also included 300 vendors, and we were excited to be included as one of their vendors.

The word for the day was HOT! The extreme heat and humidity came to a surprise to us as we were nearing the end of October. We were wilting out in the heat and welcomed the few clouds that passed by to block the blistering sun.

Finally, one of our volunteers brought a couple of big fans to get the air moving around us. We were given two ice packs to keep Max and Bailey cool. They were the round bags that were twisted up to a metal cap which you filled with ice. They were white with blue stars, and they were a hit with Max and Bailey. We were grateful that we were at least under a tent which kept the direct sun off us.

A steady crowd visited us all day, and we ended with $297 in donations and $514 in logo gear sales. Not bad for what is known as the slowest day of the event. We still had Saturday and Sunday ahead of us, so we were excited to be there for two more days.

October 30 - Day 183: New Orleans, LA

The weather did not improve as we greeted everyone who visited our booth again for the second day in a row. By the middle of the day, we had sweat dripping constantly from us. The weather did not keep the crowds from attending and visiting us at our booth. Media reps like those from Thunder Roads and Cycle Connections came by to get our story about our ride.

Carolyn surprised us by bringing a couple of carved pumpkins for our booth. One of them was intricately detailed with the Hogs for Dogs logo. They were amazing! As the sun set, we lit the lights inside the pumpkins. They were so cool and a perfect touch for our Halloween weekend at the rally.

Our board member, Steve, and his wife, Janet, came down to attend this event, so we were lucky to join them for dinner. The hugs from them were priceless! It was heartwarming to have friends from home with us and we enjoyed a delightful time catching up with each other. Steve had been doing an excellent job of keeping our large events organized. We were grateful to have him on our team.

October 31 - Day 184: New Orleans, LA

Against our hopes and wishes, the last day of the rally was just as hot and humid as the other two. October 31st and record heat! The long, hot events were taking a toll on us, and we were glad that the event ended at 6pm instead of the previous days of 8pm. The crowds continued to visit us throughout the day. Blaine took a break from our booth and he and Max went exploring. He chatted with many of the custom bike builders and took pictures of Max in front of all the cool custom bikes and choppers.

We were joined by one of the Paws With A Cause Assistance Dogs, who held the handle of a bright orange plastic Halloween bucket asking for donations for our cause. How could you resist that cuteness? People stopped and dropped donations in the bucket, which gave us the perfect opportunity to let them know what other tasks Assistance Dogs could do.

While we were at the event, a young gentleman in a wheelchair named Chad Ferrand approached us. He loved Max and Bailey and told us he was on the waiting list for an Assistance Dog. Unfortunately, he also told us that his application had been misplaced and, after already waiting for a few years, he had to start at the end of the line as they put in a new application for him. We were heartbroken to hear this and to know how long he would have to wait for an Assistance Dog. We told him we would contact our organizations to see if we could assist in any way. This story emphasized why we were doing our ride…to shorten the time it took to get an Assistance Dog.

Finally, after three exhausting days, we packed up the booth and headed back to Carolyn's house. It was nice to just chill at her house for the evening. We were grateful for the wonderful hospitality that she provided and all the hard work she put in to organize our booth at the rally, as well as rounding up so many volunteers to help us. We were again humbled by all the people who made our ride such a success.

November

November 1 - Day 185: New Orleans, LA - Hattiesburg, MS

After several days of wonderful events in New Orleans, it was time to move on to the next state, Mississippi, our 44th state. Maybe heading north a little ways would give us a break in the heat and humidity…was it really November 1st with all this heat? We packed up our bikes again and hit the road. It had been nice to have a couple of days where we did not have to unpack and pack our massive amount of gear!

Our trip for the day seemed like it would be pretty uneventful...another boring day on the interstates again. The route would take us on I-10 over the tail end of Lake Pontchartrain and then onto I-59 to Hattiesburg, MS. Heading over the bridge of Lake Pontchartrain, Blaine yelled "Ow!". "What's wrong?" I asked. "Your bike just spit up some debris, like a piece of wood, and it hit my foot! Didn't you see it?" "Sorry," I exclaimed, "but I did not see anything. Would have avoided it if I had!" There seemed to be a lot of debris around this area, but we continued onto our destination.

A little while later, I heard Blaine back in my ear. "Uh, I believe your dog needs a little help," he said while laughing. I looked over at Bailey and he was in his usual position for riding...laying down with his head hanging out the right side of the sidecar, enjoying the breeze. Only this time all I could see of his head was this big Snoopy looking nose with a white plastic bag over it! Bailey had caught a flying grocery bag onto his face! I started laughing at him and tried to get myself into a position where I could help him. We were cruising down the Interstate at 60 mph and I knew I needed to set my cruise control and get to a point where I could safely lean over far enough to reach his head on the far side of the sidecar...a difficult and dangerous task! The major problem I was having was that I was laughing so hard that I could not see because of the tears streaming down my face. Yikes! How was I going to do this? I kept thinking that he would duck his head inside or turn it to the side so the bag would automatically get blown away, but he continued to ride along with it over his nose, goggles, and ears! He just acted like it was natural and just waited for me to help him. I finally got my cruise control set and, after several attempts, was able to carefully lean over enough to snag the bag off his head and stuff it into the sidecar. Bailey gave me a grateful look that said, "It's about time you got that off my head" and Blaine and I continued to laugh at him uncontrollably for the next 20 minutes. I'm not sure how I stayed on the road because I was crying streams of tears with all my hysterical laughter. As I wiped tears from my eyes, I thought that was definitely a scene you would see in a Peanuts cartoon! Goofy Bailey again made our boring day a little brighter with his silly antics!

Later that evening, when Blaine was making his usual check-in call to Deb Davis, we found out that Chad had already contacted them and was in the process of filling out an application. While there were no promises that he would receive a dog, the ball was in motion, and we knew PAWS was going to hustle to get the needs assessment done as soon as possible. We hoped that this coming year would be the year that Chad received his Assistance Dog.

November 2 - Day 186: Hattiesburg, MS - Meridian, MS

The next morning, we got up ready to hit the Waffle House next door to the motel and then head to Meridian, MS where we would meet an old friend of Blaine's family. Blaine said he had woken up at 3AM to excruciating pain in his left foot and, if he had been given the choice at the time, he would have amputated it! He initially thought that it was caused by the board that had hit his foot the previous day, but after thinking about the type of pain he was having, the realization finally hit him. It was GOUT!

Remember when we went to get our physicals to make sure that we were fit for the trip? We had received the green light for the ride with one (non-fatal) warning. Blaine's uric acid was close to the levels that would cause the very painful arthritic condition called gout. After 185 days, the doctor's prediction came true -- painfully true! He realized that he had eaten several things the previous days that contributed to his elevated uric acid levels...peanuts, shrimp, and beer.

Blaine tried to stand up, but he yelped and sat back down on the bed. I worried that we would not make our trip that day...and how many days after that? He took some Advil and, after realizing what it was that was actually causing the pain, he took his medication for gout that the doctor had given him. We were really thankful that we were prepared for this problem and the doctor had given us medication just in case it occurred during the trip! Thank you, Dr. Griffin!

I told him I would feed and take the dogs out for the morning. After getting the dogs settled, we headed next door to the Waffle House for breakfast if Blaine could hobble over there. He managed to hobble, and we tried to enjoy our greasy, but yummy, breakfast. One more challenge for the ride was facing us. We were both concerned that Blaine could not switch gears on the motorcycle with this condition. We discussed our options and finished our breakfast. As we walked back to the motel, Blaine decided that he would give it a try to see if we could make our destination for the night, Meridian, MS. We only had 85 miles to travel that day, so it would be one of our shorter days. I let Blaine rest his foot while I packed the bikes with the gear and got the dogs ready to go. We headed out, and I told Blaine that his pain today was nothing compared to the challenges facing the people we were riding for everyday. He agreed and was a trooper that day...bearing the pain with every gear change and being very thankful that the day was again a long interstate ride, keeping the gear changes to a minimum.

Unfortunately, it was also a very wet ride, so we were all thrilled to get to our motel for the evening.

Thankfully, the rain kept our stops short with nobody stopping to talk to us. Therefore, we reached our destination in a record-breaking amount of time compared to all our other days.

Blaine's friend, Don Shehane, lived in Meridian. Blaine knew Don from long ago when Blaine was growing up overseas. Don lived on the navy base with Blaine in Iceland and then again in Hawaii. Since Blaine's dad was often on a navy ship, Don became like a second father to Blaine. He taught him how to play baseball and his mentorship helped Blaine develop his giving nature. His influence stayed with Blaine throughout his adult life.

That evening, we went over to Don's house to meet his family and then they took us out to dinner. It was fun catching up with them.

November 3 - Day 187: Meridian, MS - Auburn, AL

Blaine woke up with less pain in his foot, which was good because we had a very long day ahead of us. The route for the day took us up Interstate 20 for about 20 miles and then around 125 miles on Highway 80 to Montgomery. In Montgomery, we went back to the interstates, traveling on Interstate 65 and then Interstate 85 to Opelika. Remember the friends of ours who helped us with our first school visit near Raleigh, NC? They had moved to Alabama, and we had plans to stay with them for the night. We were excited to see them again after more than six months on the road. We knew there would be a home-cooked meal waiting for us as well.

Our excitement quickly turned to frustration as we sloshed through another rainy day. We had one of our longest riding days ahead, 218 miles, and it was a miserable pouring rain. We again had to remind ourselves why we were riding. We had to keep those images in our mind the entire ride. As each one of us got discouraged, the other one would recall one of the people we had met who still needed an Assistance Dog. Those images were the only thing that got us through that day.

As we exited off Interstate 20 onto Highway 80, we knew we were entering our 45th state. I mentioned this as we crossed over and my comment was returned with a monotone "Yay". We were not really in the mood to celebrate this accomplishment. The day was dark, the rain was relentless, the winds were gusty, and the visibility was extremely low. Highway 80 was very difficult to maneuver in these conditions. We went through Selma, Alabama, which would have been a great place to take a little time to do some sightseeing. Think of all the Civil Rights history in that town! With the treacherous weather, we had to continue on to our destination. Even though we usually loved the highways instead of the interstates, the interstate was a welcome sight when we finally got to Interstate 65. We wound our way around Montgomery and then onto Interstate 85. By this time, it was getting dark, and we were exhausted. We just wanted to get to our home for the night.

It was a very welcome sight to finally get to our exit and know we only had 3 miles to go until we arrived at our friends' house.

As I look at the journal entry for that day, there was no journal entry. The following day Blaine mentioned our ride and categorized it in our top 3 worst days on the trip. He stated the dogs stayed very dry and comfortable in their cozy sidecars and that we, on the other hand, had cold puddles in our underwear, again!

We had crossed into our 45th state, but it was so rainy and miserable that we just kept on going towards our destination with no fanfare or pictures.

November 4 - Day 188: Auburn, AL - Atlanta, GA

Max and Bailey entered their 46th state! Only two more to go! We were excited to see the sun shining as we left our friends' house and were grateful for some cooler weather. Not long after we started our 131-mile ride, we came to the Georgia border and stopped at the welcome to Georgia sign for a photo op. We were able to get Max and Bailey out of their sidecars to get a nice picture in front of the sign. With better weather, we could celebrate our crossing into our 46th state.

We were happy to stay on the outskirts of Atlanta to get to Roswell, GA which was a suburb of Atlanta. Our stay was donated by La Quinta, which was always a welcomed stay and we were happy to be settled in the same place for the next couple of nights.

November 5 - Day 189: Atlanta, GA

We did not consider that we would run into traffic, so we were a little late to our school visit at Grayson Elementary School. The students were excited to see us arrive and gave us a hearty welcome. They were very attentive as Blaine explained what service dogs could do and were enthusiastic when then finally got to pet Max and Bailey in their sidecars.

Our next stop was at The Red Bandana for our Dog Wash event. Volunteers helped wash dogs in the store's do-it-yourself dog wash for a $10 donation. They even gave Max and Bailey a wash for free. The Store was donating all proceeds to support efforts to train twelve Golden Retrievers and donate them as Assistance

Dogs for the disabled. It was a wonderful event, and we were grateful for the excellent dog-washing volunteers!

November 6 - Day 190: Atlanta, GA

They held our event for the day at Killer Creek Harley-Davidson with a full day of activities starting at 10AM and ending at 5PM. It was a tremendous event, and we were overwhelmed at everything that our friends, Robert and Carolyn Wilson, and other volunteers had organized for it.

Local businesses and individuals had donated valuable items for a silent auction. The singer Don Law rocked the crowd with his pro-bono performance. There was a demonstration by the Alpharetta Police Canine Patrol. Dogs came dressed up for the Doggie Fashion Show and Contest. Their talent was also showcased at the Dog Trick Contest, which even included a small pig in a denim Harley jacket and hat who moonwalked! Unfortunately, I was manning our booth selling logo gear while Max and Bailey greeted the crowds. However, Blaine swears that is what the little pig did!

During the event, Mayor Jere Wood declared the day to be Hogs for Dogs Day in Roswell, GA. He gave us the following Proclamation:

Proclamation

Office of the Mayor

Whereas, U.S. Hogs for Dogs is a collective effort with select organizations to amplify awareness of programs and create fundraising opportunities through unique charity motorcycle events across America; and

Whereas, U.S. Hogs for Dogs in partnership with students and schools, plant the seed for future generation of civic-minded individuals in the hopes that supporting charities and actively helping those in need will become a priority in their lives; and

Whereas, Two Golden Retrievers, Max and Bailey, and the Crew of the 2004 Hogs for Dogs Charity Ride has been supported by a dedicated network of volunteers and has been very successful in maximizing financial resources so that contributions can be distributed to the causes for which they ride: and

Whereas, The U.S. Hogs for Dogs Crew has crisscrossed miles of the back roads of small-town America and our big cities encouraging others to share in their commitment to making a measurable difference in their hometowns.

NOW, THEREFORE, I, Jere Wood, Mayor of the City of Roswell, do hereby proclaim Saturday, November 6th, 2004, as Hogs for Dogs Day in Roswell and urge all citizens to join me in expressing appreciation to the community, the volunteers, our motorcycle community, and the management of Killer Creek Harley Davidson for all their hard work and dedication.

In witness whereof, I have hereunto set my hand and caused the seal of the City or Roswell to be affixed this 6th day of November, 2004.

Jere Wood, Mayor

We were pleasantly surprised when we were visited by a couple from Fairburn, GA who we had met when we were driving through Glacier National Park. They had been following our adventures via our website journals since that brief encounter and came to our event to make a $500 donation. We were astounded by their generosity!

At the end of the day, we were exhausted after all the festivities, but were astonished at the final tally of $4,822.45 raised from the event! We were grateful for all the volunteers who rallied together to pull off this remarkable event.

The Wilsons were gracious enough to also offer us a place to stay at their house, so we could relax for the evening.

November 7 - Day 191: Atlanta, GA - Macon, GA

After a long, busy day, we were happy to have a day where we had no events. It was nice to ease into the day while visiting our friends. Eventually, we drove down the interstate for a couple of hours, taking our time with no deadlines to rush towards.

November 8 - Day 192: Macon, GA - Tifton, GA

We again were grateful for a leisurely morning where we could catch up on our rest. Around mid-day, we loaded our bikes and headed the 32 miles to the Sacred Heart School in Warner Robins, GA. It was a Catholic school, and all the students wore uniforms. It reminded me of my elementary days where I also attended a Catholic school where uniforms were mandatory...a white button-down shirt with a plaid skirt where the skirt had to be down to the middle of your knees. As usual, the students were a delight, and they enjoyed hearing about our ride and getting to meet Max and Bailey.

We continued down the interstate all the way to Tifton, GA where we found our Red Roof Inn for the night. Once Blaine logged into his email, he gave me the disappointing news. We had been communicating via email with a major network morning show and they had come back with a final reply that they were not interested in airing a segment on our ride. We were so disappointed because it would have been a perfect way to get the word out about service dogs! Our ride had proven that most people did not even know about other service dogs other than guide dogs. We were bummed that we could not educate the masses on this major network show.

November 9 - Day 193: Tifton, GA - Tallahassee, FL

B laine's journal entry for the day gave a wonderful flavor for our day:

We've seen more interstates than we ever cared to see over the last month of this charity ride. Our goal when we left home - navigationally - was to travel on primarily back roads and smaller highways. Somewhere between Texas and Georgia, we had lost our way and found ourselves staring at dashed white lines as they blinked by at 70 mph. We did not enjoy it, but it was required if we wanted to get to our events on time. Today, we found our way back to those small roads.

The day began at Little River Harley-Davidson in Tifton, Georgia. We pulled in for a picture in front of the shop for our ABC's of Harley program - a program where you take your photo in every state and at national parks, etc. What we got was more than a photo. We met great people like Don and Brad, who listened to our story and then recommended a small grill in Moultrie, GA for lunch.

Hwy 319 South was our route, and though there are four lanes (two each way), the drivers all had that small town, wave-as-you-go kind of attitude. We smiled all the way into Moultrie, past the beautiful old courthouse and around the corner to Vern & Firewaters Blue Sky Grill, where there was a parking space right up front. If you're wondering - Interstates do not lead you to places like this.

Max & Bailey were already surrounded by men in ties and women in their business clothes as we found two stools at the bar where we could see the dogs. The people inside ran the gamut from business folks on their lunch break to a woman's group and us two bikers at the bar. We made friends easily, had the local paper show up for an interview, and the Grill's proprietor buy our lunch - and several T-shirts, too.

Yes, indeed. We had been missing these people while we were out chasing dashed lines on the Interstate highways. Today, we came home.

Thank you, Don and Brad, for the lunch recommendation. A very special thanks to Randy Banister for buying our lunch and to Deb and Christie for making our visit to the Blue Sky Grill so relaxing and delicious. And thank you Moultrie, Georgia for reminding us of what we'd been missing while we raced from place to place on Interstates.

We had a wonderful, laid-back ride on the back roads that day; happy to be off the interstates for a change. Our stop at the Blue Sky Grill reminded us again of small-town America and our search for the true heart of America. Everybody in the restaurant came to chat with us and many went out to greet Max and Bailey to give them pets. The owner bought our lunch for us and $70 worth of T-shirts! We also received an interview with the local paper. As we left, we felt it had been a very successful lunch, spreading the word about our cause.

After an awesome lunch, we felt invigorated by the small-town hospitality. This was what we had been looking for when we started our ride. It did indeed still exist out there and we were elated to find it once again. We continued on as we entered our 47th state, Florida! Only one state to go in order to hit our final 48-state mark! We were getting excited that we were so close to our goal of traveling all 48 states!

Our ride ended at yet another cheap motel. While we usually stayed at cheaper motels to keep costs down for the organization and most of them were pretty decent, this was not one of them. This was one of those times where we just had to take one for the team! It was hard to know what the surrounding area would be like when I booked a motel. Wish I had Google Maps back then! We debated on whether to find another place to stay since we had 3 nights to stay in Tallahassee, but decided we had events that would keep us occupied during the days, so we opted to stay. It was dark and seedy, but I decided I would keep Bailey with me any time I needed to be outside of the room without Blaine. Not surprising to see years later that the motel no longer exists!

November 10 - Day 194: Tallahassee, FL

Happy to leave our seedy motel, we arranged to meet some of our volunteers at Cracker Barrel before our events of the day. We met our volunteers and planned out our day. We had originally reserved our time that day to be on the old State Capitol Building lawn for an event. We had invited the state's legislators and Florida's new agency for people with disabilities to join us for an event to promote their local programs to support their citizens living with physical disabilities. But they failed to respond to our invitations.

We decided to appear at the State Capitol Building and our volunteers had arranged for the local TV station, WCTV, to interview us about our ride. We met their news anchor and filmed a nice piece for their Peculiar Pastimes segment to tell their viewers about our ride.

We spent our afternoon outside of the prestigious Maclay School teaching their middle school students about service dogs. While the students sat on the bleachers overlooking their soccer field, Blaine explained why we were doing our ride and what service dogs could do. We had two volunteers from PAWS with their demo dogs join us to demonstrate many of the tasks that service dogs can do. One student from the school's Animal Club sat in the wheelchair as our volunteer for the demonstration. The students enjoyed the presentation and demonstration, but definitely loved the time they got to greet and pet Max and Bailey. The Animal Club pledged a $200 donation to our cause with the other students also collecting to increase their donation.

November 11 - Day 195: Tallahassee, FL

In honor of Veterans Day, we attended the Veterans Day parade in downtown Tallahassee. For this parade, we were not participants, but instead were on the sidelines. We found a great parking space where we could park the motorcycles next to the parade route. We took Max and Bailey out of their sidecars for a bit so they could greet the PAWS volunteers and demo dogs that had joined us. After a while, we put them back into their sidecars to continue watching the parade, and I sat sidesaddle on my motorcycle, chatting with people as they came to visit Bailey. The parade participants smiled at Max and Bailey with their patriotic red, white and blue bandanas as they lounged in their sidecars enjoying the parade.

After the parade, we went to Barnaby's Pizza for a casual meet and greet. Always happy to go to events where there is pizza!

It was threatening to rain on our way back to the motel, but when we passed a Petsmart on the way we decided to risk the rain and pick up some dog food since we were running low. Because of the rain threat, I told Blaine I would make a quick run in and purchase the food. But Bailey would have nothing of it! He knew it was Petsmart and that he always got to pick out a new toy when visiting. I do not know how he knew it was a Petsmart, since we had never been to this location before, but it must have had that "Petsmart smell". He would not allow me to leave him in the sidecar. He whined and tried to climb out of the sidecar, which is something he had never done after 194 days on the road. Giving in, I took him with me, so we could get some dog food and, of course, a new toy for Bailey.

November 12 - Day 196: Tallahassee, FL - Ocala, FL

I had downloaded two routes in my GPS for this section; one which was 172 miles and a scenic route and another which was 176 miles and was on the interstate. We awoke to rain with a forecast of just more rain. We had a very uneventful, wet, sloppy ride on the interstate down to Ocala. Along the way, we discussed the fact that we really should buy new rain gear, since ours was not really keeping us all that dry at this point. But we decided we were getting close to the end of the ride, and we would just continue to slosh along in the gear we had.

After trudging through the rains, we were excited to finally get to our La Quinta hotel and get into a dry room. Of course, the dogs were dry in their nice, covered sidecars, but they still enjoyed being off the bikes and into a dry room as well.

November 13 - Day 197: Ocala, FL - Tampa, FL

We headed out on the 94-mile trip to Tampa, FL, where our event for the day was being held. It had been a nice day for most of our trip, but about 20 miles from our destination, the rain began to fall. We were so disappointed. Not another rained out event! We rode up to Brandon Harley-Davidson, and they gave us a warm welcome. The sun appeared, but they had a nice big tent set up for us to park under, so we would stay dry if it rained again. They even made sure our bikes were super clean for the event! Nice!

We had one of the PAWS field reps helping us at this event, along with one of the PAWS recipients. Unfortunately, since it had been raining earlier in the day, we did not get a good turnout of folks coming out to see Max and Bailey. We still had a great time. They had a cool orange-red colored U.S. Mail stagecoach parked next to the building, so we went to get a few pictures of Max and Bailey in the stagecoach as well as a picture or two of Max and Bailey looking like they were pulling the stagecoach. We had a fun time with the pictures and have the cutest picture of Bailey with his head hanging out of the stagecoach window.

When the event was over, we found our La Quinta where we would spend the next four nights, since it would be an excellent central location for our upcoming events.

November 14 - Day 198: Tampa, FL

Today we had a special welcome as a local volunteer, Mike Denson, and a group of about ten riders escorted us from our hotel in Tampa to Fletcher's Harley-Davidson in Clearwater. We had fond memories of Clearwater from our sailing days, and we all enjoyed that smell of salt air again. Even Max and Bailey had their noses in the air. I also especially enjoyed the ride because I did not have to be the navigator for the day!

The event coordinator at Fletcher's had our parking place marked off with orange cones and we received a huge welcome as we arrived. A large group of riders that were there for our organized ride that started at 11:30 greeted us. While we waited for the start of the ride, large crowds came over to meet Max and Bailey and to buy our logo gear. We were even greeted by puppy raisers from three of our charity partners.

After a successful event, we spent the evening at our volunteer's house. Mike gave us a relaxing meal and even helped us bathe Max and Bailey so they would be clean for the school visits the next day. Again, we felt blessed to have met wonderful new friends and to enjoy their hospitality.

November 15 - Day 199: Tampa, FL

It was going to be a busy day. We headed the 48 miles to Pol Elementary in Lake Wales. We were happy to have a PAWS representative attend both of our presentations to be able to demonstrate what her demo dog could do.

After two presentations, we had to race 22 miles to the Karen M. Seigel Academy, which was a school dedicated to teaching students with moderate to severe physical disabilities. They escorted us into a covered circular pavilion where the students encircled that area. Unfortunately, the acoustics were terrible, so we had a hard time getting our message across. Even the service dog was distracted and could not even follow the well-known sign language commands. The echo just reverberated too much. The students still enjoyed the presentation, as well as meeting Max and Bailey. We were exhausted but satisfied with two more successful school visits. We appreciated being able to continue to educate students so they would learn the value of service dogs.

November 16 - Day 200: Tampa, FL

It was time for a rest day where we could catch up on emails, accounting, routing, and future events. We took a break in the middle of the day to travel to Largo to visit our friends at the Island Packet factory. The sailboat we owned was an Island Packet, and we were friends with many of the staff at the factory. They had invited the four of us for a factory visit.

It was a sweet reunion with many of our friends there. We had met them at many Island Packet rendezvous events and had become good friends with them. It was nice to be back at the factory that had manufactured our boat and to visit with our dear friends. While one of the staff took care of Max and Bailey, we took a tour of the factory to learn of the new editions being built. We also were able to take a picture of everyone along with us, the pups, and our bikes. It was such a fun day!

November 17 - Day 201: Tampa, FL - Naples, FL

Our morning was a leisurely one, where we continued to catch up on emails and accounting. In the afternoon we headed the 150 miles to Naples, where we were staying with Debbie's father and stepmother. We already knew them as we had visited them one Christmas when our boat was on the west coast of Florida. It was nice to see them again, and we appreciated their hospitality. It was always more relaxing to visit someone's house instead of being at a hotel. We spent the evening catching up with them over a quiet dinner.

November 18 - Day 202: Naples, FL

It was another busy day as we started it with two presentations to the third, fourth, and fifth graders at Tommy Barfield Elementary school on Marco Island. They split them into two groups, so we had presentations at 9:30am and 1:15pm. It was perfect timing since the students had just finished a section on Guide dogs as part of their reader series. While we were there, we noticed the cafeteria was lined with boxes filled with canned goods, ready to be picked up by the local Salvation Army. It was refreshing to see the students learning about service dogs and donating to a wonderful cause. We were impressed!

Unfortunately, our evening event was not as successful. We showed up at the church to find it locked up with no one around. We finally ran across one church member who was familiar with our ride and was mortified that, after all the emails asking us to join them, they had failed to actually set up the event! Disappointed, we headed back to our hosts for the evening. This was only our second cancellation in 202 days on the road, so we felt that we still had a successful ride so far. We ended the day with a delicious Chinese meal with our hosts as we enjoyed our last evening with them.

November 19 - Day 203: Naples, FL - Miami, FL

We said goodbye to our great hosts and started our race to Miami so we could get our balding back tires replaced. Our route was 132 miles along Hwy 41, which was also called Tamiami Trail. It went right through the Big Cypress National Preserve. We decided we had to at least stop and say hi to the local wildlife, so we stopped at one of the pull-offs to see them. Well, it was more of Blaine's idea to say hi because I really wanted nothing to do with them!

Alligators! I made sure it was a very quick stop. Blaine was interested in getting lots of pictures of them. I was not getting far from my bike! I had no clue how fast they could go and how high up they could reach, so I was not leaving Bailey there as bait! I kept encouraging Blaine to hurry up with his pictures while I kept inching back to my bike. He was finally satisfied that he had enough pictures, and I breathed a deep sigh of relief as we headed out of there.

When we got to Peterson's Harley-Davidson in Miami, our hearts sank as we found out they did not have any record of our appointment that Blaine had made the day before. We begged and pleaded with them. We told them about our trip and that we had been traveling and working almost every single day for 6 ½ months and we were just about to take a 3-day break in the Keys. If we could not get our tires replaced, we would not be able to enjoy our break. They were remarkable and jumped on the project immediately, even though they had a full house of bikes in their service department.

Thankfully, they were able to get our tires on and we were so grateful to them for saving our weekend off! We thanked them again and headed off to our Red Roof Inn for the night with our sights on the Keys the next day.

November 20 - Day 204: Miami, FL - Key West, FL

We sprung out of bed with excitement knowing we had the next three days off! We stopped by Peterson's Harley-Davidson on the way out because they said they would give us a bike wash before we headed out of town. While there, we met Debbie Campbell, who had recently completed a 48-state ride in 48 days for her 48th birthday. What an accomplishment! After having ridden through 47 states, we knew how much effort that was and to do it in 48 days was shocking. We immediately hit it off, and I thoroughly enjoyed chatting with her while we waited for our bikes. Before we left, she traded us two Peterson Harley-Davidson shirts for one of our Max and Bailey T-shirts.

With our bikes sparkling, we headed down scenic Overseas Hwy (Hwy 1) into the Keys. We could smell the salty air and see the Atlantic Ocean on our left side and the Florida Bay on our right side. The sun was shining, and we were in heaven! There were numerous bridges along the way as we island hopped our way down to Key West. We passed through Key Largo, Islamorada, and Marathon. Then the clouds moved in and started darkening...followed by rain. At least it was a warm rain, and we were in the Keys. We rode on.

With just 30 miles to go, we were tested again when my bike's shifting linkage broke! I told Blaine of my mishap as I slowed down and moved to the side of the road to stop. Nooooo! We were fit to be tied! I just wanted to cry. We sat there with deflated spirits on the side of the road, trying to figure out what to do. There was no Harley-Davidson dealership in the Keys. We both took a deep breath and tried to figure out a solution. Blaine's journal entry explained our solution:

All my boating skills came racing back to me. We were in the Keys, after all. I quickly reached for my tie-wraps and engineered a temporary fix to get us to Key West. If it breaks again, I have another set of tie-wraps ready for the job. We will not be deterred from enjoying a few days off. If anything else goes wrong - I am armed with duct tape, too!

We were back in business quickly and finished the last 30 miles into Key West. We navigated to the Center Court Bed & Breakfast, just a block off Duval Street! As we walked in, they greeted us with big smiles, and they started asking us questions about our ride. We had a good time telling them about our cause and the many miles, sights, and experiences we had so far, and that this was our weekend off. To our surprise, we ended up with a free night of lodging in one of their exquisite rooms, The Romantic Retreat. It was such a cool tropical room, and we felt like we were getting pampered. It was awesome! We took the dogs out to stretch their legs and then found a rum punch to sip as we relaxed outside of our room.

Along with the surprise of the free lodging, they handed us a package from Jay. It contained one of the Postcards from the Road calendars! Remember the process of us trying to pick out the best pictures of our trip? This was the end product, and Jay had done a tremendous job of designing the calendar. It was freaking awesome! Every time we turned to the next page, we were astounded at how phenomenal it looked. We were so excited by the final product and could not wait to offer them for sale.

Since Jay had them printed with a company that he had used in the past, they were outside of our normal logo gear distribution. Therefore, we ended up selling them through our website aside from our other logo gear and we asked for a volunteer who could keep track of the orders and mail them out for us. Remember Deb Davis in Michigan with Paws With A Cause? Her Mom, Mildred Simpkins, graciously volunteered to be that person. We were overjoyed that we could sell these cool calendars and have them quickly shipped out to our supporters!

Our evening ended with a walk down to Duval Street to grab a bite to eat and enjoy all the famous Key West entertainment. After the low of having another bike mechanical failure, the day certainly turned around with seeing our amazing calendar and being able to enjoy the excitement of Key West!

November 21 - Day 205: Key West, FL - Islamorada, FL

With excitement, we awoke to anticipation of a homecoming in Islamorada! But first we had to check out of our cottage and thank them for their impressive hospitality. It was a beautiful place, and we wished we could have stayed there a couple more nights.... especially since it was only a block away from Duval Street.

Before we left Key West, we decided on seeing all the famous sights, so we headed down to the Southern Most Point monument for a picture with the pups next to it.

We then wandered around Key West to see many of the places we had seen while cruising, as we enjoyed all the interesting looks we got from all the tourists. We went looking for the Wyland mural since he was one of my favorite artists. He had painted a beautiful underwater scene on the side of a building with many sea creatures in it. There were sharks, rays, turtles, and brightly colored fish swimming in it. It was phenomenal! We parked the bikes in front of it and took a picture of Max and Bailey with the mural.

Next, we drove to the famous post with all the wooden directional signs. Each wooden sign attached to the post showed a direction to a place with the distance in miles, such as Marblehead, Ohio 1342, Tucson, AZ 2057, Mobjack Bay, VA 925, and San Juan, Puerto Rico 1901. Many of the signs were faded, but this was an iconic stop in Key West. Again, we parked the bikes next to it and took Max and Bailey's picture.

We then had a fun ride back up the Keys to Islamorada. We enjoyed the smell of the salt air and the beautiful waters on both sides of us. Our destination for the night was very familiar to us. While cruising on our sailboat, we had visited Islamorada many times by boat where we anchored off the famous Lorelei's restaurant. It was a difficult anchorage to get to with the 5-foot draft on our boat, but we always managed to squeak on through without running aground.

Upon finding the little pink oceanfront resort for the night, we checked into the Sands of Islamorada. It was nicely surrounded by palm trees and was right on the ocean. We unpacked bikes and headed out to our favorite spot, Lorelei's, for a frosty tropical beverage. With Max and Bailey in their Doggles, we found a table on their white sand beach to relax and listen to the live music. We felt like we were home!

November 22 - Day 206: Islamorada, FL

We spent the day relaxing and catching up on emails, accounting, routing, and planning. As always, our big decisions of the day were where to eat for lunch and dinner and Lorelei's won both battles. With it being on the beach, having great food, and allowing the dogs to be with us, it won hands down.

While listening to the live music at Lorelei's the prior evening, we found out that one of our favorite singers was now playing at another bar down the road, so we had dinner at Lorelei's and then took the dogs back to lounge in our room while we headed to the other restaurant/bar to see Michael Crissan play. He remembered us from our cruising days when we had stopped and listened to him at Lorelei's. We shared our newest journey with him and listened with enjoyment to him playing his guitar and singing. We felt very relaxed and content on our last day off before heading north to the last few days of our ride.

November 23 - Day 207: Islamorada, FL - Miami, FL

With reluctance, we packed up the bikes and headed back to Miami. Goodbye Florida Keys...we will miss you! We headed along our 62-mile route and enjoyed our short ride up along the light blue waters. Our destination was, once again, Peterson's Harley-Davidson. They were surprised to see us back, but we showed them my bike and Blaine's makeshift fix using tie wraps. They were very impressed by Blaine's repair saying they had never seen a fix like that before, but it was quite ingenious! It did not take them long to fix my shift linkage, and we were on our way to our hotel.

November 24 - Day 208: Miami, FL - Merritt Island, FL

Our route for the day was going to be a long 211 miles along Interstate 95. We chose the interstate because it was going to be a long trip, whereas Hwy 1 would have had too many stops and a lower speed limit. We zipped along boring stretches of I-95 up to Merritt Island.

We were excited to meet our hosts for the next two nights, Bill and Katie Scholl. We had not met them before, but Bill's story with his Assistance Dog, Zeb, had been in every brochure that we handed out for the past seven months. We were ecstatic to meet him! Here is Bill's story:

Bill Scholl - a firefighter in Brevard County, Florida - was severely injured in a 1999 fall from a fire ladder. After the accident, his wife Kate was sure she could handle the home maintenance, yard work, auto care, and many of Bill's previous responsibilities. But knowing her husband's energetic nature, she feared that Bill would become depressed about the state of his health. Kate thought that an Assistance Dog would be the perfect antidote for that particular ill.

Prior to his accident, Bill was unaware of Assistance Dog programs. He knew about leaders dogs and bomb-sniffing dogs, but he had never heard of Assistance Dogs. Not so with Kate. In addition to being a registered nurse, Kate had once worked as a professional dog groomer. She had cared for numerous Assistance Dogs and knew what they could do.

Only one month after Bill's accident, Kate insisted that the family apply for an Assistance Dog from Paws With A Cause®. It was suggested that Bill take one year to adjust to life in a wheelchair. Kate and Bill took this advice, but Kate always knew that Bill would eventually have his Service Dog.

During his adjustment period, Bill did indeed become very depressed. He did not socialize with his friends or leave the house. Bill wondered what he could ever accomplish from within the confines of his wheelchair. He felt defeated and hopeless.

All that changed thanks to Zeb, Bill's new PAWS® Assistance Dog.

Today, Bill has both the confidence and ability to go out and tackle the world. In fact, he is currently training to become a certified teacher. His ultimate goal is to become state-certified to teach not only public school, but vocational firefighting, as well.

Kate feels that she, too, has benefited from adding Zeb to the family. Before Zeb arrived, Kate was uncomfortable leaving Bill at home alone. She has found that Bill's increased sense of security has allowed her to forge ahead with her life, and is now quite comfortable working and going out into the world, secure in the knowledge that Zeb is there for Bill.

Kate has also increased her commitment to PAWS. She has been instrumental in writing hospital policies regarding the care and handling of Assistance Dogs when their owners are in the care of ambulance personnel, medics, hospital workers, and long-term care workers.

Zeb helps Bill reach his true potential in many ways. He picks up dropped objects and fetches the phone, he opens and closes doors, and he can push an emergency button linked to a local alarm service. He even takes the clothes out of the washer! Bill, however, says Zeb's main duty lies elsewhere. He quips, "Zeb is a smile for the soul."

We finally made it to Merritt Island and found their house with no problem. They greeted us with open arms and got us settled in for the evening. Then we had time to sit, relax and hear more about how Zeb had made a tremendous difference in Bill's life! These were the reasons we had done this ride, and it was so inspiring to see the great things that Zeb could do for Bill and how it changed his life.

November 25 - Day 209: Merritt Island, FL

We had always spent our previous Thanksgiving holidays with our families, so we were a little disappointed that we would be away from both of our families this day. However, Bill and Katie had made special plans for us to celebrate Thanksgiving with the guys at Station 43 of the Brevard County Fire and Rescue, where Bill used to work. We looked forward to meeting the guys and sharing a holiday dinner with them.

We drove up to the station, were introduced to all the firefighters, and then had a photo op with everyone gathered around our motorcycles with Max and Bailey in their sidecars along with Bill and his Assistance Dog, Zeb. We were honored to share Thanksgiving dinner with these heroes! Next, the four of us wandered around the fire station snapping Max and Bailey's pictures as they sat near fire trucks and in front of all the firefighter's gear hanging behind them on the wall of the station, ready to be donned when the fire alarm sounded.

It was fun visiting with everyone while some of their family members prepared dinner for us all. As they were making the final preparations with dinner and the anticipation of that delicious dinner was mounting, the sirens went off and they dashed for their gear and headed out on a call.

We were extremely disappointed! Those of us left behind went ahead and ate dinner. Thankfully, it was not a major call, and they were back fairly soon to finally enjoy the meal. It was very touching to be included in their "family" for Thanksgiving since we were away from ours for the special holiday.

November 26 - Day 210: Merritt Island, FL - Orlando, FL

After posing for a few pictures with us on our bikes along with Bill and Zeb, we said our goodbyes and again thanked Bill and Katie for the wonderful hospitality. We had met such wonderful people along the journey who had opened up their houses to us and it warmed our hearts.

We had a short drive of only 62 miles, so we took a side trip along the Space Coast and got pictures of Max and Bailey in their sidecars in front of the Space Shuttle at the Astronaut Hall of Fame. We then drove through Christmas, Florida, and stopped in front of their post office to get pictures of Max and Bailey in Christmas.

November 27 - Day 211: Orlando, FL

Our event for the day started in Daytona, so we drove the 45 miles to Daytona to meet up with one of our charity partners along with the Fire and Iron Motorcycle Club. The event was the first annual Magical Motorcycle Tour with a ride from Daytona to Orlando ending at the Orlando Magic for the game. The local PAWS rep had brought a table for us to set up our Hogs for Dogs gear. We met two of the Orlando Magic Dancers as they got their pictures taken in front of the sidecars with Max and Bailey.

One of our charity partners organized the event and we were able to meet some of their volunteers who helped put the event together. After all the riders registered for the ride, we followed the Fire and Iron Motorcycle riders on our ride to Orlando. We made one stop at a gas station, and everyone enjoyed coming over to pet Max and Bailey. We continued to our destination and saw all the tents set up outside of the arena on a nice grassy area.

When we asked where they wanted us to park, we were told a parking place that was a good distance from all the other event tents. And we were right next to the port-a-potty. How convenient. We had some attendees trek over to our bikes, but most of the activity remained in the other area. We were feeling like outcasts. Even though we felt humiliated, we stuck to our end of the agreement and presented our charity partner with the usual $1000 initial check from our ride.

Eventually, the rains moved in and we were lucky and thankful that the PAWS rep had brought a tent in her van since we were the only ones not given a tent to be under for the event. When it began to sprinkle, we quickly threw the tent up and inched the bikes closer to fit under the tent. It rained harder and harder, and we realized the event was essentially over.

We had tickets to the game, but we soon found out that we were not in the same section as the others from our charity partner and the dogs were not allowed into the game. Of course, the other dogs were allowed because they were service dogs, but nobody made any effort to get permission to let us bring Max and Bailey into the game and nobody told us this news until we were ready to go in. We finally called it a day and went home in the rain. Disappointed, we left with a measly $11 in donations and only a few logo gear sales.

Even though we had an agreement with our charity partners that all proceeds from their events with us would go to the Hogs for Dogs charity, we did not get anything from their event. Even days later, we received nothing and no word from them. Their lack of compliance along with our treatment at the event tugged at our hearts and we were still so very disappointed.

After several days of contemplation, we finally decided we did not agree with their actions and their lack of following our charity partner rules. They had exploited Max and Bailey's notoriety to gain profits, which were not shared with us as all the other charity partners had done. We discussed this with our Board of Directors, and they all agreed. We wrote a polite letter to them that they were no longer our charity partner since they did not comply with our agreement about the fundraisers held for us and, with a heavy sigh, we sent it on its way. We took their name off our website, and they received no more funds from us.

November 28 - Day 212: Orlando, FL - Brunswick, GA

After being in Florida for the past 18 days, we were finally heading back into Georgia for a day. We said goodbye to our host and headed out on the road for our 178 miles to the St. Mary's waterfront. Yes, we were going a bit out of our way for a very special reason; we were meeting some friends from our sailboat cruising days. We had met Dave and Peggy Scott while we were cruising on our sailboat, and the cruising community is a very tight-knit community. We had kept up with them via single sideband radio with the cruising community morning check-ins where each boat would check in with their location and we would keep track of each other...especially for those boats that were offshore. Dave and Peggy had continued to track us as we went riding around the country on our motorcycles and they updated the cruising community with our progress via the single sideband check-ins. They kept in touch with us, and we found out that they would be in St. Mary's at the same time we were passing by. We could not turn down an opportunity to see them.

There is a tradition in St. Mary's where the town invites the cruising community to stop in and have a Thanksgiving meal with their families. For this particular year, they had 40 cruising boats anchored off their town docks and over 100 people enjoyed the hospitality and home-style Thanksgiving dinner with this generous town. With many of our friends in St. Mary's, we just had to stop in to say hi and let them see the dogs in their sidecars.

We rolled up into St. Mary's and had a warm welcome from Dave and Peggy, along with many other cruisers. It was like a homecoming! It was so good to see them. We showed off the dogs and the bikes and chatted about our trip. We found a good parking place in order to park the dogs outside of the window of Seagle's Waterfront Cafe and Saloon, and we went inside to catch up with everyone. It was an awesome afternoon!

Unfortunately, we could not stay the evening in St. Mary's, so we tearfully said our goodbyes and gave everyone hugs. Then we headed up the 42 miles to Brunswick. We settled in for the evening with great anticipation for the next day and what was in store for us.

November 29 - Day 213: Brunswick, GA - Charleston, SC

We awoke with excitement of our day ahead. We quickly packed our bikes and headed out on our 170-mile trip for the day. We headed up I-95 and about halfway into our trip we crossed into our 48th state! Woohoo! We stopped at the South Carolina sign for pictures of us and the dogs crossing our last state in our ride. We were bursting with excitement to have accomplished this tremendous milestone! I'm sure we got many very odd looks sent our way as we did our celebration dance on the side of the road...like we were not a spectacle already with two dogs in sidecars!

After our pictures and celebration dance, we hopped back on the bikes to head through South Carolina and on to Blaine's parents' house for the next couple of nights. Our anticipation mounted as we drove the last 30 minutes. Finally, we arrived at Blaine's parents' house, and it was so good to see them! We received quite the welcome, and we all fought back tears of joy. As we settled into their house, the dogs got a chance to run around outside in their fenced-in yard. Boy, were they happy pups! We were off for the day. Blaine's mom had been busy setting things up for us and Blaine had an interview with NewsRadio WSC-FM 94.3 before we could relax for the evening.

It was fantastic to be back in a familiar place after spending most of our 212 days in very unfamiliar places. Plus, we got a delicious home cooked meal by Blaine's Mom. It was a wonderful day indeed!

November 30 - Day 214: Charleston, SC

After a nice homemade breakfast, we made our 30-minute trek to the Charleston Day school in downtown Charleston. Their students were K-8, and they were a great bunch of students. Their athletic director, Cindy Branscome, had followed us for months via our website and she made special arrangements with their headmaster to move their normal Monday morning assembly to Tuesday to allow us to visit. After a great presentation by Blaine, we were both presented with Charleston Day shirts! The students were then allowed to see Max and Bailey in their sidecars and pet them. The local news station, NBC affiliate WCBD, Count on 2, even came out to do a story on us and it aired that evening on the 5:00 news.

We then headed to Lowcountry Harley-Davidson to beg them to change our oil/transmission fluid within the afternoon timeframe, so we could be ready to head out of town the next day. We ended up staying for the entire afternoon as they found one thing after another that was wrong with Blaine's bike. At least it was not mine again. Our mechanic, Rob, did a superb job of making sure we were all set to hit the road again to continue our journey the next day. Their entire staff was awesome!

After they were finally done with our bikes, we headed back to Blaine's parents' house to enjoy one more evening with them and another home cooked meal by his mom.

December

December 1 - Day 215: Charleston, SC - Myrtle Beach, SC

After another bittersweet goodbye, we headed out again on the last stretch before our ride into North Carolina the next day. Blaine and I spent a lot of time during our 101-mile ride reminiscing about the journey and chatting on the CB about our most unforgettable memories. We laughed and cried over the memories and wondered what type of impact we had on America. After teaching thousands of students across the country about service dogs, would it make a difference in their future volunteer and philanthropic efforts? We would probably never know.

We rode up Hwy 17, which consisted of a lot of forest and a few towns, and it was a nice leisurely ride. Our excitement mounted as we neared Myrtle Beach because our board member, Jay, was meeting us in Myrtle Beach in order to ride with us for the last two legs of the trip.

It was so good to meet up with Jay. He came by car instead of bike and had his little Chihuahua with him, so we had to pick on him for not being on his bike. We had a fun evening catching up with him and discussing our events for the next couple of days.

December 2 - Day 216: Myrtle Beach, SC - Wilmington, NC

As we packed our bikes, we could not contain our excitement about crossing back into our home state. The 96-mile trip took us to the North Carolina State Line. After crossing the line, we pulled over to get pictures in front of the "Welcome to North Carolina" sign and I just wanted to hug that sign! We were back in our home state! We just could not stop smiling.

A little ways into North Carolina, we detoured to the small town of Calabash - "The Seafood Capital of the World". They are known for a distinctive type of fried seafood which is now called Calabash style. We wandered in, picked out our restaurant and parked our bikes with Max and Bailey chilling in the sidecars.

Yum! We had missed this type of fried seafood. After a tasty lunch, we got back on the road and headed back to Hwy 17. A little while later, we turned onto Hwy. 210 in order to head to Southport. We were disappointed we could not stay in Southport because it is one of our favorite little towns, but instead we were going to catch another means of transportation to get us closer to Wilmington. We were catching the ferry.

After purchasing our tickets, we waited in line for the ferry. When it was ready for loading, we inched up as they directed everyone to their parking place. We got quite the interesting looks while they loaded our bikes onto the ferry. After we were away from the dock, the attendant came down to chat with us and pet the dogs. It was so cool to be on the water sitting on our motorcycles! We felt right at home in those brackish waters surrounded by pine trees and smelling that salt air. Max and Bailey had their noses in the air, smelling that familiar smell.

Once we arrived at Fort Fisher, we disembarked and continued our ride up to Wilmington. Upon arriving in Wilmington, we headed to the house of Pat Nowak. She had graciously let us use her house for the two nights we were in Wilmington. We unpacked our bikes and let Max and Bailey relax for a bit while we got ready for our evening event.

Our event for the evening was sponsored by Carolina Canines for Service, and they had done an awesome job organizing it. First of all, you know our highlight of the day was usually dinner! Well, they had savory North Carolina barbeque! Barbeque is such a regional thing; depending on what state you are in and even what part of the state you are in, the barbeque can be different...some ketchup based, some mustard based, and some barbeque sauce based. But this was a true Eastern North Carolina barbecue, which meant it had a spicy vinegar sauce on it. My Fav! Wow, was it good!

Then they had excellent entertainment with the ladies of the Azalea Coast Chorus, followed by the Craig Woolard Band. We had a fabulous time, as did Max and Bailey as they greeted all the service dogs and service dogs in training.

421

Many of our board members and volunteers had also come down for the event, so it was exciting to catch up with all of them.

Later in the evening we were asked to say a few words and, when Blaine finished talking about our trip, we got a standing ovation to honor our journey. Wow! The emotions swelled in us as we saw their response to our 216 days on the road spreading awareness for service dogs. Next, we got a chance to present Rick Hairston, the founder of Carolina Canines for Service, a $1,000 check, which was our standard down-payment to our charity partners with more to follow when the ride was completed.

After the presentation of the check, we were honored to have Rick Catlin read the Proclamation of Dec. 2, 2004, as Service Dog Awareness Day. The proclamation read as follows:

Proclamation

WHEREAS, *December 2, 2004, has been designated as "Service Dog Awareness Day" to celebrate and recognize service dogs, trainers, advocacy groups and people with disabilities; and*

WHEREAS, *disability is a natural part of the human experience and in no way diminishes the right of individuals with disabilities to live independently, enjoy self-determination, make choices, contribute to society and experience full in the economic, political, social, cultural and educational mainstream of American society; and*

WHEREAS, *family members, friends and members of the community can play a central role in enhancing the lives of people with disabilities especially when the family and community are provided with necessary support services such as service dogs; and community citizens are aware of the needs of people with disabilities to receive the life enhancing assistance of a service dog; and*

WHEREAS, *goals of this city include providing individuals with disabilities the opportunities and support to make informed choices and decisions; live in homes and communities where such individuals can exercise their full right and responsibilities as citizens; pursue meaningful and productive lives; contribute to their family, community, State and Nation; have interdependent friendships and relationships with others; and achieve full inclusion in society; and*

WHEREAS, the City of Wilmington acknowledges and recognizes the profound contributions of the U.S. Hogs for Dogs team as they near completion of the 218-day Ride Across America to raise awareness and funds for guide and service dog organizations and its own organization, Carolina Canines for Service, for their contributions and success in providing quality trained service dogs to people with disabilities.

Now, therefore, I, Spence H. Broadhurst, Mayor of the City of Wilmington, do hereby proclaim December 2, 2004, as SERVICE DOG AWARENESS DAY in the City of Wilmington and call upon citizens of Wilmington to observe the day with appropriate programs and activities. Furthermore, I encourage the citizens of Wilmington to seek counsel and input from any person or group with knowledge and expertise in matters concerning disabilities.

Spencer H. Broadhurst, Mayor

After he read the proclamation, he presented it to Blaine and me. We were humbled. Next, Rick Hairston brought up two of the recipients of their service dogs and talked about their stories and what service dogs could do to assist their person. Then the band started up, and we enjoyed an evening full of fun, entertainment, and great times. Rick, Pat, and their volunteers had done a fantastic job of organizing a very special celebration for us.

December 3 - Day 217: Wilmington, NC

We started our day with a visit to Ashley High School for our last school presentation on the journey. Blaine's journal entry describes why it was such a special visit:

The visit was extra special because Carolina Canines has partnered with the school in a program that offers students the opportunity to be foster puppy raisers for future Assistance Dogs. PAWS (Positive Achievements With Students) is an in-school project that is just beginning and has great potential for students, the dogs and the people with disabilities who are waiting for Assistance Dogs.

As we walked into their school, we commented on how beautiful it was and their auditorium was quite impressive! It was so cool to see the students with their puppies that they were fostering. It would be so awesome if more schools taught the rewarding experience of volunteering. The students enjoyed Blaine's presentation, and we had such a fun visit with the students.

On the way to lunch, we had two stops to make. The first one was at Coastal K-9 Bakery to meet the owner, Jackie Owens. She presented Max and Bailey with two big bags of Christmas cookie treats. They were a tremendous hit with Max and Bailey! While we were there, Blaine said he was afraid to get Max out of his sidecar because he was so food-driven that he might not have ever gotten back in the sidecar to leave! We thanked her for the delicious treats and then headed to our second stop.

The next stop was an unusual one, so we went with the unusual approach! We stopped by the Bank of Wilmington to meet one of the Carolina Canines volunteers and the rest of the bank staff. This was our first publicity stop at a bank, so we pulled Max and Bailey's bandanas over their noses in true old-west bank robbery style. The staff enjoyed it, but I would not recommend it for your next fundraising campaign.

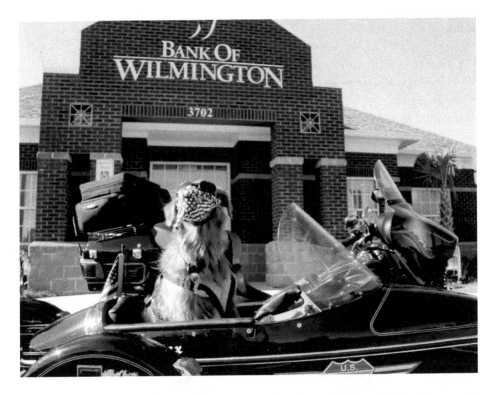

After our two stops, we finally made it to lunch and then took the afternoon to relax. In the evening we headed on over to one of our favorite restaurants in Wrightsville Beach, Dockside. It was a popular rustic restaurant on the Intracoastal Waterway, and it had a marina along with it. There was outside seating, plus you could sit inside and look out on the boats and the water. We had visited it many times while we were sailing, so we felt right at home. With lovely food and atmosphere, we had a fun time relaxing with many of our friends who came down to support us on our ride home. Some of our board members, volunteers, and friends had joined us and it was a fun low-key homecoming with everyone before we started the final trek home the next day with all the associated hoopla. It was a very sweet and special evening for Blaine and me!

December 4 - Day 218: Wilmington, NC - Raleigh, NC - Last Day - The Ride Home

We awoke with anticipation of our last day! It was a very strange mixture of feelings. We were so excited to have come full circle to end the ride in the exact same place we had started the ride. But we also had feelings of dread and disappointment since it had been such an epic adventure and we hated to see it end. The elephants were back in my stomach as I anticipated the events of the day.

Our day kicked off at Britt's Motorsports in the morning. We had a great turnout and were greeted by a growing crowd of people who had followed us throughout our journey. Volunteers from our ride and our charity partners came to celebrate our final journey back to Ray Price Harley-Davidson in Raleigh, NC where we started our ride seven months prior. I knew it was going to be an emotional day, but it started to set in as I saw more and more people show up to join our last leg of the ride. The local TV station, WWAY, came out to interview us about our ride home.

While we were in the middle of all the chaos of our last ride kickoff, I saw Blaine take a phone call and step to the side. He is usually really animated when talking, but I noticed that he was kind of somber and quiet. I was concerned and immediately questioned him when he returned. He told me he had just received a call from Deb Davis. During the call, Deb told him that PAWS was able to direct the funds from our ride to the service dog, Hayden, that was being trained for Chad, the young gentleman who we had met in New Orleans. Blaine had been quiet during that call because, as we prepared for our final day of riding, we finally saw the impact that our ride would make. We had made that happen! We had made a difference! Blaine gave me a hug as we drank in the feeling of humble satisfaction of attaining our purpose for the ride...to make a difference if only in one person's life.

At 11:00, we headed out of Britt's with an escort by the Wilmington H.O.G. chapter. Blaine had offered his back seat to Pat for our final ride; a volunteer had offered to carry his luggage, so Pat had donned Blaine's extra helmet and happily joined us.

427

Our last leg was 127 miles, and we would have two rest stops along the way. The rest stops were not only to take a break and stretch our legs but were also meeting points. For anyone who wanted to ride in to Ray Price Harley-Davidson with us, they could start with us in Wilmington, or they could meet us at either of the two rest stops at pre-designated times. We had around 25 bikes riding with us from Wilmington to our first rest area on I-40. Steve, who had escorted us on our "Get Out of Town" ride, was our final road captain and escort on our ride home. We followed behind him as he headed out behind our police escort.

Jay had opted out of riding his motorcycle with us, so he could race ahead of us and take pictures of all the riders via overpasses.

We knew the event invited other riders to join us at the two rest areas between Wilmington and Raleigh, but we were not prepared for what we found at the first rest area. There was a crowd of motorcycles as we entered our first rest area, and we were greeted by cheers from this crowd as we rode in. It was so emotional to see all these people come out to join us on our final leg into Raleigh. It was hard to imagine the support we had on our last day on the road! Blaine and I were so humbled by everyone who wanted to join us for this celebratory ride.

It was surreal to watch all the motorcycles line up for our ride to the second rest area. Our support team was growing larger the closer that we got to Raleigh.

As we approached our second and last rest area before the final destination, we could not have imagined what we would find. As we were entering our last stop, the scene made me break down in tears. There was another large group of motorcycles parked and ready to greet us. It was humbling to see this many people come out to celebrate our very last leg with us. The entire rest area was filled with motorcycles, leather, and welcoming smiles. We were extremely overwhelmed by the crowd as they came up to congratulate us on our successful journey. I recognized many people from the Raleigh H.O.G. chapter and many of the female H.O.G. members came over to give me a hug and congratulate me. The more I talked to people, the more I realized what a true accomplishment it really was. The immensity of it was beginning to sink in.

The media was also there to welcome us. We took some time to talk to them and tell them about our ride and to share our overwhelmed feelings at the final hour and the tremendous welcome we had already received; we had not even arrived at the Harley dealership where our Welcome Home party was going to be held.

We headed out of our last rest stop with an entourage of motorcycles following us. I could not even imagine what we would find at our ultimate stop at Ray Price. As we entered Wake County where our last stop resided, we watched a Wake County Sheriff's car race ahead of us to escort us for our last miles. These escorts always gave me chills!

As we were riding along, I suddenly heard a deep voice in my ear. We were connected to many riders in our group via CB and Steve had said "Final 10 miles". His baritone voice resonated through my earpieces with the finesse of a radio announcer, and it caught me by surprise.

I had been going with the flow of our events all day, not really overthinking anything, but the reality that our ride was coming to an end startled me. After riding over 25,000 miles through all kinds of conditions and through endless unknowns, it felt surreal that we were only ten miles from being HOME!

I listened to Blaine respond and could tell that he was choked up. I had tears streaming down my face and did not know if I was going to be able to gather myself up and regain my composure to get through this last event.

They say your life will flash before your eyes during the last few minutes of your life, and suddenly, the last seven months played out in my mind during these last ten miles. I thought about how hard we worked the first few months before our ride. Remembered all the times we were told that we were crazy and that it could not be done. All the times that Blaine slept in the sunroom stressing that we would not be able to make this trip. I thought about the extensive planning and thousands of details we painfully worked through to make this ride happen.

Then I heard "9 more miles". I remembered the sick feeling in my stomach as we left for our Get Out Of Town ride. I was petrified to think of Blaine and me being out on our own...just the two of us...relying on my not-too-reliable GPS. It was just the beginning of the daily riding, emails, route planning, accounting, and marketing.

At "mile 8", I remembered being sideswiped by a truck that almost derailed our entire trip. It took every ounce of strength to get back on that bike and fight the fear of another accident. All I wanted to do was to quit and protect my beloved Bailey and instead I got back on my bike and continued for our cause...pushing the fears aside with each mile.

In my ear, I heard "mile 7." My mind replayed so many stories of all the Assistance Dog recipients that we had met along the way. From "you're the man" Edmond to Phyllis beating MS to Lindsey conquering seizures to Bill surviving his fall from the fire ladder. They were all heroes in my mind, as they had overcome the hurdles of their disabilities with their service dogs by their sides.

During mile 6, I recalled all our breakdowns during our trip. The broken spokes, the failure of my brakes, my gas tank leak, the failed transmission, more popping spokes on Blaine's bike, another transmission, and lastly, my gear shifter. Each one of them could have derailed the trip for days. How in the world did we manage to get all those Harley-Davidson dealerships to expedite those crazy, out of the ordinary fixits? I believe it was Max and Bailey, along with our cause, that made them put in the extra effort to get us back on the road so quickly.

Steve's voice resounded in my ear again..."Mile 5". My mind raced across all the puppy raisers that we met throughout the country. The sacrifices they made every day were tremendous, and I didn't see how they could be so selfless as to put the assistance dog recipient ahead of their needs. They spent months training a puppy to turn around and give them back for training. Kudos to those brave souls.

During "mile 4", I remembered the heart-wrenching stories like the dog booties given to Bob during 9/11 and how two of their booties were given to us in order to encourage us to keep going. This is where the heart of America cheered us on to power us through our problems to finish the ride.

Steve's voice boomed with "three miles to go". This mile brought a sense of gratitude for the three most memorable visits during our trip. We were able to attend those three remarkable visits because Max and Bailey were certified therapy dogs. Those visits were all side trips aside from our cause and they became ever the more memorable. First, the Chestertown nursing home. Second, the MDA camp. Third, the VA hospital visit with Virginia and others. I was unbelievably grateful that we were fortunate enough to attend those visits and that we made it to our visit with Virginia one day before she passed away.

At the announcement of "two miles to go", I remembered the endless volunteers that always came to our rescue throughout the entire country and the generous people who opened up their homes to us...even people we did not know! I thought about the unbelievable number of events that were held for us by our charity partners and even volunteers who did not know us but embraced our purpose. I was grateful that our charity partners had embraced our ride and supported us.

Then, there it was...Steve's voice..."One mile to go!" Wow...one mile! I thought of the fear that I had when riding that first mile on my motorcycle, alone for the first time, and the first mile of our ride. In a whirlwind tour of 7 months, 48 states, and 25,000 miles, we were on our final mile! It felt like just yesterday that we had left North Carolina with a mixture of fear of the unknown and the excitement of discovering the lower 48 states of this magnificent country. Yet, at the same time, it seemed like we had been away for a lifetime.

As we rode along that final mile, my emotions were all over the place...jubilation for the accomplishment, disappointment at the ride coming to an end, feelings of self-esteem and confidence for being a female who handled this massive bike for that distance, gratitude for a safe and successful ride, along with the uncertainty of how to move forward with life after so many days of intense focus on our goals and purpose. What was our new purpose going to look like? I was sure we were going to feel lost with no destination to dash off to in the morning.

There was one thing that was for certain; while it was just our little family of four riding each day, we had the support of people around the country and, through teamwork, I knew we made a difference that changed people throughout America. For this final mile, I celebrated all of our little victories that would result in greater independence for the people receiving their Assistance and Guide Dogs. I silently thanked America for believing in us, supporting our cause, and becoming advocates for Assistance Dog organizations everywhere.

As we neared our destination, it felt surreal to be entering the same Harley dealership where we had left 218 days before. Our Wake County Sheriff's escort blocked the traffic of the opposite lane, so we could make the final left turn into the dealership.

As we rode into Ray Price Harley-Davidson, we heard the crowd cheering. While we had left this dealership with only a small crowd of people who believed in us, we were welcomed back by a massive crowd who saw that we had actually accomplished it. Even Ray Price and the Mayor of Raleigh were part of this welcome home crowd. It was a far cry from our Get Out of Town ride.

They directed us to our reserved parking places, and it was a bittersweet homecoming as we got off our bikes. Blaine and I immediately hugged as the cheering continued. It was a long, tight hug as the realization of our massive accomplishment hit home with us. We were finally done with the daily chores of emails, event planning, school visit planning, routing, and financial accounting. No more getting up early in the morning to make our daily miles to get to our next destination and no more being "on" every minute of every day to market our cause. We would be able to eat a meal with no interruptions asking about our dogs/journey. We were done! It felt amazing and scary at the same time.

The Mayor of Raleigh, Charles Meeker, and Ray Price, along with his wife, were waiting next to us and immediately shook our hands and congratulated us on our accomplishment. Next, there was a constant flow of people coming over to congratulate us and we were both completely overwhelmed. We were greeted by so many people who had supported us through our entire trip...volunteers, supporters, charity partners, puppy raisers, and our board members.

We saw our dear friend, Frank Vester, in one corner of the parking lot roasting a whole pig for the pig pickin'. Our board member, Steve, had won the bid at our auction for the pig pickin' and had donated it to our welcome home celebration. I was disappointed that Larry and Pete did not make it, but I was very glad to see Frank over there. I waved to him and said thank you.

Of course, more media was there to capture our return, so we completed a few interviews.

We were eventually ushered into the dealership where they had a stage set up. Ray Price addressed the crowd and talked about our ride.

He then introduced the mayor of Raleigh, who greeted us with a proclamation designating that day as Hogs for Dogs Day. We were so honored! His proclamation was as follows:

PROCLAMATION

WHEREAS, *Hogs For Dogs is a national volunteer-based coalition charity whose motorcycle-riding members are dedicated to supporting canine-related not-for-profit organizations; and,*

WHEREAS, *two North Carolina members of Hogs For Dogs—Blaine and Janet Parks of Goldsboro and their Golden Retrievers, Max and Bailey—departed from the Ray Price Harley-Davidson dealership in Raleigh on May 1, 2004 to begin a cross-country trip to raise funds and awareness about Assistance Dogs for citizens with disabilities; and,*

Janet Charbonneau

WHEREAS, *Blaine and Janet Parks returned to the Capital City on Dec. 4, 2004, after traveling through the lower 48 states of America over a 25,000-mile journey, primarily using their own money to finance the trip; and,*

WHEREAS, *the couple raised at least $150,000 to help provide specially trained dogs to people with disabilities at no cost to the recipients.*

NOW, THEREFORE, *do I, Charles Meeker, mayor of the City of Raleigh, North Carolina, hereby proclaim Dec.4, 2004 as*

HOGS FOR DOGS DAY

In Raleigh and encourage every citizen to acknowledge all members of the organization for their unselfish devotion to charity work and specifically, to applaud Blaine and Janet Parks - as well as Max and Bailey - for taking the time and effort to travel our vast country to promote the importance of Assistance Dogs.

IN WITNESS THEREOF, I have
Hereunto set my hand and caused the
Great Seal of the City of Raleigh,
North Carolina, to be affixed this
Fourth Day of December 2004.

Charles Meeker
Mayor

Next, Ray Price asked Blaine to speak about our trip. I was glad that he asked Blaine to talk because I did not think I would have been able to hold it together enough to utter a coherent sentence. Blaine again did an amazing job of talking about our 48-state ride along with giving examples of those with disabilities that could benefit from a service dog. He knew how to tug at your heartstrings with these examples and it reminded me of those that indeed benefitted from our last seven months of challenging weather, grueling miles, endless school visits, numerous events, and 218 days on the road.

As a follow-up to show how successful our ride was, Deb Davis next took the stage and announced to the crowd that our ride had funded the dog that was going to be placed with Chad, the gentleman we met at the Steele Pony event. Usually, a prospective client was required to raise their own donations to offset the cost of their service dog. However, PAWS decided to put the funds donated by our organization to fund his service dog. After Blaine's talk and the announcement from Deb, there was not a dry eye in the room.

We were grateful for our sponsors for the event:

Ray-Price Harley-Davidson
Cindy Mease of Irwin Mortgage
Irina Bennett of Keller Williams Realty
Steve Metz, Raleigh H.O.G. Activities Director and Hogs for Dogs Board Member

We were also humbled by our event volunteers and the sizeable crowd that greeted us as we rode back to where the ride started.

After all of the overwhelming excitement from the events of the day, we ended up at the same Red Roof Inn, where we stayed for our kickoff ride. They had given a special discounted price to everyone who attended our event, and we were grateful for their hospitality. Once Max and Bailey were settled for the evening, we went out to a local pub to join our board members in celebrating a successful seven months.

After 218 days on the road filled with events and school visits, we craved a very peaceful and quiet celebration. As a culmination of our crazy yet successful ride, it was just what Blaine and I needed. We were home, surrounded by our caring friends and supportive team who had cheered us on every day. This was priceless! This picture of some of our volunteers, including Annette and April, shows the elation at the end of our wildly triumphant ride.

I sat watching the celebration around me and wondered what impact and change we accomplished with our ride. Did more businesses now know about service dogs and welcome them in? Did our ride initiate a ripple effect where people we had met along the way would spread the word about Assistance Dogs to others? Who would have thought that two people with a dream and no clue how to accomplish it would have been able to pull off such an astounding trip?

As I continued to reminisce, one thought suddenly dawned on me. I realized that while we set out looking for the Heart of America, I believe the Heart of America found us.

Epilogue:

Ever have one of those days where you just do not know if you can go on? You have just had it and you wonder how you will survive to the next day? You do not even want to get out of bed. But you then try to put everything into perspective. I am grateful I have a roof over my head. I was able to enjoy a nice cup of coffee this morning. I had a nice warm bed to sleep in last night. Sometimes you have to go even more basic…I am glad that I am alive this morning. I am grateful for being able to have two arms and two legs that enable me to do what I want to do. I am grateful that I am healthy. I am grateful that I am free to go where I want to go. I am grateful that I feel grateful each day.

While I was on the road, I did this exercise a lot. Some days were very hard to get through. Some days, I just wanted to roll over in bed and throw the covers over my head. These were the days that I thought of those people who we were riding for that did not have all these conveniences. Those that did not have the freedom that I had. Those that needed to depend on others to help them accomplish the simple things in life. Those that could not even take a shower by themselves and needed someone to be there for them just in case. Those who needed assistance when they dropped their pen on the floor. Those that needed assistance when THEY fell on the floor.

My pains in those days subsided when I realized that I had a lot to be grateful for each day and that I was blessed with many things that I just took for granted daily. There are simple things that we always take for granted that many people do not have. One thing that we rarely think about is freedom. We have the freedom to make choices each day and the freedom to do what we want to do. Many people do not have that freedom. That is something most of us never even think about when we think of things for which to be grateful. Another thing is independence. Most of us take that for granted, but those with a physical disability may not have that independence. A service dog can grant that person independence and that is what I was riding for. That is why I was riding in sleet, rain, hail, extreme heat, extreme cold, and running from tornados. When I felt I could not ride another mile or get up and leave a nice warm bed to go out into the icy rain, I would remember those that lacked independence, and that was the reason I was riding another day.

As I finish writing this book and scanning dozens of newspaper and magazine articles about our ride, I ran across the Spring 2005 edition of Dogs for Dignity, which was the PAWS newsletter. Deb Davis had written an article about our ride, and I believe this excerpt from that article expertly sums up our ride.

As I sit and begin to write this article, I reflect back upon the notes I made for our original meeting with Blaine and Janet Parks of U.S. Hogs For Dogs. Blaine and Janet came to PAWS in November of 2003 with a wild idea to ride around the country on Harley-Davidson motorcycles with their two Golden Retrievers, Max and Bailey, in sidecars. Thoughts I jotted down in my notes included "Why", "What is their personal connection", and "Are they crazy?"

After working with and getting to know Blaine and Janet over the past 18 months, my answers are "Why not", "No personal connection", and "No, they are not crazy. Just adventuresome!" How else would one describe two people who have traveled on motorcycles for 7 months and 25,000 miles just to bring awareness to the Assistance Dog industry? How else would one describe two people who got up each morning, despite the weather or illness, and pushed on toward the next event or presentation because people were waiting to meet Max and Bailey? How else would one describe two people who welcomed all of Mother Nature's children — Snow, Sleet, Rain and Hail were all along for the ride — as just another obstacle to conquer, much like the obstacles in the daily life of a person with a disability?

The 2004 U.S. Hogs For Dogs Charity Ride provided educational presentations to tens of thousands of Americans on the important work of Assistance Dogs. Everywhere they went, Max and Bailey turned heads and stopped traffic (even in New York City!) as they traveled the byways of America and visited with its inhabitants. Volunteers from numerous Assistance Dog organizations throughout the country lent a hand and many of those volunteers still keep in touch with Blaine and Janet, as friendships were formed across dinner tables throughout the Midwest.

Not a meal was eaten without being served with a side of education. Brochures were handed out in Walmarts; donations were made in McDonald's parking lots. Demonstrations were conducted in school parking lots and on picnic tables at universities across the country. Max and Bailey were riding across America on an awareness journey;

America came out to meet Max and Bailey and walked away with an education on Assistance Dogs.

As Deb stated, we spent the majority of our meals being interrupted to talk about our journey and our cause, but that was why we were out there. Every stop along the way was a chance to meet people, get to know them, share our passion about the ride and cause, sell T-shirts, and gather donations for our amazing charities. We met people from every walk of life, every ethnicity, and every type of background, but we found everyone willing to come together to work towards the common good of helping our Assistance and Guide Dog charity partners. We learned so much about people, but it did not matter their circumstances; their hearts stood out with kindness and generosity.

While looking back at our accomplishments, it still astonishes me how word about our trip got out to so many people with just emails and a website...no social media. I learned many years later about the law of attraction, but I believe this was living proof that the law of attraction works. The law is essentially the fact that like attracts like. Positive thoughts and energy attract more good things. Negative thoughts and negative energy attract bad things. Our positive energy continued to attract all the unbelievable things that came our way. We started by attracting our phenomenal board members. We did not seek them out; they came to us when they found out about our ride.

Next came the multitude of volunteers across the country. We certainly felt the heart of America throughout our ride as hundreds of people set up events for us and opened their homes for us to lay our weary bones for the night. We were blessed to see the helping hands and generosity of so many people along our journey. We did all of this with only a website, emails, and word of mouth. We could not have succeeded without our core group of board members who helped keep us organized with events, school visits, volunteers, and our daily website changes. A couple of months after our ride, Blaine and I treated our board members to a steak dinner. We gathered at the house of one of our board members and I broke out that magnum of wine that I had won at the charity auction and shared it with our team. It was a small token of our appreciation for all the help in making our ride successful.

Our team was grateful for all the outstanding Harley-Davidson dealers that we visited who went above and beyond to get our bikes serviced or fixed to help keep us on our schedule!

We found that small town America was still there with the many Mom and Pop diners we cherished along the way. The generosity we met helped raise money for our six charity partners in order to lessen the wait time for Assistance Dogs. We donated over $43,000 to our charity partners. However, an even greater outcome of our ride was that we spread the word about Assistance Dogs to tens of thousands of people with far more outreaching effects.

One of these effects was that our ride opened the door for a new foster puppy raiser in Florida. The principal of Barfield Elementary School had been considering being a foster puppy raiser for years. Once she was introduced to PAWS via our visit, she volunteered to foster a puppy for PAWS. She fostered a black lab named Opal, who was named by the students. As I am finishing writing this book, I ran across an article that tells Opal's incredible story and the difference this one dog made:

https://assistancedogregistry.com/barfield-elementarys-school-dog/

Learning about this new foster puppy raiser reminded me of the butterfly effect. It essentially states that a small action can have a large effect in the future. I realized that the small effect we had on the students and teachers triggered the desire of the principal to want to foster an Assistance Dog in Training. This fostering experience allowed the entire school to learn about assistance dogs, which eventually led to other Marco Island families fostering other service dogs. The butterfly effect was blooming.

If you remember us meeting Chad in the New Orleans area, then you probably want the rest of the story. Chad received an Assistance Dog from PAWS. His name was Hayden. We were ecstatic! It was a very tangible outcome from our ride. Unfortunately, less than a year later, we were informed that Chad had fallen ill after Hurricane Katrina hit New Orleans. He had to be relocated multiple times to get more extensive healthcare and ended up with complications. We were devastated to hear that he had passed away shortly after receiving his Assistance Dog. Thankfully, his Assistance Dog was able to go to another person with a similar disability, so there was minimal training needed to make that happen.

However, the best part of this story came from news from his dad a few months later. His Dad contacted Deb Davis of PAWS and relayed a journal entry he found written by Chad. It was from Chad as a high school student, and it relayed the delight and desire that Chad would receive when he finally achieved his dream...receiving his Assistance Dog. It described the freedom he would have when he finally attained this dream. His dad did not know how much this Assistance Dog really meant to him. We totally melted when we realized our ride had allowed this young man to achieve his dream. We were humbled at what our ride had accomplished.

Wonder what happened to those Dirty Dozen puppies that were named in honor of our ride? Three of them did not make it through the program for various reasons, but were kept by their foster parents. How sweet! Eight of them were trained and placed as service dogs, and one was trained and placed as a hearing dog. They were placed with recipients in Illinois, Michigan, Florida, South Dakota, and Arizona. Therefore, three-quarters of them went on to assist their partners and give them independence. That is an awesome end result. Way to go, Dirty Dozen!

A couple more changes since our ride...after Ray Price passed away, the dealership was sold. It still stands today in the original location, but its name is now Tobacco Road Harley-Davidson. Also, Rick Hairston and Pat Nowak eventually got married. They are no longer with Canines for Service, but they started a new Assistance Dog organization called Four Paws and a Wake-up, www.k94pawsnc.org.

Several years after our ride, I was able to volunteer with Canines for Service (previously known as Carolina Canines). They moved their Canines for Veterans (CFV) branch down to Charleston, SC where I was living at the time. Their program was a triple win: the dogs in the program were rescued from shelters, the dogs were trained by military members in the brig (military prison), and the Assistance Dogs were placed with Veterans. I started out volunteering for events. Then I became a board member, eventually becoming the Chair for the board. I started taking out dogs for weekend socializations. The dogs were being trained in the military brig, so they were not getting the socialization experiences that they needed. As a socialization volunteer, I would take dogs out on the weekends to take them on as many different experiences that I could. The Charleston RiverDogs baseball team set up a table during their Friday home games for this CFV program where we sold t-shirts and introduced their fans to Assistance Dogs in Training. It was the perfect opportunity to get the dogs socialized in sizeable crowds, as well as the fireworks at the end of the game. The dogs would go everywhere with me, 24/7, when I had them for the weekend.

I loved taking the dogs out for socializations and would normally get to take the same dog out several times before they were placed with their Veteran. It was hard not to become attached to them. It was always bittersweet to see the dog start their team training with their Veteran. I knew I was going to deeply miss the dogs but knew the Veteran's life would change by giving them more independence and confidence. The most memorable placement of one of the dogs

I had socialized was announced on Independence Day on the field of the Charleston RiverDogs. A Vietnam Veteran was placed with his Assistance Dog, and I was honored to be on the field during that presentation. He was practically in tears as he heard the entire baseball stadium cheering for him. He admitted to me later how much that meant to him as he stated it was a far cry from the humiliation he received upon returning from Vietnam to riots disgracing our Vietnam Veterans. That realization for me was powerful, and I felt grateful that I had helped with his Assistance Dog's training.

I also fostered two dogs for an extended period of time. One was brought into the program as a puppy and was not mature enough to be placed with a Veteran after she was fully trained. I fostered her for a few months while she matured and was eventually paired with her Veteran. A second pup was pulled from his Veteran after CFV found out that the dog was being abused by the Veteran. After receiving reports of odd behavior by the dog, the CFV staff made a trip to visit the Veteran and immediately pulled the dog. Since I had taken that dog out for many socialization outings, I was very familiar with the dog and the dog was very comfortable with me. I was asked to foster the dog until he was back to normal. I could tell by his actions that he indeed had been abused. He never regained his usual goofy self, but he got back to a normal state and was placed with a fantastic Veteran.

I was grateful that the company I worked for and the company that we were subcontracted under were both very receptive to me bringing Assistance Dogs in Training to work with me every day. The program was eventually moved back to North Carolina, but I enjoyed the many years that I could make a difference by socializing those Assistance Dogs in Training.

The non-profit, Hogs for Dogs, is still an active 501(c)(3) charity. The website is www.hogsfordogs.org. It continues to be an all-volunteer organization, so all the donation money will be dispersed to the Assistance Dogs and Guide Dogs organization that we supported during our ride. There is a Donate button where you can donate via Paypal or can mail checks to the address listed on that website. I encourage you to support these vital organizations by donating via our Hogs for Dogs website or directly on our charity partners websites. All donations to Hogs for Dogs are tax deductible.

As I reflect on our 2004 Hogs for Dogs ride, I am still in awe at what two people with a dream could accomplish. We did not know how we were going to accomplish it, but we did. We had an amazing board of directors to organize our volunteers, events, and school visits and to keep our day-to-day non-profit tasks on track. Our charity partners believed in us, supported our ride, created events, and got their volunteers and clients involved. America stepped up and gave us incredible volunteers, gracious hosts that opened their doors to us, donations on a daily basis, a willingness to learn about assistance dogs, and laughter as they saw Max and Bailey riding in their sidecars. It was a journey of a lifetime!

Board Members

Executive Board of Directors:

Blaine Parks
Janet Parks
Jay Schwantes
JoLee Southard
Seth Cortigene
Terry O'Malley

General Board of Directors:

Steve Metz
April Fort
Annette Rowan
Beth Cassels
Mary Ann Tormey
Dr. Melissa Hudson
Sherry Dodson
Jan Santel
Brad Parker

Janet Charbonneau

Charity Partners

Paws With A Cause
www.pawswithacause.org
616-877-7297

Canine Partners for Life
www.k94life.org
610-896-4902

Canines for Service (previously Carolina Canines For Service, Inc.)
www.caninesforservice.org
910-362-8181

Guiding Eyes for the Blind
www.guidingeyes.org
914-245-4024

KSDS, Inc
www.ksds.org
785-325-2256

New Life Mobility Assistance Dogs (NLMAD)
336-838-2215

Janet Charbonneau

Thank you!

Dear Reader,

Thank you for joining us on our Hogs for Dogs journey. I hope you enjoyed traveling with Max and Bailey around the country and rediscovering the heart of America.

If you loved the book and have a minute to spare, I would really appreciate a short review on the page or site where you bought the book. I believe in the power of word-of-mouth advertising, so your help in spreading the word is greatly appreciated. Reviews from readers like you make a huge difference in helping new readers discover the story of Two Hogs, Two Dogs, and a Country to Cross.

Please join my Facebook page for future updates:
www.Facebook.com/JanetCharbonneauAuthor

Thank you!

Janet Charbonneau

About the Author

Janet Charbonneau enjoys taking the road less traveled. She has spent her life chasing adventures and helping others. After leaving corporate America in her mid-30's to chase dreams of blue water cruising, she climbed aboard her Harley Davidson motorcycle, spending 218 days traveling all lower 48 states, to help people living with disabilities. To make it interesting, she did the cross-country ride with her Golden Retriever, Bailey, tucked into her sidecar. Not long after those early adventures, Janet found herself walking the historic Camino de Santiago pilgrimage. In each case, she had zero experience until the day she decided to go. Always with purpose. Always with courage and determination. For many years, she volunteered with Canines for Veterans as a board member, board chairman, and service-dog-in-training socializer and continues to support Assistance Dog organizations. She still enjoys volunteering and is currently the treasurer for the Military Appreciation Day - Charleston Chapter. She now resides in North Carolina with Holly, her Golden Retriever, working as an IT professional by day, writing books, and planning her next adventures in her spare time.